GIRLHOOD
Redefining The Limits

Yasmin Jiwani
Candis Steenbergen
Claudia Mitchell
editors

BLACK ROSE BOOKS

Montreal/New York/London

Black Rose Books No. II345

National Library of Canada Cataloguing in Publication Data

Girlhood : redefining the limits / Yasmin Jiwani, Candis Steenbergen, Claudia Mitchell, editors.

Includes bibliographical references.

ISBN: 1-55164-277-8 (bound)   ISBN: 1-55164-276-X (pbk.)

(alternative ISBNs 9781551642772 [bound]   9781551642765 [pbk.])

1. Girls--Social conditions. 2. Teenage girls--Social conditions.

I. Jiwani, Yasmin II. Mitchell, Claudia III. Steenbergen, Candis, 1972-

HQ777.G5749 2005   305.23'082   C2005-902391-0

Cover design: Associés libres

C.P. 1258	2250 Military Road	99 Wallis Road
Succ. Place du Parc	Tonawanda, NY	London, E9 5LN
Montréal, H2X 4A7	14150	England
Canada	USA	UK

To order books:

In Canada: (phone) 1-800-565-9523 (fax) 1-800-221-9985
email: utpbooks@utpress.utoronto.ca

In United States: (phone) 1-800-283-3572 (fax) 1-651-917-6406

In the UK & Europe: (phone) 44 (0)20 8986-4854 (fax) 44 (0)20 8533-5821
email: order@centralbooks.com

Our Web Site address: http://www.blackrosebooks.net

Printed in Canada

Contents

Preface

The inspiration for this anthology comes from numerous sources. One is our recognition of the still-burgeoning field of girlhood studies as a viable and valuable realm for innovative and much-needed work. "Girls" often have been spoken for and about as a homogenized group without agency and often without acknowledgement of the complex power relations that weave through their diverse experiences. Second is the obligation for work on girls and girlhoods to be intersectional and interlocking: describing and critiquing the interconnectedness of gender, race, sexuality, age and class in both framing identities and analyzing power relations. Finally, the dearth of compilations on the subject of girls and girlhoods within our very particular national context provided the immediacy and necessity of a book such as this. For this project, we sought to highlight the voices and experiences of girls in the predominantly Canadian context and to locate them within the broader scope of girlhood studies.

Many of the authors in this volume begin with an interest in and concern for girls at the level of everyday lived realities and subsequently expand their analyses to address the ways in which those realities have been influenced by larger social-structural forces. In so doing, they balance multiple dimensions of girls—as both mediators and mediated—from interdisciplinary approaches and in vastly variant domains. As a result, we have learned much from these contributors and their multiple sites of girlhood, as well as from their diverse educational, political, methodological and experiential approaches to their written work. We thank them for their multi-faceted contributions to this still-growing body of literature.

Some of the chapters here originated as presentations at the first International Conference on Girlhood, Agency and Power, entitled *Transforming Spaces*, that was held at Concordia University in Montréal on 21-23 November, 2003. The conference was a collaborative effort between POWER Camp National/Filles d'Action, Concordia University, McGill University and the Alliance of Five Research Centres on Violence Against Women and was supported by GirlSpoken: Creative Voices for Change, Laurentian University, and dozens of generous volunteers. It brought together over two hundred girls and women from Canada, the United States, the United Kingdom, Uganda, South Africa, Pakistan and Russia. The event created a space where girls and those working with them could raise and address fundamental issues in their lives and imagine possibilities for change. Dedicated to dialogue, collaboration, reflection, and building bridges between the academy and grassroots organizations, the conference provided an invaluable foundation from which further research and action on girls could surface.

We would like to recognize the Social Sciences and Humanities Research Council (SSHRC) for a grant that made the conference possible. As well, Status of Women Canada, the Ontario Trillium Foundation, The J. W. McConnell Family Foundation and CIDA/L'ACDI helped support some of the research presented here. The Alliance of Five Research Centres on Violence deserves particular recognition for spearheading research on Canadian girls and their experiences of violence and for facilitating the research presented in the chapters by Pamela J. Downe, Yasmin Jiwani, and Marnina Gonick. Finally our thanks to our contributors, many of whom have worked tirelessly with us through numerous iterations to complete this collection.

We would especially like to thank Linda Barton from Black Rose Books for her unflinching conviction in the merit of a book on girls and girlhoods. We are grateful for her time, patience and copyediting that helped bring this book to fruition.

We would also like to acknowledge our families, friends and colleagues and most especially, Iqubal, Marc, and Ann for supporting us on the home front and our respective departments and universities for providing space and moral support to undertake this work.

Yasmin Jiwani, Concordia University
Candis Steenbergen, Concordia University
Claudia Mitchell, McGill University

Introduction

Girlhood: Surveying The Terrain

Yasmin Jiwani, Candis Steenbergen, Claudia Mitchell

Girls, Girls, Girls!

The last fifteen years have witnessed a proliferation of books, articles, magazines and products on and about girls and young women in North America. "Girls" (and/or their behaviour, dress, relationships, education, consumption habits and more) have prompted frequent newspaper headlines, driven investigative documentaries, and fuelled plotlines for countless mainstream films and prime-time television dramas. Often framed in terms of declining moral standards, rising hemlines/plunging necklines, increased aggression, and the demise of feminism, popular attention about or directed at girls has been considerably—and consistently—bleak. Recent captions read: "Protect Young Girls," "From Schoolgirl to Siren: Why 13-year-olds go Wild," "Nasty Clique Behaviour among Girls Draws New Attention," "Never Easy, Being a Girl is Harder than Ever," and, simply: "What is Happening to Our Girls?" In addition, young women have become a valuable target market stemming in part from the exploitation of "girl power" scripting girls and young women as commercially lucrative as well as a hyper-sexualized population.

Reaction to the "new" girl of the millennium has been as diverse as it has been swift, due in part to the ambiguous definition of who actually constitutes a "girl." In 1985 (the International Year of Youth), the United Nations advanced the idea that "youth" were "persons between fifteen and twenty-four years old." Four years later, the UN Convention on the Rights of the Child (which called for the protection of the rights of the girl-child) considered "children" as persons under the age of eighteen. Prompted by the World Summit for Children, the 1990s were declared "the Decade of the Girl Child" and at the UN Fourth World Conference on Women in 1995 the Girl Child was considered "one of the Twelve Critical Areas of Concern" of the Beijing Platform for Action. While extremely significant, this designation served only to emphasize one element of girls' multiple realities: their vulnerability.

Outside legal frameworks, the category "girl" has been used freely as a signifier of a wide range of groupings. The very word "girl" is highly context specific: it can connote community and inclusiveness among friends ("one of the girls," "you go, girl!") or denote status (little girl, young girl, older girl). It is an index of age. It can also be an insult ("you throw like a girl"), condescension ("the girls at the office"), or a term of endearment. Overlapping definitions—coupled with often-contradictory meanings —illustrate that "girl" is a far more complicated word (and identity) than many acknowledge.

While the amount of attention that the category "girl" (however loosely defined) has increased in recent years, there remains a propensity among researchers to favour an ostensibly more encapsulating focus on "youth" rather than concentrating on the multifaceted nature of girls' lived realities; to collapse gender differences to examine a theoretical "whole." This tendency has also translated into a blurring of age distinctions by focusing on the category of "women" in general. Either way, any and all elements—as well as the nuances—of "being a girl" vanish. Simultaneously, these categorizations have been accompanied by a strategic move that dismantles differences between and among girls and young women—differences based on their location at diverse intersecting and interlocking sites of societal and structural forces.

Similarly, "girlhood" tends often to be confined within the realm of "childhood." Childhood, of course, has strong connotations of innocence, purity, and naivety. "Children" as a homogenous group move, it seems, in very linear fashion from childhood to adolescence and adulthood. The transition appears *natural*; particularly within the context of a market economy that privileges a specific construction of this space as an area to be simultaneously exploited and protected.

This construction of "childhood" is also a particularly Western one; a condition made abundantly clear when one contrasts the North American situation with other parts of the world, where the shift from childhood to adulthood can occur almost overnight. Yet these differences underscore the fact that neither stage of life can be viewed in an essentialized manner. Girlhoods in other parts of the world are often used to reinforce ideological binaries, as in the "traditional, oppressive East" versus the "libratory, progressive West" (Berman and Jiwani, 2001). We would argue that such binaries are strategic as are the very notions of "childhood" and "adulthood." We agree with Chandra Mohanty (2002) that while there are differences, there are also linkages. And in the interests of building solidarity, we need to deconstruct not only what may appear as "natural" categories but also highlight the ways they cohere around commonalities that throw into relief the interconnectedness and linkages that characterize our current global situation.

This book embraces a more holistic approach towards girls and girlhoods; with chapters emphasizing the power, agency *and* complicity of girls in resisting and negotiating oppression and inequality within the matrices of structural forces that constrain, impose limits on and contribute to their vulnerabilities. Indeed, we contend that childhood is always a *gendered, raced, sexed and classed* space, inscribed by particular behavioural dictates, social norms and mores and ways of seeing the world. It is also context-bound; rooted in language and the politics of location. Like the category "girl," "girlhood" is also a highly contested space, determined and sometimes over-determined by social forces. Our interest here lies in surveying the confluence of the various dimensions that shape and define contemporary girlhoods, especially as they are constrained by prevailing social forces and articulated by girls themselves.

Girlhood: The Canadian Terrain

Broad brushstrokes of existing works that epitomize the vast and varied landscape of girlhood studies have already been conducted (see, for example, Harris, 2004) and indeed, most of the chapters in this volume are indebted to these works. It is difficult to separate out Canadian texts from the broader literature on girls, especially given that Western girlhood studies include many works by Canadian scholars and activists. While Canadian monographs are scarce, rigorous research is being conducted on girls in multiple sectors. Since the 1990s—a decade signalling an enhanced awareness of the situation of the "girl-child" globally—Canadian research on girls has grown exponentially.

In many ways, girlhood studies in the Canadian context has followed a trajectory similar to its American and British counterparts. Of the academic texts that have been published recently, many have enjoyed considerable success; particularly Artz's *Sex, Power and the Violent Schoolgirl* (1998), Currie's *Girl Talk* (1999), Handa's *Of Silk Saris and Mini Skirts* (2003), a study of the ways in South Asian girls negotiate, imagine and construct community and identity through mediated discourses of race, nation and culture, Gonick's *Between Femininities* (2003) which explores the discursive map of femininity as played out and performed by a group of girls in Toronto, and more recently, Mitchell and Reid-Walsh's *Seven Going on Seventeen* (2005). These texts have also been accompanied by themed issues in various journals such as the *McGill Journal of Education* (edited by Mitchell and Blaeser, 2000) and the special issue of *Canadian Woman Studies* entitled "Young Women: Feminists, Activists, Girls" (2001).

The latter half of the 1990s witnessed a veritable explosion of texts both created by and providing spaces for girls and young women to speak on, about and out on issues that pertained directly to their own lives. *Fireweed*'s (1997) special issue, entitled "Revolution Girl Style" was one such compilation, assembling everything from personal experiences, rants, raves, and essays to comic art—with contributions from girls located across the nation. Girls, it seemed, had a lot to say on a spectrum of issues; and once the valves opened, the writing kept coming. Sara Torres' (1999) anthology of essays, *That Body Image Thing: Young Women Speak Out!* contains practical narratives written by young women aged thirteen to nineteen on issues ranging from eating disorders and depression to body modification through dancing and sport, to the body in relation to cultural traditions. Azmina Ladha (2003) edited a collection for the FREDA Centre with a similar mandate—by girls, for girls—four years later.

2001 saw another burst of production on girls and by girls. Sharlene Azam, founder of *Reluctant Hero* (the first magazine in Canada produced by and for teen girls), published her *Rebel, Rogue, Mischievous Babe: Stories About Being a Powerful Girl* that year, showcasing articles that break prevailing myths around the realities of girls' relationships with their bodies, their families, sex and sexuality, bullying, violence and racism. In the same year, Sumach Press published *Turbo Chicks: Talking Young Feminisms* (Karaian, Rundle and Mitchell, eds), which contained a number of pieces that either spoke to girls, were voiced by girls or addressed issues of girlhood. These works deal more specifically with a younger generation of feminists who, despite self-defining as "girls," were already well into adulthood; illustrating once again that the categorization is indeed a slippery one.

Last year, Melinda Mattos and Nicole Cohen founded *Shameless* magazine: "Canada's independent [English language] voice for smart, strong, sassy young women." Proudly independent, *Shameless* is a grassroots glossy produced by a team of volunteer staff members, with content spanning the arts, culture and politics, all guided by a teen advisory board and feminist perspectives.

In November 2003, *Transforming Spaces: Girlhood, Agency and Power*, the first international conference on girlhoods was held at Concordia University in Montréal. The overwhelming success of the event prompted a report that captured snapshots of the conference—as well as the reactions of participants to the unique and often-challenging assemblage of academics, grassroots activists, youth advocates and girls and young women—in a multi-voiced document (Steenbergen, 2004). The conference and its retreat component were both facilitated and attended by organizations in Canada with girls as their primary concern, including its host, POWER Camp National/Filles d'Action, GirlSpoken: Creative Voices for Change, New Opportunities for exploring Values and self-Awareness, The Ontario Young People's Alliance and the Real POWER Youth Society. Other organizations have been established across the nation over the last decade as well, corresponding with the growth and breadth of girlhood studies as a field. For instance, the Centre d'encadrement pour jeunes filles immigrantes works to improve the social, cultural, economic and civic lives of immigrant girls and young women, and GirlSpace's student volunteers facilitate girls' free expression through a variety of workshops. WAVES (Women Active Vocal Effective and Strong, with multiple chapters) promotes feminist politics with an anti-racist, queer positive and transpositive agenda, running camps and workshops. What is unique about these particular organizations is that they were created and exist principally for girls and young women and not as off-shoots or sub-groups of larger women- or youth-focused associations, illustrating the viability and necessity of separating and focusing on issues of special significance to girls as a distinct, albeit diverse, group.

In conceptualizing this terrain, it becomes clear that mediating the various realms of inquiry and their thematic points of concern—at the level of lived realities as well as institutional forces—are factors that both enable and constrain constructions of "girl" and girlhood. These include hegemonic femininities as articulated through preferences which are race, class, ability and sexuality-based.

Balancing and negotiating competing demands is a hallmark of contemporary girlhood. Whether this involves balancing school and home, diverse cultural dis-courses or peer cultures organized around sexuality, race, and ability, this act of bal-ancing—of finding momentary spaces through lasting connections—is itself an expression of the agentic capacity of girls; of utilizing available resources, making in-vestments, and charting directions that allow for an articulation of a sense of self that speaks to their own truths and that resonates with experience.

Yet, and in spite of these agentic capacities, the weight of structural consider-ations cannot be under-estimated. Constructions of femininities are not only mediated by but also determined by issues of race, class, ability and sexuality. In that sense, femininities which are raced are contingent on the processes of racialization inherent in society. How racism mediates expressions of girlhood depends then on the con-structions of raced girlhood that are available, acceptable and sanctioned in the larger society. These might take the form of the dependent girl from a war-torn country seeking refuge in the West or the "oppressed" Muslim girl typically shown shrouded in a burqa. Such a construction not only permits for a degree of benevolence and pity on the part of the dominant society, which in turn reinforces national mythologies (Razack, 1998) but also allows for the reassertion of similar power relations as in-scribed in our colonial history. Similarly, a raced construction of girlhood that de-pends on the exoticization of difference is also rendered acceptable and available as a script, given that it resonates with the bedrock of historical associations rooted in colo-nial encounters.

What is allowed and disallowed in prevailing and dominant constructions of girlhood then serves to demarcate the boundaries of this terrain at the socio-cultural and political levels. For girls who are presented with these dominant scripts, the task becomes one of negotiating and navigating this terrain, its various cul-de-sacs and spaces of safety, and its hyphenated third spaces. What we have said of race here could easily be applied to issues of sexuality and class, albeit not as separate and mutually exclusive categories, but rather as experiences articulated through a framework of pa-triarchal and capitalist structures of power. Underpinning all of these hegemonic ide-als are ambivalences which once again border on and define the acceptable and unacceptable. But between these bordered edges of dominant ideals lies a nebulous, fluid and dynamic landscape, one marked by complex layers, intersecting and inter-locking mediations with their variegated outcomes: the girlhoods of today.

This volume captures some of these shifting, fluid and dynamic realities; locating them, in a rather momentary way under an analytic gaze so that we can interrogate, disrupt and re-examine the depth of these negotiated realities in transition.

Organizing *Girlhood*: Redefining the Limits

This anthology focuses on diverse yet connected issues confronting girls today: the construction of girlhood and communities of girls; encounters with violence; agency, resistance and articulation; narratives of sexuality and the body; identity formation and popular culture; and more. Our subtitle, "Redefining the Limits," allows us—as editors and contributors—to interrogate the very categories that have strategically limited, contained and defined girlhood in highly specific and ideological ways. To us, the space of girlhood is one of contestation; marked by conflict, resistance and change.

A collection like this could be organized in several ways, and we oscillated between various possible permutations that clustered chapters around common sites (technology, popular culture, school), shared methodologies (ethnography, textual analysis, narrative), and recurrent themes (racism, identity, violence, sexuality). However, this rather artificial "framing" into neat sections with definite titles seemed to do an injustice to the very notion of 'redefining limits'; confining the pieces under hard-and-fast headings and categorically constricting their movement. While the ordering we eventually selected reveals a certain thematic coherence, currents of similarity run throughout, enabling a play of resonance between the various chapters and revealing the complexities of "girlhood" in ways that we couldn't have predicted.

As fitting reminders of historic instances of violence marked by uprooting and displacement, we begin with chapters by Pamela J. Downe, and Hourig Attarian and Hermig Yogurtian that poignantly capture the legacies of colonialism/imperialism and exile. Haunting and painful memories constitute a well-spring through which identity is recreated and reproduced anew at each location of migration both temporally and spatially. Though creative in its process of renewal, revival and recuperation, the task of identity formation through a prism of violence can also be devastating. But rather than portray girlhoods as quintessential sites of victimization, these chapters demonstrate the individual and collective resilience and strength of girls, and reflect on the myriad ways in which memory can be invoked to restore and re-invigorate a sense of self-determination.

A number of chapters target and ask difficult questions of the multivariate discourses that work to construct girls and that have helped shape the emerging field of girlhood studies in the Canadian context. Rachel Gouin and Fathiya Wais note that the field has thus far only minimally included Francophone girls and their perspectives, and even then much of this research is confined to French texts dealing specifically with Quebec. English texts, on the other hand, have tended to exclude references to the French experience and failed to consider the realities and experiences of French speaking girls living outside of Quebec. They take a much-needed first step here by calling linguistic categories into question and proposing a more equitable framework for future research.

Yasmin Hussein, Helene Berman, Romy Poletti, Rian Lougheed-Smith, Azmina Ladha, Ashley Ward, and Barb MacQuarrie chart the language of gendered violence, examining its expression, impact and outcome in the lives of girls and young women. They ask: What does it mean to "do" participatory action research with girls and young women? Why is girl-centred research important? And what is accomplished or gained by engaging girls in the research process? Their chapter outlines some of the issues they have encountered in presenting their work to diverse audiences, working with girls who are differently situated, and the experiences of violence that mark their own lives. In a self-critical and insightful manner, their voices weave through the text, punctuating a discussion on girl-centred research with personal reflections.

Yasmin Jiwani and Jo-Anne Lee specifically address racialized violence against girls. Jiwani focuses on the violence of racism as experienced by girls and young women of colour. Drawing on a study conducted in Vancouver, she argues that racism as a form of violence tends to be erased, trivialized or dismissed by those in positions of power. The violence of racism also tends to be internalized and over time and is reproduced through the naturalized hierarchies of power that prevail in schools and peer groups. While Lee makes a similar argument in her study of girls and young women of colour in Victoria, she underscores issues of citizenship and locality. Through an analysis of the community development/participatory action research paradigms, she outlines the ways in which exclusion is mediated in the dominant white landscape of Victoria. Here whiteness becomes both a physical feature of the environment and the dominant gaze under which girls and young women of colour live their lives, mediating different realities and worlds, and navigating between the corrosive effects of denial and dismissal and the affirming yet problematic dynamics of a participatory process.

Tatiana Fraser and Sarah Mangle also cast a critical eye on the spaces in which they work and the methods used to fulfill their organizational mandates. Using their involvement with/in a national non-profit organization whose goal is to raise awareness and mobilize around the elimination of violence and discrimination for girls and young women (and organizations working with them), they illuminate the challenges that emerge in attempting to bridge multiple strategies for change. Sharing examples, they discuss the creative possibilities that emerge from such tensions, and offer useful tactics for identifying, articulating and dealing with conflict.

Are queer girls, girls? Marnina Gonick argues that if we understand "girl" as a category which is socially produced rather than simply a naturally occurring biological and developmental phase in the life course, we can better appreciate the restrictions that limit the diverse reality of girlhood. Her question suggests that even more may be involved than the already complicated project of creating more inclusive categories. It demands that we look again at the intersecting discourses of femininity, age, agency and sexuality and the social and cultural practices that constitute "girl" as category, and consider the institutionalized norms that regulate the boundaries of the category as well as girls' responses to them. In documenting the various ways in which queer youth are vulnerable to violence, Gonick also problematizes the discourse of risk and considers the numerous ways in which queer youth manifest agency and activism, sometimes using queer identity strategically to obtain much needed resources and services.

While the concept of resistance has been much celebrated in recent academic and popular writing, few have undertaken to interrogate this concept critically. Rebecca Raby provides a nuanced analysis of the differences between modernist and postmodernist constructions of resistance. Resistance, she argues, can include subtle and often covert acts as well as larger more pronounced oppositional actions against structural forces. Among girls, acts of resistance tend to be confined to the day to day interactions with peers and those in positions of authority. Similarly, resistance is often expressed through the language of style—reflecting girls' agency, but one that is undoubtedly delimited by the latitude that girls are afforded through gendered scripts and prescriptive guidelines.

Is meanness a form of resistance? Dawn Currie and Deirdre Kelly's provocative chapter explores the economy and currency of meanness between and among girls in the context of the school. Commonly understood as "relational aggression" or "lateral violence," they argue that meanness is a direct outcome of the dominant constructions of femininity that are articulated within the hierarchical structures inherent in peer groups and within the larger school culture. More importantly, such meanness reflects the agency of girls as they strive to navigate between competing constructions of "good girls" and "bad girls" and attempt to gain a level of popularity and inclusion in the economy of peer cultures. Meanness, they contend, becomes a currency through which such inclusion is obtained and maintained.

Based on an ethnographic study of girls at "East Side High" in Vancouver, Shauna Pomerantz explores style in relation to girls' identity construction; offering an alternative reading to both the "Ophelia genre" and moral panics surrounding girls, their bodies, and their clothes. Framing clothes as "social skin," Pomerantz argues that style "functions as a significant form of embodied subjectivity for girls" that locates power within the body. It also draws attention to the complex social processes that girls negotiate on an everyday basis, highlighting the multiple ways in which they carefully and creatively make meaning out of their complicated lives. Through their construction and articulation of stylized identities that purposefully challenge traditional femininity, the ethos of popularity, and their sense of disenfranchisement, girls express their own individuality and agency.

Issues surrounding girls' bodies is a theme further explored in the next few chapters. Using the dominant North American narratives of menstruation sites of inquiry, Michele Polak examines the secrecy, fear, discretion and embarrassment typically associated with the onset of menses and its perpetuation by the feminine hygiene industry. Based on an extensive study of girls' personal web pages, Polak moves from history to corporate advertising to the online world and discovers that a considerable rewriting of that narrative has been taking place, one that is "unflinchingly descriptive and seethingly honest." She argues that online space has provided a place where traditional menstruation narratives are not only being disrupted, but reimagined.

Prompted by her own visceral reaction to her "discovery" of the online world of preteen modeling websites, Sophie Wertheimer examines the construction of the North American girl as simultaneously embodying asexual innocence and the erotic. Situating preteen modeling websites within the often-contradictory and always-constructed social, cultural and discursive framework of "childhood," Wertheimer argues that dominant discourses render girls as passive objects—not as agents in their own right. In an attempt to move beyond this narrow construction, she offers ways to read these spaces—and girls' participation in them—as more complex and nuanced, reflecting their agency and complicity in the consumerist ethos of contemporary society.

Taking the theme of representation further, Michele Byers explores Canadian television programming in terms of how girls are positioned within the national imaginary. Byers argues that while much of teen programming is constrained by the commercialized format of the genre, Canadian programs such as *Degrassi Jr. High* and *Renegade.com* make a concerted effort to produce programming that is girl-centred and which speaks to a specifically Canadian audience. Drawing examples from these two popular series, she demonstrates how the series differ from their American counterparts, and how in fact—despite its limitations—Canadian programming remains quite faithful to Canadian girls and their varied realities.

Individually, each chapter interrogates "girlhood" as a site of resistance, complicity, survival and celebration. Taken as a group, they point to the inherent interdisciplinarity of girlhood studies, highlighting the necessity of including multiple perspectives and multifaceted analyses of an area of inquiry. They also underscore the need to see all borders (both geographic as well as conceptual) as constructions that need to be interrogated, scrutinized and negotiated in the interests of improving the lives of girls and young women.

Girlhood: Redefining the Limits offers a panoramic view of a largely un-mined and very rich emerging area—namely, girlhood studies in Canada. We recognize that the collection is far from complete, given the complexity of issues that exist within our national framework. At the same time, it strikes us that this is precisely the time that girlhood studies in Canada might serve as a much-needed catalyst to the feminist community and society at large to see age, across the life span of girls and women, as a broad category for analysis and activism.

This anthology is dedicated to the strong, smart, funky, savvy and courageous girls and young women we have had the good fortune to know and from whom we continue to learn more than we could ever adequately express.

And to those girls and young women who shared so much of their lives, realities and experiences and whose incredible resistance against structures of domination continually inspire us in our commitment to social change.

Chapter One

Aboriginal Girls In Canada:
Living Histories Of Dislocation, Exploitation And Strength[1]

Pamela J. Downe

> Children are the heart of the community, and are precious spirits over
> whom we must watch. —Kim Anderson (2000: 162)

Children have traditionally been central to Aboriginal communities in Canada, figur-
ing prominently in the prevailing worldviews of the diverse First Nations and Métis
peoples across the country.[2] In its profile of Aboriginal women, the Saskatchewan
Women's Secretariat (1999) depicts one such worldview as a series of embedded and
concentric circles:

> The inner circle is where everybody begins as daughter, son, granddaughter
> or grandson. In the first outward ring we are the sister or brother. As the
> rings move progressively outward, we are the niece/nephew; cousin;
> friend; wife/husband; and finally we are the mother/father. At one time
> there was no word that described orphan or the concept of foster care.
> When a child was without parents, individuals in the other rings became
> parents. Every child, when they reached a certain age spent time with the
> Elders to learn their wisdom (35).

Nested at the centre of society, protected and educated by the surrounding layers of
community, children are represented as a link from the present to future. They represent the cherished continuation of tradition and culture. Children also constitute a
greater proportion of the Aboriginal population with the birth rate among First Nations women being almost twice as high as among the general Canadian population
(Indian and Northern Affairs Canada, 2001). The average age of Canada's Aboriginal
population is approximately thirteen years younger than the non-Aboriginal population and children under the age of fourteen constitute over 33% of those identifying as
Aboriginal, compared to the 19% of those who are non-Aboriginal (Statistics Canada,
2003). The relative youth of Aboriginal communities is seen by some to be a cause for
hope and a celebration of strength and vitality.

Set against this child-affirming ideology, though, is a starker picture of apprehension, abuse and invisibility. As Maria Campbell points out, the reality of hardship

and marginalization is often quite different from the ideal: "I know some of the most dysfunctional, disrespectful families, who all have their Indian names, and they have done all their ceremonies, but there is no respect for the spirit of the children" (qtd. in Anderson, 2000: 163). The problems of neglect, abuse and violence are rooted not only in individual family dysfunction but in historical processes of colonization. Through years of displacement, marginalization and oppression, communities have become stressed to and beyond their breaking point. We now have a situation where children face heightened risks of violence and oppression, and it appears that girls are forced into positions of particular vulnerability.

There is not much written about the daily lives of Aboriginal girls in Canada: how or to what extent they experience the vulnerability to various forms of violence, how they cope with cultural dislocation and uprootedness, and where the sources of strength and pleasure lie. In fact, Aboriginal girls remain among the most invisible and silenced in Canadian society, erased from even the most exemplary postcolonial work in the area of Indigenous rights and identity construction. The intent of this chapter is to attend to the experiences of Aboriginal girls, examining how the history of child apprehension and residential school regimes established a pattern of dislocation, uprootedness and abuse that continues to characterize the lives of those Aboriginal girls who today face sexual exploitation and homelessness. I seek to explore how the colonial history of Aboriginal dislocation and uprootedness is very much a lived history; kept alive not only through the oral traditions of Aboriginal memory-making but through the ongoing "traumatic disconnection" of Aboriginal youth from communities where a sense of home and be-longing can be safely fostered (Chansonneuve, 2005: 43).

Although it is a surprisingly under-theorized concept, the notion of "lived history" is particularly useful in this analysis because it requires us to make inter-generational connections between the gendered experiences of residential school dis-placement in the early- to mid-1900s and the equally gendered experiences of uprootedness, homelessness and sexual exploitation that many Aboriginal girls cur-rently face in the early twenty-first century. Employed most frequently by historians to refer to the re-enactments of past events or the engagement with artefacts and her-itage buildings of bygone eras, the idea of a lived history can be extended to mean the ways in which past events are narrated to contextualize and make sense of ongoing and present-day situations.

In his analysis of Kwame Appiah's book *In My Father's House*, Tsenay Serequeberhan (1996) employs just such a meaning by examining how a history of African colonization is a lived history, playing itself out in the individual and collective constructions of African identities today. "We are all inheritors of a past," Serequeberhan argues, and although he believes the past to be beyond individual con-trol, it infuses who we know ourselves to be in any given context (116). The abuses experienced by Aboriginal girls over the past 130 years are not isolated occurrences; they are connected through a pervasive colonial ideology that sees these young women as exploitable and often dispensable. However, the lived history of girls' uprootedness is also characterized by an intergenerational strength that is too often overlooked in depictions of gender- and culture-based violation and abuse. While we must not—in any way—diminish or disregard the suffering and hardships faced by Aboriginal girls and women through the years, we must not allow stories of violence and exploitation to eclipse the equally powerful stories of survival and determination that are also told.

Residential Schools And Child Apprehension

For they killed the best that there was in me
When they said I must not return
To my father's lodge, to my mothers arms;
When my heart would burn—and burn!
For when dead is a daughter's womanhood
There is nothing left that is grand and good.

—E. Pauline Johnson

This verse from an originally unpublished poem appears in Charlotte Gray's (2002) biography of the nineteenth century Mohawk and English writer, E. Pauline Johnson (266). It was written in response to the plight of dislocation, cultural alienation, exploitation, coercion and abuse experienced by Aboriginal residential school students who were forced to leave their home communities to attend Church-run schools in non-Aboriginal settlements so that they could become culturally less Aboriginal and more European. Since the early 1600s, Christian missionaries had attempted to educate First Nations and Métis children so as to instil European values. By the mid-1800s, with the Bagot Commission Report of 1842 and the Gradual Civilisation Act of 1857, this enterprise was endorsed by the Canadian state when an effective relationship between religious offices and the Government was built in order to "solve" what was commonly known at the time as the "Indian problem" of resistance to colonial rule (Miller, 1996; Milloy, 1999). The 1889 Annual report of the Department of Indian Affairs described this bluntly:

> The boarding school disassociates the Indian child from the deleterious home influences to which he would otherwise be subjected. It reclaims him from the uncivilized state in which he has been brought up. It brings him into contact from day to day with all that tends to effect a change in his views and habits of life. By precept and example he is taught to endeavour to excel in what will be most useful to him (qtd. in Gray, 2002: 267).

With its reference to the singular and masculine Aboriginal child, the passage above reflects the androcentrism of colonial rule and policy in the late nineteenth and early twentieth century Canada. Although it has not received a great deal of attention, the gendered policies of the residential school system complemented other federal legislation, most notably the *Indian Act* of 1876, that took away Aboriginal women's legal and cultural status, as well as women's traditional rights to land, if they married a non-Aboriginal man, a man from another community, or if they sought a university education. In other words, the administration of residential schools worked in tandem with the *Indian Act* to erode the vitality of Aboriginal communities in part through uprooting Aboriginal women and apprehending the children. Together, these initiatives were devastatingly successful. Between 1840 and 1980, approximately 150,000 Aboriginal children attended these schools and the effects have been long-lasting. James Waldram (2004) explains that "Residential schools [were] 'total institutions'… in which every aspect of the child's life was regulated. Sleeping, eating, playing, working, and learning were all regulated [and] often supported by strict codes of conduct and corporal punishment" (229). To meet its assimilationist objective, these schools imposed strict rules prohibiting children from speaking their own languages and requiring them to wear European-style clothing (sometimes military-style uniforms) and to don European-style haircuts. Threats and physical reprimand were used to enforce these rules. According to Amnesty International (2004), these punishments "included beatings, chaining children to their beds, or denying them food. Cloaked by society's indifference to the fate of these children, individual staff carried out horrendous acts of physical and sexual abuse" (9).

Agnes Jack (2001) offers stories from former students at the Kamloops Residential School where the abuses against attending children were considered "atrocious" and the "pain of sexual advances," to which the girls were particularly subjected, "extreme." Jane Willis (1973) recalls how she came away from the Anglican-run James Bay Residential School in Quebec with a profound disillusionment and shame at being a young Cree woman which, she was taught, meant being dirty, unkempt, and "inherently rape-able" (155). Edna Brass, a respected Elder and counsellor in Vancouver, recalls her 13-year residential school experience in British Columbia and she describes the intergenerational effects of her trauma:

> I was sexually abused, I was raped, I was beaten. [Years after] I felt like I didn't belong anywhere and my children have faced the same. They don't know my family. They don't know my community. I never felt like my reserve is my reserve. I just try to fit in where I can. My daughter suffered because of this (Amnesty International, 2004: 10).

The Aboriginal Healing Foundation (AHF, 1999) explains that "When trauma is ignored and there is no support for dealing with it, the trauma will be passed from one generation to the next. What we learn to see as 'normal' when we are children, we pass on to our children…This is the legacy of physical and sexual abuse in residential schools" (5). The AHF (2005) also understands that intergenerational trauma not only refers to the effects suffered by subsequent generations, but it also affects ascending generations including the parents, grandparents and Elders in the communities from where children were forcibly removed. Concern for the proliferating and enduring damage done by residential school abuse has given rise to the elusive and still-undefined phrase "Residential School syndrome." Although the meaning and application of this "syndrome" is hotly contested, the public retellings of the institutionalized violence of residential schools certainly resonate with many and create what psychiatrist Laurence Kirmayer (1996) calls "a public space of trauma" (189).

Although references to gender are scattered throughout the testimonials of former students, this public space of racialized and colonial trauma to which Kirmayer refers has not been extensively excavated for the gendered effects of the experience. There is evidence to suggest, however, that residential school education was itself decidedly gendered. Historian Jim Miller (1996), for example, describes the "fanatical segregation" of boys from girls, believing that the Aboriginal girls' greater autonomy and control over their bodies contradicted colonial British norms of female subservience and shame (234). Sexuality became a means through which the children, and by most accounts especially the girls, were punished. Fournier and Crey (1997) cite Mary Chapman, a Sto:lo woman who recounts being taught that female bodies were shameful and sites for discipline:

> When girls were caught doing something like…talking Halq'emeylem, the nuns would make them stand in a long line, then lift their skirts right up. They had to stand there, in front of everybody, naked… [Other times] the nuns would strip the girls naked from the waist down and force them to lie face down on their beds. Then all the rest of us were told to parade by the girls and hit them as hard as we could on their bottoms. The nuns would just stand there and watch (121).

Children learned that the female body was the source of pain and shame, something to be controlled and disciplined. Girls at Blue Quills Residential School in Alberta were required to wear a long flannel nightgown (referred to as a "bathing suit") in the bath so that they would learn "to be modest in dress, chaste in behaviour, and free of pregnancy" (Miller, 1996: 235). Although boys at other schools were sometimes required to wear shorts in the shower, the girls had a heavier burden of imposed modesty and restricted sexuality.

European defined labour roles were also imposed on the children in gendered ways. Due to a shortage of funding, Canadian churches designed many of these institutions as working farms which the children's labour made viable. Ironically, it was the children themselves who, through their exploited and coerced labour, funded the very institutions that undermined their own well-being. The intense agricultural training that students obtained in many of these schools was highly gendered, with the boys learning to be farmers and the girls learning to be "domestic helpers" (Lomawaima, 1994: 82). During the summer months, girls were sent to wealthier Euro-Canadian homes to work as domestic servants, a practice referred to as "outing." Dian Million (2000) argues that the practice of "outing" had as its goal the domestication of young Aboriginal women, requiring them to enter "circumscribed relationships with white women as low-paid drudges. Many Native women, and specifically Northwest coastal women, had no equivalent role historically except for slave...Many of these women, removed from their Native communities for years, were adopted or married out to white husbands and never went home" (96). This allowed the racist hierarchy of White privilege to remain intact with Aboriginal women paying the price through the disenfranchisement from their families and ways of life.

The disruptions to Aboriginal families and communities, and the removal of Native children did not end with the last closure of Church-run residential schools in the 1980s. For decades, provincial and federal child welfare systems apprehended Aboriginal children who were suspected of being abused, whether or not those suspicions were ever substantiated. Once in a system of rotating foster- and state-care, many children completely lost contact with their families of origin and home communities. Maureen McEvoy and Judith Daniluk (1995) explain that "[t]his system culminated in the 1960s with an apprehension rate so high that some Reserves lost nearly a generation of children to child welfare authorities" (223). The report of the Royal Commission of Aboriginal Peoples (1996) notes that the number of Aboriginal children in British Columbia who were taken from their homes and placed in state-sponsored care rose from twenty-nine in 1955 to 1 446 in 1965. By the late 1980s, the apprehension rate had slowed somewhat but was still six times that of the national average (Arvard and Haney, 1989).

There were political and economic reasons for this rapid escalation in apprehensions. The 1951 amendments to the *Indian Act* transferred responsibility for the healthcare, welfare and education of non-status Aboriginal peoples to the provinces. Because the federal government was still financially responsible for Status Indians, it negotiated with the provinces how much it would pay, per capita, for the resources invested in this population. As Fournier and Crey (1997) point out, "[o]nce the provinces were in charge, and guaranteed payment for each Indian child they apprehended, the number of First Nations made legal wards of the state quickly ballooned" (83).

It is important to stress that in some cases children were removed from homes because they were facing undue hardships and the charges of abuse, neglect as well as endangerment were substantiated by Aboriginal and non-Aboriginal investigations alike (Palmer and Cooke, 1996). However, in other cases, "children were taken from parents whose only crime was poverty—and being aboriginal...The white social worker, following hard on the heels of the missionary, the priest and the Indian agent, was convinced that the only hope for the salvation of the Indian people lay in the re-moval of their children" (Fournier and Crey, 1997: 85, 84). It is ironic that those who found themselves living in the poorest conditions were the children of former residen-tial school students, and they themselves were now at risk for apprehension because of dysfunction wrought by that system. According to Bridget Moran (1992), a former government social worker in British Columbia, Aboriginal families were given next to no resources to help them alleviate the poverty, unemployment, or health problems that they faced. Instead, their children—who were often loved and cherished—were removed to foster homes "about which we knew next to nothing, no matter how we cloaked our actions in welfare jargon, we were putting those children at risk" (139). As Campbell puts it, "In our stories, this [scoping of children] is known as 'the time of the black car'" (qtd. in Anderson, 2000: 162).

Some foster- and adoptive- home situations were safe and warm environments. However, many authors charge that whereas "residential schools incarcerated chil-dren for ten months…they always knew their First Nation origin and who their par-ents were…In the foster- and adoptive- care system, aboriginal children typically vanished with scarcely a trace, the vast majority of them placed until they were adults in non-aboriginal homes where their own First Nation and even their birth names were erased, often forever" (Fournier and Crey, 1997: 81). Exacerbating this situation was the Euro-Canadian misinterpretation of Aboriginal behaviours. Until the mid-1980s, it was commonly assumed that Aboriginal parents were not interested in hav-ing their children returned because they did not aggressively fight for them in an ad-versarial court process. Of course, many Aboriginal adults, particularly those from more isolated and traditional communities, were unfamiliar with this process; with no help or guidance, they had no realistic possibility for success.

This situation began to change by the mid-1980s when new legislation was in-troduced giving Aboriginal governments more control over the welfare and placement of the children in their communities. *The Ontario and Child Services Act* of 1984, for ex-ample, stated that "Indian and native people should be entitled to provide, wherever possible, their own child and family services, and that all services to Indian and Native children and families should be provided in a manner that recognizes their culture, heritage, language and traditions, including the concept of the extended family" (in Palmer and Cooke, 1996: 716). By the late 1990s, Ontario had thirteen Aboriginal agencies providing support to Native families and recruiting Aboriginal foster- and adoptive-care homes. However, there are not enough Native foster homes, particu-larly in urban areas, to serve the needs of children apprehended into state care and, de-spite attempts to alter evaluative techniques, the criteria used to assess child neglect are still predominantly mired in Eurocentric values (Anderson, 1998). Moreover, chil-dren placed in non-Aboriginal care facilities frequently encounter race-based discrimination at the same time as they are becoming increasingly alienated from their home communities (Palmer and Cooke, 1996).

The gendered implications of these child apprehensions by the provincial welfare systems have not been explored to any significant degree. However, we do know that the history of community dislocation wrought by both residential school abuse and child welfare apprehension often informs how Aboriginal women and girls make sense of the violence and exploitation that they face in disproportionately high rates today. Pursuing how the links between past and present abuses are made, and how they come to inform what it means to be an Aboriginal girl in Canada, is particularly important given the ongoing and devastating profile of violence. Young Aboriginal women holding Indian status are five times more likely than other women of the same age to die of violence (Indian and Northern Affairs, 1996), seventy-five percent of Aboriginal girls under the age of eighteen have been sexually abused (Lane, Bopp and Bopp, 2003), and seventy-five percent of Aboriginal victims of sex crimes are girls under eighteen, fifty percent are under fourteen, and seven percent are under seven (Hylton, 2001).

McEvoy and Daniluk (1995) offer many examples of adult women survivors of childhood sexual and physical abuse who cast their experiences in light of the history that they feel created a tacit acceptance of violence and a prevailing belief that Aboriginal girls are less worthy and more dispensable. More formally, the Royal Commission on Aboriginal Peoples (1996) makes the connection between past and present apprehensions:

> The dysfunction of today is a legacy of disrupted relationships in the past, but the effects are broader and more diffuse than can be traced in a direct cause-and-effect relationship. There are entire communities whose members are imbued with a sense of violation and powerlessness, the effect of multiple violations having reverberated throughout [the generations and across] kin networks (36).

However, set alongside the individual and community-wide stories of the devastation brought about by the apprehension of children into residential schools and state-sponsored foster- and adoptive-homes, are companion stories of strength, resilience, and healing. These stories must also be told.

Aboriginal girlhood is not constituted exclusively by uprootedness and violence but also by tenacity, innovation and survival. Agnes Grant's (2004) collection of fourteen survival stories told by women with first-hand experience of residential schools offers an excellent overview of how strength and resourcefulness were and are exhibited even under the direst constraints. Rita Joe, an acclaimed Mi'kmaq poet and recipient of the Order of Canada, tells Grant that after winning the approval of the Catholic teachers and administrators at the Shubenacadie Residential School in Nova Scotia by learning to be "quiet, humble and acquiescent," she decided to decline the offer to stay on at the school. She chose instead to take a job at the Halifax Infirmary:

> As the train [for Halifax] pulled away, Rita cried. The school had been her home for four years. She had no home to return to and, at sixteen, she felt she was truly alone in the world. However, she also felt great freedom and vowed that never again would anyone else regulate her life. Most of all, she vowed that her spiritual life would be her own (43).

Rita's sense of uprootedness and trepidation, then, is countered by an opposing sense of freedom, possibility and self-actualization.

The strength and resilience of residential school students is also captured well by Shirley Sterling (1992) in her fictionalized account of a young girl at a British Columbia institution. Although based on her own adult and autobiographical recollections of childhood residential schooling, Sterling's novel provides one of the only child-centred perspectives of these schools. The book takes the form of a journal written by twelve-year-old Seepeetza as she endures the trials and violations of the educational system into which she was physically forced. Although fear is the predominant emotion captured in her diary, readers come to appreciate Seepeetza's strong and independent will, only one example of which is Seepeetza's superficial acceptance of the Christian name "Martha" that is bestowed on her by the school but that she repeatedly and defiantly rejects by re-inscribing her own name in her thoughts and journal entries every night. We also come to know Seepeetza as incredibly funny, resisting the daily indignities of the institution with humour so skillfully employed that the other girls recognize and appreciate its subversiveness but it eludes the watchful and harsh Sisters.

In her forward to Grant's (2004) collection, Marlene Starr argues that the lived history of residential schools and child welfare apprehensions reverberate throughout Aboriginal communities:

> It came as a great relief to me that finally there is a book that does not treat us as 'history' but rather as living, breathing human beings who still exist today…In residential schools we were carefully tutored, through both direct teaching and role modeling to accept the inequality of the sexes as right and just. The 'might makes right' philosophy of the residential schools has done immeasurable harm to our communities" (xi).

And yet, as Starr also notes, this history is one marked not only by violence and dislocation but by triumphs over the emotional, physical, mental and spiritual abuses experienced by so many (viii). The stories of girls' strength and community reconnection are beginning to emerge in the literature on residential schooling and they resonate with those young Aboriginal women who currently face related challenges of disconnection and isolation.

Living The History: Self-Determination Amidst Sexual Exploitation

> We survive, and we do more than survive. We bond, we care, we fight, we
> teach, we nurse, we bear, we feed, we earn, we laugh, we love, we hang in
> there, no matter what. —Paula Gunn Allen (1986: 190).

The physical and sexual exploitation and abuse of Aboriginal children sanctioned by the
Canadian residential school system in the early- to mid-twentieth century established a
pattern of violence that has become normalized and accepted by many in the surrounding and dominant Euro-Canadian communities. The common disregard for the
kidnappings, sexual assaults and murders of Aboriginal women and girls that the much
publicized 2004 Amnesty International report documents would not be seen if White
women and girls were succumbing to the same fate in the same numbers. Stories of
these unnoticed disappearances circulate in many Aboriginal communities, and particularly among Aboriginal girls, as public secrets which are collectively known but rarely if
ever confronted or redressed (Taussig, 1999). In addition to living with grandmothers,
mothers, aunts and cousins who, as children, may have endured residential schooling
and state-apprehensions, Aboriginal girls today are connected to historical patterns of
uprootedness and violence every time they hear these secretive stories of 16-year old
Felicia Velvet Solomon from Norway House, Manitoba (raped and murdered in 2003),
Pamela George from Sakimay Saulteaux Nation, Saskatchewan (raped and murdered in
1991), Maxine Wapass from Thunderchild Cree Nation, Saskatchewan (missing and
murdered in 2002), Moira Erb from the Fort Alexander First Nation, Manitoba (missing
and murdered in 2003), or the countless others whose names are not known. In this
context, Aboriginal girls learn quickly that they are at risk.

The dangers of injury, assault, exploitation and displacement that Aboriginal
girls face are exacerbated by the fact that they are two and a half times as likely as
non-Aboriginal girls to live in poverty (UNDP, 2000). Moreover, Aboriginal girls can
look forward to being, as young adults between the ages of eighteen and twenty-four,
over twice as likely as non-Aboriginal women to live below the low-income cut-off
line. The probability of being poor increases when these young women have children,
particularly when they are the sole providers (Statistics Canada, 2001). Additional
children and pregnancies worsen poverty levels and although Aboriginal women living with a co-parent experience less poverty on average than a single mother, financial
dependence also elevates risks of violence (Davies, McMullen and Avison, 2000: vii).

Aboriginal children living in poverty frequently find themselves in sub-standard
and over-crowded housing. In Canada, fifty-two percent of Aboriginal households
—the majority of these headed solely by women with children—do not meet the Canadian Mortgage and Housing Corporations standards of affordability, adequate repair,
or space. In Saskatchewan, a province with one of the largest Aboriginal populations
in the country, the situation is even worse with seventy percent of on-reserve house-

holds being below housing standards (Saskatchewan Women's Secretariat, 1999: 33). In response to the pronounced poverty and inadequate housing characterizing most on-reserve communities, Aboriginal girls are far more likely to move from one community to another than are non-Aboriginal girls. Michael Hatfield (1997) explains that very often girls, like boys, relocate voluntarily, or are relocated by parents or guardians, to poorer and predominantly Aboriginal neighbourhoods in larger urban centres where they are subjected to racism from surrounding areas. Uprooting children from their home, school, peer group and community can, as was evidenced in the residential school regimes, lead to isolation and desperation. For relief from the pressures of economic hardship and cultural isolation, an increasing number of girls are turning to drugs and gang involvement (O'Nell, 1989). Rates of solvent inhalation (glue- and gas-sniffing in particular) among Innu girls in Labrador, for example, have been rapidly increasing and are attributable, in part, to the history of displacement from one home community and then another. A Sheshatshiu woman described the situation within her community: "Sniffing has been going on for years and years... These children feel that the only way to forget these sort of things [abuse and neglect] is...gas sniffing. It's not their fault the way they are today. I would call them victims of our history" (qtd. in Denov and Campbell, 2002: 27).

When young Aboriginal women find themselves disconnected from home communities, mired in poverty, deflated from ongoing racism and violence, and often facing challenges of addiction, they turn in great numbers to the urban-based sex trades; particularly prostitution (the exchange of sexual access for material remuneration). The sexual exploitation of youth through systems of prostitution has drawn considerable attention lately (Downe, 2003). Depending on the location, it is estimated that anywhere from fourteen to eighty-five percent of youth involved in prostitution in Canada are Aboriginal, though Aboriginal girls and young women constitute upwards of ninety percent in the street-based trades (Kingsley and Mark, 2000: 41). In Regina, the stroll where street prostitutes most commonly work has been described by the city police as "a world of drugs and prostitution, and most of all, as a space of Aboriginality" (Razack, 2002: 141). This racialized space is also one that is defined by the youth of the workers. On average, the age of entry into prostitution for Aboriginal girls is around twelve, lower than for non-Aboriginal girls for whom the average age on entry is fourteen (Kingsley and Mark, 2000: 9). Boys and young men certainly have a presence in Canadian sex trades, and once again, there is an over-representation of those with Aboriginal ancestry; however, the vast majority of those involved in prostitution are young women and girls.

The predominant reason for their involvement in prostitution is survival and yet, ironically, the risk of violence and murder faced by young sex workers is elevated with every month spent in the trade. Several of the young women participating in Kingsley and Mark's (2000) study describe the situation well:

> In Toronto, there's no one girl alive [who I knew from] when I was four-
> teen, and in Winnipeg, there's only two of us left. That's the reason I want
> to stop…I don't want to die (Winnipeg).

> The numbers [of women I knew in the trade] are getting smaller and smaller.
> The last time I went home, there was only one person still alive that I knew.
> All the rest of them had died…being shot, drug overdoses (Halifax).

> I have a lot of friends who have died from drugs, from murder, from even be-
> ing beaten. I've been to the lowest of lows, getting beaten as badly as you can
> get beaten, waking up in a ditch wondering where the hell I was (Mission).

The sexual exploitation of young Aboriginal women and girls, then, is a site of violence wherein racism, sexism, and poverty collide as the lived history of colonial displacement and devaluation.

The deaths and disappearances of the young women described above are largely
invisible and are reminiscent of the residential school students' experiences. Marlene
Starr recalls an incident at the Sandy Bay Residential School in Manitoba when a classmate was forced to stand in full view of the entire class with her blood-stained underwear over her head:

> While she stood there, we treated her as if she were invisible. We saw it as a
> way of maintaining the dignity of the victim, whereas in truth we were
> validating the unjust treatment by simply accepting it. We were well
> trained to ignore it and remain silent (qtd. in Grant, 2004: viii).

The lessons of acquiescence, silence and invisibility learned by girls in residential schools
were also learned by girls—many of whom were the same ones—apprehended by child
welfare services. And these lessons are once again learned by those Aboriginal girls and
young women who find themselves on the streets with limited options and ongoing
sexual exploitation. However, in my own research into the involvement of Aboriginal
girls and young women in prostitution, it is obvious that they learn other, more empowering lessons about friendship, strength in numbers and belonging as well.

In the seven years of partaking in participatory research with nineteen Aboriginal
girls and young women who are involved in primarily street-based prostitution in Saskatchewan, I am struck by the extent to which stories of sexualized violence, racist harassment by local residents, repeated police abuse and continual displacement are
balanced by stories of friendship, strength and resilience. One young woman, for example, has lived in a succession of foster homes and, at fifteen years old, saw selling sex as
her only viable option for economic independence. In 2000, she spoke at great length
with me about how the challenges she faces today are associated with the province's colonial history:

> I'm not sure where I belong…I mean I'm not Indian like the Cree 'cause, you
> know, I'm Métis so I guess I don't really count, you know? Like, I know I feel

this way 'cause the government drew lines to divide people, saying that you are one thing and I'm another. But they're lines that really seem to matter because I don't have no place that feels like mine. I feel like I don't really matter to nobody. Like, if I got hit bad or something or went missing, like who would really know? Like the kids who got shuffled off to the schools, you know? If something happened to them, like, who really knew?

On the heels of this testament to the lived history of colonial control of indigenous identity and residential schooling, however, this same young woman offered a different perspective of street-involvement:

Like, I hate having no real home, you know? That just totally sucks. But I feel good when I'm with Leanne and Karen [pseudonyms] and them, you know? We make each other laugh so hard. I peed my pants the other day 'cause we got laughing so hard. I never knew nobody like them. I know if I need something, I got them. And you know, if something bad happened to me, like, maybe nobody else would give a damn, eh, but I know that they sure would. They know how to say my name right. Ashley-Mika [pseudonym]. They say it like they know who I am. It's like we feed off each other, helping each other out, always having each other's backs, you know? It feels good knowing that there are girls who are like I belong with them, you know? When I'm with them, it's like I really like being only part White and part Indian.

Although there certainly is hardship and violence in Ashley-Mika's life, there is also pleasure and a sense of community that is fostered with other young women who, while sharing a personal and political history of displacement, create a sense of belonging and place. Many of the Aboriginal youth participating in Kingsley and Mark's (2000) study expressed similar sentiments. One young woman from Goose Bay explained, "You gotta' have people there with you through the whole thing, helping you out. You can't just get up and go [from the sex trade], but have people there for you when you need them" (65).

The sense of camaraderie forged among Aboriginal girls and young women who are involved in prostitution offers an informal but predictable sense of community that, in many cases, has served as a first step towards individual and collective self-determination. As with many residential school survivors and those who, as children, were apprehended and removed from their home communities, the girls and young women involved in prostitution frequently find themselves in high-risk, stigmatized and racially-charged environments. However, as the quote from Paula Gunn Allen at the beginning of this section attests, these same young women "hang in there" to build relationships, to enhance their strengths, and to live their history together.

Conclusion

Tsenay Serequeberhan (1996) claims that social identities are not, as many theorists claim, invented artefacts to be used only for strategic purposes. Instead, social identities—involving how individuals and communities see themselves and how they are seen by others—are lived histories born of "a context of concrete social, political, and historical struggles and success" (117). To be an Aboriginal girl in Canada does not, of course, mean that poverty, assault, sexual exploitation or childhood apprehension are inevitable. However, it does mean that the history of residential schooling, child welfare apprehensions, discriminatory federal legislation and cultural displacement visits itself—through family recollections, public secrets of disappearances and murders, impoverished living conditions, prevailing racism and displacement—upon the girls, informing how they see themselves and what possibilities their futures hold. Given the over-representation of Aboriginal girls and young women in prostitution and given the devastating levels of violence and oppression that colonial rule has left in its wake, creating connections between past and present conditions of abuse and sexual exploitation allows us to appreciate the intergenerational continuity and strength characterizing Aboriginal girlhood.

For many, childhood experiences of violence and abuse are paramount, devastating and undeniable. But few Aboriginal women recall these experiences as being all-encompassing. Amidst the violation and displacement is strength, resilience, friendship and occasionally laughter. These positive aspects should not be used to justify, excuse or negate the exploitation that characterizes the lived history of Aboriginal girls, but neither should the remarkable characters of these girls and young women be denied. Given that stories of strength, resilience, resistance and community connection are emerging in the published and formal recollections of residential school survivors, those of us who work with Aboriginal girls would do well to turn our attention more systematically to the ways in which they Aboriginal girls today exhibit similar strengths. And we should do so with the hope that Aboriginal girls will transcend the long-standing abuses that they face and they will be unencumbered to live their history with due reward.

Notes

1. Portions of this chapter were written as a background paper for the Alliance of Five Research Centres on Violence.

2. The term "Aboriginal" is used throughout this chapter to refer to people of First Nations, Métis and/or Inuit heritage in Canada. In the context of studies conducted in the United States, this term is also used to refer to American Indian and Alaskan Eskimo peoples. "Native" is used to refer to those of First Nations and/or Métis heritage in Canada. Occasionally, the colonial labels of "Status Indian" and "non-Status Indian," imposed by the Canadian state, are used in order to be consistent with the literature discussed.

Chapter Two

Survivor Stories, Surviving Narratives: Autobiography, Memory And Trauma Across Generations

Hourig Attarian, Hermig Yogurtian

My memory will retain what is worthwhile. My memory knows more about me than I do; it doesn't lose what deserves to be saved.
—Eduardo Galeano, (2000: 20)

Beginnings

These are the stories of several girlhoods told in three voices; that of Pergrouhi, Hourig and Hermig. Our voices come together in a contrapuntal narrative, telling the stories of many young women who lived through the horrors of war and genocide in different places and at different times.

As we originally envisioned this piece, we were especially concerned with staying faithful to the storytelling aspect and were faced with a decision to find an appropriate representational form that would reflect this concern. Thus came our choice of fusing the aural, oral and textual aspects of narration in a structure, where a cascade of voices flow into each other in a cyclical form instead of a mere linear recounting of events. This is both an aesthetic and a conceptual choice in our writing. Moreover, we have tried to step back to let all the voices, Pergrouhi's, our grandmothers', and our mothers', come forward on their own, in equal measure with ours. By doing this, we particularly want to acknowledge the role of Pergrouhi and her collaboration with us, in weaving this text. To further the analogy of counterpoint, the layout of the narratives, the transitions from one voice to another, the deliberate fusion of the roles of narrator and interpreter in the stories, all intertwine to share the reverberations of one ultimate narrative of survival.

Pergrouhi was a little girl in 1915, when the Ottoman Turkish government launched its genocidal campaign of mass killings and deportations of Armenians from their historic homeland of western Armenia. To this day the Armenian genocide remains unrecognized and actively denied by the modern Turkish Republic, a direct inheritor of the Ottoman legacy. Together with her mother, Pergrouhi was deported from her hometown and forced into the death march, with hundreds of thousands of other Armenians, through the deserts of Der el Zor in northern Syria, then part of the

Ottoman Empire. She survived, reached Iraq and lived there until she joined her children and grandchildren in Canada in 1978.

We met Pergrouhi when she was ninety-five years old, while we were working on a community project to bring survivor stories alive. Her name in Armenian means joy; a strange name for someone who had experienced so much suffering in her life. What impressed us most about her was the spontaneous way she connected to us and instantly held us captive with her storytelling. Despite her harrowing experiences, she was full of love, serene and attentive towards us. Encountering her was a true joy.

Through her story, we became engaged in a personal quest into our own inherited matrilineal life stories and memories of trauma. In both our families, all our grandparents were genocide survivors. As we were recording, translating, and editing Pergrouhi's story, we started remembering and retelling the stories of our own grandmothers, great-grandmothers, and great-aunts. Trauma for us is not simply constituted by inherited memories of genocide stories. Before making Canada our home, we had lived through fifteen years of civil war in Beirut. Soon it was our own memories of war and violence that we were writing about, something we had avoided doing for many years.

The civil war in Lebanon erupted in the spring of 1975, just as we were turning twelve. We had attended the same school and lived on the same street since early childhood. The war for us marked our years through high school, college, university, and work; it ended shortly after we had both immigrated to Montreal. Here too we always stayed close; though revisiting our horrible days during the war was a subject we actively avoided.

Our encounter with Pergrouhi brought everything to the fore; our childhood memories of genocide stories told at bedtime by mothers and grandmothers; our first-hand experiences of war, re-evaluated this time through the experiences of Pergrouhi when she was only a little girl.

In the pages that follow you will read some of those stories. Some lived, some heard, some recorded. All true. All spoken words that try to unburden the unspeakable horrors of war and genocide experienced by young girls who lived to become women, and tell the stories.

An Armenian's Fate

Voice 1—Pergrouhi[1]

My name is Pergrouhi. My mother's name was Hadji Mariam. My father's name was Boghos. I don't know my family name.

I just remember the walk. On and on and on and on we walked, for endless days, and endless nights. There were gendarmes around us, mounted on horseback. They had whips and canes and they would urge people on. Oh how frightened I was of those whips and the soldiers. My mother would tuck me under her arm; cover my eyes not to let me see what was going on around me. There were other children around us, all crying and wailing.

The villagers would bring bread; barley bread, corn bread. They would give a piece of bread to the mothers and take their children in return. That's how the children would be sold, for a piece of bread.

There were bodies lying all around us. Corpses were lying all around us, but we had to walk on, on and on, with no food and no drink, just the occasional piece of barley bread. Some bodies were hung from walls. They would lay the little boys on the ground; hit them, hit them and kill them. But we had to walk on.

Finally we reached Der Zor.[2] I remember crossing a bridge, and then they told us, "You are in Der Zor." There was a huge crowd, lots and lots of people. I lost my mother in the confusion. My mother was crying out for me. I was crying, looking for her, running around and crying, "mother, mother," until we finally found each other again.

People had made up songs about Der Zor—

A Burdened Silence

> I went through Der Zor,
> I drank the bloody waters.
> There are many sick and wounded in Der Zor,
> But don't come doctor don't bother,
> For there is no cure,
> We only have God to turn to.
> I woke up early and looked into my bag,
> With tears in my eyes I threw it over my shoulder,
> I left my father and mother in the desert,
> This is an Armenian's fate; this is an Armenian's fate...
> —Eduardo Galeano, (1992:11)
> *To remember, From the Latin record is: Passing back through the heart.*

Voice 2—Hermig

My great-grandfather Sarkis died quietly in Beirut[3] on a day when the fighting was intense, and was quickly buried in the Armenian cemetery. He didn't get his wish, even in death, to be joined with his beloved Nouritza, and to rest his bones with hers.

Grandfather Sarkis came to the city when he was a century old. He had never bothered with dentures and when he came to live with us he only had two yellow teeth in his sunken mouth. When he inhaled the smoke from his hand-rolled cigarettes, his cheeks would hollow out completely, his two teeth stuck out, and his jaws outlined the cave that was his mouth.

He wore a long camel-hair *abaya*[4] that I would snuggle in when I sat down at his knees to hear his stories. His gaze would fix a point not in space but in time, and my eyes would meet his at that imaginary dot which would magically bond us in his past. How he'd loved Nouritza; how he'd fought in the Ottoman army; how he'd tricked the Turks; how he (still) loved Nouritza; and how they had never, ever, bowed either from pain or hunger.

"But now!" he would rage, "NOW!! They've brought me to this cement box to die and they will probably bury me here. I have to go back to the village. I want to be buried on top of Nouritza…"

They were my parents, who thought he was too old to be capable of living on his own. *The village*, at the southernmost tip of Lebanon, was where he'd spent his entire life after the deportation.

Everyday at dusk he would let out a sigh that came from the deepest folds of his soul, "*shketsin mer sarere*; our mountains have cast their shadows." *Mer lernere, mer sarere*. "Mountain" is an elevation on the landscape in English; *mer lernere, mer sarere* have a nostalgic sadness that does not translate. He had lived in Lebanon for almost eighty years but this was still not his country. He yearned at every sunset for *yergire*,[5] "our country," and now he was doubly deprived, forced to watch the sun set not behind the mountains but behind the neighbour's laundry drying on the rooftop.

My parents brought him to Beirut in the heat of the civil war, and his only wish was to die quickly. When the street fights were raging, he would go out on the balcony in the hope that a stray bullet would free him of his misery. "Oh god, spare the life of one young person, take mine!" he kept saying. He thought god had made a mistake in his ledgers and counted him with the dead, while he still had to suffer the drudgery of life far removed from everything that had ever meant anything to him. Indeed god could have been forgiven for forgetting him, for he had died a long, long time ago, in the desert.[6]

Sarkis was my maternal grandmother Azadouhi's father. My paternal grandparents had always lived with us. They too had stories—of hardship, of beatings by the gendarmerie, of children dying on the deportation route, of hunger, humiliation, of the endless desert trek. Their stories deeply troubled my little soul and I didn't want to hear them. I got weary of my grandmother showing me her curled up toes, crooked from the long march in the desert, exhorting me not to ever forget their significance. But how different it was to listen to my "new," or rather "new-found," grandfather. His were stories infused with courage and strength, and of struggle rather than submission, of defiance, rather than a sad resignation to the fate that had befallen them. I think, even at that age, he derived his inspiration from Nouritza. His wrinkled eyes would glow like a forlorn seventeen-year-old's when he mentioned her name and told her stories, and I never had enough, *noren*,[7] I kept saying, *noren*, again…

Sarkis and Nouritza had met and fallen in love during the deportation march. He was taken as much by her courage and character as by her beauty. Nouritza never hung out with the women. She wore pants, smoked a pipe and discussed politics with the men. Even the Turkish men treated her with much respect. Her beauty wowed them and her courage awed them.

"She could bring a horseman down from his horse," my grandfather would boast. This woman, this legend, was so different from the other women in my life, and she soon became my hero, the one who inhabited my dreams, and the woman I wanted to become when I grew up.

When my grandfather asked to marry her, she shunned him, saying, "What difference is it going to make, you're as poor and as hungry as I am, and we probably won't live for much longer…" but in the end she gave in, and they were married somewhere along the deportation route.

Their first child, my maternal grandmother Azadouhi[8] was born on a ship that was carrying the refugees to the port city of Tyre in southern Lebanon. A childless woman on the ship stole the baby and hid her. But through my great-grandfather's rudimentary detective talents, and given the fact that the baby cried at a very critical moment, my grandfather found her and brought her back to Nouritza. This was only the beginning of Azadouhi's misfortunes.

After living for a while in the refugee camp in Tyre, most of the Armenians moved to Beirut. Work was available there, and refugee relief more accessible.

My great grandfather Sarkis, however, went in the opposite direction, further south, and settled in the village of Ain-ebl, just off the border with Israel. Some other Armenian families had settled there too, but eventually they all moved to Beirut, where there was a large concentration of Armenian refugees. All his relatives' exhortations for him to move to Beirut didn't convince him. He had work and made a decent living, and so he stayed. He ended up being the only Armenian in the village, and was known as *Sarkis el-Ermeni*, Sarkis the Armenian.

When Sarkis and Nouritza settled in Ain-ebl, Azadouhi was still a baby. She would grow up, witnessing her parents' struggle to adapt to the norms of a new country whose language they had to learn, and to a new village, where they would always remain outsiders.

I have heard the rest of the story from my mother. For my grandfather Sarkis, history ended when they reached Ain-ebl. His stories always ended there, and fast forwarded immediately to the present moment when he would grumble again about why he had to go back to the village to die, and be buried next to Nouritza. For all the years in between, his stare would focus on a suspended point in the room, and he would remain silent. A silence that my mother would later populate with her stories and characters; the silence of the women, whose lives were relegated to being written on the margins of men's destinies and decisions.

After Azadouhi, Nouritza bore one child after another, but they would quickly get sick and die. When my grandmother Azadouhi was almost a teenager, her brother Antoine was born. He was a weak and sickly child. Surely he would also die, like all the others before him. But he lived. It was my grandmother Nouritza who took sick and died shortly thereafter. Azadouhi became a mother before she could become a sister. As the years passed, Azadouhi blossomed into a beautiful young woman. Sarkis could see that the youth of the village were eying her differently. Yes he had stayed on in the village, but there was no way he was going to let his daughter marry an *odar*.[9]

He arranged a marriage for his daughter with an Armenian family from Constantinople. The groom and his family came over for a visit. Azadouhi, as was the custom, would come into the room from the kitchen only once to serve the coffee, so that she would be seen and be approved of. The short encounter was enough for her to sense her imminent exile.

The men drank the coffee and agreed on the dowry arrangements. The dignified Armenian family specified a date when they would return to make the necessary arrangements for marriage, and returned to Constantinople. Rumours circulated in the village that Azadouhi had been betrothed and was to marry. My grandmother learned the details from friends she played with on the streets, and from their mothers who had started looking at her pityingly. "Poor Azadouhi, she'll never see her brother again."

This struck terror in Azadouhi's heart. She could not yet grasp the impact of her father's decision. She wouldn't dare ask him. Never see her brother again? Her brother? More like her son, whom she had reared like a mother, though she herself had been motherless all these years. She couldn't abandon him and leave him to die.

The women of the village felt they had to do something, if only for the sake of Nouritza's memory. How could this heartless man separate his orphaned son and daughter? What crazy notion was this, which would almost seal his son's fate, but wouldn't let his daughter marry an *odar*, a non-Armenian?

The whole village seemed to be seething with the news. There was a young man, Maroun, who had been spotted by the women eyeing Azadouhi as she went to the spring for water, or played on the streets. An arrangement with Sarkis was unthinkable. So a plot was hatched, orchestrated mainly by the neighbourhood women, and one night Maroun came and Azadouhi secretly mounted his steed to flee her fate in Constantinople, and stay in the village with her brother.

They had barely made half the stretch of the village, when Maroun started to waver. How could he abduct Sarkis's daughter? This man who had fought in the Turkish army, *Sarkis el-Ermeni*, who feared nothing and no one? He returned when it was almost daybreak and knocked on the door, shaking with fear. He told Sarkis the full story. "Listen," he said, "I have not laid my hand on her, and I've brought her back as she left this house only a very short while ago." Sarkis raged. "She has stepped beyond the threshold of my house! She is no longer my daughter!" He struck a blow to Maroun which hurled him a few meters beyond the porch. "Get out of my sight, the two of you, and if you want to live, make sure I never see you again."

My grandmother left her father's house with lowered eyes, resigned to her fate with this stranger, this new man, with whom she had barely exchanged a few words. That blow, its humiliation, would always stand between them, and mark their relationship permanently.

They lived down a few streets in the village, but Sarkis had disowned her and would neither talk to her nor allow her in his house for twenty-three years. She had to pay for *his* humiliation as well. Hadn't he promised his daughter, man to man, to that family from Constantinople, and hadn't she forced him to bite his tongue and tell his prospective in-laws that his daughter had eloped with someone from the village?

Azadouhi had to hide behind walls and watch her brother Antoine play. She was not allowed to go near him or speak with him. They had a few hens in the yard. She would keep the fresh laid eggs not for her children but for her brother Antoine, and send it secretly to him with one of the neighbours. She hid behind walls and watched her paternal hearth. Banned and exiled. She went back to her husband's home, a stranger place still, and a stranger man.

She bore Maroun twelve children. And after all married and left, after her husband died, her brain started to slowly erase the unpleasant pasts.

After our encounter with Pergrouhi there was one thought that lingered once the volcanic surge of emotions slowly subsided. What was my Nouritza grandmother's name? Her family name. Her identifier—that label which we inherit from our fathers or append from our husbands but don't bequeath to our daughters.

I called my mother in Los Angeles. "What was Nouritza grandmother's family name?" There was a short, surprised silence. Why this question? Why now? Then my mother gathered her thoughts together. "She married grandfather Sarkis during the deportation. In the old country, she had been married and widowed, so she probably carried her first husband's surname. Or her paternal surname? I really don't know. Maybe grandmother Azadouhi would remember. I think she still has some occasional lucid moments."

My mother was referring to grandma Azad's degenerative brain disease which was slowly spreading to different patches of her memory.

I call my sister in Beirut. "I need to know Nouritza grandmother's family name. Call Azad medzmama,[10] or go see her, see if she remembers."

I know I'm asking too much of my sister. My Azad medzmama still lives in Ain-ebl in southern Lebanon. Access is complicated.

My sister is hesitant, but sensing the urgency in my voice doesn't cut me off abruptly and promises to try. She calls me back within a week after getting in touch with aunts and uncles who still live in the village. No more lucid moments for Azad medzmama. No, her health is otherwise not bad but her brain has shut down. She doesn't remember anyone. She remembers nothing.

When we are old and alone with only our memories, when the ghosts from the past haunt us incessantly and it becomes too much to bear, perhaps the brain wills itself into a shut-down, into a silence.

> After all my children can bear the burden of my memory. I wish to be released from its chains. I wish to die with a blank slate, in my primordial state of innocence when that wicked woman on the ship stole me from my mother's bosom and my father retrieved me. Let me be.

Is this how my medzmama feels, I wonder? I cannot know but I wish to have been able to unburden her silence, if only slightly. I want to unburden *her*, somehow, and yet I consciously, daily, repeatedly burden my daughters with Nouritza's memory; I burden them with Azad medzmama's memory, with the countless memories of all who perished in the desert, all whose bones rot under the slow slumbers of its sands. I burden them with the heavy weight of exile and genocide.

I wish, and hope against hope, that they will be given the chance to forgive, and bury the burden.

Not Yet Twelve And In Grade Six

Voice 2—Hermig

We had hardly taken in the full impact, the immensity of our grandparents' stories when our war started. Not yet twelve and in the sweet twilight zone of childhood, that borderline space where realities and fantasies flow in and out of each other seamlessly, still trying to make sense of the deportation stories, my grandmother's toes, my grandfather's defiance, Nouritza's mythical aura, my father's insistence on how despite being a star student he'd had to leave school after grade six, so he could work and get the family out of the refugee camp...Barely twelve, when our first rush of hormones and our first infatuations had landed upon us with full force. Grade six, and awaiting that most important of all events in a young person's life, graduating from primary school, the celebration, the heady expectation of going on to high school and making our grand exit from the realm of childhood and being accepted into the world of grown up people, so we would be able to go to the parties that previously only our elder sisters were allowed to attend, and perhaps be allowed to wear bell-bottom pants...

Barely twelve, when our war started.

It was April 1975, when the first incident occurred. It was a shooting on a bus carrying civilians.[11] We were lost trying to make sense of the grown-ups' confused conversations, some insisting that this was only an "isolated event," and others ominously insinuating that this was only the beginning of much more blood to be shed. How or for how long they couldn't guess, but they knew this was only the beginning. I would have lied if I said that we desperately wanted the first camp of optimists to have been in the right. Sure, we did want that year-end ceremony, but we'd also had a week off from school because of that first incident, so these "events" (nobody was calling it a war yet) held a wicked excitement for us too. We held on to the fairy tale belief that it was possible for incidents to happen that were not grave enough to kill people or for all-out war to start, but that would be serious enough for the schools to be closed.

Little did we know then that this was only the start of a long and drawn out civil war that would last fifteen years and consume not only our teenage years but last through college, university and first jobs, and it would be our long march in the desert that our grandparents had gone through in their time, only different in its intensities and experiences, but nonetheless a baptism in blood and fire. And we, like them, would love and study and work and marry throughout the bloody civil war, the numerous booby trapped car bombs, the overnight shelling, the sniper fire, the invasion and occupation of southern Lebanon, and the blowing up of the American marines.

The bus incident was a story we only heard on the news, but soon the real fighting spread all around Beirut. It would usually start with rounds of machine gun fire. Then we heard the militia yelling at people to empty out the streets, stay indoors, and stock some food…This would send my parents into a flurry of first making sure that everyone had returned home from wherever they were, and then closing all the shutters and ordering us not to go near the balconies. There isn't anything an eleven year old wants to do as much as disobey her parents and of course this for me was like a direct directive to go and watch what was happening on the streets through the slots of the shutters.

And I did.

A man was tied from his feet to the back of a pick up truck and was being dragged around in the streets. The gravel was tearing him apart, and he was all bloodied. It was a very short glimpse, but enough to catapult me full force into a new world, where suddenly my grandparent's stories of death and hunger stopped being "stories" and acquired the full force of reality. I reproached myself, oh so profoundly and with all the penance that an eleven year old is capable of, for my jubilation at skipping school for a week. Oh dear god, I'll go to school Saturdays and Sundays too, study until the late hours of the evening, please let this not happen. Deep down I knew that my pleas were in vain, and ours wasn't going to be an adolescence of bell bottom pants and parties…

Another experience was soon to complete my rite of passage.

Soon after the fighting started, the government collapsed, and regional militias took over. I have no memory of how our garbage was collected before the war. My first childhood memory of garbage is how it was piled up on the street corner for a couple of days, and then burnt, as there was no authority responsible for collecting it any longer. Surely the militia had more important matters to attend to. The sweet stench of the smoke that wafted through the air was unbearable, but like all horrors that eventually become "normal" in any war, this too, shortly, just became part of our daily smells, together with the exhaust fumes of diesel from the militia trucks and the smell of gunpowder.

One day though, the smell was different. It was almost nauseating. My little head got to thinking its very first deeply profound and philosophical thoughts. Why does the burning garbage not smell the same every day? Is it what people eat? Is it the kind of plastic bags they use? Is it me? I went down with my mother to deposit our daily share of garbage that was to go on the pile. My mother was holding my hand and we were walking at a brisk pace, not hurrying yet, but there was the sound of automatic rifles coming from a distance, better get back home as soon as possible.

My mother pulled on my hand forcefully and turned my head the other way. But it was too late. I had already seen the charred remains and bones of what was surely a human figure, shrunk, shrivelled and black.

This was the summer of 1975. My twelfth birthday had come and gone in May of that year. It was a very hot summer and September brought relief neither from the heat nor from the fighting, and the schools stayed closed for the whole academic year.

We had turned twelve, and now, everyone was calling it a war.

The Year I Turned Twelve

Telling stories about the past, our past, is a key moment in the making of our selves. To the extent that memory provides their raw material, such narratives of identity are shaped as much by what is left out of the account —whether forgotten or repressed—as by what is actually told. Secrets haunt our memory-stories, giving them pattern and shape. —Kuhn (1995: 2).

Voice 3—Hourig

Hermig and I grew up together on the same street in Beirut, amid the chaos of civil war, our blossoming friendship our lifeline to sanity, our defiance to the turmoil engulfing us.

The year was 1975. The day April 14.[12] Three days before I turned twelve. It was a bright spring day. The early morning ritual when our whole household was up always started with the aroma of coffee my father brewed for himself and my mother. Then he would open the green shutters of the veranda, to let the sunshine and the waking street noises in. This morning though there was an eerie silence on the street and my father behaved in a strange way. Instead of finding him in the kitchen boiling the coffee, I saw him peering outside through the cracks of the green shutters. My mother was standing next to him. They talked in low whispers. "No school today, go back to bed," was their response to my and my brother's bewildered looks. "It is not safe. There has been an incident." I couldn't understand why the shutters had to stay closed. I couldn't understand why the sunshine could not be let in. It was only three days before I turned twelve.

The events that unfolded in the coming days and weeks though proved to be a lesson in honing my comprehension skills overnight.

The summer I turned twelve, I had my first period. The day I walked through the threshold of womanhood is imprinted in my mind as the time I bled out the pain I felt in my heart. The summer I turned twelve was a very hot one. My bedroom window that overlooked the garage of a neighbouring building stayed open at night, in the hopes of carrying a waft of a breeze inside. Instead, what invaded my bedroom were the moans and cries of the blindfolded young boys I saw hurled into the dark abyss of the garage during the day.

The year we turned twelve, Hermig and I met daily to talk about the books we read, the boys we had crushes on, the school we would go to if the roads were safe again, and the childhood that was robbed of us.

Disconnections

Voice 3—Hourig

It isn't easy to talk and write about trauma, especially if it is your own. Some of the stories unfolding in these pages belong to a different generation, a different time, a different dimension. Yet the distance time affords does not prevent them from haunting us. How does the plot of ghost stories usually develop? The ghosts revisit the living until justice is done. In this case the ghosts of the past have not even had that poetic justice. This is the story of the generation of my grandparents, of my parents, of mine and of those who come after us. Some years ago I tried hard, very hard to avoid writing about it. In the process, I realized then that my only way of coming to terms with the countless stories of my grandparents' generation was by letting go of the pain. Ninety years ago, a million and a half Armenians were left to perish in the sands of Der el Zor. Six years before that, thirty thousand of them were butchered in one city. Fourteen years before that, three hundred thousand of them were slaughtered. Do I need to go further back? My dictionary has run out of synonyms for the word "murder." Ninety years, ninety-six years, a hundred and ten years, what difference does it make? We still carry the burden.

I feel torn. How can I reconcile my belief in pacifism with the reality of the anguish my grandparents (and through them my people) suffered? I question my parents' wisdom. Why instil the essentials of love, brotherhood and freedom in their children? Didn't they know we wouldn't fit in a society obsessed with violence? My adolescent years were spent in war-torn Lebanon. I watched my whole world shatter with every bullet, every shell. The humanism my father taught and cherished was dismembered slowly, painfully, crippling my sanity and my hold on life. I grew up in a matter of hours and days. I felt how the insane rage of the absurd war was defining my helplessness and I could not come to terms with it. The arbitrary absurdity of it all entrenched in me an obsession with peace. Peace, peaceful, pacifism. I suppose my inward drive for pacifism sprang from the very absence of everything peaceful in my life then. The more outspoken I became about non-violence, the more silent I was about the growing pain inside me and its after-effects. Until now.

There are too many parallels stretching across the generations from my grandparents' to mine to ignore. The pain, the trauma, the disconnection, the shattering of everything around us are only some of the common points. During times of reckless shelling, when the whole family rushed downstairs to the relative safety of my grandparents' corridor, and I tried to huddle under the protection of my father's or mother's arms, I often wondered how the madness I lived through must have been similar to what my grandparents experienced long, long before my existence was thought of. They weren't even teenagers when they were forcefully deprived of all that is known as home, family, love and warmth. And now they had come full circle. They were the orphans of the lost homeland. We, their grandchildren, carried on the legacy of that orphanage. How else could I describe the terrors I felt every time a shell exploded nearby, every time I witnessed a corpse dragged behind a truck with a group of onlookers cheering the scene…

The horrors, our respective generations lived through, could have been different in their variety, but there must have been a streak of similarity in the pain they caused. Worst of all was the issue of recognition and retribution. How did my grandparents manage to cope with their suffering in the face of constant denial of the validity of their life stories? How did governments continue to proclaim the genocide my grandparents survived, to be an "alleged killing" or a mere "tragic event?" How did I live "normally" in spite of the daily butchering of all the ideals I was brought up with? The anatomy of our survival has deep, very deep roots. Resurrection was not a grace from heaven, but an imposed survival mechanism. This is what countless teachers have taught generations of Armenians. "You will avenge yourself by living/Living a thousand fold more stubbornly" wrote one poet.[13] And so I have lived.

I was brought up with the stories of my grandparents. The deportations, the massacre, the suffering. They were robbed of their childhood, of their memories, of their way of life. Hurled into the wilderness of the desert sands. Their stories scorched from the desert sun. Every time my grandfather told his story, every one knew exactly where he would stop to catch his breath, when he would suddenly stumble over his words and swallow the tears in his eyes. Every time we urged grandmother to tell her story, we knew she would refuse on the pretext of not remembering anything. These stories live in me. Through me they will attain new flesh and blood or will be lost forever. It is too heavy a burden to carry. But the journey back is an inevitable one. "To recount the past is to reclaim it, to reevaluate our selves in relation to others" writes Andra Makler (1991: 46). Our past bonds us to our futures. It is only then that we can attempt to become complete.

In recent years, in my attempt to come to terms with the painful memories of my adolescence, I have sought answers in the harrowing tales of the survivor generation. Their compelling narratives have been a source of inspiration. The more I have listened to them, the more I have been able to untangle the hidden knots that make up my life story.

Creating Memory: The Story of Anoush[14]

Voice 3—Hourig

April 24, 2003.[15] I decide to listen to the last recording I made of my grandparents' stories. I feel a bit ambivalent. I know listening to their voices ring out so real when they are not among us anymore, telling stories about their past—a past that was painfully erased from their lives but one they insisted on making part of their present and mine as well—will be difficult to deal with. The intensity a bodiless voice can trigger, the memories it embodies, will inhabit the world of my mind and become more real than the one I live in daily. Nevertheless I insert the tape in the recorder and press the play button. I watch painfully as the tape rolls. I hear my voice announce the date. 1992. There is a questioning in my grandfather's voice as I ask him to state his full name. I explain it is for the sake of formality and for the family archives. My grandmother clears her throat in the background. My grandfather plays along with me and speaks out his full name with an actor's flair. A few minutes later I ask the same question of my grandmother. "Why do you ask? Don't you know it?" she retorts in her genuinely surprised voice. I laugh out loud. So typical of medzmama, I think instantly. After a few minutes they both go on to enumerate the names of their parents, grandparents, aunts, uncles and siblings. My grandparents were second cousins and shared a close-knit family circle. I check my notes as I listen to the tape and scribble down the names. A sudden thought hits me. I stop the tape. I count the names I've jotted down: Varteni, Hampartsoum, Haroutioun, Marinos, Pilig, Hovhannes, Hagop, Khatchig, Arsenouhi…All perished during the death march or in its aftermath, yet my grandparents and their surviving siblings make sure their memories live on by naming their children after them. All that is, except Anoush. Her name does not appear again. It is wrapped in veils of secrecy in the family memories.

Anoush was/is my grandfather's younger sister. I first heard her story from my mother when I was in my teens. I even remember that I was the one who asked medzhayrig,[16] my grandfather, to tell me the real story about her. It struck me that in a family history full of so many old photographs, I had never come across hers. I realized that she once existed in my grandfather's painful memories and continues to live on in my mother's faint recollections of a passing, vague face.

It all started in 1915. In all the stories medzhayrig told us, until then he led an idyllic carefree childhood in his native village of Khasgal,[17] a close distance from Istanbul. Then one day, the order for deportation came. He was only twelve and remembered how his parents and grandmother entrusted the family papers and the house key to their closest Turkish neighbours. They were like family, he always said, his own grandmother like a mother to them. It was the first of many painful separations and unending tears. Thus started the beginning of the end of his family as he knew it —his grandmother Varteni, his father Hovhannes, his mother Marinos, his elder brother Mihran, his elder sister Srpouhi, his younger sister Anoush, and his younger brother Hampartsoum.

There were inevitably gaps in the story. How many days and months did it take them to traverse the country in a forced death march, to pass through the living hell of the Der Zor desert,[18] to finally reach a caravanserai in Kerkuk,[19] I will never know. I will never know what courage my then twelve year old grandfather must have mustered to survive. I know though, that every time I trace the enormous distance on a modern map with my fingers, between the one dot that signifies Istanbul and the other that shows Kerkuk, I shudder. On that invisible line I trace from one city to the other, I know he lost his mother, his younger brother, his grandmother and finally his father. In that fateful caravanserai in Kerkuk, his father's last thought was to save his young daughter Anoush at all costs, from the grim destiny that awaited them all. During the day he had seen some Bedouins from the region come in to ask if there were any young children for sale.[20] He decided Anoush must live. She was not yet ten. Although grown very skinny and weak from their ordeal, she was still very beautiful and so young. The tears streaked down Anoush's delicate face as she pleaded with her father to stay with them. Surely no life would be worth living without whatever remained of her dismembered family. My grandfather's voice breaks as he retells the story. Anoush is "sold" the next morning, while her father perishes, unable to bear the anguish. The rest is the story of my grandfather's orphanage days. Out of a family of eight, three only had survived the horror.

Years pass. The twelve year old orphan transforms into a young man. He finds and marries his second cousin who also has survived. She had reached the shores of Greece. Together they settle in Mosul[21] and have five children. He then decides to move his family to Beirut.[22] The year is 1952.

On his return to settle the family affairs after a few months, his neighbours tell him of a mysterious Arab woman who often appeared on the corner of the street and gazed through the courtyard to where my grandparents used to live. After a few days she approached the neighbours and asked where the family of five children had gone.

Her eyes had a clouded look and her lips trembled. The neighbours were curious. Why did she want to know? "They moved to Beirut," one of them blurted out. A loud wail cut the neighbour's words short. The Arab woman crumbled to the floor. The women of the courtyard scurried around her. "I lost them. I lost them twice," the Arab woman mumbled. Then under the caring gaze of the women, she revealed her story. My grandfather is incredulous. He stopped believing in miracles in 1915, the year of the desert sands. And yet thirty-seven years later, he is now to come face to face with one.

I will never know how it feels to meet a sister you have lost for thirty-seven years. I will never know what words you say to a brother you find thirty-seven years later. I want to know though how the eyes caress and the hands embrace to repel the memory of the loss.

She has tried, always tried to find them. She has never forgotten. She has family and children of her own. Her sons are already married. They never understood who she looked for. Surely this family she talked of, the father, brothers and sister, they had all died back then. She herself said they were doomed to die. So why this insane search now? Why forsake what she has for something that is not? In time their questionings turned into a deep frustration and a sense of betrayal. Persuasion techniques gave way to subtle threats. In it all though, she never wavered once. Especially after she finally traced her brother's family to Mosul. So many times she came and stood at the corner of the street, watched the family of five children discreetly, saw the kids—her nephews and nieces, her own flesh and blood—play joyfully in the courtyard. She never dared come nearer, for fear the subtle threats in her family would become real. Until now, when the compounded feeling of a second loss made all else irrelevant.

I try to imagine how Anoush would have felt and cannot. How can a woman, her life torn asunder in layer after layer after layer, have found courage to live on, to birth, to nurture, to hope, I wonder.

Surely a reunion with her brother's family would have meant yet another lesion in her life—this time with her husband and sons. Unable to find any way to reconcile her two worlds, Anoush makes the difficult decision to stay with her brother. She agrees to meet him secretly a few days later to go into hiding, while my grandfather secures legal backing for their case. At the appointed time and place however, she is not there. For many agonizing months to follow, my grandfather searches for her in vain. All his influential friends, all his efforts, all his wanderings come to naught. The rest is shrouded in silence in the family narratives.

Over the years, in endless recountings of his survivor stories, medzhayrig kept a stubborn silence over this episode. Even to the end of his days, when the memory of his younger brother's killing would still bring tears to his eyes; he could never reconcile himself to talk of Anoush. Was it because the loss of his other family members was more defined through their death I wondered, yet with Anoush he was never sure? On my part, I try to reconstruct/(re)imagine Anoush's face through my mother's faint memories of a strange veiled woman on a street corner, intently gazing at them. I sometimes think of her as only a face—a disembodied face. It appears in a hazy background. I shudder to think that even in my imagination I cannot find a body for her. What does that say about her story and about her place in our family memories? How can I remember someone I have never seen, I ask myself? How can I mourn her three-fold loss? Yet I feel I know Anoush; I have felt her pain; I have lived her loss; I live her absence. My attempt at sketching her narrative is my tribute to finally give body to her voice. Isn't this what the afterlife of memory is meant to be?

How Will I Forget

Voice 1—Pergrouhi

When we went to Yaremja,[23] they let us sleep in the barn. The animals would return to the shed after having grazed the whole day, and we were allowed to sleep there, in a pit, almost. But the heat, the fleas, and the lice were unbearable. My mother would always keep reminding me, "listen, my child, your name is Pergrouhi, my name is Hadji Mariam and your father's name was Boghos. Don't you ever forget that."

During the day I would go and play with the Turkmen[24] kids in the field. I was playing one day, and noticed that my mother was lying on the ground. I went closer and saw that her eyes were open, so I spoke to her, but she wouldn't answer me back. I went back to play. I was only a child, barely six years old. I would play during the day and go and sleep next to her at night. For three days I slept like that in my dead mother's bosom. After three days, my cousin's mistress, the old lady said to my cousin, "Go tell her, her mother's dead." So she came and told me.

Four Turkmen brought a hemp sack, opened it, put my mother's body in the sack and took it out. I was crying and running after them. They took her out in the fields and buried her there. I guess they just covered her with some earth and came back.

I would go every day to where her body lay and cry endlessly, "Mother, mother, please come back, please get up, mother, please." But my mother wouldn't answer back. They would come and take me back in and tell me not to cry. They would give me a rag doll to console me. On the third day, I went to where she was buried again. Her arm was sticking out of the ground. Like a piece of wood. I was very frightened. The next day I went back. The dogs had pulled her body out of the ground and were ripping her apart. Those village dogs were very ferocious. Those dogs were very ferocious.

I have so many more things to tell, but I cannot go on anymore.

Epilogue: A Single Red Carnation

Voice 3—Hourig

Everyone who had met Pergrouhi was always surprised at her lucidity and her flawless memory. She knew intricate details of family stories, the dates of weddings, births, deaths, baptisms of all her near and distant relatives, great grandchildren, grandchildren, children as well as the minutiae of their places of birth and residence, addresses, phone numbers. In the recesses of her mind, all memory was parceled neatly. Yet, she had no recollection of family records indicating her exact date of birth. The official papers from the orphanage though, where she spent her childhood after her mother's death, stated her birth date to be January 1, 1907.

After a short illness, Pergrouhi was hospitalized in the late winter of 2005. She was very weak and had gone totally blind. However, she remained lucid as ever, always reciting a poem from her orphanage days, singing a song, murmuring a prayer, recounting a story for me on each of my regular visits to her. She charmed everyone around her and certainly took me under her spell. Every time I was about to say good-bye to her she would tell me, "You are so busy, you have so many things to do, you don't have to come again. I know you are thinking of me and that is enough." Every time I entered her room and she heard my voice, she would say, "It's you my Hourig, I was waiting for you…"

In her hospital days, the stories Pergrouhi retold took a different sense of urgency. Even though I had heard them from her countless times, I felt they attained a distinct and unusual reality. They hovered between worlds—mine, Pergrouhi's, my grandparents', of the living and of the dead. They got under my skin. She had known my grandparents in Iraq, in a diasporic landscape of displacement where a generation of survivors had tried to patch their lives together. I had met her long after my grandparents had passed away and had always wondered at what mystery lay behind that coincidental encounter. In the early days of my acquaintance with Pergrouhi I was mesmerized with what she would be able to tell me of the early years of my grandparents I knew relatively little about. Little details about the street they lived in, the courtyard my mother and her siblings grew up in, the houses they inhabited, all attained vivid colours through Pergrouhi's memories. What I was not prepared for however, was the intriguing way Pergrouhi's story kept unfolding in my life. On numerous occasions during my hospital visits, she would speak to me of lucid visions of my late grandfather who would comfort her or be a soothing presence. All these stories of encounters left me without words. My grandfather had passed away in his sleep, in the early morning hours of April 24th, 1997. At that time, I was haunted by that symbolism and could not believe it to be coincidental. Now I felt the presence of the past ever stronger.

My last visit to Pergrouhi was on Sunday, April 24, 2005. There was a single red carnation in a vase, next to her bedside. The evening before, an interfaith ecumenical service in the St. Joseph Oratory of Montreal had commemorated the ninetieth anniversary of the genocide. Red carnations were handed out to the very few remaining survivors during the service. Pergrouhi's grandson had accepted one in her name. With a proud and serene smile on her face she recounted to me how her grandson had brought the carnation to her and how her name was read aloud during the service. She then repeated to me her vision of my grandfather. Her voice was very tired. As I held her hand to say goodbye, she told me, "Thank you for coming, thank you for not forgetting me." It was to be my last visit to her, her last spoken words to me. Two mornings later she passed away. Dignified even in her suffering and her pain, she was gone as so many of her generation, leaving us trying hard to comprehend the symbolism of their lives.

What will always remain engraved in my memories of Pergrouhi is the image of her as a little girl. On one of my visits, she was asleep when I entered her room. As I sat next to her, holding her hand, her daughter insisted on waking her up so Pergrouhi could talk to me and tell me about the nightmares that were troubling her. She certainly was not her cheerful self when she heard my voice that day. "As soon as I closed my eyes I heard them coming, I heard them coming after me," she said in a trembling voice. All I could do was squeeze her hand softly and mumble a few comforting words to her. "The dogs are coming; they are barking loud, they are fierce. They're going to rip me apart just like they did my mother." She sounded so helpless. In an instant, she was the little girl who had witnessed it all. I didn't know how to comfort her. I felt a helpless rage inside me. Ninety years had not been able to wipe away the fear. Ninety years she had lived with this pain. Ninety years and the wound is still raw.

For Dr. Ingrid L. Semaan, our mentor and lifelong inspiration, and in memory of our grandmothers, Tefarig Der Arsenian and Azadouhi Touloujian.

Notes

1. All parts of Pergrouhi's narrative in this chapter are excerpted from Attarian, H. & Yogurtian, H. (Producers), *Survivor Stories, Surviving Narratives: Pergrouhi's story* [Video documentary]. Montreal: Par Productions, 2002.

2. Refers to the Der el Zor desert in northern Syria, then part of the Ottoman Empire, where the death marches led to during the 1915 genocide of the Armenians. It has now become the site of annual pilgrimages.

3. The capital city of Lebanon.

4. Abaya is a long, ankle length mantle, usually worn by local Arabs.

5. Literally meaning the world, *yergir* is an endearing term referring to the ancestral homeland in Western Armenia, from where the Armenians were subsequently deported in 1915 and led into the death marches of the Der el Zor desert in northern Syria.

6. Refers to the Der el Zor desert, which became synonymous with death camps during the Armenian genocide.

7. Noren means again in Armenian.

8. Azadouhi means freedom in Armenian.

9. Odar, here signifying non-Armenian, literally means foreigner. Among a generation who had just survived a horrific extermination, marrying an *odar* was a stigmatizing experience and tantamount to betrayal and loss.

10. Grandmother in Armenian.

11. On April 13, 1975 in Beirut, the right-wing Phalange party militiamen shot at a bus full of Palestinian women and children, which was passing through the Beirut suburb of Ain el Remmaneh. 27 people were killed as a result. An incident intended to provoke armed conflict, it is seen by many as the trigger to the fifteen-year-long civil war in Lebanon (Fisk, 1992: 78).

12. See above note on April 13, 1975.

13. Excerpted from the poem *Mtorumner djanaparhi kesin* [Reflections midway in the journey] by the East Armenian poet Silva Kaputikian (Kaputikian, 1996: 225).

14. A common female name, Anoush literally means sweet in Armenian.

15. April 24 is the Armenian genocide commemoration day.

16. Grandfather in Armenian.

17. Literally meaning "fertile land" in Armenian, the village is located in the region of Adapazar, a short distance from Istanbul. Hourig's grandfather told of how the village was famous for its orchards and especially mulberry trees, which played an important part in the budding local silk industry. In 1962, when he visited his native village a last time, he was shocked to find the area completely barren, with no trace of its once very fertile agricultural lands.

18. See notes 2 and 6.

19. City in northern Iraq, then part of the Ottoman Empire.

20. In a last-minute effort to save their lives, many parents during the deportations and subsequent death marches resorted to "selling" or giving their young children away to the Arab Bedouin tribes in the region.

21. City in northern Iraq.

22. In the period from the 1920s to the 1960s, there were internal demographic movements within the Armenian diasporan communities in the Middle East, which led to an important concentration of Armenians in Lebanon, especially its capital city of Beirut, making the community there the "backbone of the Armenian diaspora" as it became to be known. In the years preceding the Lebanese civil war, the community numbered around 250 000 strong, with a vibrant infrastructure of numerous day schools, daily newspapers, and cultural centres.

23. Refers to a town near Kerkuk in northern Iraq.

24. Refers to the Turkmen of Kerkuk.

Chapter Three

Les Filles Francophones Au Pluriel:
Opening Up Girlhood Studies To Francophones

Rachel Gouin, Fathiya Wais

In the last 25 years, not only has the field of girlhood studies emerged; it has already taken new directions. And yet the focus of this field has largely been on western and Anglophone girlhoods. Few contributions have been made from a Canadian context and the few that do exist often have not included Francophone perspectives or even research on French speaking populations. Studies that address the realities of girls from linguistic minorities, girls with (dis)abilities, rural and First Nations girls are sorely missing (Ward & Cooper Benjamin, 2004: 21). This chapter is a first step in addressing one of these gaps, namely the study of girls from linguistic minorities; particularly, Francophone girls living in Canada. In this chapter, we call into question linguistic categories, review the current literature on Francophone girls in Canada and propose a framework for future research that breaks the silences around the intersections of racialization, class, ability, gender, sexuality and age in the lives of girls. We argue that an anti-racist approach would expose "Francophone" as a complex category, and consider the impact of racist policies on the many Francophone groups that constitute Canadian society. Furthermore, we underscore the need for research with a social justice agenda; research that not only looks at girls' realities, but also identifies the barriers that maintain their precarious living conditions. In making these connections, it is our hope to stimulate research that advocates for equal opportunities and the redistribution of wealth—that is, research that does not silence one oppression in favour of another but that works with the intersecting systems of oppression as they manifest themselves in the lives of girls.

Our intent in drawing attention to this neglected area of research rests on our desire to de-centre the Anglocentric focus on girls by researchers, the media, public programs and services, given that it constitutes a powerful form of surveillance and homogenization which silences diverse and alternative stories of girlhoods (Harris, 2004b, 186). Drawing on the work of Harris (2004a), we begin by outlining the past and current themes of girlhood studies (xix-xx). We then unravel the categories "Francophone" and "Anglophone" in order to move beyond a dichotomous and fictitious vision of Canadian society [see Jiwani, this volume]. We follow this discussion by examining the literature on

Francophone girls in Canada, focusing on the issues that have been explored, the research lenses that have been used, the particular groups of girls that have been studied, and the ways in which this research silences specific issues and girls.

Starting from the understanding that there are multiple Francophone experiences, our goal is to provide direction for doing research that looks at girls as members of social groups who seek to forge their own identities. If girls are to be considered agents, we must start by analyzing the ways in which they are victimized. In other words, research on girls must first illustrate the ways in which victimization operates and limits the exercise of girls' agency. This would allow us to understand how girls who are part of marginalized groups become agents for social change. To this end, we propose a framework for research that privileges an anti-racist analysis and a social justice lens.

Francophone Girlhood Studies?

Harris (2004a) argues that three issues have been fundamental to girlhood studies to date: "the relationship between popular cultures, material conditions and gendered identities; the role of social institutions such as schools and the media in shaping femininities, and the places and voices young women utilize to express themselves" (xix). She identifies newly emerging directions within the field; research that questions the so-called freedom of girls in light of the widening gap between their access to resources (xx). A second direction has been that of studying the differences among young women rather than collapsing them into a universal and homogeneous category (xx). Finally, Harris identifies the increasing number of young women, once researched as "girls," heading their own research initiatives and thinking critically about whether to participate in others' research (xx). Most of this research has been conducted in English and addresses the lives of western girls. What little research exists in French or about Francophone girls in Canada has either not looked at, or has failed to mention the realities of girls who have been contained and marginalized within the categories *minorité visible*/visible minority, *communautés culturelles*/cultural communities, and *groupes ethno-culturels*/ethno-cultural groups.[1] Rather than simply including these groups in future research, we propose that such categories be disputed.

Girls And Young Women In Québec

In 2002, the Québec government produced an information document on young Québécois girls between the ages of fifteen to twenty-nine (Conseil du Statut de la Femme). "Des nouvelles d'elles" offers a general overview of what girls in Québec are up to, who they are, who they live with, what they do in school, their employment, their financial situations, their relation to issues such as suicide, violence, eating disorders, smoking and sexuality and finally, how they occupy their leisure time. Québécois young women, it is reported, are characterized by their diversity. The 1996 census indicates that 56 385 young women between the ages of fifteen and twenty-nine had immigrated to Québec at various ages (10). This represents eight percent of the 710 582 young women in Québec. Montréal is even more diverse, where one young woman out of five is a minorité visible (15). The groups most represented in this age group are: Black (thirty-four percent), Arab and West Asian (fifteen percent), Latin American (twelve percent), South Asian (twelve percent), Chinese (eleven percent) and South-East Asians (nine percent) (11). First Nations girls represent one percent of the population of this age group whereas (dis)abled girls represent six percent (11-13). The report makes no mention of linguistic diversity.

Highlights of the report include the observation that young women attain higher levels of education than the young men in their age group. This does not necessarily translate into the workforce, where their options are often limiting (35). Jobs held by young women are increasingly precarious, part time and non-unionized (47). The salary gap between young women and young men is greatest for fifteen to nineteen year olds (57). Importantly, the report notes that young women under thirty in Québec represent seventy-five percent of Sexually Transmitted Infections cases and forty-one percent of women are victims of violence (63-69). It is also mentioned that suicide rates have doubled for young women and that they have significantly less free time than their male counterparts (69, 79). The report ends on a positive note, highlighting young women's ambitions in education, careers, families and social participation (89).

Given that this document was meant to support parents and community groups in understanding girls in Québec, there is little analysis provided. Readers get the sense that some girls—although we are not told which ones and for what historically specific reasons—are not doing so well but that generally, 'the girls are alright!' No call is made for research that would delve deeper into various areas. Although the reader is initially informed of demographic information pertaining to girls in Québec, the remainder of the document does not give any specific information relating to these 'groups' of girls. This leads to a homogenization of girls' experiences specifically related to their employment, schooling and other activities.

Calling Into Question Linguistic Categories

By definition, an Anglophone is someone whose mother tongue is English, while a Francophone is someone whose first language is French. The term Allophone refers to someone whose mother tongue is other than English or French. Discussions on language in Canada are generally articulated around the fiction of two founding nations. People who are linguistically categorized as other, Allophones, must try to fit into legitimate and institutionalized categories—they must strategically choose to speak French or English. The choice that is made by Allophones is determined by economic and historical factors (for example, immigrants already fluent in French may choose to learn English to facilitate access to employment). Consequently, language is an issue of power and recognition. As Bourdieu writes, "Linguistic exchanges, being modes of communication par excellence, are also relations of symbolic power where power is expressed among speakers or their respective groups" (1982, 14). ["Les rapports des communications par excellence que sont les échanges linguistiques sont aussi des rapports de pouvoir symbolique où s'actualisent les rapports de force entre les locuteurs ou leurs groupes respectifs" (1982, 14).] In other words, there are political, social and cultural complexities tied to debates on language, which reflect societal structures already in place. In order to understand French language as an identity in Canada and Québec, we must consider Francophones' historical struggles for survival as oppressed people. Demonstrating these relations of power, this chapter is written by two French-speaking women living in Québec, and yet it is written in English in order to facilitate the diffusion of this information to a wider audience. Beyond a too-simple French/English dichotomy, there is diversity within these linguistic categories, and they too must be addressed.

Speaking French is not only a matter of language, but also an expression of power (for instance, different accents, and expressions, have the power to mobilize more or less wealth). For example, Rachel's family migrated from Québec to Ontario a few generations ago. While French is her mother tongue, and despite being educated in French, her vocabulary is speckled with English words. Rachel does not speak "proper" French, which creates barriers for her in certain contexts (in university settings where a certain style of French is expected, for example). In Ontario, she learned English to survive, remaining very conscious of her French accent. In English Canada, Francophones and Québécois are seen as backwards and inferior. Yet there is a hierarchy of Francophones in Canada. Since moving to Montréal a few years ago, Rachel finds herself part of a French-speaking majority and yet her accent haunts her. Because she has lived in a context where English is the norm, people think she is Anglophone. Her 'outsider' status in Québec however, is mediated by her access to the 'inside' as a white woman.

To be French speaking and Black outside of Québec delimits the freedom of marginalized groups. Fathiya, a Somali, French and English speaking Black woman living in Québec, is seen as a threat to the survival of 'de souche' (old stock) Francophones and as part of a group of people who are, in and of themselves, construed as 'problems.' Richard Bergeron, leader of a municipal party in Québec writes:

Immigration, to the tune of 37 000 people per year, as we witnessed in 2001, constitutes an adequate response to low birth rates under an economic angle, but not from the angle of a collective project for a 'distinct' society. Over a medium to long term period, immigration, rather than birth rate, leads to a replacement of the population and therefore to a transfer of the rights and privileges attached to territory. Québécois 'de souche', by choosing not to reproduce, have begun to give their territory away to whom ever wants to take it. Because it is an extraordinary territory, takers are busting down the door (Bergeron, 2002: n.p.).

[L'immigration, à la hauteur de 37,000 personnes par année, comme nous l'avons fait en 2001, constitue une réponse adequate à une trop faible natalité sous l'angle économique, mais pas sous celui du projet collectif d'une société se voulant "distincte"...Car sur moyenne et longue période, l'immigration, plutôt que la natalité, conduit à un remplacement de population et, par le fait même, à un transfert des droits et privilèges attachés à la propriété du territoire. Les Québécois "de souche", ne souhaitant plus se reproduire, ont entrepris de céder leur territoire à ceux qui veut bien le prendre. S'agissant d'un territoire extraordinaire, les repreneurs se bousculent aux portes (Bergeron, 2002 : n.p.).]

Such a discourse constructs white Québécois as valiant guardians of territory and language, whereas immigrants are seen as a threat to the very survival of 'de souche' Francophones in Québec. Bergeron's concern with territory erases the colonization and takes for granted the conquest of First Nations peoples by the French. Moreover, this way of thinking demonstrates how immigration, is seen as a threat to a "distinct" Québécois society. It is an example of how non-white groups are demonized and subjugated, while others are legitimized as the first Francophone people in Canada, the protectors of territory, democratic values and language which carry their histories, their identities and their commonalities. We then ask the question: Is the subjugation of others (the Francophones by the Anglopohones or 'visible minorities' by Francophones) a precondition for the construction of a Canadian or Québécois identity?

In order to understand the category *filles Francophones* it is necessary to consider the ways in which groups in our society are categorized and racialized according to their languages and so-called cultures. For instance, *filles Francophones*, by definition, excludes girls whose mother tongue is not French. If we were to speak of immigrant and refugee girls whose second language is French, we would need to speak of Allophone girls, a distinct and separate category that inflects their Otherness in relation to the hegemonic power of the 'pure laine' Québécois. These divisions and exclusions are problematic to say the least. Who defines girls? The process of separating girls into categories is not natural, but rather, is presented to us as naturalized (Hall, 1996: 5). In a context where racialized girls pose a threat to Québec as a nation and Québécois as a people, what does it mean to identify with a linguistic group, particularly that of Francophone? Who is included and excluded in the categorical distinctions defining Allophones, Francophones and Anglophones? We maintain that the racialization of these categories is an enduring legacy of colonization. Hence, Haitians in Québec will always be seen as Haitian and Allophone because they are Black, they speak Créole and because they do not exist in the collective imaginary of what it is to be Canadian and Québecois.

Canadian society is a racist society, which constructs and maintains whiteness as a measure of purity—not as a racial category[2]—against which all others are defined. Francophone identity in Canada has been built on the categories *Francophone de souche*, *minorité visible* and *communauté culturelle*. The particularity of Francophones in Canada is that they are French-speaking in the context of an English dominated country. Francophone identity in Canada *is* a 'minority' identity, which exists in relation to 'the Other' except in Québec, which has its own history and struggle for sovereignty. As Juteau notes, the Québec nation "was built on a movement to abolish the domination suffered by French Canadians and keep 'the others' away" (2000b, 70). Khan (1995) argues that this division, as it is manifested in Québec, constructs a notion of French identity that promotes the assimilation of the Other into an assumed superior Québécois culture that is backed by economic and political power (149). Similarly, Handa argues that "the moral superiority of white Canadians is restored by a narrative that portrays 'other' cultures…as backward. Youth, and especially young women, are instrumental to this narrative" (32).

Lambert (1997) draws our attention to the ways in which the Canadian nation state has institutionalized and classified its population into different categories using the Official Languages Act of 1969, the Indian Act, and multiculturalism policies:

> The 'founding nations,' English Canadians and French Canadians, 'Aboriginal peoples,' Amerindians, Inuits and Metis, and 'ethnic groups' having immigrated after the 'founding peoples,' such as Ukranians or Italians. A fourth category, 'visible minorities,' non-whites who are excluded from full participation in Canadian society, includes Aboriginals and Canadians who do not have a European origin.

> [*Les 'peuples fondateurs', Canadiens anglais et Canadiens français, les 'peuples autochtones', Amérindiens, Inuits et Métis, et les 'groupes ethniques', ayant immigré après les 'fondateurs', comme les Ukrainiens ou les Italiens. Une quatrième catégorie, les 'minorité visibles', soit 'les non- Blancs qui ne participent pas à part entière à la société canadienne', regroupe tant les autochtones que les Canadiens d'origine non-européenne (np).*]

It is important to understand that these categories are fluid; they have been transformed over time and continue to be influenced by internal and external dynamics. Québec stands as an illustration of the importance of history in the creation of identities to which people adhere strategically. In response to English colonization and the continued oppression of French speaking people by English Canada, the Québec State constructed itself as a Nation in the 1960s when white French Canadians began calling themselves Québécois. The Québécois converted their cultural minority status within Canada (including their language) into a political project with the creation of the Parti Québécois in 1968. Acadians, Franco-Ontarians and other Francophones in Canada did not follow the same strategies and although they were affected by Québec's political ambitions, they became defined as "Francophones outside Québec," thereby maintaining their minority status.[3]

The construction of Québécois identity was redefined again following the defeat of the 1980 referendum. The idea behind this adjustment was to create the winning conditions for sovereignty predicated on the political separation of Québec as a separate nation from Canada. The loss of the 1980 referendum exposed the need to recognize and take into consideration ethnic and cultural minorities in political discourses. This was done through the creation of the *ministère des communautés culturelles et de l'immigration*—the department of cultural communities and immigration—in 1996 with a mandate promoting respect and reinforcing the development of non-Francophone cultural communities [non-white Allophones]. These developments did not occur in isolation; Canada was also going through a similar process of inclusion with the Canadian Multiculturalism Act of 1988 (Juteau 2000b: 70).

The second failed attempt at Québec sovereignty in 1995 brought about new changes. With the creation of the *ministère avec les citoyens et l'immigration* in 1996, the opposition between the categories Québécois 'de souche' and minorité culturelles was replaced by the idea of equal citizens. The prevailing legal discourse at the millennium was that all Québécois were equal regardless of their language, origins and differences (Juteau, 2000a: 12). Also erased in the construct of "equal citizenship" are issues of racialization, gender, social class, age and ability. Cultural minorities, who were once relegated to the margins in the 1980s, have now been erased from legal discourse by the creation of this new ministry, whose mandate is to manage problematic people. Inhabitants of Québec were collapsed into the category *peuple Québécois*. This new category has never been defined, nor has it been the subject of public debate. However, until the political, social and economic concerns and realities of oppressed people are taken into consideration, we cannot really speak of a *peuple Québécois*. In practice, there is no such category. It is only another version of soft multiculturalism, which aims to add "colour" rather than truly listen, respect and be challenged by what non-dominant groups have to say. Without this, dialogue—requiring reciprocity—is not possible. When the concerns of these groups are reflected in the political, economic and cultural project of Québec, then, and only then, will we be able to speak of a true and radical democratic system—a diverse Québécois society.

The dominant political idea is that citizens of Québec, as in the rest of Canada, are all equal in their differences. Citizenship is discussed in only two ways: as rights and obligations. In this context, cultural differences, although recognized as rights, are perceived as a threat to public space. Girls who are visibly 'different', for example, girls who wear the hijab, are seen as a threat to public spaces such as schools. The hijab is seen as a political statement and is thus interpreted as a threat to Québécois democratic values and tradition; that is, western traditions of liberty and equality. Cultural rights (such as the right to celebrate religious holidays) and social rights (such as equal opportunities and the right to vote) are separated into a false and dangerous dichotomies. No link is made between the recognition of cultural diversity and poverty, sexism, racism, ableism, or the like. The idea of equal citizenship thereby erases race, class and exploitation (Razack, 2001: 60).

It is all the more problematic when we speak of girls who, because of their age, are not even considered full citizens and are framed as being in need of protection. [see Lee, this volume]. Only when we link economic equality and cultural equality can we gain a better understanding of why groups identify with certain pre-determined categories. If we consider the exclusion of Franco-Ontarians from certain spheres of activity, we gain a better understanding of where they are coming from and why French as a linguistic/political category of identification is central to their existence. Similarly, research in two Montréal schools demonstrates how "English is sometimes intentionally used [by second generation Haitian youth] as a confrontational strategy in order to define a personal identity vis-à-vis teachers and other Francophones" (qtd. in Potvin, 1999, n.p.). Clearly a focus on language alone cannot explain the historical and economic situation that would make using English a form of resistance among Haitian youth.

Who is included and excluded in the category *filles Francophones*? How is this category constructed and why do girls identify as Francophones or not? When we speak of Francophone, Anglophone and Allophone girls, we often forget to mention that the creation of categories has a purpose: that of sidestepping history. Why are some groups being asked to trade in their history in exchange for an alleged equal citizenship, while descendants of French colonizers are entitled to hold on to their history of struggle against the English colonizers? These unequal relations illustrate a hierarchy of oppression where non-white French-speaking groups are being denied their trajectory whereas Québécois, Francophones outside of Québec and even Anglophones in English Canada hang onto a glorified history of colonization.

Existing categories have served to nurture a discourse focused on difference and racialization, a "process through which white society has constructed and co-opted differences in bodily characteristics and made them the marks of hierarchical social categories" (Martinot, 2003: 180).[4] Racism therefore is "the system of racialized thoughts and acts by which the white supremacist society maintains itself and its hierarchy of social categorizations" (180). In Québec, as in the rest of Canada, we are less likely to speak of different races and more likely to speak of different cultures. As Razack explains, "cultural differences perform the same function as a more biological notion of race...once did: they mark inferiority. A message of racial inferiority is now more likely to be coded in the language of culture rather than biology" (19). In this context, the debate around the hijab is presented as a clash of cultures issue; "as a conflict between equals, obscuring the fact that white Canadian [and we argue white Québécois] is a more acceptable ethnic/cultural identity" (Handa, 2003: 7).[5]

Across Canada, certain girls—and Muslim girls in particular[6]—are positioned as in need of protection by their own communities and by mainstream Canadian society. Girls' bodies act as locations where cultural anxieties are played out; they are physical sites for debates around culture, religion, tradition, secularism and 'cultural backward-ness' (Handa, 2003: 54). We draw on the case of Emilie Ouimet, a young woman who was expelled from a Montréal high school for wearing the hijab, as an example. Ouimet, it should be noted, was a relatively new convert to Islam. Todd (1998), who conducted an analysis of media representations of the incident, notes two major concerns:

> First, the right to public education was denied to a student on the basis of her religious dress. Second, the question of what is to be 'tolerated' in a multicultural society became a crucial issue. The discourse of individual rights, community responsibility, and the relation of religion to the state were deeply embedded in Canadian reports of the incident...the concerns raised had less to do with the specific details of the case and more to do with larger questions of social policy and definitions of the Anglophone and Francophone communities. (438).

In other words, attention to the personal consequences of this expulsion for Ouimet were sidetracked in favour of a debate between the French language press (who saw the hijab as a threat to a secular and equal society) and the English language press (who saw themselves as victims of an intolerant Québec nationalism).

The violence that is done to girls in the name of culture has little to do with culture, but rather with white supremacy and the consequences of the policies in place which categorize and maintain them, and their families, in poverty:

> Minority groups' claims are not exclusively cultural...they consist of social relations that have economic, political and cultural dimensions, which are at the basis of categories, which, without being homogenous, do share distinct interests. (Juteau 2000a: 5).[7]

> [Les revendications des groupes minoritaires ne sont pas exclusivement culturelles...il s'agit bien de rapports sociaux aux composantes économiques, politiques et culturelles, qui fondent des catégories, qui, sans être homogènes, possèdent néanmoins des intérêts distincts (Juteau 2000a: 5).]

If we are to pursue research with Francophone girls, we must deconstruct the traps laid out by false linguistic dichotomies that erase girls' pluralities—their historical, economic and cultural trajectories, as well as the complete translation of their experiences into the language of culture.

Jean-Loup Amselle (2001) makes a similar argument, noting that no culture is explicitly closed onto itself. He writes: "Unplugging civilizations from their purported origins is probably the best way to escape racism, or, similarly, to touch on the universal" (9). [*"Débrancher les civilisations de leurs origines supposées est peut-être le meilleur moyen d'échapper au racisme, ou, ce qui revient au même, de toucher à l'universel"* (9).] In the case of Francophone girls in Canada, the category of Francophone 'de souche' is stripped of its authenticity and alleged superiority when we demonstrate its historical roots in colonialism and migration. All Francophones in Canada have either migrated to this continent from France or from countries that were colonized by the French. First Nations people in Canada were colonized by the French who, in turn, were colonized by the English. There is no authentic French-Canadian. As Amselle has argued, the categories 'traditional' and 'modern' as they are applied to cultures do not exist (8). Similarly, the minoritized category of Anglophone in Québec needs to be interrogated especially when we observe its capacity to mobilize resources and survive for generations without being assimilated. This is not the case for Francophones outside of Québec. Debates on who is, and who is not *de souche* or *minoritaire* silence the central problem of the distribution of wealth and territory and the power that goes with it.

To gain a better understanding of the mechanisms of domination that regulate the lives of Francophone girls, we must consider the ways in which the two dominant linguistic groups in Canada manage minorities. As demonstrated, the categories that have been created to control diversity are the result of a racist institutional logic. Francophone girls in Canada are linguistically, economically and historically plural. As we illustrate in the next section, research on Francophone girls does not reflect nor address this plurality.

Current Literature On Francophone Girls In Canada

In this section, we outline some of the main themes in the Francophone literature on girls in Canada to provide a general sense of which girls are being researched, what issues are being explored and from what perspective. We have reviewed literature with a specific focus on filles, adolescentes and jeunes femmes.

Adolescent sexuality

As evident in the Anglophone girlhood studies literature, adolescent girls' sexuality and its regulation has also been an area of interest for Francophone researchers. Identifying how sexual education was institutionalized in Québec, and discussing the current context in which it is being called into question, Boucher (2003) takes a critical feminist look at the social representations of sexual education in the province (133-136, 122). Reviewing the literature and reflecting on the characteristics of sexual education programs, she observes that adolescent girls' sexuality has been predominantly addressed as a social problem both in research and intervention (123, 128). She demonstrates how sexual education in Québec privileges a biological rather than a social approach and is taught from an essentialist and individualistic perspective, thereby omitting the issues of gender and power at play in sexuality (139). Boucher calls for change in sexual education and is currently conducting research that will integrate young women's perspectives on the issue (147).

Regarding the sexualization of pre-teen girls by the media, Bouchard and Bouchard (2003) have argued that the aggressive and early sexualization of girls increases their vulnerability and susceptibility to violence (5). In the first phase of their research, they reviewed the literature on education, communication and consumerism, focusing on information communicated through the press and the internet. Although they do not exclusively focus on French-Canadian girls, they do examine Québécois publications in terms of their role in commercializing and selling sexuality to young girls. Bouchard and Bouchards' desire to understand the links between this sexualization and issues such as poor body image, eating disorders, dependency and sexual exploitation led them to a second phase involving interviews with nine to twelve year old girls on their reactions and understanding of the contents of a popular teen magazine (62).

Adolescent motherhood has also been addressed in the literature, albeit as a consequence of girls' sexual activity. Charbonneau interviewed thirty-two young women in their twenties who were living in Montégérie and who had delivered their first child in their adolescence (1998: 43). Focusing on intergenerational relationships between parents and their children, and on the correlation between youth and society, she used young mothers' negotiation between autonomy and dependency as a point of reference in her analysis. After providing an overarching view of the history of the young women interviewed, she presents preliminary findings which indicate that having a child during adolescence is likely to create a stronger sense of solidarity between a young mother and her family (1998, 49).[8]

Similarly, Quéniart and Vennes conducted exploratory qualitative research with young women between the ages of eighteen and twenty-five, which addressed the lack of research on young women's perspectives on their maternity, their family and their relationships with their child (75). Having already done research on young fathers, this second phase began with analyzing the representations of young mothers' pregnancies and their passage into adult life (77). Using grounded theory, they interviewed eighteen young mothers. The authors provide some descriptive information pertaining to the respondents' age, the type of family they have, their occupation and their income. They also describe the interviewees as: "*toutes francophones et québécoises d'origine*" (78). Interviews were semi-structured and young women were asked to talk about their experience of being a mother. They found that motherhood provides young women with social recognition and a sense of becoming someone, but that paradoxically, is also a source of isolation (98).

Also of interest is Côté's genealogy of discourses on adolescent mothers in Quebec, from 1940 to the present (287). She asks how the framing of adolescent mothers further empowers the state in its regulation of bodies: "How is power exerted when adolescent maternity is constructed as problem, and in the application of solutions that control the body through abstinence, contraception or abortion?" (299) *["Comment s'exerce le pouvoir dans une construction du problème de la maternité à l'adolescence et dans l'application de solutions de contrôle du corps que sont l'abstinence, la contraception ou l'avortement?" (299).]* Rather than further problematizing pregnant adolescents, her approach outlines the ways in which these young women have been constructed and treated as problems by the state for various reasons that are historically specific to Québec.

If we rely on the existing Francophone literature on girls' sexuality, we cannot conceive of a sexuality that is not about pornography, lack of agency, pregnancy or disease. The principal arguments around girls' sexuality continue to perpetuate an image of vulnerability and victimization, which denies girls the ability to make informed decisions regarding their own sexual identities. This allows adults to, under the guise of 'saving' girls, mobilize funds and offer services without sharing power or the necessary information that would support girls in making informed decisions about their sexuality. Furthermore, this literature homogenizes girls as a group. It erases the exoticization of girls of colour; it completely silences the sexuality of (dis)abled girls and First Nations girls. It is also makes it impossible to view pre-teen girls as sexual and desiring people. Bouchard and Bouchard's research does not inquire into how the bodies of certain girls are exoticized and how this increases their vulnerability to violence. Gender is the only lens they use but it does not do justice to the complexity of girls' sexualization. Who is sexualized and in which ways? How is sexualization racialized? Asking these questions shifts the tone considerably and we would no doubt be accused of diverting the subject from sexualization to race. But it is about both. The silence weakens Bouchard and Bouchard's case.

Media studies

In the area of media studies, Currie (1999) and McRobbie (1991, 2000) have conducted extensive studies of gendered representations in popular teen magazines. Building on this work, Caron conducted a content analysis of teen magazines in Québec (2003a, 2003b). Caron's objective was to find out which messages were being disseminated about femininity, male/female relations, personal development and societal issues (2003b: 8). Her findings confirm research previously done by McRobbie:

> Our analysis converges, for example, with the semiotic analysis of McRobbie, exposing four codes illustrating the ideology of feminine adolescence in the British magazine Jackie: heterosexual romance, personal and domestic life, fashion and beauty, and popular music (2003a: 3).

[Nos résultats convergent, par exemple, avec les analyses sémiologiques de McRobbie, qui ont dévoilé les quatre codes connotatifs de l'idéologie de la féminité adolescente dans le magazine britannique Jackie: romance hétérosexuelle, vie personnelle et domestique, mode et beauté, puis musique populaire (2003a: 3).]

Caron's findings also corroborate those of Currie, in that the contents of the magazines were found to be ethnocentric (focused on white girls and boys). Caron (2003b) proposes that future research address the ways in which Francophone girls themselves read and interpret the magazines, something which has not yet been done. Media plays an important role in the construction of young girls as (hetero)sexual and desirable beings. This is intimately tied to consumerism and an increase in girls' vulnerability to violence (Bouchard and Bouchard, 2003).

How do girls who do not fit the mainstream beauty standards negotiate their identity vis-à-vis these dominant media images? This is an area for future research that needs to be pursued.

Young women's political involvement

Curious about young women's political involvement, Quéniart and Jacques (2001) examined young women's engagement both in political parties and in groups rallying around various social justice issues (10-11). The authors interviewed Francophone females between the ages of eighteen and thirty who were involved in the liberal party of Québec, the Québécois party and the Fédération des Femmes du Québec. They provide each respondent's socio-economic background, as well as those of her parents' (18). Quéniart and Jacques explore five themes:

> 1) The trajectory of engagement (motivations, catalytic elements, origins of political interest, etc.); 2) The meaning of engagement (definitions, representations, etc.); 3) Concrete practice of engagement (description of daily or time limited activities); 4) Life history (family and school trajectory); 5) Social representation (perceptions of Québécois society, social issues, etc.) (2001, 47).

> *[1) La trajectoire de l'engagement (motivations, éléments déclencheurs, origines de l'intérêt pour le politique, etc.) [motivations]; 2) Le sens de l'engagement (définitions, représentations, etc.) [their understanding of their involvement]; 3) La pratique concrète de l'engagement (description des activités quotidiennes ou ponctuelles) [concrete practice]; 4) L'histoire de vie (parcours familial et scolaire) [life history]; 5) La représentation du social (perceptions de la société québécoise, enjeux sociaux, etc.) [how they perceive society] (2001, 47).]*

The authors found that young women are far from apolitical and that their political actions are driven by a cause rather than by their dedication to the groups within which they act. Additionally, grassroots work is valued over more mainstream politics, which young women judge to be happening behind closed doors. Finally, political involvement provides spaces within which young women may socialize and develop friendships (2001, 52).

As yet, research that focuses on the political involvement of young girls is lacking. How do girls under eighteen, who are by law dependants and excluded from political involvement, negotiate with allies in bringing forward their concerns? Is it even possible to speak of citizenship and participation of young girls? Quéniart and Jacques' research does not consider the political participation or community engagement of girls but rather of young women (eighteen to thirty). We have included it here because it is the *only* research that takes a gendered look at young women's political involvement in the Québec context. Future research could address this gap and also inquire into questions such as: how racialized girls negotiate their participation as "citizens" when their very existence is perceived as a threat to the survival of Francophones 'de souche' within and outside of Québec? How, in light of the fact that their religion, history and culture are seen as private, rather than public issues, do these girls engage in political processes? What does political participation mean to them?

Education

Pierrette Bouchard, St-Amant and Tondreau (1995) have examined the gap between boys and girls' school success in Québec, and challenge the myths surrounding this discussion (11). They argue that boys are not being discriminated against by western education systems but rather that girls are disciplined, ambitious and have developed strategies for collaboration and competition (12). They recommend that efforts be made to help both girls and boys who drop out of school. In addition, they propose that girls be supported in their school success so that their achievements can be reflected in their search for equality in socio-economic spheres (24). Dallaire & Rail (1995) have also studied equity in schools, specifically in physical education with Francophone populations both in and outside Québec. Particularly interested in exploring the reasons why a high number of girls drop out of gym classes, they propose strategies for teachers to encourage female participation in physical education.

Although a response to masculinist discourse is provided by this research, we contend that when an exclusively gendered analysis dominates this discussion, it erases the complexity of *which* girls succeed and the barriers that exist for different groups of girls in other social and historical locations. In what ways are schools failing certain girls? How does racialized dominance play out within the school? Research on second-generation Haitian youth in Québec answers some of these questions, but gender rarely factors in their analyses. Potvin (1999) offers an understanding of the school realities of Haitian youth; realities which include stereotypes, harassment, racism from teaching staff and school authorities as well as situational ethnic boundaries and racism which surface during sporting events or fights. In terms of school performance, "[r]esearchers tend to confirm that the problems experienced by all youths in underprivileged environments are the same: poor linguistic and academic performance, an absence of teaching 'models' from their social environment, and displays of negative attitudes toward them" (Potvin, 1999). To understand these educational realities, we must consider how violence is a vehicle and a catalyst influencing school failure or success.

Violence

Sylvie Normandeau (1999) reviewed the Francophone literature on violence against children. She found that "although violence against girls has been studied extensively, a great deal of research still remains to be done, especially on the factors associated with the effective prevention of violence and on the socialization of girls and boys" (n.p.). Research relating to the violence children experience is rarely gender specific. Providing a short inventory of violence prevention programs in Québec, Normandeau also found that most of the interventions were not gender-specific and focused mainly on domestic violence and dating violence, reflecting a growing concern about these issues in Québec. Again, the differences within groups of girls and boys living in Quebec are not examined.

The criminalization and criminal involvement of girls in gangs is a subject that elicited some attention. Fournier, Cousineau and Hamel (2004) examined girls' experiences of victimization in Montréal. They met with thirteen girls between the ages of fourteen to twenty-four who were living in a rehabilitation centre. Some of the girls were still involved with a gang, while others had left the gang entirely. Fournier et al. asked the young women about their experiences starting from the moment they were first in contact with a gang—*le récit d'expérience*. The authors reveal the different forms of victimization girls experience, namely physical aggression, controlling and violent intimate relationships, isolation, sexual violence as well as fear and threats. Interestingly, they observe that the girls' understanding of victimizing behaviour and that of the researchers' differed considerably, and suggest that this should be taken into consideration by practitioners when working with girls in gangs.

Once again, the exclusively gendered perspective adopted by Normandeau and Fournier, Cousineau and Hamel, does not do justice to the complexity of violence against girls. Violence and racialization are not separate issues. Racialization *is* violence a point the authors have neglected to investigate. If the violence that was done to Emilie Ouimet—by refusing her access to her school—is not concrete enough, there are examples such as the brutal beating of fifteen year old Aylin Otano-Garcia by an explicitly racist classmate,[9] which illustrate the need for research and action around this issue.

Analysis And Ways Forward: Anti-Racist Research

The research we have reviewed here looks at a broad spectrum covering fourteen to thirty year old "girls." Francophone research has not overwhelmingly taken a gendered perspective and research that is specific to girls rarely addresses the realities of young girls. Bouchard's studies on the sexualization of young girls, as well as her research on girls' school performance, are notable exceptions; focusing exclusively on pre-teen and teenage girls. Nevertheless, the contributions we have highlighted offer useful starting points for continued work on Francophone girls. Unfortunately, these studies reflect a limited amount of girls' studies scholarship, often relying on texts that have been critiqued for being ethnocentric (Pipher's (1995) *Reviving Ophelia*, for example).

There are many possible directions for future research but the most important gap is around the intimate relationships between gender, ability, race, violence and identity formation among Francophone girls. How do girls who have been excluded from citizenship because of their age, their (dis)ability, their visible 'difference' or other status, negotiate an identity for themselves in Québec or in English Canada? Current research perpetuates the view of Francophone girls as a homogenous group in need of adult protection and surveillance; this is deeply patriarchal. Ignoring the existence of systems of oppressions—capitalism, patriarchy, racial ideology—in favour of working with one manageable category such as gender, does an injustice to girls. It is impossible not to work with these intersections and trajectories. If, in the city of Montréal for example, one out of five girls is categorized as a visible minority, it is a violence to do research that does not adopt an anti-racist, historical and gendered lens. An anti-racist perspective means something different to us as authors in our daily lives. For Rachel, racism is an urgent question of power and morality; for Fathiya it is an everyday matter of life and death.

In this light, research on Francophone girls must take into consideration the historical, social and political contexts in which these girls live, so that we may understand their strategies for survival and gain a better understanding of how violence and domination are produced and reproduced within specific spaces (within the family, schools, state, and religious institutions). By being unclear as to whom we are speaking of when we say "filles" or "jeunes femmes," and by silencing a discussion on racialization, the illusion of girls as a homogenous group is maintained. Only when their histories are recognized can we see to what extent girls share commonalities and to what extent they differ. This opens up a possibility for moving towards what Mohanty (2003) suggests as: "solidarity in terms of mutuality, accountability, and the recognition of common interests as the basis for relationships among diverse communities" (7). Thus, "[r]ather than assuming an enforced commonality of oppression, [in this case "girlhood"], the practice of solidarity foregrounds communities of people who have chosen to work and fight together" (7). The solution does not lie in adding diversity to the mix, but rather in taking into account the intersecting systems of oppression that play out in girls' lives both historically and currently.

We contend that it is not possible to address the issue of Francophone girlhood without calling into question the very existence of Francophone girls as a group. None of the research we have reviewed has done this, nor has it drawn on literature that addresses the issue of Francophone identities and its fragmentations.

Researching For Social Justice

As in the Anglo-centred research on girls coming out of the United States, Britain and Australia, the research we have reviewed on Francophone girls reproduces quite problematically the "public interest in young women that is centered around their study, work, recreation, and consumption, [which] is often in the service of constructing a new subject who regulates herself onto a success trajectory" (Harris, 2004b, 188): that is, who becomes a consumer. Research on girls must include a social justice lens. The idea of social justice is not easy to define when we consider the complexity of the issues it calls upon such as political systems and economies. Moreover, its definition will vary according to different schools of thought. Drawing on and going beyond the work John Rawls, Philippe Van Parijs (1995) proposes that social justice be concerned with equal opportunities and redistribution of resources (10). Doing research with a social justice lens illustrates the links between the issues facing Francophone girls and their living conditions. It breaks the silences that currently dominate academic spaces. Research with girls needs to consider issues such as poverty, age, education, health and relations with others in order to identify the spaces in which their exclusion is produced and reproduced. We adhere to Van Parijs' vision of social justice, which includes free and accessible education and health systems, the right to housing and a subsistence wage, all reinforced by fundamental rights. In following Mohanty's vision, this includes racial equality, the freedom of choice on issues such as reproduction, marriage and love, the redistribution of wealth, ecological sustainability and the freedom to participate meaningfully in society regardless of social location (3-4). Research can contribute to this vision if researchers and communities act courageously.

Conclusions

The silences we currently observe in the literature serve to maintain marginalized girls in precarious living conditions. For example, research on violence against girls that fails to look at the violence done to racialized, Aboriginal and (dis)abled girls perpetuates violence against girls. Research is not neutral, it plays a role in maintaining the status quo. It is possible for research to play a role in subverting the status quo—in fact we argue that it must. Research that makes connections between girls' realities, their access to resources and opportunities, and that advocates for social justice and redistribution, is sorely missing in both Francophone and Anglophone research in Canada. Researching French-speaking populations in Canada and Québec is not only a matter of language or of including French-speaking people in our samples. This would not bring anything new to the field beyond a little added 'colour'. What we are calling for is not a matter of diversity; it is a matter of social justice. Girls should be engaged in research with as many lenses as it takes to understand and struggle against their continued oppression as Francophones, Allophones, racialized, Aboriginal and (dis)abled girls who are not even entitled to political participation and power. As researchers, we must consider how the language we use may be embedded with violence, serving to further marginalize and alienate girls.[10] The goal should be to create a platform where people's histories, their economic, social and political realities can be given importance. Using our cultural capital[11] we can create spaces where girls may access spheres of power, all the while working to minimize our domination over the girls with whom we are allied.

Our experience in working with young economically marginalized girls in Ottawa and Montréal reminds us that communicating across knowledge barriers is a constant challenge; we offer no magical recipe for doing research with girls. Rather, we propose a clear intention: to be allies and vehicles of change. Our aim in writing this chapter has been to identify a first step in broadening the field of girls' studies to include research on Francophone girls that does not just add the language ingredient but rather expands research to question who is considered a girl in the first place and what systems of oppression act to maintain girls in precarious living situations. We consider this first step to be an interrogation of the dichotomous linguistic categories that cleave national identity and the ways in which they silence the realities of Allophone girls.

We have briefly outlined themes in the literature on Francophone girls in a Canadian context, while pointing to its limitations. These limitations can be extended to the broader girls' studies literature. We have broken the silence that pervades current research, inviting researchers to reflect and act on the ways they contribute to further marginalizing girls. We have been particularly interested in providing potential directions for future research on Francophone girls, arguing that one cannot assume a universal Francophone identity but rather complicate it by addressing the structural violence girls and their families face. Finally, we call for an engaged research that would not only propose changes, but also advocate for social justice. With this in mind, research on Francophone girls has the potential for making a valuable contribution to the field of girls' studies by avoiding specious categories, whether they are based on language, racialized identities, (dis)ability, sexuality or age. We are inspired by the words of Cornel West in asking our own question: Do we have the intelligence, humour, imagination, courage, love and respect to challenge racism, sexism, poverty and all forms of subjugation so that we can understand and work with girls?

Notes

1. "Communautés culturelles/cultural communities," and "groupes ethno-culturels/ethno-cultural groups" refer to communities other than the dominant French and English.

2. Race as a biological category does not exist. Whiteness is a measure of purity in that "one is white only if one's ancestry is purely white" (Martinot, 2003:21).

3. As Cardinal (1994) explains, it was not easy for Francophones outside of Québec to maintain an identity without access to territory: "But French speaking populations outside of Québec, not having a state or territory to which to identify, have experienced these developments with more difficulty. The gap has been covered up by the discovery of provincial identities, Franco-Ontarian, Franco-Manitoban, Fransaskois, Franco-Albertan and so on, but on the national level, the very expression francophones outside of Québec points to the exclusion of a territory, something which has never ceased to cause an identity malaise" (71). ["Mais la Francophonie hors Québec, n'ayant pas d'État ou de territoire auquel s'identifier, a vécu ces développements plus difficilement. Le vide a été recouvert par la découverte d'identités provinciales, les identités franco-ontarienne, franco-manitobaine, fransaskoise, franco-albertaine et ainsi de suite, mais sur le plan national, la francophonie hors Québec, qu'exprime présisément cette appellation qui dit l'exclusion d'un territoire, n'a jamais cessé de vivre le malaise identitaire" (71).]

4. Martinot looks at the roots of racialization within colonialism.

5. Amita Handa's (2003) work on the identity formation of second generation South Asian girls living in Toronto sketches a framework for doing research that does not fall into racist 'clash of culture' theories (7). Using "a survey of articles in mainstream media, interviews with young women, and discussions within the South Asian community" (23), she demonstrates how "white identity has been constructed in reference to an outside community" (163).

6. Since the end of the cold war, the new enemy of the western way of life has become Islam. With September 2001, there is a new legitimacy and authority to annihilate Muslim 'terrorists' and protect the so-called democratic values.

7. Many of the strategies adopted by people to navigate Canadian society (eg. veiling) are both the product of and answer to domination and unacceptable living conditions. In this sense, they have much more to do with access to resources than culture (see Amselle).

8. Charbonneau has recently published a book on the issue entitled *Adolescentes et mères: histoires de maternité précoce et soutien du réseau social*, which we have not reviewed in this chapter.

9. Otano-Garcia was targeted by her classmate because of her perceived 'ethnic' background despite the fact that she had moved to Québec at a young age.

10. Stephanie Higginson, Email Communication with Rachel Gouin, 2004.

11. We use cultural capital in the sense that Bourdieu defines the term.

Chapter Four

Violence In The Lives Of Girls In Canada: Creating Spaces Of Understanding And Change

Yasmin Hussain, Helene Berman, Rian Lougheed-Smith, Romy Poletti, Azmina Ladha, Ashley Ward, Barb MacQuarrie

In May 2003 I was asked to participate and represent the London Centre for Research on Violence Against Women and Children along with other members at the National Congress on Child and Youth Health in Vancouver, B.C. This was an extremely large conference with organizations from all over the world. I was able to sit in on a lecture from an organization in Chile and I met a woman from New Zealand. This was all in a few days and I was preparing myself for the day the Centre for Research on Violence Against Women and Children presented itself and the Girl Child Project.

It was at this conference that I became emotional for the first time. I had spoken about my experiences before, but I had one of those moments when a painful memory breaks you down for a minute. I couldn't help but cry at that podium. I was able to compose myself and finish my speech.

I find that moment funny now but I think I made it a bit more real for those who had been at the lecture that day. I was approached by so many after and congratulated on having the courage to speak out. When you hear things like that from complete strangers you know that representing the Girl Child Project is worth so much. —Ashley Ward.

What does it mean to 'do' participatory action research with girls and young women? Why is girl-centred research important? And, what is accomplished or gained by engaging girls in the research process? The Alliance of Canadian Research Centres on Violence Against Women and Children continuously revisits these questions in our work examining experiences of violence in the lives of girls and young women. We explore and discuss these questions in conversation with girls and young women who have participated, and continue to participate, in our work as co-researchers. Ashley Ward is one of those young women. Here she tells how she has given voice to her experiences and then, how she connected with them emotionally. Other girls comment on what happened to them as they participated in the research throughout this paper.

This chapter is a collaborative effort undertaken by a small group that has been involved in research in various capacities over the past few years. In this paper we consider the role of research as a mechanism for moving forward social agendas related to the improvement of the everyday lives and contexts of girls and young women. We begin by presenting a brief overview of the historical background and context for conducting our research. We then examine issues that relate to the development of research frameworks that include the participation of girls and that examine girls' own knowledge of their daily realities. We include a brief look at how knowledge about girls' lives is constructed in academia and prevailing popular discourses. This analysis is followed by a discussion of intersectionality as a conceptual approach for the comprehensive understanding of violence in the lives of girls. Finally, we explore the experiences of research with and for girls and young women. We examine these issues by sharing our reflections regarding participation in the research.

This paper provides an important opportunity to examine the context of our research on violence in the lives of girls. Thus, we see this process as furthering reflexive dialogue on critical issues of theory, methodology, and researcher-participant relationships in participatory action research with girls and young women. Reflexive discussion plays a key part in the process of generating knowledge and research practices that are both meaningful and empowering. We sincerely hope that this paper helps to engage with and challenge conventional research methods and relationships by demonstrating the potential of collaborative research approaches with and for girls through the shared creation of spaces of expression, connection, commitment, and transformative engagement. Ultimately, we hope to creatively devise research approaches that are personally and politically meaningful for the researchers and the girls; approaches that contribute to positive change in understandings of girls' lives and that enable girls and young women to consider their experiences in previously unseen ways.

Background And Context

Our research stems from the recognition that violence is a daily reality in the lives of girls and young women (Berman and Jiwani, 2002). It is our assertion that this premise holds true for girls who grow up in loving homes where mutual respect and care are valued and enacted, as well as for those who are raised in homes where violence and aggression are common occurrences. Beyond the home setting, violence permeates girls' lives in a multitude of subtle and explicit ways in our schools, communities, media, and society. Our research has developed a complex understanding of violence that is interwoven into the daily fabric of interpersonal, community, institutional, and structural relations. Though all girls experience overlapping forms of violence in their lives, vulnerabilities to violence and experiences of victimization are multiple and varied, reflecting social inequalities and differentiated social locations and identities. In essence, there are no groups of girls that are immune to the violence that is woven into the fabric of everyday life.

Why the "girl child"? Gender discrimination has been a reality in the lives of girls for many years. However, it wasn't until the 1980s that the distinct challenges faced by girls received international attention. Several key international initiatives were instrumental in bringing these concerns to light. Among these was the adoption of the phrase "the girl child" by UNICEF during the 1980s. Several international organizations subsequently declared 1990 "The Year of The Girl Child," and the 1990s as "The Decade of the Girl Child." At the United Nations Fourth World Conference on Women in Beijing in 1995, the focus on girls was subsequently incorporated into the *Beijing Declaration and Platform for Action*, which was ratified by Canada.

The notion of the 'girl child' was first articulated in reference to girls in the developing world, where some languages have no term for "girl," and where girls and girlhood are concepts that simply do not exist. This fact is highlighted by Taslima Nasrin who wrote about her experiences of growing up female in Bangladesh. In her book, *Meyebela: My Bengali Girlhood: A Memoir of Growing up Female in a Muslim World*, Nasrin tells the often harrowing story of her journey from birth to adolescence. It was necessary for her to create new language to denote this passage, as none existed in her native tongue. The Bengali term for childhood is *chelebela*: boy-time. *Meyebela*, an act of radical linguistics, means girl-time.

While the English language clearly includes distinct terminology for males and females, attention to gender often becomes obscured, or blatantly negated by the ubiquitous use of the term "youth." Government documents employing a gender analysis almost exclusively refer to inequalities in the lives of adult women, with virtually no mention of girls and young women. Similarly, an examination of national and international conventions to which Canada is a signatory reveals a notable absence of any consideration as to the unique needs and challenges faced by the girl child in Canada. Instead, concerns related to girls are consistently subsumed under the gender-neutral categories of "children" and "youth."

In recognition of the obstacles, challenges, and vulnerabilities faced by the girl child in Canada, a multi-phased national action program of research, funded by Status of Women Canada, has been conducted by teams of community and academic researchers from the Alliance of Canadian Research Centres on Violence. This Alliance is comprised of five Centres across Canada that were established in 1992 as part of a federal initiative to promote research related to violence against women and children following the 1989 murder of fourteen women engineering students in Montreal.

The initial research started in 1998 and produced the report "In the Best Interests of the Girl Child" (Berman and Jiwani, 2002). Referred to as "The Girl Child Project," the study was designed to examine the diverse ways in which girls and young women

are socialized to expect violence in their lives. A second aim of this research was to examine how social policies, legislation and institutions alleviate, or perpetuate, the
problems faced by this population. A third objective was to explore the varied dimensions and manifestations of the connections between systemic forms of violence, such
as racism and sexism, and violence occurring within intimate/familial relationships.
Finally, our fourth objective was to propose constructive and meaningful strategies
for implementing policy and programming changes geared towards the prevention of
gendered violence and the promotion of egalitarian interactions in the lives of girls.

Collectively, the investigations of the "Girl Child Project" revealed numerous layers of violence present in the lives of girls. A continuum of violence exists in the lives of
girls, linking individual lived realities to systemic institutional structures (Berman and
Jiwani, 2002: 8). One recommendation was for the inclusion of a gender analysis in all
policies and programmes affecting girls and boys, young men and young women.
Otherwise, gender-neutral perspectives in legislation, policies, and programmes will
continue to support the reproduction of both discursive and material violence against
girls. Another important finding was that girls who experience violence in the form of
sexual harassment or racism have few places where they can turn for help or support.
As a result, we put forward a strong recommendation regarding the need to create
"safe spaces" where girls have opportunities to build connections and develop structures of support (174-175).

Theoretically, our thinking has moved from a feminist analysis, whereby gender is
viewed as central to understanding the experiences of girls, to an intersectional analysis.
Through the stories of racialized girls and young women, including those from Aboriginal, immigrant and refugee backgrounds in the "Girl Child," it became apparent that
racism was, and is, the key form of violence they encounter. Further, we learned that
acts of violence seldom occur in isolation; instead there is a confluence of various forms
of violence and oppression that girls encounter in daily life. How violence is experienced
has a great deal to do with one's social locations, identities, and positions of privilege.

Researching Violence In The Lives Of Girls

She had hit me. It wasn't the fact that my jaw hurt, the fact that it had been
uncalled for, or even that it had been embarrassing that bothered me, it was
something that one of my friends had said to me afterwards: "You're making a pretty big deal out of this, it was nothing". She hit everyone all the
time; it was nothing special that she had hit me harder than everyone else,
why should I care? I found myself wondering, since when is one person using violence against another nothing, and why did no one else see it as anything out of the ordinary? Why was it that by taking offence to someone
hurting me I was the one doing something wrong? I knew that I did not

want to hit her back, but I also knew that I did not want to stand by and do nothing. I found it bizarre that while the majority of my peers would tell me violence is wrong, none of them even blinked an eye at the fact I had been hit. It was the fact that I was bothered by it that drew the most attention, as if that's all I wanted, attention. —Rian Lougheed-Smith

I was invited to participate in a panel to share some of my experiences as a means of illustrating the reality of violence in the lives of young women. A few months later, I was asked to participate in a national panel in Ottawa focusing on perspectives and experiences of violence in the lives of young Canadian girls originating from various locations and backgrounds. After sharing my experiences, listening to the narratives of other young women, as well as my involvement with the research on violence in the lives of girls, I started to develop definitions for violence and vulnerability. For the first time I understood gendered violence was not only extreme physical violence that so many young girls believe it is, but also that violence can be emotional and psychological. After this startling realization, I opened my dossier of memories and it appeared that I had experienced forms of violence all those times when the explanative "boys will be boys" was used or when I had to change the way I acted/behaved in order to not be placed in a vulnerable situation. —Romy Poletti

How do girls define and understand experiences of violence in their lives? How do experiences of violence affect them? How are intimate forms of violence shaped by broader social, cultural, and political constructs? What language and discursive means of expression do girls use to articulate their individual experiences? Rian Lougheed-Smith and Romy Poletti, participants in the Girl Child Study, begin to give shape to this discussion with their comments above.

A central theme underpinning our work has been an attempt to determine how to most effectively and sensitively discuss the issue of violence with girls and young women. During our earlier research, a definition of violence was developed by the research team, which at that time was comprised primarily of community and academic researchers. While girls were becoming increasingly involved in the research, they did not participate in the early formulation of our definition of violence. Nor did they like it. From their perspective, the definition was both cumbersome and pedantic. These reactions reminded us that we needed to carefully consider how to engage in discussions about violence with this group. More importantly, we gained a deeper understanding of the fact that if our work is to be meaningful, girls and young women must be involved in the process from the earliest stages of conceptualization.

Through further dialogue between the researchers and the girls, common understandings regarding violence emerged. Inherent in our definition of violence is a recognition that it exists as a dialectical process linking discursive and material practices and continuously unfolding between social structures and individuals (Solis, 2003: 16). Our responsibility lies in tracing the social and political origins of violence (28) and building integrated and differentiated understandings that enable us to grasp its multiple impacts on the lives of girls. It is important that we seek to understand how girls internalize experiences of violence by listening for the meaning they give to what happens in their interpersonal relationships and their experiences within structures of oppression.

Understanding The Construction Of Girls' Lives: Whose Knowledge?

The Girls Advisory culminated in a very large project which emphasized the importance of having girls and young women directly involved in research. In June, 2003, more than 100 girls, the majority of whom were from traditionally marginalized communities, gathered at the SFU Harbour Centre in Vancouver, BC for Keepin' it Real: Girls Speaking Out about Diversity. The conference was a safe and comfortable forum where they spoke out about issues of identity. It was a place where they stood with their hands linked for an Aboriginal prayer, where they gave a standing ovation to the mixed race woman who presented a play called "an understanding of brown", and where they attended workshops like "Being a Leader and Feeling Good about It" and "Act Out Your Thoughts and Emotions." While the girls said that they enjoyed the specific activities and workshops, I was personally struck by their commitment and their desire for change. It's not everyday that 100 teenage girls give up a sunny Saturday to be inside a university building discussing issues of marginalization, oppression and to devise strategies for change! —Azmina Ladha

In 1999 the Muriel McQueen Fergusson Centre in Fredericton, NB, began research at my school in the form of awareness creating workshops regarding violence and healthy relationships. I had been involved in these workshops as a participant for about a year at the time the girl hit me. I became further involved in the workshops at my school. The workshops were really something great, the students enjoyed them, not only because they were being held during class time but because they were fun! The workshops involved gender-segregation and mixed gender groups. Giving both sexes a chance to have discussion and activities within separate groups, but also a chance to come together as a whole for activities. The workshops were highly successful, teaching students about healthy violence free relationships and lessons about violence in general. The most important thing I found about these workshops was the fact that they were accessible. We were never told what was right for us, but instead asked. Students who had initially been participants in the workshops were then trained to facilitate. Participating in and learning to facilitate the workshops changed my perspective in many ways. —Rian Lougheed-Smith

How are the experiences of girls portrayed in academic research? How are girls framed in popular public discourse? How are girls' lives (re)presented? And why should we listen to the voices of girls? Azmina Ladha and Rian Lougheed-Smith lead the way into a discussion of these questions with their reflections.

Feminist scholarship has long looked at the political nature of research and knowledge production. Far from being "objective," knowledge is shaped by the unequal material and discursive conditions in the realms of social, gender, race, economic, sexual, cultural and global relations and interrelations (Berman and Jiwani, 7). Feminist theory has challenged what counts as research and knowledge using approaches that place women's experiences at the centre of inquiry, thereby valuing women's "ways of knowing" (Belenky, 1997). This work has taught us to see that how we frame our research and how we engage in the research process affects the kind of knowledge that is created and the potential for change. Thus, engaging in non-traditional research methods that challenge dominant theories is crucial to the development of social understandings, policies, and institutional settings responsive to women's experiences and perspectives (Lesko, 1996: 142).

It is clear that the complex diversity and specificity of girls' experiences has not been widely researched. Girls and young women have often been lost in the research agenda as a result of inappropriate approaches to understanding their lives. The lack of specificity along lines of gender, race, class, sexuality, ability and attention to the manner in which identities and social relations intersect in conventional research has served to objectify, exclude, and silence girls and young women in society. A gender-neutral, decontextualized, and undifferentiated examination of the experiences of girls conceals the root causes of violence, fails to reveal how girls' lives are variously impacted by violence, disconnects violence from unequal social structures and relations, and does not capture the interconnected and relational quality of violence.

While girls and young women have been ignored as subject participants in prevailing research agendas, girls are simultaneously absent and present in popular perceptions and discourses. Harris (2003) and Gonick (2004) have commented on the cultural fascination with girlhood and the discourses used to fashion girls' identities in society. Gonick has discussed the continuous supply of constructed stories detailing a "crisis" in girls and girlhood (395). For example, in recent years, public conscious- ness has been focused on the rise of the "mean girl" with such books as *Odd Girl Out* (2003) by Rachel Simmons, *Queen Bees and Wannabees* (2002) by Rosalind Wiseman, *Fast Girls* (2002) by Emily White and Sharon Lamb's *The Secret Lives of Girls* (2002). In addition, movies such as *Mean Girls* (2004) and the documentary *It's a Girl's World* (2003) by Lynn Glazier have sensationalized the actions and behaviours of girls through a targeted focus on destructive and anti-social behaviours of girls and how these behaviours shape their friendships. Gonick has argued that the behaviours of girls are naturalized and objectified (395-396). Declarations regarding the existence of psychological "warfare," exclusionary practices, and fights between girls are presented as 'ethno- graphic curiosities' (ibid) alongside alarmist explanations and earnest interventions.

Anita Harris (2003) has also explored the representations of girls in public debate. She talks about constructions of 'girls as risk-takers' and on-going discussions about various "inappropriate" behaviours. This public discourse is laden with moral overtones as stories and images of teen pregnancy, girl gangs, drug taking, sexuality and STD's take hold. Narratives of "girls as risk-takers" are linked to notions of "girls at-risk," and both build on a belief that the behaviours and actions of girls are the source of experiences of violence, pain, and hardship in their lives. Girls and young women are discussed and represented as violent, irresponsible, and uninhibited in their actions (40). Other sources of interpersonal, institutional, or structural violence are rendered invisible. As with the discourse on "mean girls," discussions and images of "girls as risk-takers" and/or "girls at-risk" inform policy recommendations and institutional responses, and support agendas for further study.

As both Harris and Gonick have indicated, these discourses and images are circulated without an exploration of the material contexts of girls' daily realities. Such popularized conceptualizations of girls fail to acknowledge and examine the specific circumstances of girls' lives and identities. The choices that girls make with respect to engaging in violence, participating in gangs, and on issues of sex and pregnancy are discussed and labelled without placing their actions and decisions into context or understanding them as negotiated strategies. The focus of these discourses is not on the complex, shifting, and differentiated social locations in which girls find themselves, but on their individual actions and behaviours. The experiences of girls are trivialized by a refusal to understand issues of aggression or "risky behaviour" by girls in the context of their relationships to peers, both male and female, the social environment of the schools they attend, and their neighbourhoods and homes. Missing is an intersectional analysis exploring the position of girls within and between uneven social terrains as determined by relations of gender, race, class, sexual orientation, (dis)abililty, language and geographic location.

Furthermore, as Harris has rightly pointed out, while these discourses and images individualize the issues by focusing on the choices and actions of girls, they also contribute to "a splitting of young women" along lines of race, class, (dis)ability, sexuality, and geographic location (40). Thus, discussions of "girls at-risk" and "mean girls" not only find fault with girls themselves, but also with their communities. The images and identifications produced by "at-risk" discourses, thus serve to produce and reinforce hierarchical separations between constructed groups of girls (Bessant, 2001:41). Images and constructions of "girls at risk" or "girls as risk-takers" most often refer to girls from racial and cultural minority communities and girls living in socio-economically marginalized communities. Hence, public discussion and theorizing of the concept, 'at-risk', and the accompanying prevention and intervention strategies support the continued delineation of boundaries between homogenously constructed groups and communities by disengaging from such issues as poverty and racism. In this way the discourses reproduce exclusionary social practices that target minority and disenfranchised girls.

While these popular discourses problematize the violence enacted by girls, in actuality violence is being carried out on multiple fronts, in particular against girls from minority communities and marginalized social locations. First, discursive violence is unleashed upon girls in the creation and circulation of images and narratives that moralize about the "violent and inappropriate" actions of girls and that isolate groups and communities of girls for disciplinary attention. By refusing to trace the multiple and overlapping relationships and social processes that shape the social contexts of girls' lives, these public discourses serve to reinforce complex and intersecting gendered, raced, and classed narratives of judgement. These narratives, in turn, enable the production of differentiated public strategies that support the development of "expert knowledge," which further serves to victimize girls (Bessant, 33). Second, the isolation of girls' actions from their social contexts diverts our attention from the reality that girls experience various forms of violence in their everyday lives. As Berman and Jiwani (2002) make clear, given the pervasive nature of violence, all girls must be considered to be vulnerable (6). Constructions such as 'girls at risk', 'good' and 'proper' girl behaviour, or 'problematic' girls, do little to further our understandings of violence, and in fact, impede any meaningful understandings.

The above discussion on academic research agendas and prevailing social discourses indicates that while there is knowledge available *about* girls and *on* girls, the current landscape still does not provide substantial opportunities for girls to be a part of the production of knowledge regarding their own lives. As the contributions of the four co-authors illustrate, girls are interested in developing frameworks of understanding that reflect their lived experiences. They are eager to see spaces of dialogue, connection and action develop; and they want to generate knowledge grounded in their daily realities and on issues of consequence affecting their lives. Meaningful and valuable knowledge about the multiplicity of girls' experiences and concerns can only emerge once research agendas based upon appropriate frameworks and processes are developed. Inherent in these frameworks must be a process that affords girls a central role.

Building Knowledge On Violence In Girls' Lives: Intersectional Understandings

"Hey, baby—you're a tootsie-roll," my second grade male peer with the braided rat-tail whispered to me. My immediate reaction was total outrage that my gender had been explicitly identified and degraded and I wondered why this young and (probably) unknowing boy felt entitled to say that to me. While the words, "baby" or "tootsie-roll" may seem inconsequential, that experience has remained with me because it was the first time I remember feeling vulnerable as a female.

Now, flash-forward to grade twelve and I was the girl in high school who had the 'girl revolution' patch on her backpack. I ended up becoming the spokesperson for any and all comments relating to feminism. It was during this time that a friend and I started a Riot Grrrl chapter in our city. Riot Grrrl was an all-grrrl defined collaborative which created a space where young women felt comfortable to speak about topics relating to health, relationships, media and politics. For months we enjoyed our safe space—until we were made aware of a website titled "Project Kill Grrrl" containing personal information about members and ways in which the grrrls were to be murdered. While I was totally shocked and outraged and wanted to seek preventative measures by introducing a third party, not everyone in the group agreed. Many believed that this particular website was only a 'natural' reaction by our male peers to our all-grrrl organization.

It is because of this particular experience that I wanted to try to understand why young women 'naturalize' and excuse violence. I was extremely fortunate to find a forum for my questions when I became involved with the London Centre for Research on Violence Against Women and Children. — Romy Poletti

In the winter of 2000, I was a participant in a focus group for immigrant and refugee girls, organized by the FREDA Centre for Research on Violence against Women and Children. The Centre, part of the Alliance of Five Research Centres on Violence, was conducting a series of focus groups with marginalized girls as part of a research project on Violence Prevention and the Girl Child. Over the course of two days, we discussed issues such as race and gender, and more importantly, their effect on one's integration into Canadian society. There was no general consensus over why the majority of immigrant girls felt as though they did not fit, but there was definite agreement over the fact that they were treated differently by other seemingly more "Canadian" girls. Most often, being Canadian was equated with being white, being a member of a religious majority, speaking without a noticeable accent, wearing "cool" clothes, and doing "cool" things. I place the word "cool" in quotation marks primarily because the definition of this word changed with the latest fad or trend. As far as clothing went, cool was equated to name brands, tight or fitting clothes and clothes which resembled a celebrity's look. As for acting "cool" or doing "cool" things, this meant having a boyfriend, drinking and/or taking drugs, and being invited to parties. —Azmina Ladha

In that same year I went to Victoria, B.C. to attend the "It's About Us! Girls on Race and Identities" conference at the University of Victoria in 2002. It's About Us was the first conference for girls of different races, that was a huge goal to accomplish and it was good to see they had done it for themselves. I was able to identify with so many young women there concerning issues with race. It was interesting to hear about their stories and know that they weren't much different from my own. Just because my skin is a different colour doesn't make me any less human, nor because my nose is wider and my hair is thick and curly. Examples such as this are what we shared. —Ashley Ward

How then, do we begin to support contextual understandings of the everyday lives of girls and young women with respect to experiences of violence? And, how can we create conceptual frameworks that enable us to produce knowledge that is responsive and meaningful to the complex, multiple, and differentiated experiences of girls?

As the reflections presented here reveal, girls and young women are seeking to grasp and frame their experiences. They are sorting out issues, experiences, and emotions that inform their conceptions of society and their sense of identity and place within these contexts. The theorizations of girls about their material realities and daily experiences offer the foundation from which integrated conceptual frameworks can develop and further our understandings of the linkages between and among social processes that structure our life worlds. As Gina DeBlase (2003) has noted, when girls are sharing their stories they are telling personal and collective histories that are connected to such structures as gender, race, and class (323).

In order to produce research that is relevant and meaningful to girls and that supports strategies for change, we must build conceptual frameworks that enable us to 'hear' what girls are saying about their lives and that capture the diversity of their experiences. We need to invest in frameworks and approaches that move us past essentializing the identities and experiences of girls. They must also enable the development of spaces where girls can produce knowledge and images that counter the prevailing discourses and representations that exist as expertise about their lives and identities. A theoretical framework that is founded upon the belief that violence in the lives of girls is best explored solely on the basis of shared gender identity will not generate meaningful, comprehensive understandings of the experiences of girls from marginalized and minority communities.

It is important to challenge the notion of gender constituting a foundational oppression, since it creates a situation where oppressions in the lives of girls on the basis of class, sexual orientation, race, (dis)ability, and geographic location are viewed as less significant. Further, conceptualizations that use an additive approach to understanding differences or that create a hierarchy of oppressions ultimately retain separated and bounded understandings of different social identities and experiences (Shohat, 2002: 68). Thus, in order to enrich our understanding of the complexity of girls' identities, their agency, their social experiences, and their concerns, our conceptualizations of girls' lives must be positioned at the intersections of race, gender, class, geographic locations, (dis)ability, sexuality, language and cultural heritage. Experiences of "being a girl" are intrinsically tied to the multiplicity of social processes that interact to shape our social contexts and identities.

Intersectionality, then, offers an integrated framework that enables us to explore the complexity of social experiences as shaped by the interplay of various social processes on multiple interacting levels. Avtar Brah (1996) has discussed intersectionality in terms of a conceptual grid where the multiple processes that shape the social, economic, political, and psychological realms come together to produce specificities of experience and identity (181). Individuals and collectivities are thus positioned in uneven relation to one another by multiple relations of power that intersect in complex and shifting ways (Stasiulis, 1999: 194).

Employing a framework of intersectionality builds an awareness of the contextual and relational quality of social identities and experiences, and enables a mapping of the complex societal relationships that produce inequalities. A relational understanding of our social experiences and identities is central, along with an understanding of the differentiations that result from social processes and structures that protect and reinforce power imbalances. Sherene Razack (1998) has indicated that differences in experience exist in relation to one another; or more specifically, they exist in unequal relation to one another (69, 153). Thus, as we draw connections between the experiences and locations of violence in the lives of girls and the material realities of their everyday contexts, we must trace not only how girls from differentiated social locations and backgrounds experience unlike forms of violence, but also how they are positioned in relation to one another within multiple pre-existing hierarchies.

As we begin to create research frameworks that enable the lived experiences of girls to inform our theories and concepts, multiple terrains of struggle begin to emerge. These struggles connect various social processes and structures, and they interlink social contexts with the personal and the psychological. Our goal, as we learn from the narratives of girls, is not to develop a comparison of the experiences of girls, but to create a map that simultaneously explores the commonalities, the differences, and the hierarchies among and between them. Intersectionality as a framework for research creates conceptual openings for the integrated incorporation of experience, identity, inequality, and context into the questions and issues we seek to explore with girls from a diversity of social backgrounds and locations.

Building Knowledge On Violence In Girls' Lives: Relationships Of Research

We are a group of academics engaged in girl-centered research." This statement sounds very progressive and engaging; however, I often wonder about the extent to which girls and young women are actually involved in such research. As someone who has been a part of numerous research projects, both as a subject and as a researcher, I know that working with girls is not simple. But doing research on girls and young women as opposed to with them is not an effective option. For research to be relevant and applicable, it must come from a partnership between academics, community activists and front-line workers. Most importantly, the research must directly involve the very girls it speaks about. Over time, I have found that it is important to make sure that the girls are involved in the 3P's, namely the programming and the products and that they receive payment for their participation. —Azmina Ladha

I wasn't sure what to expect but I remember the room was full and that I was nervous. All those pairs of eyes looking at you can be intimidating. The weird thing was as I introduced myself and began talking I relaxed. Everything I said came out so real and I wanted all the researchers, teachers, school board members, etc to hear that and understand how I experience violence. After that forum I was asked to do more I couldn't believe it. At age sixteen I was speaking at these important engagements and adults were listening. It's not often a teenager feels that way. —Ashley Ward

While it would seem that shedding light on experiences of violence in my life would prove to be painful, in actuality, it was liberating. I found agency by sharing my narratives because I felt in some way I was illustrating and validating one perspective of the reality of violence in the lives of girls in Canada.

These personal experiences shared by girls and young women with researchers are imperative to help understand girls' lives and their relationship to violence and vulnerability. However, it is important not to define the girls' identity by these stories and experiences. While conducting research with girls it is vital to create a sense that there is not a rated level of violence—every girl's experiences of violence are both valid and important. —Romy Poletti

I attended the Alliance of Five Research Centers on Violence conference held in Ottawa where the Alliance was presenting their research from a phase of the Girl Child Project. I and one other girl from my school had been asked be part of a panel of 8 girls from across the country, from different research centers and from very different backgrounds. I realized that while we were all looking at violence from a slightly different angle, we were all working towards the same goal: making violence in all forms something that was no longer considered normal. —Rian Lougheed-Smith

How can we produce knowledge that is shaped by the experiences, perspectives and conceptions of girls? What roles can/should girls and young women play in the research process? What are the impacts of participating in girl-centred and action-oriented research for girls? And, what are the impacts of their participation on researchers? As Audre Lorde has written: "[I]t is not our difference which immobilizes us, but our silence" (1984: 44). This quote underscores the need for personal stories, and for conversations such as those included throughout this paper. These conversations enable us to connect in our efforts to achieve social change.

In our efforts to understand the landscapes in which girls' everyday experiences of violence occur, we have sought to create a participatory process for girls in which they are supported in their efforts to generate meaningful knowledge and action. An integral component of this process is the provision of a space where girls can define their realities using their own language through the sharing of stories. Research spaces can simultaneously constitute spaces of community when collaborative approaches are girl-centred. These spaces create a context for interaction and connection between researchers and participants. While not free of power differentials, they do facilitate the development of personal and collective empowerment and strategies for change. Current studies support the view that when young people, both male and female, are given opportunities to tell their stories we hear complex accounts and explanations of the multiple factors that affect their well-being.

Yet, a number of challenges and important ethical concerns exist concerning the conduct of participatory action research with girls. This research must be carried out with great sensitivity, responsiveness, and responsibility. Burman (2001) and Howell (2004) have discussed the "politics of disclosure," noting that as researchers we must always question and reflect upon our motivations and actions. In providing meaningful opportunities for girls to share their stories, we must be mindful of the fact that we may be opening up possibilities of misappropriation of voice and experience and we may contribute to further pain. Indeed, we need to be careful that our processes do not cause further violence in the lives of girls (Burman, 2001:450; Howell, 2004: 325-326).

As Romy Poletti has stated in her reflections here, we need to handle the stories shared by girls and young women in a manner that acknowledges strengths and resilience in their lives, and not just experiences of violence. Too often, the examination of violence and victimization have been linked to the production of 'victim identities' (Pollack, 2000: 83). In our examination of experiences of violence in the lives of girls, we view violence as a significant and concerning dimension of girls' everyday experience that intimately affects their sense of self and that influences how they view their social worlds. However, it is important not to reduce the personal histories and social identities of girls to a single experience or dimension of that experience. Rather, the multifaceted quality of their agency and lived experiences must be recognized.

Our efforts focus on the development of strategies that capture the contextual diversity and multiplicity of girls' everyday realities. We seek to validate, honour, and contextually frame the diversity of experiences shared by girls in a responsible and accountable manner. In our work with girls our commitment lies in producing knowledge that is politically and socially meaningful, and that has the capacity to contribute to change at both the individual and broader structural levels.

In her work with girls and young women from disenfranchised and minority communities in the United States, Katherine Schultz (1999) learned the importance of providing spaces for young women to talk and to connect both with one another and with caring and supportive adults. These connections provided the necessary support for many of the young women to realize their own goals. Similarly, our conception of a research agenda includes the creation of spaces where the agency of girls is nourished through connection and engagement. Such spaces help to break isolation and support the creation of community between and among girls and adults, and the development of opportunities for 'connected learning' (Surrey, 1991: 171).

The notion of "connected learning" enables us to appreciate the value of developing collaborative research processes and spaces of community (Surrey, 1991: 171). Surrey has written (1991) that spaces of connection support empowerment for those involved by developing opportunities to engage with each other's perspectives and experiences. This builds mutual recognition and understanding (163). Girls experience power and growth by 'being together' and 'acting together' (Surrey, 163). Spaces of connection offer valuable and creative environments for girls and researchers to act together in new ways. Providing opportunities for girls to express themselves, in different and powerful ways, builds community. They identify with and learn from the experiences and emotions of other girls.

The voices shared throughout this paper illustrate the theoretical idea of empowerment through collaboration and connection. These narratives of reflection illustrate the nourishment, support, energy, and knowledge that can be gained from participating in a girl-centred process with other girls and young women, and caring and supportive adults. Further, these reflections reveal how involvement in research may result in a sense of personal transformation. In brief, the sharing of stories through research participation, at conferences, workshops, and other forums and the engagement in collective activities are powerful ways to influence one's sense of self, sense of belonging, and sense of place in the larger world.

Conclusion

The guidance counsellor at my school asked me to help her train other students to facilitate the workshops we had done about healthy relationships. I was again shocked to find that many students thought things such as extreme jealousy, lack of trust and possessiveness were key to a healthy relationship, even above respect, honesty, and friendship. Many people thought that we were being silly when we listed teasing and ignoring as forms of abuse. I find doing the workshops inspiring to see students come up with their own answers, and to see that look in their eyes "I know how that feels", or "I've done that", to see even a few people make that one tiny change in their thinking that changes almost everything you see.

The feeling of inspiration is contagious, and whenever I meet with members of the Alliance, the Muriel McQueen Fergusson Centre, or girls and women at conferences like Transforming Spaces, you can feel the enthusiasm we share. Spaces like Transforming Spaces are important, they bring together people from across the country who other wise might not have met, and we can all learn and benefit from each others experience!
—Rian Lougheed-Smith

Exposing myself to this organization and being researched changed how I view people around me. I no longer feel the same way about myself and about how violence affects women and girls. I was forced, in a good way, to re-examine myself at a young age through my work with the Centre for Research on Violence Against Women and Children. I believe I matured in a way different from my peers, at school I noticed people differently. I have gained so much knowledge about this issue that my eyes were opened a bit more to everything around me.

Am I grateful for that?...Yes, absolutely. Working with the Centre for Research and its members has been so fulfilling and has motivated me to be better in so many avenues of my life. My learning experiences over the past four years have been enormous. Not just from the conferences, forums, lectures, and reading material, but also from all the women I have met. All of us share this common thread of knowing what violence is. We all want to contribute to the end of violence against women and our courage to let others know through our involvement is our way of showing others what we can do. Without this research many young women would not be able to feel as if they had a voice. I am proof as well as many others that we do.

—Ashley Ward

The narratives of girls are powerful. They initiate conversation with other girls, with researchers, and with adults and institutions willing to listen. The telling of their stories is linked both to action and change. Minh-ha (1989) has talked about the 'circularity of stories' by referring to their movement and energy (123). A story is a contribution to knowledge. In sharing their personal narratives, girls and young women are generating knowledge by initiating new discussions. The stories and perspectives shared by girls create conversations and dialogue that challenge prevailing images and discourses; in other words, the assertion of their experiences and identities creates oppositional knowledge (Flores, 2000). In essence, such narratives offer a correction to our social views and understandings by presenting an alternate portrayal of daily realities. The inclusion of the voices, perspectives, and concerns of girls from differentiated backgrounds and social locations is particularly important since it fills significant knowledge gaps. The girls' personal accounts about their everyday lives and realities powerfully re-work our understandings of the past and the present, and serve as a valuable guide for a better future.

Our collaborative research experiences and the resulting space of community re-affirm the belief in feminist practice that participation and action is a form of theorizing (Shohat, 2002: 71). The reflections of the four co-authors who participated in the research show that collaborative research practices can facilitate the creation of spaces where girls are able to give meaning to their experiences and allows them the opportunities to "rethink, review, and rework" (Bertram et.al, 2000: 734) their identities, their relationships, and understandings of society. Such research spaces offer locations of understanding, connection, and change. Through the development of new ways of doing research with girls and young women, we are able to build knowledge by engaging theirs.

We gratefully acknowledge our friends and colleagues from the Alliance of Canadian Research Centres on Violence Against Women and Children who, since that first meeting in Manitoba, May 1998, have generously shared their ideas and their vision.

Chapter Five

Racialized Violence And Girls And Young Women Of Colour

Yasmin Jiwani

We must conceive discourse as a violence which we do to things, or in any
case a practice which we impose on them; and it is in this practice that the
events of discourse find the principles of their regularity.
—Michel Foucault (1981: 67)

When we think of girls and young women of colour in the Canadian context, we most
often think of them as 'immigrants' and refugees. Whether they are first, second or
third generation, girls and young women of colour—like their male counterparts—are
often assumed to be Others. As Others, they are positioned outside the nation; never
quite belonging, never wholly 'Canadian.' Typically, these girls and young women are
asked the perennial question: "Where are you from?" Never an innocent question, the
issue of querying another's origin is itself predicated on the assumption that you are
not from here, cannot be from here, and will never be from here. What 'here' signifies
is the 'fantasy' of Canada as a white, imagined nation; a country built on the mythology of two founding races—the British and the French, and built on the premises of
equality and liberation (Razack, 2004).[1] Such a mythology negates the reality of race
and racism, erases the history of colonization and violence meted out to First Nations
peoples and dismisses through trivialization and containment, the ongoing violence
perpetuated against those who are considered to be outside the nation.

 In looking at the lives and realities of girls and young women of colour, these discursive strategies of violence—this trivialization, dismissal and containment—serve to
'keep them in their place' as subordinate, inferiorized Others whose access to Canadian
identity is contingent on assimilation and denial: assimilation into the dominant culture, which is based on consumerism and a patina of liberal values; and denial of the
violence of racism and sexism. It is the intersecting influences of the discourses of race,
class, gender, sexuality and ability that make this denial on the one hand, and the lure
of assimilation on the other, possible. At the same time, affinities between patriarchal
structures within minoritized groups and those in the dominant state often work together to shape the lives of girls and young women of colour as boundary markers,

bordering their communities, and as Others, bordering the Canadian nation. Nowhere is this most apparent than in the brutal murders of Aboriginal girls and girls of colour by those outside and inside their communities. Within this context, girls of colour signify 'cultural purity' as future reproducers of their communities and hence their transgression of social-cultural norms often results in violent reprisals; and as Others bordering the nation, they signify the exotic and/or expendable Other who can be used and abused by those within the dominant society either under the guise of benevolence or ruthless exploitation.

In this chapter, my intent is to explore this bordering both from within and outside communities of colour. I begin by problematizing the very notion of community, and then follow with a discussion of racist violence and gendered racism directed at girls and young women of colour in the English Canadian context. In pursuing this line of inquiry, I draw heavily on a research project conducted in British Columbia,[2] to demonstrate some of the salient aspects of the lives and realities of girls and young women of colour in Canada.

Notions Of Community

Himani Bannerji (2000) reminds us that communities are constructed entities. In other words, though they may be based on biological and social linkages, it is the salience of these linkages that marks these groups as bounded and defined communities. Such communities are formed in response to existing structural circumstances. In applying this notion of the constructed community to the Canadian landscape, it becomes increasingly apparent that racialized communities were and are formed as a result of immigration practices, and have solidified in response to state policies (Thobani, 2000).

It is in this context that the situation of racialized girls and young women of colour needs to be located. In communities that are formed in response to state interventions and in a milieu that is hostile and exclusionary, girls' and women's bodies occupy a particularly symbolic role. On the one hand, girls' and women's bodies are used as boundary markers; on the other, they represent the essentialized embodiments of culture. In other words, girls' and women's bodies become signifiers of culture. Anthias and Yuval-Davis (1992) note that these designations are contingent on women's perceived roles as biological and social reproducers of the community. Through their child-bearing and child-rearing roles, women thus constitute a category that demands protection and safeguarding in the interests of cultural preservation and continuity, and as registers of cultural specificities. As future mothers, girls' bodies acquire the same aura of cultural specificity and anticipatory boundary markers. In this sense, girls' and women's bodies become the hallmarks of cultural identity, preservation and morality. They signal not only the specificity of particular cultural communities but also symbolize the future of that community. Such cultural specificity acquires its own aura of 'authenticity' based on the presumed link with tradition, but also emerges in opposition as that which is seen as different and unique from the outside, dominant society.

Within the terrain of Canadian multiculturalism, however, this emphasis on girls and women's bodies within constructed reified communities engenders another dynamic; namely, the erasure of differences within cultural formations, and pressures on girls and women to conform to a single, privileged interpretation of culture (Bannerji, 2000). These pressures and the emphasis on a singular and preferred interpretation of cultural formations do not occur in isolation. They are an implicit and implicated outcome of the construction of a community *as* a community, of the closure or inward retreat of members of a group into a community in order to avoid, confront or challenge the racism and exclusion they experience from the dominant society. In effect, this dynamic leads to the hegemonic affinity between the patriarchal structures inherent within all communities and the patriarchal structures inherent in the dominant society as they seek to contain, define and position girls' bodies as signifiers of 'culture.' Grewal and Kaplan (1994) have called this the "scattered hegemonies" that operate within a transnational context—a context marked by diasporic communities that are located throughout the world but that are linked to and sustained by a connection to ancestral lands and cultures of origin.

Racialized And Gendered Bodies, Inside And Outside The Nation

The continuities between the scenario outlined above and the realities of racialized girls of colour pivot around their role as carriers of culture and their embodiment of an essentialized, gendered and dominant interpretation of culture. This dominant and dominating framework is imposed on them and often internalized by them to make sense of their realities. Thus, it is not surprising to hear girls and young women from various racialized and minoritized communities speak of their conflicts in their language of culture, and to see their own cultural communities as being highly traditional and oppressive. Within such a framework, notions of race and racism are evacuated. Instead, the language defining such realities becomes one of culture. Race becomes culture, and racialized violence becomes culturalized violence (Razack, 1998).

Two dominant and interwoven trajectories emanate from this kind of cultural gaze: First, the emphasis on culture becomes the hallmark of explanatory frameworks within academic studies of racialized girls of colour; second, a culturalized framework marks and masks the discourse of gendered violence directed at these girls and young women such that that violence is no longer seen as having anything in common with the gendered violence that girls and young women experience in the dominant society.

Imam (1999) calls this the "culture deficit" model where the dominant Western culture is seen as being emancipatory and egalitarian, while minority cultures are seen as being static and frozen. Interestingly enough, these explanations are also articulated by young women of colour and reflect their internalization of the governing hegemonic ideology which posits the dominant Western culture as being an idyllic landscape of gender equity and freedom from gender-based discrimination or structural violence (Pyke and Johnson 2003).

This view of a 'frozen' and 'static' culture fixes these communities as holdovers from a primitive past. As Anita Handa (1997) argues, it converts them from dynamic and fluid entities to pre-modern, monolithic and homogenous entities. The emphasis on cultural traditions (as ways of preservation and identity formation) is construed as a sign of a lack of progress. Against this construction, the dominant Western culture is constructed as a progressive landscape and the passports to acceptance are premised on the basis of acculturation and assimilation into the dominant society.

There are major problems with this dominant perspective. For one, communities are not monolithic or homogenous. For another, the paradigms of assimilation and acculturation are predicated on assumptions that posit the prior existence of two equal cultural formations where culture A gets absorbed into Culture B. Additionally, such a paradigm negates the consequences and impact of racialization. In other words, difference cannot be assimilated when it is weighed with connotations of immutable inferiority and where economic and cultural powers are unequal. Further, such an approach fails to consider the fact that acculturation and assimilation are not linear processes: beginning at one point and ending at another. The very nature of globalization ensures that immigration occurs in a non-linear manner with transnational communities being located in numerous spaces and maintaining fluid connections with each other.

A critical outcome of this emphasis on acculturation and assimilation as the lens through which violence against racialized girls and women is viewed revolves around what Uma Narayan (1997) calls "death by culture." In effect, the violence enacted on bodies of girls and young women of colour has often been attributed to the peculiarities of their supposedly backward, traditional cultures. Thus, girls and women of colour are seen as victims of infanticide, female genital mutilation, dowry deaths, honour killings and the like (Arat-Koc, 2002). Rarely are these forms of violence situated in comparison with the violence that girls and young women in the West endure. Instead, the focus on culture serves as the explanatory vehicle by which these practices are made sense of and utilized to fuel 'rescue missions' to save racialized girls and young women from the clutches of their cultural traditions. Such a move strategically underscores the benevolent and progressive nature of Western societies while at the same time, deflecting attention away from structural factors such as poverty, gender inequalities, and the violence of deskilling and relocation.

From within communities of colour, girls and women's lives are morally and socially regulated. In her study of Filipino youth in the United States, Espiritu (2001) notes that girls' sexuality and behaviours are highly regulated in response to what is perceived to be a failing of the dominant society. Thus, while girls and young women in the white, dominant society are regarded as being sexually promiscuous, lax in moral behaviours and values, Filipinas are supposed to signify the opposite—the 'superior' morality of the community as reflected in chaste behaviour and restricted sexual expressions. Espiritu observes that, "the immigrant community uses restrictions on women's lives as one form of resistance to racism. This form of cultural resistance, however, severely restricts the lives of women, particularly those of the second generation, and it casts the family as potential site of intense conflict and oppressive demands in immigrant lives" (436)

Drawing attention to intimate or familial violence occurring in such a context becomes extremely difficult for girls and young women of colour. Bannerji (2000) notes that one outcome of being in a stigmatized racialized community is a reticence and reluctance to involve outside authorities for fear of criminalizing an already marginalized community. Fear of being deported, of family members being imprisoned, and fear of betraying familial and community ties are very real. Yet, while instances of intimate and familial violence are pervasive, it is the persistence of racism that continues to mark young women's lives, shaping their realities and influencing their response to different forms of violence.

Racism significantly influences girls and young women's life chances; it impacts and informs their identity formation. But this does not mean that girls and young women are simply victims of racism. Rather, they negotiate the racist environment in which they live and at the same time, negotiate the internal moral and social requirements imposed on them from within their own communities. Nevertheless, this bordering in the form of racist exclusion, stigmatization and othering does force girls and young women to turn inward towards their communities, which in and of themselves, are highly constructed and have emerged in response to a hostile and exclusionary environment. Racism thus constitutes a major form of violence that permeates the lives and realities of girls and young women of colour.

In internalizing the dominant preference structures and idealized constructions, girls and young women also interiorize the valuations that the dominant society affixes to their families, communities and cultures of origin. Often this takes the form of internalized racism wherein they reject their own cultural communities in favour of what they perceive to be the freedom afforded to them by the dominant society. In an effort to find a sense of belonging, girls and young women often buy into what Melinda de Jesús (1998) has called the 'fictions of assimilation.' These are the illusory promises that suggest to them that if they behave in particular ways, if they become more like girls and young women in the dominant society, they too can share the rewards of such privileged membership in the sense of being accepted and being more like their white counterparts. On the most apparent level, these fictions suggest a path of consumption: purchasing products and goods that will make them resemble girls and young women from the dominant white culture. On a deeper level, these fictions translate into value judgements that they make amongst themselves and of other communities of colour.

Intra-ethnic violence is one example of internalized racism and the different values that are attached to assimilation. In their study of second generation Korean and Vietnamese youth in the United States, Pyke and Dang (2003) observed the existence of an inner hierarchy within these Asian American groups. At the pinnacle of the hierarchy were the 'white-washed'—those who were seen as having 'sold out' to the dominant culture by emulating its preferred and valued behaviours and lifestyles. At the bottom, were the FOBs (the "Fresh Off the Boat"); recent immigrants who had not yet assimilated the dominant cultural styles and who tended to speak in their own language. These internal hierarchies offer a symbolic map situating individuals on the basis of the degree of their acculturation into the dominant society. As Pyke and Dang note:

> Although the construction of the identities "FOB" and "whitewashed" involves somewhat different "othering" dynamics, both are constructed as an adaptive response to the racial oppression of the larger society. By discrediting coethnics who either confirm stereotypes of Asians as unassimilable or defy racial categories by attempting to merge into white society, a bicultural identity emerges that deflects stigma and defines the "normals." This process of intraethnic othering is an attempt to resist a racially stigmatized status; however, it does so by reproducing stereotypes and a belief in essential racial and ethnic differences between whites and Asians (2003:168).

It is the 'normals' in between the two extremes that try to mediate the competing demands placed on them by both the wider society and their own communities. Although assimilated to some degree, they are not "white-washed." They reflect what Indy Batth (1998) has described as the process of 'walking the hyphen': bridging the realities of their own communities and the demands imposed on them by the wider society. Critiquing the dominant paradigm, Debold et al. (1999) argue that acculturation increases the potential of internalizing the values and norms of the dominant society. They suggest that girls and young women are forced into a dilemma in which

> …'success' in middle-class terms too often means a betrayal of cultural and familial connections and the terror of isolation, whereas, on the other hand, not achieving such success can mean betraying one's own and one's parents hopes, economic marginalization, and restrictive notions of identity and social position" (1999:183).

Success is often defined in terms of 'fitting in' and 'belonging.' This notion of 'fitting in' begs the question of 'fitting into what'? Clearly, dominant social values and normative expectations are part of what girls and young women feel that they need to comply with as part of their way of fitting in. These normative standards are not only based on an ideology of consumption, but more importantly are grounded in an ideology of whiteness, heterosexuality and ableism. The comportment of an ideal-typical whiteness carries with it connotations of slimness, beauty, sexuality and a certain look. Certainly, there are variations, but even these cohere around particular notions of what is considered beauty, what an ideal type body should look like and are also assessed in terms of whether these bodies can and do attract the attention of boys and young men. Racialized girls and young women then face a more complex, intertwined and powerful confluence of normative standards which are both raced and gendered and which are articulated through class, power, heteronormativity and able-bodiedness.

Listening To Voices: Girls And Young Women Of Colour

In listening to racialized girls and women's voices, the issues discussed above are apparent and evident in their lives. In this section, I cover some of these themes as they were articulated by young women of colour who participated in interviews and focus groups on issues of racial violence. The latter were convened in Vancouver, British Columbia, though some interviews were conducted with girls and young women in rural areas as well. Given that each region in the country has its own texture of racism and its own hierarchy of racially inscribed groups, location becomes an important consideration.

Through partnerships with community organizations and community-based researchers, a total of fifty-two girls/young women were recruited to participate in the project. The youngest was thirteen years of age and the oldest participant was twenty-two. The majority of the girls were between fifteen and sixteen years old. Their or their parents' countries of origin included Antigua, Barbados, China, Congo, Ethiopia, Fiji, India, Iran, Jamaica, Mexico, Pakistan, the Philippines, St. Kitts, Taiwan, Thailand, Trinidad, and Zaire. In total, five focus groups were convened. Three were ethno-specific focus groups consisting of a Persian (Iranian) girls group, an African-Caribbean group of girls, and a Latina group of girls. The other two consisted of mixed groups of girls of colour, one of which was held at the conclusion of a two day participatory theatre workshop. In addition, individual interviews were conducted with a total of fourteen girls located in rural and urban areas.

It should be noted that all the interviewers and focus group facilitators were women of colour. Although they did not share the same ethnicity or cultural background as the participants, their position as racialized women of colour undoubtedly influenced the nature and dynamics that occurred within these interviews and focus groups. What is most interesting in this regard is that girls and young women who were interviewed did not hesitate in naming racism as the predominant form of violence they experience in their daily lives. Methodologically, this raises interesting issues particularly in light of eliciting opinions and narratives about violence and racism from those who are most immediately affected, foregrounding the importance of not only the kinds of questions that are asked in a research process, but also who asks the questions in the first place.

Voicing violence
The majority of the girls and young women who participated in this project identified racism as the dominant and pervasive form of violence they encounter in their daily lives. They defined racism in interpersonal and systemic terms: from discriminatory treatment by teachers in schools, to the minimization of their participation in the classroom, the silencing of their voices, and the erasure of their histories and cultural realities in the school curriculum. They also identified racism as acts of verbal and physical abuse that cause pain and that result in their othering, inferiorization and exclusion.

Some of the other themes that emerged from the interviews and focus groups revolved around notions of belonging: how they fit within the dominant culture, the hierarchy of racism, and the various ways in which girls and young women of colour are "othered." A significant theme was the impact of the media in negating and stereotyping their communities.

Notions of belonging
In negotiating a sense of self and their own positionality vis-à-vis their communities and the dominant society, many of the girls and young women revealed a relational identity. In other words, they would be Iranian (or whatever) in one context, and Canadian in another. Overwhelmingly, they did not see themselves as 'Canadian' when in Canada, but rather when they were visiting their cultural homeland, or within the context of their own group. For some, their perception of authentic 'Canadians' was based on the latter as being white and of European origin. As one Iranian girl noted:

> They look at you and go, "You're not Canadian. You're Persian or whatever.
> But you're not Canadian because you don't have blue eyes or blonde hair."

In her study of mixed race women in Canada, Mahtani (2002:77) found that their notions of "an 'authentic' Canadian is of either British or French blood—those 'real' Canadians who are part of a 'capital-C Canadian' society." Aujla (2000:41) makes a similar point with regard to second generation South Asian women who are made to feel "never quite Canadian enough, never quite white enough." The whiteness of the dominant identity not only serves to reinforce the 'darkening' of the identity of the Other but is constitutive of the very process by which, "the culturally dominant create the nation as home—in other words, as part of a home-making project of white Canadians." (Pratt, 2002:8fn).

In the focus group with Afro-Caribbean girls, the question of 'birthright'— whether they were born here or not—was a key factor in how they defined themselves. Those who were born here felt that they were Canadians. Those who had immigrated here did not feel the same level of comfort in calling themselves Canadian, although they were often referred to as such when they went to visit their relatives in their country of origin. The notion of 'birthright' is one of the ways in which the differentiation between newly arrived communities and those that are well-established is maintained. Yet, as the Filipino focus group participants in Pratt's study indicate, birthright does not automatically grant a sense of permanence or belonging. A recurring phrase in her focus groups was: "Made in the Philippines, born in Canada" (2002:4). Aujla makes a similar argument in articulating South Asian women's sense of exclusion which she suggests is worse for those who were born in Canada. Speaking to this issue, one of the young South Asian women interviewed in this study stated:

I feel more Indian here. Because when you go to India, there's so much more to it. So it's like you're too much Indian here and not enough Indian there.

This kind of critical interrogation of their identities and location was apparent in a number of interviews, but the majority of participants saw their Canadian identity in evolving terms: not one that was inherently theirs, but rather as one that could possibly be acquired over time via an increased facility with English, broader networks with European Canadians, and 'knowing the system.'

Fitting in
The aspects of fitting in that the girls and young women described were also highly influenced by systemic and everyday racism. As a young woman in the Iranian focus group reported:

Well they make fun of my name…White people. Well my name is [name]. It [sounds] like gonads. It's close to that. They make fun of it or they say that "Your name is stupid." Sometimes they say that…Like I want my name to be what it is. I don't have to shorten it for people to make it easier for them. I mean I have to learn their way to fit in but they can't say my name properly, spell my name properly, or pronounce it properly. Like if I don't say it right, they would make fun of me. They'd be like, "Oh, you're an FOB" (Focus Group with Iranian Girls).

Clothes—as in the wearing of trendy ones—constituted a major signifier of acceptance (see Twine, 1996). This is something shared by all girls, but for immigrant and refugee girls of colour the issue of poverty makes it very difficult for them to acquire clothing that would facilitate their fitting in. As well, informal knowledge about the normative values ascribed to clothes is something that they can only acquire over time. 'Fitting in' requires fluency in the dominant language and the ability to remain silent in the face of dismissal and erasure—in other words, knowing how to 'stay in one's place.' Many of the young women were cognizant of this implicit demand. Others, however, saw it as a normalized response to a situation in which they had little knowledge of the rules or limited access to social resources. As one of the young Iranian woman put it:

> Right now, you're under a lot of pressure. You have so many things in your mind. And plus this, this whole thing, not knowing English, and trying to fit in but you're not because your appearance is not good enough, the way you dress is different, it's a different style, it's a different taste of clothing. And other things that you want to do but you can't, that's a lot of pressure and I think it's going to be very difficult. Because at this age there's a lot of pressure you're going through (Individual interview).

Her experiences reflect the pressures of conformity—in dressing a particular way, matching the standards of attractiveness, and speaking in the language and style of the dominant group.

Another Iranian girl spoke of the self-policing that accompanies the internalization of dominant norms and perceptions:

> Persians are loud people… People would be looking and staring at us, white people. And I'd be like, "Shut up. Don't speak so loud. Everybody's looking at us." Because I don't like that kind of stuff. Like we should balance out. We don't like everybody to stare at us. We don't want everybody to say, "Oh, those people are so loud" (Individual interview).

Her quote confirms Foucault's insights when he describes the power of "a gaze which each individual under its weight will end by interiorising to the point that he is his own overseer, each individual thus exercising this surveillance over, and against, himself" (1980:155). Jennifer Kelly (1998) argues that the Afro-Canadian youth in her study live 'under the gaze' of white society. Here, the white gaze has been internalized and regulates behaviour in concordance with the dictates of the dominant society.

The ultimate form of violence within the lives of these young women, and perhaps the most profound and harmful manifestation of the desire to fit in, is the negation of self (Fanon, 1965). This process can occur through assimilation, internalized racism and sexism. The young women in the focus groups and individual interviews revealed the self-denial and self-erasure they experience in their daily lives. As one Afro-Caribbean Canadian focus group participant said, "Sometimes I feel like I have to lose my true identity to fit in." Another young South Asian woman from Fiji reported that "the only time I think I would be like Indian would be when I would go to a party, or a wedding, or a Temple." Her comments illustrate the ways in which cultural identity becomes compartmentalized and privatized, relegated to the sphere of community (Peter, 1981).

The "othering" of girls and young women of colour is achieved through particular strategies in which their differences are devalued, exoticized or distanced largely through the dominant culture's construction of such differences. As one Afro-Caribbean Canadian girl commented:

> They always ask us about our hair and they always feel our hair and it really bothers us. "Oh, is that your real hair or is that extensions?" They come up to you on the bus and start feeling your hair without asking if they can touch your hair.

This quote illustrates not only the curiosity of those in the dominant society with respect to wanting to 'touch' and 'feel' the 'strangeness' that they witness, but also the certitude with which private space is transgressed in the interests of satisfying a personal curiosity. That Black hair should be considered 'strange' reflects one facet of the ethnocentric white gaze, but that one's space can be so violated demonstrates a power relation whereby those who are crossing this space in order to assuage their curiosity feel no sense of transgression because they simply take for granted the inferiority of the person whose hair they are touching.

One of the young Black woman noted the commodification of Black popular culture as yet another mechanism by which Afro-Canadians get exoticized. As she put it:

> The hip hop thing going on. Most people try to dress like hip hop. And there's an issue also that a lot of other people from other races try to talk like us, you know what I mean, in that sort of way. A lot of them sometimes feel like they belong but, you know, I met this Caucasian girl and she told me she's Black…when people say that, I didn't say anything (Individual interview).

The process of commodification as alluded to in the above quote also foregrounds the phenomenon of the 'wannabees': those who claim a particular heritage or group membership by virtue of appropriating the symbols of that heritage. That the white girl can assert such a claim reflects her occupation of space of power and privilege. For the Black girl who might want to make a counter-claim—to claim membership in the white group—would make her the object of derision in her group where she would be accused of being 'whitewashed' and make her the object of ridicule in the dominant group; where she may be conditionally accepted but only through the erasure of her identity as a young Black woman.

Stereotyping and criminalizing were two other key strategies by which difference was underscored and devalued. Stereotyping was the more subtle strategy of the

two, and was often attributed to the media, the ignorance of peers and authority figures. This is evident in the following exchange which occurred in a focus group with
Afro-Caribbean girls and young women:

> Girl: There's this girl, she comes to me and, "I know how to talk like Black
> people." I'm like, "How do Black people talk?" And she's like, "What's up
> mon?" I get that a lot. I tell her nobody talks like that and it's not, "What's
> up mon." That's how white people say it.

> Girl: And the teachers. "Where you from?" "Jamaica." "Jamaica mon, Ja-
> maica mon."

This quote demonstrates the disdain with which other cultures are stereotyped and
mockingly mimicked. But it also reflects the element of exoticization pertaining to the
way in which certain differences are constructed. This exoticization is also laced with
inferiorization, demonstrating that even though aspects of Black culture can be appropriated, the very act of appropriation (as mimicking) underscores the simulta-
neous attraction and revulsion experienced by those of the dominant group. However,
as the last statement by one of the focus group participants suggests, these young
women are aware of the differential power relations that are being used against them
and by which they are being judged.

Criminalization was more pronounced with young women of colour reporting
that they were often followed by employees or security guards if they were in stores,
or perceived to be prostitutes if they were hanging around a street corner or waiting
for a bus. In the words of one Afro-Caribbean girl:

> I was on the street. My cousins were here. And we were waiting for the bus
> and a police car walked by and we started showing off. And they stopped and
> they walked around the block and they looked at us. And they walked
> around the block and they came back and they walked around again. And
> I'm like, "We're not prostitutes. We're waiting for the bus" (Afro-Caribbean-
> Canadian focus group participant).

Again, the assumption that race is associated with crime and prostitution reflects the
dominant construction of racialized groups as being prone to crime. 'Hanging around' a
street corner is then construed as 'loitering' or 'causing trouble.' The gendering of this
dominant construction results in a stereotype of Black women (and other women of
colour) as prostitutes or sex trade workers if they are seen in public spaces. As James
(1998:168) eloquently puts it: "White people window-shop, Black people loiter."

Inferiorization is also communicated through the institutional streaming of girls
and young women of colour into ESL (English as a Second Language) classes. As this
young woman noted:

> When I first came here, it was my second year at school. And they're like
> taking me to this room…I speak English because they were going to put me
> in ESL. I'm like, "I speak English. In my country, I speak English. That's the
> only language I know. English" (Afro-Caribbean focus group participant).

As in Pyke and Dang's (2003) study discussed earlier, being accepted or being perceived as fitting in was also predicated on being defined as different from those 'others' —notably those immigrants who were newly arrived—who had not yet assimilated. As this young women from the Iranian focus group commented:

> But I have Canadian friends too. But then they, Canadians, make fun of my
> friends. Like, "Are you hanging out with those FOBs [Fresh off the Boat]
> again. Come hang out with us. Why are you hanging out with those
> FOBs?" I'm like, "They're not FOBs just because they can't talk English, or
> …you know? But that's just making fun. That's not really…I don't think
> that's really racist.

Here, the experience of differentiating between the 'FOB's versus the more established immigrants is not understood in terms of racism but rather is imputed to the ignorance of members of the dominant society. Again, as this young woman's quote reveals, the distinction is hierarchical. At the top of the ladder of acceptance and authenticity are the 'true' Canadians, defined by their skin colour and access to informal and formal social knowledges. At the bottom are the 'FOBs'; defined by their newness, by their lack of such cultural capital, and by their cultural/racial difference. Or, as one young woman described them:

> FOB is like "fresh off the boat." It means that you're really…geeky and you
> don't know how to speak and stuff. You dress stupidly or whatever, right?
> (Iranian focus group participant).

In between are the assimilated, relatively accepted but culturally/racially different girls and young women. Aujla (2000) argues that this internal hierarchy consists of those who are assimilated, the 'honorary whites,' and the 'authentic'—those who have retained their cultural traditions. One young Iranian woman commented that:

> The ones that are new hang out with Persians, their own culture. The ones
> that aren't, they usually hang out with white people. They're called whites.
> They pretend that they're not Persian."

Facility with the dominant language is seen as the passport to achieving acceptance. It becomes a major marker (along with clothes) defining an individual's acceptance. Another young Asian-Canadian woman reported:

> Some people you meet in Canada, they look like Chinese but they were born
> here. They don't like Chinese people who have just come to Canada. I don't

know why but if you come to Canada and your English is really good, than you can speak with them freely. But if you can still speak Chinese, they think you are no good, they think you're a bad person because you come from China. If you tell them, "I don't know any Chinese, I don't know Cantonese, I was born here," they'll like you (Jump Start focus group).

Thus, knowledge of the ethnic language is similarly construed as a signifier of inferiority. However, the hierarchy resulting from this preference structure is not simply confined to an internal register of cultural identity but rather works in tandem with the external register of 'Canadian' identity in which other racialized groups are ranked in order of preference and degrees of acceptance.

This hierarchy of race was most clearly expressed in terms of the inter-ethnic/racial conflict that was endemic in most schools. Most focus group participants and interviewees reported witnessing considerable inter-group violence in their schools. Girls and young women reported that they often hung around with members from their own communities as a form of protection and because they could communicate more freely with those who shared their own cultural affiliation.

Though preferential treatment was perceived as being accorded to certain groups over others, the overall sense of these girls and young women was that the white students were given more attention, allowed more privileges and treated better than any of the students of colour. As the Iranian girl quoted above elaborated:

And then also, I don't know what it is but my teacher, when we come in late, she starts yelling at us, she starts saying, "Why are you late again? La, la, la, la." But some white girl comes in, she goes, "Oh, where have you been." She goes, "I was out with my friends, I'm so sorry," and she starts laughing. I would be like, "What the hell was going on?" Why is she yelling at us and not her and she's not saying anything. Or assignments. You hand them in one day late, "Oh that's a zero for you." But then Canadian people, I don't know what they do, suck up or whatever, and then they can get the marks.

Despite being aware of the ranking and differential privileges accorded to different groups not to mention the power and authority of teachers, the girls and young women who participated in the study did not perceive this as an interconnected issue. On the contrary, many attributed the interracial violence and hostility of their peers to the innate characteristics of different groups and to a competitive and violent school environment. In contrast, they could name the racist behaviours of school teachers and principals. This reflects how 'common sense' works to align interpretations in a way that correspond with the hegemonic values and beliefs. Those whose power is more apparent and uncontested can be seen to be violent, whereas those who share the same structural situation are seen to be more ignorant and naïve. It may also be that for these girls and young women, racism is something that adults do, not a conscious motivation on the part of their peers. On the part of their peers, racism becomes more a matter of competition and meanness [see Currie and Kelly, this volume]. As this young woman commented:

> Someone asked me if we have TV in Iran. If you see someone, and you see they're not closed-minded but because of the limitation that they have, that they don't really have a good idea of what it's like so I have to explain to them in order to get the idea (Focus group with Persian Girls, Vancouver).

The girls' and young women's comments repeatedly revealed their willingness to excuse their peers' lack of knowledge about the history and customs of racialized minorities. In this sense, their own perceptions are subsumed under the dominant discourses of denial which trivialize and dismiss the subtle and overt expressions of racism, or simply refuse to name them as such. For one, they are not given the tools of language by which to name the abuse, and second, there is no collective recognition of this racism as a form of violence. However, an alternative interpretation is that while they recognize the everyday and systemic nature of racism, they do not call attention to it for fear of having it dismissed by those in positions of authority, or of invoking potential retaliation. As Matthews (1997) observed in her study of Asian girls and boys in an Australian school, "being too quick to label can restrict and limit your social interactions and opportunities. Here the refusal to evoke discourses of racism or sexism can be seen to involve the tactical maximization of limited opportunities and thereby relocate the sites of negotiation to other grounds" (14).

The erasure of history through the lack of accurate and adequate curricular materials is another way in which girls and young women of colour are Othered and subordinated. Echoing these findings, one of the focus group participants commented:

> In school they don't teach you anything about Black people really. They don't teach you anything about your culture or anything. And if they teach you anything they teach you about Africa. That's not the only place where Black people are from. I think they should teach you about other places, not just one area (Afro-Caribbean-Canadian focus group participant).

Another girl explained how her teacher's dismissal of Canadian slavery affected her:

> In school we were learning about slavery and she goes, "Oh we all know that there was never slavery in Canada," and then it kind of made me feel bad because I know there was slavery in Canada...I went up to the teacher and I told [her] she said there was never slavery in Canada. And the teacher said, "Yeah, there was slavery in Canada but it wasn't as big a deal as the States."...They should check their research on it before they teach it instead

of reading the school books and then teaching what it says. Because a lot of the school books about African history is not true (Individual interview, Afro-Caribbean-Canadian girl).

Other studies have corroborated these observations and strategic absences in school curricula (Anisef and Kilbride, 2000; Wideen and Barnard, 1999). In effect, schools tend to delegitimize the histories of people of colour and in so doing, evacuate the reality of racism. However, what the above quote points to is the minimization of Canada's role in permitting slavery and the latter move simply serves to affirm the notion of Canadian tolerance. For these young women, such tolerance is not only communicated as 'putting up with' difference but also as a hollow, conditional and rather tenuous acceptance of their difference.

Racism in the schools was also perceived to being fostered by teachers and administrators who refused to speak out about it or simply perpetuated it. As one of the focus group participants explained:

The teachers, they keep it to themselves, the principal. They always try to keep it in secret. They don't go out and say we need to deal with this issue (Afro-Caribbean-Canadian focus group participant).

The girls who confronted their teachers over such issues explained that their concerns were often dismissed. Likewise, their attempts to correct the misrepresentations of their cultures and histories on the grounds that the latter contributed to the racism they experienced on a daily basis generally went ignored. They conceded that their histories and cultures were being erased in the context of the classroom.

Mediated violence

A key issue raised by the focus group participants and the girls and young women that were interviewed dealt with the media's role in disseminating stereotypical representations of their respective communities. As these participants from the Afro-Caribbean-Canadian focus group noted:

[TV] portrays all the bad things like it's known for marijuana or ganja or whatever drugs. They always come up to me [at school] and go, "So do you know where the drugs are?" "No I don't. I don't even know what the tree looks like." So I always tell them saying, "Yes, I have some in the back yard of my house and if they want some, they can come over later." Because I'm sick of it. That's about all you hear.

Racial and cultural stereotypes in television and film media have been noted as having a negative effect on the self-image and peer acceptance of immigrant and refugee youth (Kunz and Hanvey, 2000). These types of racist media images coupled with sexist media content can deeply influence the identity formation of the refugee and immigrant girl child. Social messages about who is and who is not desirable and what characteristics constitute "beauty" converge to effect the self- esteem and self-image of racialized girls. The results include self-consciousness about body image, low self-esteem and eating disorders. Schooler et al. (2004) found that Black girls who had a choice in viewing Black programming did not identify with mainstream images of white women's bodies or standards of beauty. This analysis is reflective of the necessity to provide alternative and community media that affirm cultural and racial identities and act as a protective force against the pressures of assimilation.

Aside from this indirect influence, many of the girls and young women, by virtue of being minorities, carry with them the 'burden of representation.' Kobena Mercer (cited in Cottle, 2000:106) uses the term to describe Black media producers' quandary in being held accountable by their communities for representing them in the best possible light while attempting to create a product that speaks to their own truth and reflects their own interests. Here, I extend the concept to apply to those who are subjected to the same feeling of accountability for their 'entire' group regardless of whether that group shares any degree of homogeneity.

An Iranian girl mentioned in her interview that she was highly embarrassed and shamed by the teacher's screening of the film, *Not Without My Daughter* (1991), which portrayed Muslim cultures as backward and brutally patriarchal. In recounting her experience, she said:

> I start[ed] crying and I was so upset and I talked to my teacher and told her
> this is not how it is for me. Now I realize that all the people who (are Chinese,
> Japanese, from all over the world), would think of Iran based on this...

Another girl of South Asian origin pointed to the discrepancies between exoticized and depressing representations of India, her cultural homeland. As she put it:

> [The media] shows it [India] being very exotic, with Madonna, her mendhi
> [henna], saris being turned into drapes, and the masala and everything being
> exotic...It's [also] shown as a welfare culture. It's the kids on the UNICEF ad.
> So on one hand, it's like this big rich silk industry which does henna on the
> side and on the other hand, it's the nude baby with the over-swelled tummy
> on the UNICEF ad (Jumpstart Workshop with girls of colour).

The burden of representation contributes to the 'ambassadorial' role in which racialized children and youth are commonly cast. Here they become representatives of their entire cultures and groups, and as experts on whatever practices are considered as 'peculiar' and demanding of explanation (see also Pratt, 2002).

Though faced with what appear to be insurmountable structurally mediated forces of violence, these young women have developed their own strategies of resistance. The latter include the formation of tight peer groups with members who share the same cultural ethos, asserting their own perspectives and definitions when compelled to do so, and defending their cultural communities. As this young Iranian woman states:

> The thing about me is I don't like to change myself. Why should I change myself for other people. So the thing is that if I like my culture, if I like whatever—now is the fasting time right? and I'm fasting—if someone calls me and says, "You can't fast. This is Canada." That's none of your business. This is my culture, this is me, I want to keep it. You can't tell me how to change it. So I don't change the culture because of other people. I change it if I don't like it. Then I'll change it. I don't change it because other people tell me Persian culture sucks or whatever (Individual interview).

The assertion that this young woman makes is itself grounded in a cultural terrain. So rather than see the issue of imposition as one of power, she translates this into an affirmation of individual will and cultural identity. As in the news media, the language of power and conflict are culturalized.

The confidence that underpins any assertion of identity needs to be grounded in a sense of self that has remained intact or that is somehow supported in the struggle to remain intact (hooks, 1992). Family and community provide such anchoring and protection. A mark of that surety of identity comes through in the following quote by a young Iranian woman:

> …like when you're talking to white girls, you talk to them and have different opinions and you're like, "Yeah, okay, you have a different opinion about something. And if there's a fight in school, my white friends are like, "Yeah, you Persian girls fight all the time." And now that upsets me because I'm with Persians. Before it was like, "Yeah, Persian girl fights. Who cares?" Now it kind of upsets me. "What do you mean Persian girl fights all the time?" Now I defend myself. I think I defend my friends of Persian [origin]. Like, "No, Persians don't fight all the time. That's the way it is." If somebody says something to me, I'm going to defend myself.

Above all, this last quote highlights the necessity of such a defence—a necessity derived from the need for solidarity in opposing violence in all its different manifestations. Such solidarity is organic in terms of its emergence and evolution in sites of support and affirmation.

Conclusion

These interviews and focus group data reveal the complexity of the negotiations that racialized girls and young women are engaged in daily, both in terms of identity formation and in securing a place for themselves in society as a whole. They also disclose a number of interesting insights which parallel the experiences of women in violent relationships. Many of these girls articulated definitions of violence which they equated with racism. For them, racism is a significant aspect of their everyday reality. They were also cognizant of the power of the authoritative structures in the school and the absence of any representations of their histories and communities in the curriculum. However, they were unable to perceive how the hierarchy of races that was in place served the interests of the dominant group. Further, they often attributed racism to ignorance on the part of their peers—a reflection that reinforces elite notions of racism relayed by the media in which racism is portrayed as being due to a lack of education or the ignorance of 'a few loonies out there' (van Dijk, 1993). Like women who experience violence, their stories revealed that there are few services or safe places available to girls or young women from racialized communities of colour. Rather, they are often faced with little choice except to turn to their own communities—to friends and family within those communities—to deal with these issues. And in this sense, they continue 'walking the hyphen' between the mediated, tenuous and conditional constructs of Canadian identity and those afforded to them by their own communities of colour.

Notes

1. I use the term 'fantasy' here based on Ghassan Hage's work *White Nation: Fantasies of White Supremacy in a Multicultural Society* (2002). Hage argues that "This White belief in one's mastery over the nation, whether in the form of a White multiculturalism or in the form of a White racism, is what I have called the 'White nation' fantasy. It is a fantasy of a nation governed by White people, a fantasy of White supremacy" (18)

2. The project was conducted through the FREDA Centre and focused on racialized girls and young women of colour. It is part of an ongoing study by the Alliance of the Five Research Centres on Violence (see also Jiwani, Janovicek and Cameron, 2001).

Chapter Six

Locality, Participatory Action Research, And Racialized Girls' Struggles For Citizenship

Jo-Anne Lee

This chapter reflects on a three-year study with racialized minority girls and young women living in Victoria, BC that was conducted between 2000 and 2003. It contributes to the field of girls' studies by bringing analytical attention to racialized minority girls' complex relationships to citizenship as locally and relationally constituted. In highlighting the importance of locality as a factor mediating racialized minority girls' processes of citizenship identity formation, as spatially and contextually grounded relations, the chapter draws on intersectional, transnational, feminist frameworks that problematize space, place, gender, migration and identities. Transnational feminist frameworks are also helpful for understanding the dialectical relationship between research practices and locality. This study employed a variety of qualitative research methods intended to facilitate research subjects' participation. Research methods included traditional methodologies such as interviews, focus groups, participant observations, and literature reviews as well as non-traditional research approaches such as community development (CD) and participatory action research (PAR) methods such as, popular theatre, participatory photography, and journal writing. To discuss the interaction of cultural locality, identity, and research practices through transnational feminist frameworks, I draw on three moments in the PAR process: focus groups; the "Its About Us" Girls' Conference; and the popular theatre workshops that included photo-journaling and group discussions.

This research into racialized minority girls' processes of citizenship identity formation helps to shift analytical focus away from concerns over girls' engagement with popular culture and consumption and their impact on girls' identities. By explicitly naming and interrogating whiteness as a cultural formation that influences racialized minority girls' lives, the research study engages with cultural practices beyond the emergence of "girl/grrl culture" (Aapola, 2005; Gonick and Harris, 2005). Much of this literature overemphasizes the role of teen popular culture on girls' lives, and fails to consider the multiple and alternative influences shaping racialized minority girls' lives and their mobility across several cultural and social worlds, such as citizenship and racialized nationalisms. It also extends understanding of girls' agency and resistance, beyond the limited realm of popular culture and the idea that there is a crisis of "girlhood," fueled by the "Ophelia industry" (Pipher, 1994).

By moving away from an emphasis on *the* "girl" as a central category of analysis with its attendant concerns with becoming *a* girl within gendered regimes of masculinity and femininity (Griffin, 2004), I hope to draw attention to regimes of cultural citizenship that mediate girls' subjectivities. As Chandra Mohanty (2003) argues, any naturalization of analytic categories such as "woman" (or "girls" in this case), ends up mystifying difference, especially differences between boys and girls, and differences between and among girls and women. Claiming "girlhood" as an act of construction or deconstruction is not in itself a liberatory or emancipatory act because the question of liberation for which girls is never asked. Instead of simply claiming, or reclaiming, "girlhood" as a time of innocence and latent power, I am interested in the constitution of located subjectivities in everyday interactions and experience.

On Citizenship, Identity And Locality In Victoria

The concept of locality, as discussed by feminist geographers, brings theories of space and place into feminist analyses. Yet locality is more than a spatial form or a geographical region that women occupy in paradoxical, ambivalent and unequal ways. Appadurai (1996) understands locality as referring to the social relations that take place in cultural contexts of places. As individuals increasingly move across space and time in imagined and material ways, our understanding of subjects and their constitution must now theorize locality as well as globality and their interconnections. Knowledge claims, too, are influenced by researchers' and research subjects' embodiment in localized places and times. This idea is captured in Donna Haraway's (1991) concept of situated knowledge. Haraway argues that knowledge is derived from specifically grounded realities that challenge erasures resulting from the universalisms and overgeneralizations of traditional epistemology. Social practices such as research are not neutral but are also located within hegemonic citizenship regimes and their webs of power. Despite the liberatory or transformative intent that research methodologies such as PAR claim, when translated into actual decisions in everyday life, these intentions lose their grip. Each moment in the research process is an opportunity to rethink taken for granted, normalized assumptions in regimes of citizenship and the identities that are made to matter and not matter.

The specific content and social relations in localities or places offer particular symbolic resources upon which social identities are crafted, making it necessary to problematize localities as important mediators of citizenship identities. Attending to the specificity of place or location helps to guard against a tendency to over pluralize, over generalize, and over universalize leading to erasures and reproducing hegemonic discourses about the "other."

This chapter examines Victoria, British Columbia as a locality that possesses unique features that not only affects the identities of racialized minority girls, but also mediates research practices and the interpretation of research findings around citizenship formation. I focus on intersecting dynamics of locality, racial ideology, gender, cultural practices, and shifting identities among researchers and research participants caught in similar webs of power, as these factors played out in PAR in Victoria, BC.

On Citizenship, Transnational Feminist Theories And Racialized Girls' Identities

With respect to citizenship and belonging to the nation, Benedict Anderson (1991) observes that residents of a sovereign territory can never directly experience "the nation," they can only imagine the nation as it is represented through mass communication media and texts. A person's most intimate knowledge of themselves as a member of a nation occurs through face to face interaction with the small number of people that they encounter in everyday life. For Anderson, national cultural identity is forged through daily practices of representation and material interactions. If citizenship is understood as an ongoing process of identity formation, rather than as a set of rights, or as a status, then intersecting issues of cultural representation and recognition in social relationships must be considered in discussions of social cohesion and citizenship (Jenson, 1998; 2002). Although Anderson's insights into citizenship as an imagined identity are useful as a way of moving beyond abstract debates over models of ideal citizenship, he fails to address issues of race or gender as factors in forming citizen identities. If, for example, racialized minority girls' everyday interactions are mainly with white-identified subjects, and take place in a context of cultural "whiteness," their identities as citizens may be mediated through these encounters as well as imagined through dominant forms of media and communication.

Nevertheless, Anderson's thesis does help explain the complexities and disparities in experiences of citizenship and why citizens' sense of belonging to and identification with the nation varies. In Victoria, a mid-sized provincial capital city in Canada where those of Anglo-European backgrounds are demographically and culturally dominant, racial minority girls and young women, a numerical and social minority, encounter a social reality where their "difference" is obvious, but paradoxically, negated and erased (Minh-ha, 1989). The relentless pressure to accommodate to the dominant culture coexists with a lack of spaces to affirm one's distinctiveness or nurture an oppositional consciousness (Mohanty, 2003).

Osbourne (2001) claims that national or provincial capital cities like Victoria are rich with symbolic meanings carefully selected to convey myths of national identity. These symbols or signs may be found in statues, commemorative plaques, monuments, architecture, flags, and streetscapes and signal Victoria's civic identity as a celebration of its colonial heritage. As seen in tourist literature, Victoria fashions its civic identity temporally, in the 19th century, at the height of British colonialism. Geographically, it situates itself on the North Atlantic by affiliating its cultural identity with Britain and Europe, rather than with Asia and the Pacific Rim. Spatially and temporally, the city represents itself as a city on the edge of empire, while culturally, it symbolizes an imagined British colonial identity that is "more English than the English." These enduring, invented cultural representations inform subjectivities of citizenship and national belonging. Through complex systems of cultural symbols, discourses, and practices, Victoria normalizes whiteness as a hegemonic cultural formation in the hearts and minds of its citizens. As others have demonstrated, cultural practices of white hegemony are important mechanisms for establishing norms of nationhood, class, and empire through race, class, gender, and sexual signifiers (Razack, 1998).

Victoria, BC, Canada, can be viewed as a localized site of Canada's hegemonic citizenship regime. Citizenship regimes are enacted in and through particular, situated, and context-specific historically emergent, cultural, political, economic, and social interactions (Isin, 2000). For example, public and media reaction to the arrival of "illegal" boat people from China's Fujian province off the coast of Vancouver Island in July 1999, exposed underlying premises in the dominant regime. Local and national media coverage of the incident repositioned Victoria residents of Chinese and Asian backgrounds on the margins of the nation (see *Globe and Mail*, July 21, 1999). In addition to several recent media representations of "others" stemming from the Gulf Wars, the World Trade Center attack on 9/11, the SARS epidemic, or other local incidents of racial violence, threat, or crime—to name only a few that have associated violence with a particular racialized ethnic group—remind individuals from affected groups of their ambiguous and paradoxical status in Canada (Jiwani, 2005). Their/our citizenship is called into question regardless of their/our legal status, length of tenure, birthright, or desire to belong. Positioned on the "colourful" end of the white/non-white pole of national cultural identity, an enduring legacy of the nation's colonial roots, racialized groups cannot take their citizenship for granted (Razack, 1998). For many, marginalization in the nation deprives us of a sense of well being that comes from a securely belonging to the nation. Racialized citizens, displaced to the margins of the nation, are continually reminded of their border status.[1]

Belonging to the nation—and by this I mean acquiring a self-identity as a citizen, and not merely the possession of a certificate, or passing some residency test, or having access to a set of rights, all of which are important dimensions of citizenship—is constituted in the realm of everyday life. One is formed as a citizen of a nation through daily dialogical processes of self-making.[2] This occurs in everyday life as one's racialized, ethnicized, sexualized, gendered, classed, linguicized, and other socially constructed and signified identifications are manufactured in relation to others in one's immediate social environment.

Discourses of citizenship as legal status, a process of identity formation, a framework of entitlements and responsibilities, and/or a mode of political participation are never neutral in their constitution or effects. For example, minority ethnic and racialized women, children, and youth of different social identities, are rarely discussed when debating citizenship since they have already been positioned outside of the prerequisites of liberal notions of citizenship: masculinity, rationality, autonomy, property ownership, and, in Canada and other white settler nations, whiteness.[3]

Citizenship has only recently been centered as an issue in feminist research and activism. Chandra Mohanty (2003) argues that questions of nationalism and citizenship must be integrated into feminist research of women and girls' inequality. Given contemporary realities such as globalization and the feminization of migration, female subjects are increasingly positioned across real and imagined borders and boundaries through governmentality and citizenship regimes.[4]

Racialized minority women and girls living in white settler nations cannot afford to take their citizenship for granted, or to continue having their issues left aside as tangential to feminist activist agendas because citizenship has become a mode of regulatory power. When citizenship is understood as already gendered, racialized, and classed, as feminist theorists argue, and not as neutral and universal as suggested in liberal philosophical approaches, then its operation as a regime of power that produces social inequality must be seen as a crucial site of analysis (Mohanty, 2003). Many feminist scholars are calling activists to take up critiques of discourses of universal citizenship as a way of uncovering mechanisms by which hierarchies of citizenship are organized by the state through the signification of "difference" and through the normalization of "whiteness" in white settler societies. Jacquie Alexander (1997) argues that democracy should be reconceptualized as a practice of decolonization, and more importantly, as a way of thinking ourselves out of the limitations in Western liberal formulations of democracy.

Aiwah Ong's concept of "cultural citizenship," defined as "the cultural practices and beliefs produced out of negotiating the often ambivalent and contested relations with the state and its hegemonic forms that establish the criteria of belonging with a national population and territory," bridges the distance between identity formation and everyday practices of citizenship (Ong, 1999: 264). She argues that hegemonic ideas about citizenship connect with state and civil society through institutional practices. Drawing on Foucault's concept of governmentality, as a set of rituals and rules that produce the consent to be governed, Ong includes those regulations that control the conduct of individuals within a given sovereign territory. The state is not a monolithic and coherent enterprise, and state institutions recruit institutions within civil society in governmentality through downloading, devolution, and interpenetration of their governance structures. This is evident in the ways in which the state harnesses the voluntary, non-profit sector to do its work.

Ong's conceptualization of cultural citizenship returns analysis of citizenship to concrete practices and values in everyday life, away from traditional political philosophical approaches that are more concerned with debating citizenship as abstract ideal type, a discussion most often found in liberal political philosophical debates. Indeed, liberalism's hold on citizenship discourses in western societies is achieved through its underlying moral promise of full inclusion and social equality contained within its conception of universal citizenship. In addition to investigating material practices, we must continue to interrogate debates over moral values and beliefs about the ideal citizen since unstated norms and beliefs about the characteristics of the ideal citizen also have material effects on peoples' lives.

Locality, Citizenship And Participatory Action Research (PAR) With Racialized Minority Girls And Young Women

I chose to employ PAR as a research method while investigating citizenship as a productive set of material practices in which racialized minority girls and young women actively participate. My decision to use PAR was motivated by a desire to support racialized minority girls and young women in becoming active agents of change in an environment where they have been made invisible despite their marked difference from the majority population.

Most research on visible minorities, immigrants, and racialized populations in Canada originates from larger metropolitan centers like Vancouver, Toronto, and Montreal, while experiences in smaller, less cosmopolitan, urban centers like Victoria, remain under studied. There is a huge difference between Vancouver and Toronto, and Victoria in the "visible minority" youth population; a graphic reminder of the need to exercise caution before generalizing too readily from research emanating from multicultural metropolises. According to a 1999 Statistics Canada report, in Vancouver and Toronto, visible minorities constitute over seventy percent of those under the age of twenty-five years, while in Victoria, only ten percent of this age group are visible minorities (Mata and Fernandez, 1999). These social statistics fuel a need to consider locality as an important aspect of citizenship formation.

Locality, as a situated relational and contextual concept, should also be acknowledged in research practices. For example, the distribution and isolation of racialized minority girls in Victoria posed several challenges for PAR, such as finding research collaborators and research participants. The research team found that youth who grow up in white dominated localities such as Victoria did not necessarily perceive themselves as racialized, gendered, and classed subjects, given the pressures to present themselves as "the same." It was also difficult to find appropriate community-based research partners because there were very few specialized services or representative organizations in Victoria. In comparison, Toronto and Vancouver have over 200 immigrant serving, multicultural, and ethno-specific organizations while Victoria has only two organizations serving immigrant groups, a handful of ethno-specific organizations, and only one unstably funded program designed for immigrant youth. In most discussions of PAR, there is an assumption that PAR researchers will work with an already existing community-based partner (Park, 1993). This was not the situation in Victoria.

Post-structural, transnational, feminist conceptual frameworks support the argument that racialized, transnational female subjects must be understood as holding multiple identity positions and that they are capable of exercising agency in constituting selves. But under what conditions do they exercise this agency? In the context of Victoria, where they are relatively few in numbers, categories such as "immigrant," "South Asian," or "racialized" were not meaningful or relevant to minority girls' sense of who they are given their need to see themselves as belonging to and surviving in the majority culture. Any attempt to hail, or call out to girls assuming that they will respond to a given named identity assumes an already existing "natural" identification and "fixes" them in a social category they may or may not see themselves fitting into. Social categories such as these are constituted through relational processes of representation and recognition that take place in specific localities; they cannot be assumed.

As much as we were aware of this in theory, we found it difficult to extricate ourselves from hegemonic thinking about taken for granted social identity categories. When recruiting research subjects, we initially approached school officials for permission to contact racialized minority girls, but they assumed that we were referring to students in English as a Second Language classes. There was an assumption that only newly arrived immigrants are racialized, and that anyone Canadian-born or raised, must be white. Although this way of thinking may seem terribly antiquated and even illogical to anyone working in Vancouver and Toronto schools, it is a fairly common position in an ethnically and racially homogenous city like Victoria.

Members of the research team designed and circulated in schools, a poster asking for girls to participate in the study.[5] We found ourselves unwittingly reproducing colonial images of the "other" by using a Microsoft Word clip art image of a "brown" girl wearing a school uniform, one of the few images of a non-white girl that we found. We had one response to the poster. Later, in discussions with girls, they told us that the image was "old-fashioned" and no one would see themselves reflected in such an image. The image that we used was of a girl in a school uniform, which is an artifact of British colonial schooling practices. Our chagrin was palpable after this discussion.

We were unconsciously enmeshed and complicit in essentialist thinking around identities, even though we thought we were familiar with the dangers of essentializing identities and cultures (Lee, 2005). We, too, as researchers, had learned to accommodate to whiteness. From the beginning, we had bracketed our concerns around identity categories and our pragmatic approach to language and identification gave rise to several unforeseen repercussions. With humility, I offer some examples of missteps and slippage encountered in the research study.

Focus Groups

The basic design of the project's focus groups was premised on racial and ethnic identifiers as the basis of recruitment and grouping. We conducted thirteen focus groups in total, with approximately sixty-five racialized minority participants. Participants in these focus groups were arranged into ethno/national/cultural categories that reflected our own perceptions of those we recruited. One focus group was formed around the topic of health. We divided the Chinese background group into Mandarin-speaking Chinese, and Canadian-born Chinese; there were two South Asian focus groups, one for older and one for younger girls; and we constituted the remaining focus groups as Latina, African-background, Kosovar, mixed-race, Muslim, and South East Asian backgrounds.

These labels are not innocent. Each label covers over diverse, heterogeneous realities. Namings, labelings, and groupings reveal how the research team enacted relations of power by classifying and inserting research participants into preexisting categories of identification. We distinguished girls through specific ethnic, religious, nationality, and racial identifiers, and once assigned to a group, we continued to count and manage them within these categories (we had intended these categories to be "provisional"). Organizing the participants into focus groups had seemed a small, logistical issue. Indeed, the groups that we formed did make it easier to keep track of participants, but we quickly began to perceive them as though they actually belonged unproblematically to *these* groups, and no others.

We had strategically used essentialism, the idea that individuals can be "known" through a few "natural" characteristics, in the recruitment phase (Spivak, 1988). When we called the girls on the phone, depending on their reactions, we would use phrases such as, "Other girls like you;" "Most are Canadian-born and grew up here"; and "Not an immigrant." We were signaling which differences mattered as we dialogically negotiated their identities with them. Once we confirmed their willingness to participate, we further constituted them as subjects/objects through technologies of conceptual power (Smith, 1987). For example, to keep track of participants, we recorded personal information on Participant Profile Forms (PPF). These forms ironically "formed" a fixed identity for the girls as a paper mask and this masking continued through to the completion of the research. When analyzing the transcripts and writing up results, I continued to position their responses within the categories that we had first generated to "administer" the research project. The PPFs contained certain biographical information, but left out other salient and crucial information. For example: How many generations had their families been in Canada? And, for those who immigrated to Canada, what were their ages when they arrived?

A central topic of discussion in the focus groups circled around girls' self-identities in relation to others "like them." Differences emerged within the focus groups around discussions of ethnicity and identity. Not only were focus group participants from different class locations, citizenship status (immigrant, refugee or Canadian-born), national and religious backgrounds, and different degrees of language fluency in English, they were also differently located in terms of their own and others' perceptions of their popularity, and "coolness"—categories of identity that mattered to them. The focus groups that we had formed around a presumed common ethnic identity gave way to multiplicity. There were many more factors differentiating the girls in our focus groups than were shared.

Other issues arose at the time of data analysis. In analyzing the results, we easily drew conclusions based on categorical identifiers such as: "the South Asian girls," the "African-background girls," and so on. But to what extent did our research practices seep into and complicate our analytical practices? For example, were long discussions over positioning and re-positioning of selves more about how we had arranged them into groups, or about how they thought about themselves outside of these focus groups, or some combination of both? Were we observing and listening to hybrid, diasporic self-identities, or were we observing contestations over social relationships played out in the context of constructed categories that the research project itself had imposed? To what extent were the narratives emerging *"in situ"*? Participants may have experienced the constructed focus group discussions and our tracking technology as another occurrence of living under dominant whiteness, even though all members of the research team were members of racialized groups. After all, in the context of living in Victoria, the focus groups were a unique opportunity to share a usually invisibilized "otherness." When reflecting on their experiences in the focus groups, most participants said that they enjoyed the opportunity to talk to "others like me." To what extent then, were research activities and relations already constituted as a sub-locality in relation to and within a dominant white locality? Yet, despite these misgivings, the groupings that we had arranged around "provisional" identity categories offered a sense of belonging to the girls as we were later informed.

Feminist researchers have long acknowledged interactions between the researcher and the researched and false claims to objectivity and neutrality. In raising these issues, my main concern here is not the interactions between the subject positions of researcher and participant as they relate to knowledge production, but rather, it is to highlight the spatial, social, and cultural contexts of the research study. We had initially seen focus groups as conversational moments built on provisional and shifting identities. What we had not foreseen was that over the course of the research study, these "provisional" identities would become concretized as "real" in the process of doing the research. Upon reflection, we came to realize that social interactions among research participants in focus groups could not be understood by abstracting them from the larger social context in which the focus groups occurred.

The Girls' Conference: "Its About Us"

At the conclusion of focus group discussions, several girls expressed their desire to continue meeting and to share the opportunity to talk about identity issues without having to be concerned about how their words would be heard or misheard by their white friends. This led to the idea for a conference; to give racialized adolescent girls and young women a platform and space to talk about issues of identity, racism, sexism, classism, and sexuality in their own language and in ways that were meaningful. The conference, which they named "Its About Us," was a key turning point in the PAR process. It brought together, for the first time, 100 racial minority girls and young women, in one place to talk about growing up and living in Victoria. At this point, the research study had morphed into a combined community development and action research project. I was committed to supporting these girls in their desire for more opportunities to connect because they had expressed a sense of isolation from one another. They wanted opportunities to come together to develop a sense of "oppositional solidarity" (Tatum, 2002).

In the context of Victoria, an opportunity for racialized girls and women to gather and talk about themselves on their own terms was rare. In Toronto, Vancouver, or other large cosmopolitan city, an event like the Girls' Conference might seem ordinary, since minority youth see each other in public spaces as a routine occurrence, and have opportunities to be in gatherings where they are not the social or numerical minority. In Victoria, I cannot emphasize how unique it was to see a hundred young racialized girls and women come together in one room. Participants continually expressed a sense of amazement at their collective presence throughout the Conference.

Our main research strategies now shifted to ethnographic approaches to document our interactions with the girls and the girls' discourses and interactions with each other. Planning a conference and participating in popular theatre workshops with the girls enabled the research team to undertake a feminist ethnography of girls' everyday lives, and through PAR, to have racialized girls actively participate in producing knowledge about themselves, for themselves.

Conference Planning Advisory Committees

The Conference was intended to offer a venue for participants to speak to each other in their own voices. Because racialized teens are rarely given leadership opportunities where their issues are the focus of attention, two advisory committees were developed, one with younger teenaged girls, aged fourteen to eighteen years, and the other with young women mainly in their twenties, to help design and establish the goals for the workshops and conference. In addition, two conference organizers, racialized minority women themselves, were hired to coordinate the conference. They consulted and listened carefully to the advisory committees even though this was often a slow, cumbersome, and difficult process for them. Organizing a youth conference brought different challenges than planning a conference for adults. For example, it was initially difficult to recruit and maintain the energy of young girls given their busy lives. It was also difficult to explain the importance of the Conference to many youth who did not identify themselves through their difference, nor had given much thought to issues of racialization and citizenship in their everyday lives. There was also vast difference in experience and understanding between the youth and the organizers that made decision making a challenge. There were many different experiences and visions for the conference. Power differences were unconsciously being played out when some of the younger planning committee complained of feeling silenced by their older, more activist sisters.

The research team and I came to realize, through trial and error, that we had to be sensitive to age and stage of life experiences. Younger girls would quickly retreat into silence, feeling intimidated by older and perhaps more experienced and articulate volunteers. We had to slowly overcome differences in life experiences and assumptions through trust building exercises and open dialogue. We could not assume any uniformity in experience based on a shared experience of "otherness" and "difference."

Based on the advice of the youth planning committees, the conference did not have keynote speeches delivered by experts or famous personalities. They wanted workshops where they could acquire skills, do "fun" things and just hang out. The key event was a performance by a popular theatre group on issues that they faced living and growing up in Victoria. To bring issues out into the open, we planned a speak-out at the close of the Conference. A local First Nations Chief opened the Conference and welcomed us to his people's territory, and his wife, an Aboriginal spiritual leader, gave prayers. When they entered the room and saw members of their family present, they expressed surprise. They remarked on how unusual it was to come to the University, and see members of their family in the audience. It was also unusual in the sense that racialized minority and First Nations girls rarely interact outside of school, and even in school, they often occupy separate spheres.

"Locus in Parenti"...I Don't Think So!

The need to assure the safety and security of young teenagers was an element that arose in the later stages of organizing the Conference. A member of the research team brought to our attention that we were legally responsible for the safety and security of those under the age of fifteen years. We had to know where youth were at all times. We had to keep parents and guardians fully informed, and to obtain their written, informed consent before youth under the age of fifteen years of age could attend. Legal liability issues added an entirely different level to organizing a conference.

The need to recruit many more volunteers to help with "supervision" proved to be a blessing in disguise because it necessitated the involvement of adult women. This became the catalyst for involving about thirty-five committed volunteers, the majority of whom were students at the university and who continued to provide leadership to the formation of Anti-dote, an organization for "multi-racial girls and women" that developed out of the Conference (see www.anti-dote.org). It was not difficult to recruit thirty-five racialized women in the twenty to thirty years of age group. Once they learned about the purpose of the conference and the need for volunteers, a typical immediate reaction was, "that's a great idea, I wish I had that when I was growing up," or "count me in, this is really important."

Despite their initial willingness, though, some volunteers interpreted our compliance with legal requirements to supervise minors as not in keeping with feminist principles. Instead of adopting a maternal, protectionist stance they argued, girls should be taught that they have the right to free mobility, and that adopting the stance of "victim" should be resisted. In the end, those who were willing to comply with the law that sees the "girl- child as non-citizen, in need of saving and protection" remained, while those who felt they were participating in patriarchal domination left. Again, we confronted politics around difference. The issue reminded us that "youth or child citizenship" is a category made real in everyday life. The legal requirement to safeguard children's mobility is part of the regulatory apparatus of governmentality through which gendered female citizen-subjects, girls and women, irrespective of age, are unable to move freely through public spaces without a "responsible" adult (usually understood to be male) accompanying them. The problem is not the girl child or adult female subject, as feminist scholars have pointed out, but with what bell hooks (1994) accurately calls a white supremacist capitalist patriarchy that promotes and accepts violence against women and children as the norm and not the exception. On the other hand, our decision to comply with legal requirements was a strategic act and not cooptation.

Popular Theatre

Augusto Boal, known as the originator of popular theatre, created theatre exercises and forms called the "theatre of the oppressed." Aligned to Freire's (1970) pedagogy of the oppressed as a form of knowledge production, popular theatre is intended to enable those most knowledgeable and affected by oppression to enact their own realities, tell their own stories in their own voices, and reveal their otherwise hidden realities to others (Boal, 1971; 2000). The popular theatre skits that the workshop participants developed were not easily created. Developing skits and rehearsing them for performance was a long process that developed over a six-month period. Group solidarity and trust had to be built. Not all participants were ready, willing, and able to make the commitment that the project demanded, and different allegiances and alliances existed and developed among participants, between participants and the research team, and between members of the research team that needed to be negotiated and bridged. When it came to working together, we could not assume our ability to find common ground and common language for communication; instead, we had to patiently build community day by day.

Combining PAR with popular theatre extended principles of PAR in new directions.[6] Approximately ten girls who were focus group participants expressed interest and volunteered to participate. The dynamics surrounding this aspect of the research were also revealing. However, one observation is that as a cultural form, theatre, and acting, exercise their own demands. Theatre is a collaborative and collective process requiring mutual and shared commitment. Three participants dropped out; the girls with part-time jobs, child-care responsibilities, and unstable family arrangements found it hard to remain committed, and there were also difficult interpersonal relationships among the girls and between us and the girls. There were constant negotiations over logistical details such as, start and ending times, transportation, snacks, and honoraria. As researchers, we participated in reproducing hierarchies of privilege as the popular theatre workshops tended to privilege middle-class girls from stable homes. Still, popular theatre enabled the remaining eight girls to speak about issues in their lives that they had not spoken before about publicly.

Within the popular theatre project, we used photography and journaling to engage girls as researchers of their own lives. The use of photography brought another dimension to the process. Over a period of a week they were asked to take pictures with a disposable camera and to think about questions such as, "who I hang out with, where I feel most/least at home, where I feel I do/do not belong, and where I feel I fit in and where I feel I don't fit in." They were asked to record their thoughts in a journal which we provided. We told them that the pictures could be concrete or abstract and other than those rules, along with some tips on framing and lighting, we left it to them. We called this phase the "Shooting Back" project.

When the girls reassembled a week later, we discussed the photos and the notes that they had recorded in their journals. We were surprised and moved by what the girls chose to reveal through their photographs and journal writing. We learned that two girls had fathers who had recently passed away and that they were dealing their grief and loss privately, "by writing in my diary to get it out" and "by just sleeping." Others revealed their loneliness at school, while others took several pictures of their schools, their classrooms and their friends showing that they were well connected and involved in school life. In group discussion, we found that girls had a wide range of daily experiences and there were many factors that helped to shape a positive or negative set of experiences. For example, those girls attending a working class high school where there were other racialized girls, depicted their school as a place of connection and belonging. But another, who attended a school in the suburbs where there were few other racialized girls, showed the school as empty of people. The spatial dimensions of belonging and locality were highlighted in these photo journals. As researchers, we gained access to the girls' own narratives of their lives only when the girls themselves became researchers of their lives.

The photographs and the stories that accompanied them enabled them to show us what was on their minds. The photography exercise exposed the complicated cultural knowledge that they possessed in terms of negotiating their multiple and intimate social worlds. There were different strategies of presentation depending on which cultural world and space they were crossing into or out of. Journal writing revealed a vast knowledge of cultural negotiation in sites and sights: *"I'm different with my family and my friends."* Each girl selected two photographs for as a slide show/spoken word performance at the Girls' Conference.

Our plan was to present skits developed in the popular theatre workshops around everyday experiences with racism, sexism, citizenship and identity formation to Conference attendees. It would be a way of reflecting back an often unspoken reality of "difference" in girls' lives from their "insider" perspectives. The performance at the Girls' Conference also enabled us to deepen and broaden our co-created observations and analyses with peers—other racialized girls and women. We believed girls could perform their created knowledge, making visible conscientization through analysis and performance.

In becoming 'actors,' the girls were able to speak through multiple voices and social locations revealing the depth of their own culturally derived critical consciousness about racist and sexist stereotypes but without having to reveal too much about themselves, which would have placed them more at risk. The opportunity to share and validate knowledge was a crucial aspect of voicing submerged critical consciousness about their doubled selves.[7] Developing a critical self awareness is a first and necessary step to decolonizing the mind. This process involved weeks of practice and rehearsals. The girls began to see themselves in new ways. They were able to compare their values, experiences and beliefs with others who were similar to them. By performing their everyday lives while discussing and analyzing what was going on in their lives as a group, they began to develop a critical understanding of invisible and dominant whiteness in their lives. They developed a language to name and voice what they all knew, but could not speak. The process of popular theater helped them confirm the validity and "truth" of their experiences (Carr and Kemis, 1986).

In naming their experiences and sharing it with others, the girls became co-creators of reflective knowledge. For example, initially, some girls had accepted and assumed the touristic rhetoric of Victoria as 'Canada's Little England'—a white colony—and could not imagine that other girls like themselves also inhabited this landscape and struggled with similar issues of living on the margins of whiteness:

> When they said there would be this project for girls like us, I was like 'wow, there's other girls like me? Is anyone gonna show up?' I didn't think there would be, because I know who everyone is where I live and we all know who the other Muslim girls are, I was surprised to meet other Muslim girls I didn't know, it was so cool. —Parshad (17)

After five months of almost weekly sessions, the girls developed a production of three skits, which were fleshed out and refined. The girls wrote the titles, scripts and introductions to each skit. Within a PAR framework, the popular theatre process enabled us to support the girls through an engaging, active process that led to personal and social transformation. One of the skits, "Popularity" was to become a theatre forum piece, meaning that the girls would invite audience members to come on stage with them and engage the girl actors in finding solutions or potential interventions to the dilemmas posed in the skit. I have included a short excerpt from each skit below.

In the first skit, "A Day in the Life," the storyline is about racism, sexism, classism, and ageism. The central character speaks to her constitution as a racialized subject and how she is positioned into stereotypical categories. The skit is her commentary on the hidden daily messages that she receives that work to erode her self-esteem and self-confidence, and against which she consciously resists.

Excerpt from "A Day in the Life":

> Girl to teacher: "I was just wondering why I got a low mark on my current events paper."
>
> *Teacher to girl*: "Well, racism is not really a current event, I mean you were supposed to write about something in the news that week, like the hydro dispute, or housing issues, or crime."
>
> *Girl to teacher*: "But racism *is* a current event, it happens all the time, it happens in our school every day, I mean it's a part of our lives."
>
> *Teacher to girl*: "I understand it affects your life, but the assignment was about a current issue that affects the whole province, something that has been in the news."

In the second skit, "Curry Rice," the girls describe their common experiences with horizontal racism, by naming the internalization of racism and white supremacy that is part of living under whiteness. Name calling and taunting are everyday experiences and powerful expressions of gendered and racialized violence. The skit's dialogue demonstrates the complicated racisms/sexisms that challenge the dominant understanding of racism as being only about skin colour and black and white dichotomies, ignoring sexuality and other historical racisms. In developing the skit, "Curry Rice," the girls threatened each other using racial slurs and taunting, stopping short of outright physical violence.

Perceived common experiences of racism under the umbrella category, "racialized minority" were destabilized in this skit. The First Nations girls who attended the Girls' Conference discussed the violence and racism they experience daily. They felt that that the "Curry Rice" skit about trans-ethnic racism, or what some call, horizontal racism, did not represent their realities which often extended beyond name calling to physical violence. One young audience member of Aboriginal background stood up during the discussion after the skit and said that walking away from racial slurs would not have been their response, they would have hit back. The idea of "polite racism" or "democratic racism," as a particularly "non-physical" Canadian form of racism that Henry and Tator (1995) propose exists in Canada, does not fully explain the everyday racisms that these particular young Aboriginal girls experience. For them, physically violent racism is very real in schools, in malls and in the streets. Yet another girl who lived in Burnaby, a middle-class suburb of Vancouver, also found the skits did not reflect her reality. She explained that because she lived in a community where there are people of similar backgrounds as her own, trans-ethnic violence was rare. It happened, but not in ways that affected her. It was important for the conference attendees to hear these comments because it reinforced for them the distinctiveness of growing up in a white dominant space. And, it allowed them to acknowledge, contextualize, and relativize the pain of racism instead of keeping it secret and private.

The performance of the skit in front of an audience of peers enabled girls to reveal the ways that experiences of growing up under whiteness are similar and different for girls from diverse racial, ethnic and class backgrounds.

Excerpt from "Curry Rice":

Girl 1: "Why are you so upset, did your Honda break down?"

Girl 2: "What about you? Maybe your uncle couldn't pick you up in his taxi??"

Girl 3: "How would you know, I can't even tell you apart...Hinder, Binder, Jinder, you all look the same to me"

The third skit, "Popularity," tells the story of the effect of media images and popular culture on their lives. It shows how popularity, coded as white, blonde, and blue-eyed matters in their school experiences, a view confirmed in our other research interviews. Girls live in a cultural context in which whiteness is assumed and normalized as beautiful, attractive, and "popular," a pseudonym for full inclusion and belonging. This image of popularity as citizenship is one that the girls internalize and that they actively participate in regulating and reproducing. The skit they developed showed how they participate in social and moral regulation by helping to "lighten" their friend to make her "look" more "popular." Not surprisingly, given the systemic nature of racist, sexist, heterosexist, and classist oppression, none of the individual interventions in the forum theatre part of the performance helped to alleviate the situation. This clearly demonstrated to the audience the systemic and longstanding complexity of gendered racism and racialized sexuality when living through and in dominant whiteness.

Excerpt from "Popularity":

Girl 1: "Could we do something to her hair…it needs to have highlights or something…"

Girl 2: "Yeah, it's so dark… so flat… so depressing!"

Girl 1: "You definitely need some blond highlights, to make your hair look shiny, prettier…and what are we going to do about your cleavage? You're so flat! Guys like boobs."

Girl 2: "Girl, we need to stuff your bra!"

The Absence Of Queer Issues

Queer issues and identity were not addressed at the Girls' Conference. The decision not to put forward a queer discussion group grew out of experience in the research project, not out of neglect or silencing. Two research assistants, queer women themselves, had tried to recruit young girls to discussion groups, but found that the girls they approached were extremely reluctant to come forward to speak publicly about their sexual identities. Most of the girls in the age group we had targeted had little knowledge or experience about their own sexuality, or about "queerness" as an identity category. Moreover, we were sensitive not to jeopardize the few "brown" spaces in this city because some participants may not have come out to family members and friends. The fact that one participant, who had not come out to her family and community, felt comfortable enough to speak about her desire for a queer discussion group at the Conference was seen as a credit to the volunteers who created a space of safety for her.

Diasporic Heterogeneity And Experiences Of Racism

In all the groups, the heterogeneity of diasporic ethnic communities was brought up over and over again. Although girl participants recognized that having an umbrella label, such as Asian, or South Asian, or Black might be necessary in Victoria, they also insisted on their own knowledge of lived ethnicity. They had to work through the dominant group's language of ignorance and stereotypes among themselves and to recognize the diversity that exists within their diasporic communities. Focus group discussions enabled them to develop and articulate critiques of stereotypes that they held of each other, some of them emerging from within their own families and others coming from dominant group myths. Recognition of differences in their sameness was only achieved after heated discussions. Isolation and living under cultural whiteness gave them few opportunities to see themselves in relation to their heterogeneous ethnic communities. These were difficult conversations and the girls and young women involved in the project, as well as members of the research team, found it challenging emotional and intellectual work. As Maguire (1987) found in her PAR experiences with women in a battered women's shelter, the PAR process helped the women produce knowledge about themselves. Through PAR focus groups, popular theatre workshops, the girls' conference planning committee meetings, conference discussion groups, and email dialogue, the girls produced contested knowledge about themselves. The popular theatre process allowed that knowledge to be publicly heard, seen, validated as "true," and put into circulation.

Conclusion

This chapter examined some of the complexities of undertaking research with racialized minority girls and women *vis-à-vis* cultural citizenship as a dynamic and active process of subject formation through community development/participatory action research (CD/PAR) methods. I highlighted the need to consider the specific contexts of Victoria, BC as a locality not only in terms of implications for understanding racialized minority girls' experiences of citizenship, but also for using PAR as a methodology to investigate citizenship identity formation. In Victoria, ideologies of whiteness as normative, not only operated to silence girls' expressions of their identities, but, like a weightless, descending cloud, it engulfed the research process as well. Nonetheless, PAR processes did enable and support transformative knowledge and action to occur among racialized girls and young women. It helped to uncover the need to understand more fully, interactions among intra-ethnic diasporic, trans-ethnic, and dominant white/minoritized ethnic relations as crucial dimensions of cultural citizenship formation.

Appadurai (1996) observes that localities are relational and emergent; they are socially produced and productive of subjective identities. Academic writing on PAR has rarely discussed the constitution of subjectivities of research participants assuming an already available subject position on the part of research participants (Smith, Wilms, and Johnson, 1997). In this research, questions of subjective identification and formation as locatable and situated in a specific cultural place became central and by involving girls themselves in research, we came away with much greater insights into the forces that structure and mediate their everyday lives. Under conditions of dominant whiteness and invisible visibility, white hegemony was an inescapable mediating contextual factor for all involved—researchers, research participants, and volunteers.

Through CD/PAR processes, we were able to support research participants' initiatives to claim space as citizens, but not without replicating existing relations of power. Nonetheless, through an ethical commitment to social change, girls became co-creators of knowledge by joining us in the research and communication process. Their desires for change became ours. All of us who were involved developed new identities as members in a shared community that we had co-constructed. Members of the research team, like the girl research participants, were members of racialized communities and, recognizing our own isolation, joined with the girls in developing a supportive structure to continue the project of becoming and making ourselves into subjects not wholly subjectified and objectified through dominant citizenship regimes. The isolation and marginalization reported by the girls spoke to memories of growing up under whiteness that we had all experienced at some point in our lives. The PAR process resulted in the creation of a new community-based, grassroots organization for "multi-racial girls and women"—Anti-dote (see www.anti-dote.org) It is a registered non-profit society, with a part-time executive director funded through Status of Women Canada. Though still struggling to get off the ground, the organization has already made a difference in the community and to many racialized girls and women's lives. The spaces opened up by the PAR process and the Girls' Conference has slowly begun to transform the cultural landscape of Victoria. It has already transformed those of us who were able to participate in this process.

Notes

1. Robert Miles (1989) defines racialization as the process whereby particular physical traits or cultural characteristics of peoples become seen as important distinctions among different social groups. These distinctions are then used as criteria for social classification systems that reproduce ideologies of racism based on the erroneous pseudo-scientific ideas that different categories of human "races" exist to justify unequal treatment which he defines as racism. Racialization is a complex relational process of self/other identification that has a psychic dimension. Those who are perceived as "different" learn to see themselves through the eyes of the dominant and when subjected to racism's injuries learn to keep silent, to not rock the boat, and to say nothing that will draw attention to themselves. Ultimately, according to Franz Fanon (1967), they internalize the dominant culture's views of themselves as lesser, insignifi-

cant and invisible. Fanon describes the psychic effects of racialization on those racialized: seeing themselves reflected through the eyes of the dominant, they become that reflection.

2. For further discussions on Canadian citizenship see: Kymlicka and Norman, 2000; Isin, 2000.

3. Alternative conceptions of citizenship are emerging that do include women, children and youth. At the UN, two Conventions have been passed: the 1989 United Nations Convention on the Rights of the Child and the 1979 Convention on the Elimination of Discrimination Against Women. Canada is a signatory to both conventions. The Convention on the Rights of the Child suggests a model of active citizenry for children (defined as human beings "below the age of 18 years, unless under the law applicable to the child, majority is attained earlier."). This document has generated political and academic interests in young people's participation rights (Stasiulis, 2002). International recognition of rights does not, however, translate into access to rights, nor does it address the question of belonging and inclusion in the national community. We have yet to understand the complex experiences of migrant and refugee youth, and other marginalized youth living in diasporic, transnational communities as they develop their identification as citizens in the nation of residency (Brah, 1996, Yuval-Davis, 2000).

4. Governmentality is a term developed by Michel Foucault (Burchell, Gordon, and Miller, 1991) and refers to the ways that the state organizes regulatory practices, laws and policies to produce self-regulating, citizen-subjects. One important technique of governing is by organizing individuals into generalizable social categories that can be subjected to broad, administrative regulatory procedures that, over time, result in subjects internalizing these categorical identities as their own.

5. I wish to thank Eugenie Lam for bringing these insights forward.

6. I wish to acknowledge Sandrina de Finney for organizing the popular theatre workshops and assisting in the analysis. I also wish to thank Lina de Guevara for her role as artistic director.

7. By "doubled selves" we refer to Fanon's (1967) insight into the development of doubled consciousness in the "master and slave" relationship, or in dominant and subordinate social relations under colonialism. According to Fanon, the colonizer's denial of recognition forces the colonized to see herself reflected through the deliberately distorted gaze of the colonizer. Yet, when the colonized become conscious of this distortion, she gains a doubled consciousness of self; on the one hand, her self as other, as object, that contradicts her own knowledge of her self as subject, as not distorted. The development of critical doubled consciousness may lead to passive, hidden and sometimes overt resistance to the lies and practices of the colonizer that attempt to deny subjectivity and agency to the colonized.

Chapter Seven

POWER Camp National/Filles D'action:
Working With/(In)Tention

Tatiana Fraser, Sarah Mangle

POWER Camp was established in 1995 by Tatiana Fraser, Willow Scobie and Stephanie Austin who, as undergraduate students in Women's Studies, set out to bridge the gap between institutional education curricula and the lived realities of girls. POWER Camp Ottawa emerged as a result: a community-based, grassroots summer camp and school based workshop series experience for girls aged eleven to eighteen. The first summer camp programs ran in 1996 in partnership with the Ottawa Rape Crisis Center and the University of Ottawa. In 1999, Rachel Gouin expanded the program through Filles D'Action, a sister project designed to serve the Francophone community. The success of these initiatives resonated in the community and across Canada, and interest in the POWER Camp programs and approach increased steadily alongside requests for information and resources. POWER Camp chapters began to emerge across Canada in conjunction with similar projects with shared goals and with girls and young women in mind.

In an effort to seize the momentum and to guide the future direction of the organization, a national meeting was organized in the fall of 2001. Attended by grassroots POWER Camps and similar initiatives, participants met for two days to discuss the need and possibilities for a national network of organizations working with girls and young women across Canada. The meeting's first day demonstrated the importance and potential of a national network through the exchange of stories, learnings, successes and barriers. By the end of the weekend, it was unanimous that yearly retreats, electronic communications and outreach strategies would be the most effective mechanisms to connect, grow and support this ever-growing network. Later that year, POWER Camp National/Filles d'Action, a "national, not-for-profit organization that creates, inspires and supports social justice education for girls, young women and organizations" across Canada was formed.

As proactive and productive as POWER Camp National has been and remains, our organization encounters numerous challenges in bridging groups across sectors and sub-sectors; girls, young women, women, and institutions who all use different approaches, languages, and strategies for promoting equitable social change. This chapter focuses specifically on the tensions and creative solutions that have emerged from working through the challenges inherent in feminist endeavours. While tensions almost inevitably arise when working for change, we have discovered that "intentional bridging" and understanding the politics of how we work are two useful—and productive—strategies for identifying, articulating and dealing with conflict. Sharing three examples from our work as case studies, we discuss the creative possibilities that can emerge from the challenges of working through such tensions: first, within a local after school program called Girls' Club; second, at "Transforming Spaces: Girlhood, Agency & Power," the 2003 conference that officially launched POWER Camp National; and finally, with our latest venture, "Love (in)tention," a national gathering of organizers working with girls and young women.

As a national feminist organization that also works at the grassroots, we often find ourselves navigating the complexities and challenges of the Canadian women's movement. This includes a combination of funding cuts, anti-feminist backlash, differing political agendas and divisiveness. Within this context, our challenge is to identify entry points and find common ground from which we can act. Yet, in our experience, some of the entry points for transformation are born out of the very tensions and struggles we confront. As we will see in the following three examples, when these tensions are held and engaged rather than denied or erased, creative possibilities emerge.

When we participate in co-creating spaces—whether we are collaborating on a project or bringing people together to discuss the issues we face in our daily lives—we rely on certain key ingredients. First and foremost, POWER Camp National is rooted in an integrated feminist analysis. This means that we recognize that women are not a homogeneous group; they are directly affected by policies and practices in different ways depending on how they have been racialized, (dis)abled or otherwise excluded because of their immigration status, because they are First Nations peoples, because they speak French, and so on. Second, we are committed to building an anti-racist, feminist, queer positive, ability-inclusive and youth empowerment vision of social justice. Third, we draw on theatre, games and arts-based activities to support people in learning and acting on these issues. Finally, a fluid spiral of learning, reflecting, researching, acting and evaluating informs our work.

How do we work in ways that allow us to identify and move beyond tensions? There is no obvious, simple answer. As an organization, this is POWER Camp National's most important and most difficult challenge. Techniques, approaches and strategies are fluid, context-specific and most importantly, learning processes. Nevertheless, some ways of working create the conditions necessary for identifying and moving beyond these tensions. We are guided by intentions, including: bridging as a strategy for moving towards a common ground and creating transparency towards understanding the politics of "how" we work.

Intentional Bridging: Finding Common Ground

The idea of "bridging" is born out of the work of feminists of colour in the United States who propose a framework for building coalitions across difference. Many authors write of the importance of forging bonds (hooks, 1995) and creating coalitions around specific issues despite the many barriers encountered in doing so (Mohanty, 2003). Beginning in the late 1960s, American feminists of colour were building coalitions with people who lived in "similar realms of marginality" (Sandoval, 2000: 52). Much of this work involved understanding the intersections of people's histories, thereby allowing them "to begin making links with each other" (Violet, 2002: 488). This 'revolutionary interdependency' is a space purposefully located on the margins (hooks, 1995: 150), "a visionary place where people from diverse backgrounds with diverse needs and concerns co-exist and work together to bring about revolutionary change" (Keating, 2002: 520).

This approach to collaboration informs our grassroots practice and inspires our efforts to create space for those who want to engage with tensions. However, as we navigate collaborations or co-create and participate in spaces, we recognize that our location shifts. In some spaces we are more or less privileged based on how we are situated (our education, our relation to whiteness, our resources). As we reflect critically on our work, it is important that we stay conscious of our privileges and of the ways in which our actions sometimes further marginalize people. We are forced to confront tensions and anxieties related to the limits of our work, our own reproduction of the oppressions we work to eliminate, our weaknesses and our mistakes.

The Politics Of How We Work

Jill Vickers (1991) examines some of the debates concerning organizational and political processes in the Canadian Women's movement, and suggests that challenges occur more out of the crisis caused by differences in political processes, strategy and tactics than from issues of substantive policy (75). In other words, *how* we organize ourselves in our work is often a greater source of conflict than *what* we are organizing about, or the issues we are working to change. Her research also addresses the challenges of working as a feminist collective when trying to respect and authentically include women with differing points of view, life experience, values and priorities for action. Feminist collectives, as an organizing model, she argues, are most successful in homogenous formations (86). Janice Ristock also identifies the silencing of differing perspectives and the denial of power issues as common experiences within collective models for organizing (1991: 48). Ristock also notes ways in which collectives are confronting some of these issues by acknowledging power relations, drawing clear lines of accountability and responsibility, as well as by creating mechanisms to acknowledge and adapt to change (54). She explains, "The emphasis is on seeing the collective as constantly changing and evolving and therefore requiring frequent monitoring of internal processes and individual and collective assumptions" (54).

Through our work experience, we have learned the value of being transparent around issues of power and accountability, organizing processes, interests and agendas. For example, as we will discuss further in this paper, we have found it fruitful to establish partnership agreements and group norm agreements when working in a collaborative context. The purpose of such agreements is to identify responsibilities and accountabilities, thereby creating a mechanism for understanding potential power dynamics within collaborative efforts. In our experience, this supports a shared effort to 'level the playing field' throughout the group processes. Group norms provide a tool that allows us to revisit the ways we work together. They offer a starting point that we can return to when tensions surface. Additionally, applying a focused and participatory methodology, solid evaluation mechanisms also create many opportunities for us to reflect, apply our learning, and to be fluid in our approaches to working.

Grounded in these theoretical approaches, we will now explore our learning through three case studies that draw on recent experiences.

Girls' Club

Our educational approach has always combined popular education and feminist analysis with dialogue and creative expression. Programming ranges from arts-based workshops including spoken word and dance to media literacy, HIV/AIDS and sex education, as well as addressing relational issues such as bullying, communication and team building skills. Action oriented programming has included 'zine making, community engagement and self organized protests.

POWER Camp National facilitates Girls' Club—now in its third year—with girls in grades six and seven in an inner-city elementary school in Montreal. This year, the initiative has been running an afterschool program once a week for an hour and a half each session. It is facilitated by five women, ranging in age from twenty-two to thirty-three years old.

The Girls' Club Space looks like this: Two big classrooms decorated by girls' drawing and art, sunlight streaming in. There is a chalkboard with space for anyone to write whatever they feel like. There are markers, paper, and string. There is coloured cardboard hanging, signed by all the girls and facilitators, listing the ways we agree to interact in the space.

> The Girls' Club Space feels: Stuffed with potential. The room is filled with support, love, loudness, quiet conversations, critical thinking, fun, art, energy, action, big questions, truth(s). It's a space that makes room for Girls' lives, the real ones, lives that don't fit comfortably into boxes (Mangle, 2004: 43-44).

The POWER Camp approach has been especially relevant in this inner-city school setting where many of the girls face multiple levels of violence. Many girls who participate in the project face difficult and at times explosive situations at home, in the schoolyard and in the classroom. There is a high incidence of bullying, relational aggression and isolation in and among young women. According to one of the schools' behaviour technicians, many of the girls have been abused sexually and/or physically, become sexually active at a young age and are more likely to become teen mothers. The drop out rate at this particular elementary school where Girls' Club is held is fifty percent.[1] Girls at the school are faced with difficult choices and have few skills to deal with their situations in self-advocating ways. The behaviour technician has observed that some girls cope through the use of drugs or alcohol and others ally themselves with anti-social male partners. Consistent with Canadian research, the situation at the school reflects the high rates of violence prevalent in young women's lives.

Our objectives as an organization are to provide resources and support for these girls. We understand that the politics and climate of the school system leave little room to address the girls' emotional needs and unique life challenges. We understand the challenges to be affected by the girls' gender, class and racial identities. At Girls' Club, we try to have conversations about issues that the girls' have little space to talk about in the school setting. Applying a participatory approach, we aim to use language that they use in their everyday lives, with their friends. We believe that by meeting the girls at "their level," on "their terms," and as much is possible on "their turf," we will be able to validate their experiences and support them as they cope with challenging conditions. This contributes to lessening the impact of violence in girls' lives and particularly in the school environment.

The Girls' Club project navigates through many challenges. Funding poses one of the most difficult challenges. Money, of course, remains a constant struggle, and even after two years of program delivery, the program is still not fully funded. In the current climate where the dominant discourses maintain that *girls are thriving often at the expense of boys* there is great difficulty in communicating the necessity of our program to potential funders and government agencies. This concern is shared by our network members across Canada, many of whom continually struggle to sustain their much needed programs.

As we have chosen to facilitate Girls' Club in a school setting and intend to continue the program over the long term, we are also challenged regularly in our attempts to navigate the school system. While the school is generally in full support of the program, administrators and teachers call for more transparency and communication. From our perspective, they do not seem to have the time or mechanisms to allow for this exchange to happen. Limitations, including the physical space and regulations, often create barriers to maintaining the safety and intimacy of the Girl's

Club space. It is difficult to facilitate in a context where we are required to follow the rules of the system we are challenging.

Another tension we confront is the location of our work and our organization. The facilitators who organize the group do not live in and have not grown up in these girls' community. The facilitators struggle to stay relevant and effective, while at the same time recognizing the reality that we can only understand the girls' lives to a certain point. We can never fully comprehend what it means to grow up in that specific community. It is important that we recognize our limits and the contradictions inherent in this work.

In the last six months, we have responded to issues of relational violence—specifically bullying—by focusing on anti-oppression training with the girls. We have found that issues of racism, homophobia and classism underpin and inform the bullying dynamics that we have witnessed and encountered. Translating anti-oppression training for girls between the ages of eleven and fourteen was our first major challenge. Tensions also emerged when the facilitators became personally challenged through their efforts to create critical anti-oppression learning opportunities. As facilitators from diverse backgrounds, we represent different life experiences and choices. For example, one facilitator may be the only out queer person that many of the girls know. Another facilitator who doesn't have kids may be the only single, partnered straight woman in her thirties that the girls know.

The girls ask direct questions about us and speak frankly about themselves. Their behaviour is similar to that of the theories found in models of popular education, where people start with their experience as a springboard to talk about and think about broader structures of inequality. The difference with Girls' Club is that often the girls start by questioning the facilitators, in order to question and speak about themselves. Their questions can seem invasive and harsh. They ask a lot of questions: "Are you from Japan or China?" Are you a lesbian? "How old are you? And you don't have any kids?"

The girls are learning how to socially interact in new and different ways. They are crashing through identity politics by asking us pointed questions, listening to our responses and watching our body language. They are thinking about themselves, their neighbourhood and their school. When a facilitator is asked a personal question about her identity, she must decide how to respond on the spot. "I don't feel like talking about that right now," or "That's not an appropriate way to ask that question, let's talk about it another time, in a workshop," or "Yup, I'm a lesbian," or "I'm not from Japan or China, I'm from Canada, my parents were born in China, though. What about you? Where are you from?"

The girls may not be aware of how their language and behaviour sometimes perpetuates and creates racism, ageism, and other discriminations. The girls often do not intend to be offensive or discriminatory. Even though their intentions are not to perpetuate oppressions, the effects of their questions can be painful and difficult for facilitators. Facilitator debriefs and learning from these experiences are important mechanisms for facilitator support.

We are working to build safer, anti-oppressive community spaces and activities for girls. While we do this, our bodies often become the markers of learning and the targets of discrimination from the participants. We are challenged to provide important learning opportunities for the girls while also maintaining self respect, self-care, openness and self/group responsibility. Tensions emerge as we work to balance education, personal boundaries and safety. We also need to make sure we are not acting as tokens; making our bodies representations of entire communities of people. Most importantly, we need to look after ourselves. Our own self-care and personal emotional health is essential to providing consistent and quality education and care to the girls with whom we work. While we navigate and learn from these tensions, we also observe the changes and possibilities. The girls who participate in Girls' Club are planning how they will take their learning and share it with their own communities. Next year, the program will focus on using arts-based activities as a means for creative expression and skill-building action oriented strategies for change. At the same time, our evaluation indicates that Girls' Club has successfully created a cohesive, generally supportive group dynamic, and a safe space for girls to deal with issues that otherwise are difficult to express. Our evaluation interviews illustrate that the girls participating in Girls' Club, as witnessed by school staff, their parents, and themselves, are developing increased self-awareness, perspective-taking and critical thinking. They are also learning non-violent means for conflict resolution and applying them in ways that are observably benefiting their personal and collegial relationships (Kishchuk, 2005: 10).

Transforming Spaces: Girlhood, Agency And Power

Bishop, Manicom and Morrissey (1991) document the tensions and struggles that surface when activists and academics work together. In particular, they recognize class differences, resource accessibility, diverse working cultures, and the tension between theory and practice as some of the strains that work to produce conflict and, often, an uneasy alliance (299-304). They write: "It is our view that recognizing and examining how differences are socially organized is a necessary task to undertake if we are to work together honestly, respectfully and productively" (306). Community/academic conferences are one of the models they propose for activist and academics to work together (306). In this spirit, as community activists, we teamed up with feminist anti-racist academics to organize a national conference, entitled "Transforming Spaces: Girlhood, Agency & Power."

The conference emerged out of an effort to bridge what often appear to be two divided terrains: academic and grassroots practice. The idea of this initiative emerged at a time when POWER Camp National was struggling to obtain financial resources to support its efforts to connect people doing work with girls and young women across Canada. The event was designed to bring together the diverse experiences and vast knowledge of girls and young women, community practitioners, grassroots activists, service providers, academics, educators and policy makers in a space devoted to communication, collaboration and social change. Our aim was to integrate a broad range of experiences and approaches to "Transforming Spaces" as well as to address four inter-connected sub-themes: resistance, violence, sexualities, and identities as they related specifically to young women and girls. Our goals were to create strategic bridges and interventions—informed by girls and young women directly—which would draw public attention to and galvanize support for a much needed area of concern.

Canada had never had a national conference on girls and girlhoods and, as we soon found out, many people were eager to collaborate to make it happen: POWER Camp National, Concordia University, McGill University, the Alliance of Five Research Centres on Violence Against Women and GirlSpoken: Creative Voices for Change from Laurentian University. Together we created a core committee which later expanded to include a large number of volunteers from the academic and activist realms. We began our planning by establishing a partnership/organizing agreement, which outlined shared values, roles, responsibilities and—most importantly—decision-making mechanisms. Although this work was tedious, it created a much-needed level of transparency and helped us navigate through particularly difficult moments. In addition to this agreement, interests and agendas amongst the organizers were identified, communicated, and discussed.

Organizing the conference had its own moments of synergy as well as tensions. Here we focus on the pre-event process as it offers a micro-example of the kinds of tensions and challenges we experienced during the conference. The politics of representation was one site of contention. Organizers came to the table with differing analyses, experiences and expectations about how we should take action to ensure the event fore-fronted inclusion and accessibility. Moments of tension emerged concerning who comprised the membership of the organizing committees, their representation and identities and outreach strategies, as well as devising the selection criteria for presentations that were to be included in the conference. Academic, peer-reviewed blind selection processes clashed with grassroots experiences of selection criteria. We dealt with these issues—including whose voices would be privileged, and why—throughout the conference and at all committee levels.

Decision-making mechanisms were defined in the collaboration agreement, and this often helped facilitate difficult or challenging moments. However, tense moments did arise around decisions after the core committee broke into sub-committees to work on the final phases of the conference organizing. Power dynamics and communication breakdowns between committees proved to be a real challenge. Higher-level decisions that were the responsibility of the core committee process became relevant to sub-committees who were in a position to not only challenge but more accurately assess and decide what needed to be done at the ground-level. While the work became more grounded in the sub-committees, it was a struggle to maintain the links of communication, exchange and equity between the core and the sub-committees. Not surprisingly, the power imbalance between the core committee and the hard working sub-committees became a source of significant tension and, in some cases, resentment.

While anxieties did play out over the course of organizing the conference, the overall spirit of the collaboration was one of reciprocity. Certain tensions are to be expected, and from POWER Camp National's perspective, the organizing process went smoothly considering the logistics of the work involved. Academic privilege and access to resources were intentionally and generously shared to support the advancement of grassroots practice; all the while creating a platform for profiling Canadian research on girls and young women. Program development was a collective committee process; we spent an entire day envisioning ways we could thank and honour all of the participants. A combination of plenary sessions, panel presentations, workshops, art installations, and what were affectionately called 'round moments' (small group discussions) were imagined, designed, and set into motion. The overwhelming response to our call for presentations went beyond our expectations and a selection process was facilitated that prioritized the voices of girls and young women, as well as marginalized perspectives.

What happened when we brought people together across a diversity of issues, politics, perspectives, locations, personal and professional contexts? Tensions did indeed surface during "Transforming Spaces": some felt excluded, others didn't understand academic language, and still others wanted more theoretical grounding. The Canadian Research Institute for the Advancement for Women (CRIAW) has reported similar experiences in their attempts to bridge feminist research and practice. They note that these tensions "arise from the different institutional orientations to knowledge and to change" (Christiansen-Ruffman, 1991: 279). They suggest further that

> [A]n organization bridging the gap will never completely fulfill society's version of the patriarchal ideal of either side, by definition, and such dichotomous rhetoric masks understanding. Feminists need to recognize the difficulty of even small achievements…One should not minimize the importance of recognizing differences and the potential contribution of each individual, of the complement of agendas, of joint activities and of working together, and of accessibility policies that serve to counter hierarchical structures and to equalize resources, at least to some extent (281).

While there were moments of explicit tensions between academics and young activists during the conference, assuming an academic/grassroots divide masks the complexity of the tensions that actually underlie the experience of "Transforming Spaces." The tensions that surfaced touched on the possibility/impossibility of working across intersecting identities, voices and communities thereby calling into question the possibility of acting in solidarity for a greater goal (Jiwani, 2003: 21). For example, tensions around who speaks, about whom, when they speak and why; in addition to who is excluded, and what the consequences of this exclusion are—all surfaced throughout the course of the event. These are the difficult questions that we must ask and sit with, albeit uncomfortably. What we did observe, however, was willingness— at the conference, in the submissions to the conference summary report and in our continued work—to engage with these tensions and pursue the goal of finding common ground.

The conference provided an opportunity for people with very different perspectives to be heard and facilitated an exchange on issues relating to girls and young women. Through poetry, reflections, essays and art, the *Conference Summary Report* captures the "cacophony of voices on girls and girlhoods invigorated and inspired by Transforming Spaces and incorporates an expansive and eclectic collection of work from contributors from across Canada and outside our borders" (Steenbergen, 2003: 2) This report, as well as our own post-conference evaluation, illustrates the actions, collaborations and renewed energy that emerged from the event. It also captures the successes and barriers of the event, documenting a rich learning which has informed POWER Camp National's future endeavours.

Love (In)Tention: Creating Action

Every year, POWER Camp National hosts a national retreat for its members, aiming to create an opportunity for exchanging and learning across communities. The 2004 retreat brought together over 60 people engaged in grassroots work with girls across Canada. The theme of this year's retreat was violence. As suggested by the work of Berman and Jiwani (2002), we applied a broad understanding of violence which included violence to the self (self-harm, substance abuse, and eating disorders), relational violence (bullying, physical, verbal or sexual aggression) and systemic violence (racism, poverty, colonialism, homophobia and other social injustices). Our intention was to work with the stories people had gathered from their communities, exchange and build skills around anti-violence and anti-oppression, learn from and challenge each other, as well as to improve our ability to act in solidarity as a network.

Participants included a range of grassroots organizers: established organizations, self-organizing young women; young leaders working within the programs that serve them, and new initiatives. Each community was encouraged to bring a young woman engaged in their program. The age of participants ranged from twelve to fifty-something. Age differences, different levels of analysis on the issues and the vast diversity of experiences represented by participants meant that the program design would have to meet a variety of needs. We recognized that we would face many challenges, and anticipated that exploring issues of violence could become emotionally charged. The retreat agenda included popular theatre, action strategy workshops, a 'day of action' planning session, skill-building workshops, arts-based activities, and other moments for creative expression. We mapped out the various contexts in which violence is experienced and resisted using postcards that had been made by girls and young women in various communities.

Although participants shared a common ground through their work with girls, we expected that discussions challenging individual and organizational assumptions about their work and their everyday lives would arise. This is exactly what happened. The very first day, racism and its manifestations were the centre of behind-the-scene discussions, providing opportunities for people to be frustrated, cry, talk and learn. Racism needed to be named and confronted. POWER Camp National staff responded by moving anti-oppression workshops forward in the agenda, naming racism as a form of violence, and collectively revising group norms so that they would explicitly name the reproduction of racism as unacceptable. In facilitating this retreat we observed that people's resistance and their lack of knowledge and strategies for action created significant barriers to working across organizational, societal and personal realities. This was confirmed by our post-retreat evaluation when we learned more about the diverging perspectives on how racism should be identified and dealt with. Some participants were uncomfortable with our decision to name 'white' privilege. For them, this created tensions. Importantly, the resistance to using this language often reproduced racism. For example, there were comments about the silencing of 'white' people and about certain black women being behind our choices on language use and strategy. For other participants, it relieved tensions because it articulated what often remains unsaid. More precisely, the experience of racism and the subtle ways in which it infiltrates even our choice of language were named at the retreat.

While tensions are always present in every interaction, we value identifying and engaging people in moving through them. Surfacing contradictions and deeply rooted assumptions and beliefs requires a collective commitment from participants who are open to taking risks, being vulnerable and feeling uncomfortable. Following the retreat, we saw how important this commitment was when participants who had struggled during the retreat had applied their learning successfully within their communities (Gouin, 2005).

Similar to the post-conference documents, our post-retreat evaluation outlines the stories, critiques and the appreciation for the exchanges that took place. It is clear that the event had an impact on participants both personally and professionally. The retreat was an opportunity for participants to raise their awareness and to build and hone their skills on the issues of racism and anti-oppression. For some, these hard moments led to important changes and advancements.

Discussion

In the spirit of building bridges, learning from one another, creating common ground for action, we all share the challenge of working through the politics, ideas and identities that create barriers for moving towards change. Devastation and disappointment can be personal, group based/collective or systemic or all three.

Regardless of the mechanisms we put in place, we ultimately rely on the commitment of people who are willing to look at the tensions and work through them. When issues and questions that are overshadowed emerge, forward movement is dependant on the willingness to be open, honest and to learn. Creative possibilities can only emerge when participants agree to engage in the process with a commitment to working with the 'difficult' issues: issues people are fearful of naming. As Joan Grant Cummings (2001) reminds us: "we decide whether the 'difficult' issues will ever be heard or given space at the table—gender, race, class, etc." (4).

We are inspired by and learn from people who are committed to naming and confronting these issues. Young women across Canada have developed innovative techniques to creatively engage with tensions. For example, njeri-damali (Campbell), one of our facilitators at the aforementioned retreat, invited people in her workshop to make connections between their emotions, their organizing, and their visions for social change (Campbell, 2004). This approach encouraged participants to look at the connections between personal truths and organizing issues. It probed into contradictions, personal fears and the courage to act. This is an example of cutting-edge work being done by young women across Canada. It is also an example of work that calls on participants to consider transformation as both a deeply personal and community process.

What have we at learned from these experiences? Tensions are uncomfortable and often painful. As an organization that applies self analysis as one of its foundational values, we are challenged by the reality that tensions are central to our work. This also requires a willingness and openness to learn, and to be challenged. We need to remind ourselves to balance this critical reflection with a gracious mindset. Lack of appreciation for what works and the people engaged in such work can be discouraging and demoralizing. Self care also needs to be carefully balanced with our commitment to radical critique and transformation.

We are thinking more about how emotions are tied to experience, identity, politics and group processes. We are asking questions about how to honour individual emotions without sabotaging the greater purpose of the group; how to respect emotional responses and at the same time focus on the practicality of getting the work done. We are also learning how to set boundaries and to stick to them. Good facilitation skills are essential to supporting processes that engage difficult questions. Non-violent approaches to facilitating provide techniques that diffuse destructive conflict and at the same time provide insight into how dichotomies can co-exist. Transparent facilitation styles also support a power-sharing approach to group processes and conversations. We value movement, theatre-based and other creative techniques for facilitation that allow people to look beyond verbal communication.

We are also experimenting with issues around language. As we probe into understanding the language we use, we are called to understand the historical context of the language of oppressions. We are asking questions like, "How do we perpetuate the very oppressions we seek to eradicate through the language that we use?"

On the technical side, we have learned that creating safe spaces for difficult issues is most successful in smaller numbers. There needs to be a balance between the quality and quantity of the process and space. We have also learned that we can call on the experience and expertise of many people in our communities to apply innovative approaches and skills to creating transformative experiences and spaces. In addition to these approaches, we have learned a lot about the need to identify and hold a political 'bottom line'; what Cummings (2001) defines as the 'non-negotiables' (5).

Conclusion

While we shine light on the creative potential that emerges out of identifying, articulating and then facing tensions head-on, we do not wish to gloss over the often destructive outcomes of bringing these issues to the fore in ways that alienate the very people we are trying to engage. This reflection attempts to illustrate our learning and successes, and to highlight some of the challenges we face as an organization doing both local and national work with girls and young women and with organizations with shared goals. Most importantly, we write these experiences recognizing that we are engaged in an on-going effort to learn from what we do. We share the anxiety that tension and contradiction creates, but we do this because we remain committed to co-creating spaces that help unblock barriers, voice silences, and build common ground from which we can act—and empower others to act—as agents for social change.

We are well accompanied in this journey.

Notes
1. Montreal Island Council, 2001.

Chapter Eight

Sugar And Spice And Something More Than Nice?
Queer Girls And Transformations Of Social Exclusion

Marnina Gonick

Are queer girls, girls? What are the signs and discourses of girlhood and queerness that would be drawn upon to respond to this query? What are the social, theoretical and epistemological issues at stake in asking this queer question? At the outset, the task appears to require an un-coupling of normative meanings of the category girl. This task bears a certain relationship to one of feminism's most successful, difficult, contentious and unfinished projects: the redefinition of what it means to be a woman and girl. From expanding the options in girls' lives in schools, workplaces, and the public sphere, to multiplying gendered representational images in the media, curriculum and cultural production, feminists have fought to create the conditions of a more inclusive society. But, both within feminism and within the wider social world, the work of breaking down the raced, classed and sexed boundaries of who is included in the category of "girl" remains critical.

Far too often when the category "girl" is named, in the media, in feminist research, in education, sociology and psychology discourses, and in popular culture amongst other sites, it is white, middle class and heterosexual girls whose experiences are referenced. If we understand "girl" as a category which is socially produced rather than as a naturally occurring biological and developmental phase in the life course, than this narrow view presents a problem in the way it restricts possible meanings of girlhood. But, the question 'Are queer girl, girls?' suggests even more may be involved than the already complicated project of creating more inclusive categories. It also demands that we look again at the intersecting discourses of femininity, age, agency and sexuality and the social and cultural practices that constitute "girl" as category. It asks us to consider the institutionalized norms that regulate the boundaries of the category as well as girls' responses to them. Queering the category girl therefore, is about more than simply adding queer girls into an always already existing social category. Rather, it is a stance that allows us to both ask how girls become girls and to investigate the implications for those whose social, cultural, sexual and aesthetic practices position them outside the normative meanings of the term.

There is no question that there are severe consequences for those living outside normative gender/sex categories. This article explores some of these consequences, including what Deborah Britzman (1997) following Dank (1971) calls the "cognitive dissonance" of queer youth. "Most persons who eventually identify themselves as homosexuals require a change in the meaning of the cognitive category *homosexual* before they can place themselves in that category" (cited in Britzman, 1997: 194). The very signifiers of queerness, must, according to Britzman, be rearticulated in ways that are pleasurable, interesting and erotic. As well as the everyday practices that produce this cognitive dissonance, I am interested in the efforts girls use to re-signify queer identities.

Theorizing Intersectionality And Queer Youth

Just as the categories "girl" and "woman" are not singular, the category of queer girls is comprised of a wide range of racialized, class, ethnic and linguistic backgrounds. Included are people with and without disabilities and people who negotiate a range of gender identities and expressions of sexuality. Queer girls experience marginalization and oppression on the basis of sexuality and other markers of social difference, but they may also occupy positions of privilege on a range of other grounds. An approach that uses intersectionality to understand identity and theorize oppression looks at the complexity and contradictory ways people are located in relation to positions of dominance and marginality. Therefore, in considering the exclusionary practices that queer girls encounter in their daily lives, related systems of power and privilege, such as white supremacy, patriarchy and the capitalist system need to be integrated into the analysis (West, 1996).

An intersectional analysis makes the connections between homophobia, power and privilege allowing for an analysis of the ways in which sexed, gendered, raced and classed social positions intersect in shaping experiences of structural, political, physical and representational exclusion against queer youth. An intersectional focus highlights the need to account for multiple grounds of identity when exploring how the social world is constructed and experienced. For example, Kamashiro (2001) shows how the ways in which discourses of healthy gayness are constructed around "being out" may have different implications for youth of colour than for some white youth. Those who do not come out in those ways deemed "healthy" by the broader gay community may be construed or construe themselves in negative terms. He suggests that these norms may pose a problem for youth of colour, who may not "be out" to their families because of the ways gayness may be attached to meanings of whiteness in their communities. While they may not find support for their sexuality in their families and communities, Queer youth of colour may rely and depend on these same social spheres for support and survival strategies for the racism they encounter, including within the gay community. Thus, "being out" in the ways advocated in discourses of gay rights is not necessarily always a workable option.

An intersectional analysis is also important in considering intervention strategies. As Snider (1996:296) suggests, programmes need to be designed in such a way
that youth are not being asked to address homophobia separately from racism,
thereby forcing them to choose potential involvement in the Queer community over
involvement in their families' communities. To do otherwise is to ask Queer youth to
hierarchize oppressions. Moreover, an approach which challenges only one form of
oppression can often unintentionally contribute to other forms of oppression
(Kumashiro, 2001) reflecting the way society privileges some identities over others. As
Wilchins (1997) says:

> Left untouched is any problem which is about sexual orientation AND." So,
> we're not going to deal with queers of color, because that's sexual orienta-
> tion AND race. We're not going to deal with issues of working-class queers
> or queers on welfare, because that's about gay AND class. We're not going to
> deal with the concerns of lesbians, because that's about gay AND gender.
> Pretty soon, the only people we present are those fortunate enough to pos-
> sess the luxury of a simple and uncomplicated oppression. That is, their race,
> class and gender are "normal," and so go unmarked and unoppressed (83).

However, there is also something more at stake in an intersectional analysis that requires significantly more than simply adding on various facets of social difference to
an assumed always already core subject. That is, an intersectional analysis of sexed
experience needs to work from an understanding that the subject is constituted in and
through the a convergence of facets of social difference in such a way that it is impossible to delineate what is a feature of simply sexuality, race, gender or class. Judith
Butler (1993) explains:

> To prescribe an exclusive identification for a multiply constituted subject,
> as every subject is, is to enforce a reduction and a paralysis…And here it is
> not simply a matter of honoring the subject as a plurality or identifications,
> for these identifications are invariably imbricated in one another, the vehi-
> cle for one another: a gender identification can be made in order to repudi-
> ate or participate in a race identification; what counts as "ethnicity" frames
> and eroticizes sexuality, or can itself be a sexual marking. This implies that
> it is not a matter of relating race and sexuality and gender, as if they were
> fully separate axes of power…And when they are considered analytically as
> discrete, the practical consequence is a continual enumeration, a multipli-
> cation that produces an ever-expanding list that effectively separates that
> which it purports to connect, or that seeks to connect through an enumera-
> tion which cannot consider the crossroads, in Gloria Anzaldua's sense,
> where these categories converge (116-17).

Exclusionary Practices At Work

Researchers are producing a wealth of studies documenting the social consequences of challenging normative categories of sex/gender. Such consequences include high rates of suicide, depression, low self-esteem, drug use and psychological trauma from abandonment (Kroll and Warneke, 1995).

Sexual violence is not an uncommon experience for queer youth with Duncan (1990) reporting that such incidents were even higher for lesbians than for heterosexuals. One way of accounting for this is to consider the ways in which sexual violence and the threat of violence has often been used as a means of regulating and controlling women's sexuality and sexual expressions. The complex interactions of gender, race and sexuality are also a feature of this violence. As Martinez (1998), suggests for Latina women, the double stereotypes of "sexually deprived lesbian" and the "hot Latina woman," are often in play in this violence. Other stereotypes, such as the "sexually loose" Black or the "exotic" Asian woman may also be at work. Interestingly, the Human Rights Watch Report (2001) suggests that in schools, it is lesbians who identify as or are perceived to be "butch," that are punished more for violating gender norms. There is a perception that lesbians who are "femme" are punished less by their peers, largely because the harassment takes the form of boys wanting to "watch" and then "join" the girls. Girls perceive this harassment not only as an invasion of their privacy but also as an implicit threat of sexual violence. One of the trans-sexual youth in Wyss's study (2004) reports being explicitly threatened by "guys who wanted to have sex with me and [...tried] to force themselves on me." (2004: 717). Others reported being raped, sometimes more than once.

> [The boys would] drag me into the bathroom and like humiliate me and try to find out what I was...I was totally like sexually assaulted by them... People talk about how they were harassed in high school. And what them mean is they got raped... And it's bad to have things yelled at you because what that carries with it is the *threat* of something happening to you that is worse, you know? And it is humiliating to get yelled at and looked and stared at and spit at. *All* these things happened to me at that school. (2004: 718)

When adults downplay or ignore this type of harassment, they use a "boys will be boys" type of argument, downplaying the harassment as merely an expression of desire rather than a threat of violence (Human Rights Watch, 2001: 51). Trans-sexual youth push the boundaries of gender non-conformity even further which also exposes them to more harassment and violence than other Queer youth. For example Wyss suggests that many transgirls who have tried cross-dressing in high school have been ridiculed, ostracized and physically assaulted by their peers (Wyss, 2004: 710).

Social services is another area where exclusionary practices are at work. For example, queer youth in out-of-home care settings have reported data that suggest this population receives less services, are more readily labelled as difficult, experience verbal harassment and physical violence regularly, are moved more often (multiple placements), are more likely to be separated from their siblings, experience high rates of homelessness, are not often reunited with their families, and have a more difficult time attending community-based educational programmes and accessing medical and mental health services than their heterosexual counterparts (Dame, 2004). Linda Dame (2004) recounts a chilling story of a case she encountered as a social worker with the province of Manitoba. She was told that the 15 year old youth in question was considered the most difficult child in the system and when she first met "him" he was in the Crisis Stabilization Unit for his own safety. According to Dame, "I had reviewed the file before I visited the CSU, so I already know that this boy was in fact a transgendered male to female young woman and that she, not he, had been subjected to incredibly ridiculous and abusive case planning strategies for many years, if not throughout her entire young life. No note in the file referred to her transgenderism, and all notes referred to her as male and used her original male name, even though she had changed it years previous…The staff in the treatment home where she lived routinely ridiculed her and ignored the Child Advocate's Office direction to respect her chosen name, even after she launched a formal complaint."(2004: 2). The province of Manitoba spent over a quarter of a million dollars in two years housing this one teenager, who has since run away from Winnipeg.

In Canada, as O'Brien argues, "grave inequities in the treatment of lesbian, gay and bisexual youth by group homes and youth shelters" not only exist, but are reinforced as "pathological" and "deviant" through professional discourse (1994: 37). Verbal and/or physical harassment usually not tolerated by child care workers may be ignored or even encouraged when it is directed at queer youth. A common theme is the stance by group homes and foster placements that openly queer youth could not be placed in their programme because other residents would beat them up. This open discrimination is passed as an acceptable reason for denying placement of a queer youth in a home (Dame, 2004).

As suggested above, the experience of violence has also been linked to high rates of Queer youth suicide. A 1995 study concluded that Canada has one of the highest youth suicide rates in the world (Kroll and Warneke, 1995) and an earlier study indicates that Indigenous Canadians have the highest suicide rate of any racial group in the world (York, 1990). This combined with the statistic that Queer youth are six times more likely to attempt suicide lead Kroll and Warneke (1995) to suggest that suicide may appear as the only viable option in a situation where the lack of acceptance, experiences of discrimination, violence, stigmatization and fear of rejection are predominant features of social life.

A Word Of Caution On Discourses Of "At Risk"

The category of "at risk" has quite recently become one of what sociologist Nancy Lesko (1997) has termed "confident discourses" of youth in the social scientific, social service and social policy literatures. According to Lesko, the meaning of youth is shaped by shifting social, historical and economic factors. Social and scientific discourses contribute to shaping what meanings are attached to the category youth in any given place and time. Often the effect of expert discourses about youth is to place the privilege and responsibility on adults to explain adolescents. According to Lesko, the result is that "adolescents are emptied out, made liminal, and then reconstituted by scientific descriptors and schooling practices" (1997: 149). It is a process which gives clear positional superiority to adults over youth. This process is apparent in some aspects of the youth "at risk" discourse.

On the one hand, this "at risk" discourse has been useful in the bid to secure resources for groups of Queer youth that have been virtually ignored and/or demonized in the public sphere as a threat to social security and the future of national interests. This includes those "at risk" for suicide, depression, low self-esteem, homelessness, dropping out of school, teen pregnancy, substance abuse, criminal activity and violence. This designation has been a useful one for making the case for developing programming and services specific to Queer youth's needs relating to their higher than average rates of suicide, harassment and experiences as victims of violence (US Dept of Health and Human Services, 1989). In this regard, the "at risk" discourse provides an alternative framework for conceptualizing the relationship between young people and the social structures shaping their lives. In a time such as the current one, where neo-liberal social policies severely curtail the allocation of resources to support the welfare state, and where the individual is made solely responsible for the direction and outcome of their lives, the "at risk" discourse makes an alternative suggestion. It makes the case for social responsibility in providing the social services and resources such as education required to support Queer youth.

On the other hand, some commentators have pointed out how the "at risk" designation poses certain problematic limitations on understanding the experiences of Queer youth. As a highly racialized and classed discourse, "at risk" is often used as a euphemism for talking about social fears and anxieties that are projected onto young people of colour and/or working class youth. It is also used as a rationale for increased adult surveillance and regulation of marginalized youth. It is possible that through this discourse, the individualization of responsibility for social problems is rendered stronger. In this case, programmes and services for youth considered "at risk," are designed to enhance the individual's "choice" making or problem management skills. Encountering problems is thus considered a feature of poor decision making and risk management. The discourse hides structural barriers such as discrimination and limited access to job markets due to economic restructuring that marginalized youth encounter limiting their "choices."

Talburt (2004: 119) warns of another danger of reliance on the "at risk" discourse to address the needs of Queer youth. She suggests that this reinforces the associations of "gay" with "problem." Harbeck (1995: 127) cautions that an extreme and sole focus on suicide may replace one negative representation for another. Young people who are exploring their sexual identities may conclude that suicide is the consequence of being Queer. More broadly, Talburt warns that the "at risk" discourse can perpetuate essentialist views on who is really gay and who is not and of what different groups need. Young women who are not comprehensible within the terms of identity constructed by the binary discourses of youth "at risk" and counter-discourses of positive or healthy development, may be not be included in the social programmes designed to meet their needs. While Talburt urges us to refrain from closing down the meanings attached to healthy and "at risk" youth and to keep the categories open to new meanings, Cornell West (1996) underscores the importance of thinking about difference as a source of strength, rather than merely as a set of obstacles and impediments. By interrogating the meanings that get produced by the categories "at risk" and "healthy" as well as by examining the power relations involved in labeling, there may be a greater acknowledgment of the different kinds of victimization and risk as well as a focus on young women's agency in order to move beyond simplistic assertions of who and what an "at risk" victim is. In what follows, I explore some of the exclusionary practices queer youth encounter in schools, the media and in access to public space.

Exclusionary Practices At School

In her article, "What is this Thing Called Love?: New Discourses for Understanding Gay and Lesbian Youth," Deborah Britzman (1997) provides an interesting entry into how to think about the experiences of Queer youth in schools. Building on Martin and Hetrick's analysis (1988), Britzman outlines four related kinds of isolation affecting Queer youth: 1) cognitive isolation, where knowledge, practices and histories of Queer people are unavailable; 2) social isolation, where Queer youth suffer from social rejection by heterosexual youth and adults and are isolated from each other; 3) emotional isolation, where being open about one's sexuality is viewed as a hostile act, while being closeted labels one as anti-social, and 4) aesthetic isolation, where Queer youth must rearticulate received representations of heterosexuality with their own meanings while imaginatively constructing Queer aesthetics and style. Britzman quotes Joseph Beam (1991) who describes this process as "making ourselves from scratch," and Michelle Cliff (1980) who suggests this kind of identity work is about, "claiming an identity they taught me to despise." Within the context of schools, where identity making is a central, although not always clearly articulated feature of educational agendas, we can investigate the relationship between these four kinds of isolation by examining issues such as curriculum materials, social relations between peers, between students and teachers, and school policies.

The National Education Association (NEA) Report, "Grading Our Schools" (1999) shows how few school districts have policies that protect students and teachers from harassment and discrimination, provide staff with workshops and training, support curriculum that includes the lives and contributions of Queer people, and encourage the formation of groups such as gay-straight alliances. Similar results were published in the National School Climate Survey conducted by the Gay, Lesbian and Straight Education Network (GLSEN) in 2001. Writing about the Canadian context, an EGALE Report clearly states that much of the negativity Queer youth face begins in elementary schools (Boodram, 2003: 12). These include a range of incidents, such as harassment from peers and teachers, being called derogatory names, beatings, rape and occasionally murder. The response of Queer youth is often to skip school or drop out. Savin-Williams (1994) reports that Queer youth are more than four times as likely as their peers to skip whole days of school out of fear, and approximately 28 percent of lesbian and gay youth drop out of high school before graduating.

The Human Rights Watch Report (2001) includes an interview with one young woman who says that several months of verbal threats and other harassment culminated in physical violence. "I got hit in the back of the head with an ice scraper." By that time, she said she was so used to being harassed that "I didn't even turn around to see who it was" (2001: 42).

Queer youth of colour are more likely than white youth to report teachers as a source of harassment. And teachers are also more likely to single out students who violate gender norms than others (Human Rights Watch Report, 2001: 52). In one example cited in the report, a very young transgender student had a circle of friends who managed to protect her from her peers, but could not protect her from the teachers. Upset with her behavior, her teachers began to humiliate and embarrass her, telling her to "quit acting like a girl" (2001: 61). Thus, as Russell and Truong (2001) suggest the forms of victimization and discrimination experienced by queer youth of colour and white queer youth as well as those young people who push the boundaries of gender expression, may be different and of varying magnitudes. However, what is clear is that if teachers are perpetuating the problem rather than assisting to resolve it, it is unlikely that young people will turn to school officials for help when they are harassed. As one of the girls interviewed in the Human Rights Watch Report says, "we know not to say anything—it's like, unless you've been raped the administration doesn't want to know about it. They'll just say you're lying (2001: 52).

There is a double bind of inhabiting a Queer position in schools. On the one hand there is an incredible resistance to including Queer content in the curriculum. Yet, Queer people are subjected to the trauma and violence of publicly sanctioned pejoratives and are negatively marked within school spaces. As Loutzenheiser and MacIntosh (2004:152) put it, "what is invisible and markedly absent from curriculum is often rendered visible and saturated with meaning outside of classrooms."

School curricula often exclude representations of Queer people in areas where it is directly relevant, such as discussions of sexuality, family life and human rights. In addition Queer people and issues are often ignored within the broader school curriculum, in subjects such as history, literature and arts where, for example, heterosexual relationships are considered worth mentioning as relevant to a consideration of an historic figure's accomplishments or an author's work. According to Fisher (1999), crucial resources such as general information about Queer sexualities, coming out, same-sex relationships, and safe sex practices are often not carried by school libraries or counselors. In fact, schools may deliberately prohibit such materials from the premises.

A recent court case in British Columbia offers an example. In 1998, the court overturned the Surrey School Board's decision to ban the use of resources from lesbian and gay organizations and books dealing with same-sex parenting from their schools. The resolution to ban the materials was initiated by conservative parents with the support of an organization called, The Conservative Citizens Research Institute. Likewise, the case to overturn the ban was brought to court by members of EGALE BC, a parent, a student and the author of one of the banned books. Madame Justice Saunders overturned the two School Board resolutions. She stated that the one prohibiting the use of materials from lesbian and gay organizations was made without jurisdiction, was unclear and was made without relevant considerations such as the educational value of the resources being banned. She also ruled that the resolution prohibiting the use of the books was substantially influenced by religious considerations and contravened provisions in the British Columbia School Act prohibiting religion or overt religious influence in the conduct of schools.

The issue is one with far-reaching consequences for inclusivity in schools. Surrey is by no means the only Canadian school district in which these debates have surfaced. In 1997, for example, the Calgary Public School Board also banned books which they claimed promoted homosexuality. A spokesperson for a parents' group said that "a major concern is that a lot of the stories describe people who 'come out' as homosexual, which [the parents' group] finds inappropriate" (qtd. in Fisher, 1999).

Where school libraries do carry books about Queer identities, they are often shelved alongside texts on sexual dysfunction, child abuse, prostitution, and other socially stigmatized practices. Once found, a student may experience further complications accessing these materials. For example, parental permission may be required to take these books out of the library and there remains the stigma of carrying such books to the librarian's desk and the fear of exposure. These social practices are the remnants of the historic associations between homosexuality with forms of pathology and disease; the assumption of homosexuality as being unnatural; the stigma and illegalities of Queer practices; and the notion of homosexuality as contagious, where knowledge can infect innocent and unsuspecting youth.

Loutzenheiser and MacIntosh (2004: 154) argue that social change requires providing the means to interrogate power relations or the role of school cultures in limiting expressions of sexual and gender identities. They suggest further that inclusivity in and of itself is not enough to produce real change. As with anti-racist, anti-sexist and multicultural discourses there continues to be the danger that inclusivity borne of hetero-normative social institutions and motivations often results in assimilationist smoothing over of real difference and a covering up of larger ideological mechanisms of oppression.

This dynamic is visible in other everyday social practices within schools. For example, there continues to be a double standard for what is considered appropriate behaviour for same sex couples in schools as opposed to their heterosexual peers. The assumption is still that couples attending school dances will be male-female and that any public displays of affection will also be between opposite sex couples. In some parts of the U.S. some rather extreme situations have developed due to the Christian Right movements influence on school policy and government funding to schools. In one instance, students, with the backing of the American Civil Liberties Union, sued their Texas high school for the right to hold Gay-Straight Alliance (GSA) meetings, having been denied permission to do so by the school administration. The GSA was finally allowed to meet, but there were significant restrictions due to the Abstinence Only Curriculum policy shaped by Christian Fundamentalism which restricts all information on birth control and sex education beyond abstinence and sex within heterosexual marriage. As part of the settlement, youth were allowed to attend GSA meetings only with their parent's permission and they were not allowed to talk about sex at all. In fact, all discussion around sexuality had to comply with the restrictive eight-point abstinence-only-until-marriage definition. As Burns and Torre note, forcing a gay-positive student group to forward the notion that sex outside of marriage is harmful to self and society, constitutes an actual harm to youth who identify as LGBT, and/or who challenge the institution and definition of marriage. Thus, while the existence of the GSA group might constitute a sign of inclusivity, the conditions of its existence and the restrictions on what can be spoken there only reproduce hetero-normative power relations.

Exclusionary Practices In Access To Public Space

Access to public space is related to questions of visibility, recognition and inclusion in public life. Recently, discourses have emerged in some communities which link "quality of life" to increased police and everyday surveillance. In New York City, for example, Mayor Giuliani gained political acclaim for "cleaning" up the streets of the city. The effect of this campaign, according to members of the city's Audre Lorde, Center for LGBT and People of Color Communities, has been a marginalizing and criminalizing of those communities seen as threats to the "moral fibre" of the society. As a result, there has been a shrinking of public spaces due to the "re-development" of meeting places used by Queer people, and the diminishing of immigrant communities' workplaces through the outlawing of street vendors. Thus, public spaces have been privatized in raced, classed and sexed ways. Similar scenarios face youth on the streets, with an estimated 40 percent of homeless young people in major U.S. cities being lesbian and gay (Orion Center, 1986). Service providers working with this population report that has many as two-thirds have "discharged" themselves from out-of-home care—often for many of the same reasons that youths not in care leave home, including physical and sexual abuse and conflict over sexual identity (Clatts et. al., 1998: 135). In Toronto and other large Canadian cities, where a portion of young people living in the streets are Queer youth who have been kicked out of their parent's homes or have run away to escape homophobia, abuse, and discrimination in their families and communities, moves have been made to criminalize "squeegee kids" using the rationale of rendering the city safer for others. In the process, however what is eliminated is one of the few ways entrepreneurial youths living in the streets can earn a little money. Unquestioned in this process, is why certain people and communities—the poor, people of colour and Queer people—have come to be seen as more threatening than others and thus more susceptible to police surveillance. Homeless youth are also likely to be more prone to attracting police attention because there are few shelters that will accept youth residents and of those that exist, many are supported by religious organizations intolerant of sexual minorities. According to Dame (2004:15) transgendered youth are particularly discriminated against in emergency shelters and are often stripped of their gender identifying clothing and forced to stay as a member of their biological gender as opposed to their gender of choice. Thus, many may prefer the streets even if it means more encounters with the police. This includes the issue of the particular ways Queer youth of color are stopped and frisked as well as the ways transgender and transsexual women are targeted by the police on the assumption that they are all involved in sex work (Gore et al., 2001). The question of safety and protection for some becomes the issue of surveillance, harassment and abuse for others.

Exclusionary Practices In The Media

The media is one of the sites where there has been increasing visibility and a trend towards more positive representations of Queer people and issues. Images of gay life are more prevalent in North America than in previous decades, and as a result young people are able to associate themselves with 'alternative' sexual and gender categories at younger and younger ages (Human Rights Watch, 2001). Queer youth can read about or watch marches, protest demonstrations, gay and lesbian films, weddings, court cases, and if fluent in the "codes of closet," read obituaries of people who are Queer. However, the representation of Queer bodies in television shows such as *Queer as Folk, Queer Eye for the Straight Guy, Will and Grace, Xena the Warrior Princess, Buffy the Vampire Slayer* and the Canadian show *Kids in the Hall* (and *Kids'* Scott Thompson's *My Fabulous Gay Wedding*), are usually limited to the white, middle-class, urban, wealthy and able-bodied. The content of these shows also do not tend to take up questions of violence or to seriously address homophobic oppression. Nonetheless, the importance to young people of seeing positive images of Queer people is apparent in this interview excerpt with Dena Underwood a young African American lesbian. "I remember watching television and seeing a lot of stereotypical Black gay men but not very many lesbians. And I remember watching *The Women of Brewster Place*, on television and being excited that there were lesbians like in this movie and, that's really it" (qtd. In Spain, 2001).

In news coverage, positive representations as well as serious coverage of news stories on homophobic violence is rather limited. Gore et al (2001: 260) show how media coverage of violence against Queer people—especially transgender people—usually relies on hetero-normative representations and analyses. They further argue that their analysis shows that violence against male-to-female persons is not taken very seriously. Mendez (1996) reaches a similar conclusion in his discussion of media representation of Queer violence in intimate relationships. For example, he cites a *New York Times* article which included an interview with a survivor and was a sensitively written piece. However, the headline demonstrated that the news media remains a problematic site. It read "gays can bash each other too." As Mendez points out, using the term "bash" which is commonly associated with homophobic violence limits the way in which this phenomenon is understood, including the implication that there is mutuality in cases of gay domestic violence.

Access to public media spaces for the communication of issues and vital information for Queer youth also remains an issue. For example, the Calgary City Council has recently decided that a review be done on billboard advertising policies in the city. The review is the result of some complaints to the city objecting to a billboard advertising a telephone support line for Queer youth. The billboards, as well as signs in buses and malls, were sponsored by the Gay and Lesbian Community Services Association.

Thinking Through Responses To Exclusionary Practices

Critical race theory (CRT) offers some interesting and useful insights on the paradoxical nature of using, working within and rejecting a reliance on the courts or schools in the struggle for equality. These insights have also been paralleled by developments within queer theory. The limitations of the rhetoric in liberal civil rights discourse, as well as the versions of these discourses that have been used in other policy arenas such as multicultural education policies, has included its reliance on color-blind discourses that rely on assimilation as its end goal. CRT explodes the notion of color blindness or race neutrality, just as, queer theory explodes heteronormativity and sexual sameness. Within queer theory, Sedgwick's (1990) conceptualization of the terms of "minoritizing" versus "universalizing" has been extremely influential for thinking about the question of the meaning of sexuality and the process of creating social change. Minoritizing approaches frame the question of homosexuality as being relevant only to a small, distinct, relatively fixed homosexual minority. According to Britzman (1997), this approach shuts out the fact that identity is a social relation —that both homosexuality and heterosexuality are constituted in relation to each other. It is an approach which deems homosexuality as a separate and discreet category, relevant only to homosexuals. In contrast, a universalizing approach views the divide between heterosexual and homosexual as a construction and "as an issue of continuing, determinative importance in the lives of people across the spectrum of sexualities" (Sedgwick, cited in Britzman, 1997: 203). Britzman argues that if programmes and interventions are to be effective in working with all youth, they must take a universalizing view. The question enabled by this approach, Sedgwick states, is "In whose lives is homo/heterosexual definition an issue of continuing centrality and difficulty?" (1990: 40). The power of this question, Britzman suggests, is that everyone is implicated. "It theoretically insists upon the recognition that the quality of lives of Gays and Lesbians has everything to do with the quality of lives of heterosexuals" (1997: 203). Implicating everyone has the potential to disrupt the discourses which produce normalizing and regulative criteria for bodies, genders, social relations, and affectivity.

Interventions which will effectively address exclusionary practices need to do more than merely hope and plan for assimilation and acceptance on the basis of an argument built around sameness. Rather, programmes designed to create social change as well as the programmes to support Queer girls in surviving the discrimination and harassment they encounter will need to recognize, accept and celebrate radical difference and combat the ideological and structural features of hierarchical social relations producing oppression. Thus, effective interventions need to be designed around the concept of expanding the options for expressing, living and embodying a diverse range of sexualities and sexual identities. As Talburt (2004:120) argues, it is also vitally important to keep the categories of queerness open to new meanings. That is, she argues for the importance of avoiding narrow norms of who Queer youth are and what they need. In this way, interventions will be less likely to exclude young women who are not comprehensible within the terms of identity constructed by dominant discourses.

Girls' Lived Responses

In this last section, I would like to focus on the ways in which Queer girls have organized and resisted the pervasive experience of social exclusion, including violence, harassment and abuse. They have been a driving force for many of the positive political and cultural changes in recent years. As I discussed earlier, central to these changes is attributing Queer identities with positive and powerful meanings so that they may be lived that way as well. One young lesbian in Ussher and Mooney-Somers' study (2000: 194) describes her feelings,

> I love being a dyke it's sometimes I sit down like when I have time for me self in the flat like this and I scream and I think oh my god I'm a lesbian you know. It just hits me now and it's fab. It's fab since I've come out I can't relate to the person that I was before it was like two different people and I just sit down and I think who the fuck was that.

Beginning in 1996, youth activists in California have held Queer Youth Lobby Day, an event designed to bring political attention to the issues and concerns of Queer Youth. In 1999, youth played a critical role in securing the enactment of the California's Student Safety and Violence Prevention Act of 2000. In the same year, students in Naperville, Illinois, called on their district's school board to include protection against discrimination on the basis of sexual orientation policies (Human Rights Watch Report, 2001).

One of the more widespread developments, initiated by students is the formation of Gay-Straight Alliance groups in their schools. These groups provide peer support, information about issues related to sexuality and gender identity and work towards building community and a more inclusive school environment. One young woman interviewed in the Human Rights Watch Report (2001:110) says, "we held a safe schools workshop. It was a wicked good experience. We talked about gay issues, what we can do to improve schools, things like that. We have a case in our main entrance with a large rainbow flag. We have lots of fliers posted telling students where you can go, giving information on programs like NAGLY [the North Shore Alliance of Gay and Lesbian Youth]…We're going to try to put up pictures of us at Youth Pride. None of our fliers have gotten ripped down. We're not asking for complete understanding, just acceptance." The effects of such groups in schools are sometimes widespread. According to one young woman who was co-founder of a GSA in her school, "there has been a change in the general atmosphere of the school. There is an enormous awareness of what homophobia is, and that there are homosexual and bisexual students." (qtd. in Blumenfeld, 1995: 221). She adds that, since the creation of the GSA, teachers have attended workshops to manage their own homophobia and that of their students, and are learning how to help students who are struggling with issues of sexual identity. "People are now willing to interrupt homophobic jokes and slurs and now include sexual orientation when talking about diversity" (qtd. in Blumenfeld, 1995: 221).

As previously mentioned however, not all attempts to organize these groups are welcomed by school administrators and teachers. For example in September 2000, students prevailed over hostile school boards in California and Utah that attempted to deny them the right to form Gay-Straight Alliance groups, in violation of the federal Equal Access Act. California's Orange Unified School District settled a lawsuit with El Modena High School students, permitting their group to meet on school grounds and use the school's public address system to announce club meetings. Salt Lake City's School Board voted, in the same month, to permit student non-curricular groups to meet on school grounds, reversing a 1995 decision that had abolished all non-curricular clubs in an effort to prevent students from forming an Alliance group (Human Rights Watch, 2001).

Within their schools Queer girls have also challenged hetero-normative cultural practices such as school proms. One young woman, who was the first in her high school to bring a same-sex date to the biggest social event in her school, says, "I'm glad I did it for a lot of the closeted people at school. I think it was important for everyone to see that we could do it, and it wasn't a big deal" (qtd. in Blumenfeld, 1995: 221).

Queer girls have also responded by becoming politically active outside their schools. Some participate in State organizations such as Commissions on Gay and Lesbian Youth set up by State Governors in response to the growing concern over suicide amongst LGBT youth (Blumenfled, 1995). Others participate as youth representatives in demonstrations and marches, such as the historic "March for Lesbian, Gay and Bi Equal Rights and Liberation," which took place April 25, 1993 in Washington and local Gay, Lesbian and Bi Parades. One young woman who was at the Washington March says, "At fourteen, I felt like an outcast because of my bisexual feelings. I decided to be as different as possible. I joined the punk rock scene and became politically active. I went to gay marches, including the gay rights march in Washington D.C. The helped a lot because more of the time I have had to hold back being bisexual, but there I could just relax. I realized that there a lot more people who are gay than let on" (qtd. in Gray and Phillips, 1998: 130). Queer youth are also joining and creating groups which focus on culture as a site of resistance. One such group is the international organization Lesbian Avengers. According to Ussher and Mooney-Somers, who interviewed girls in a UK London based group, this is a non-violent direct action organization, whose central premise is high-profile, media-friendly, 'sexy' action to raise awareness of lesbians. They argue that becoming a member of this group provides a positive social identity, a sense of group solidarity, a source of role models, friendship and common goals. One girl in the group says,

> Now we're talking about a period like of time where I was beginning to be active in the Avengers, I started doing my own Zine, like about cartoons and stuff, I started having a social life, started having a life, I was—I was definitely much more much different, hugely different to what I was when I got there.

Conclusion

Excluded from the category "girl," from institutional sites including schools, from the media and public spaces, Queer girls encounter an inordinate amount of violence that may take many different forms including actual harm to their bodies, misrepresentations or absence of representations of their lives, psychic and spiritual damage. This exclusion has been met by systematic failure, with few exceptions on the part of the public school systems, legal systems, media and social services. Through acts of commission and omission, Queer girl's rights to safety and security have been violated. And yet, despite these hardships it would be a mistake to represent these young women as merely passive victims to a system that has neglected to recognize them. They have also refused the positions of marginalization afforded them by an indifferent and hostile society. They have joined organizations and when there were none to join they created them. They work with others to create changes in the places they live, in their families, their schools and in their wider communities. They have refused to be rendered invisible or to accept the negative stereotypes thrust upon them. Instead, they have worked to produce positive self-identifications and representations and to create the social conditions that will open up new possibilities for living life as Queer people.

Chapter Nine

Talking (Behind Your) Back:
Young Women And Resistance

Rebecca Raby

I have this teacher I really hate. I was in his class and he's like "yeah, you
should probably drop out of this." Totally screw you. Gone. So I dropped
out. That was awhile ago. Then last week, I was on my spare and I was
walking down the hall (laughs). And he was in there, in the hall and he said,
like "where are you girls going?" And we're like, "going outside." My friend
smokes, so she was going outside to smoke. And uh, he's like, "don't you
have class?" or something like that. I was like, I forget what I said, I said
something and I guess it was very sarcastic or whatever and he told me to
turn around and I said "no," he's like "come here" and I went "no," so I finally just went over there and he just got all mad at me because I was being
sarcastic or rude or whatever and I was just like, I hate you, well I didn't
say that. —Tracy (seventeen, white)

Is Tracy rebelling? Resisting? If she is resisting, then is this resistance narrowly directed towards the teacher who embodies authority and a prior rejection of her? Or
does the teacher stand in for a wider hostility towards school—where she wants to get
good grades but cannot seem to, where they are installing surveillance cameras which
she objects to and where the "jocks" seem to get all the breaks as her interview, taken
as a whole, suggests? And finally, in the end, is Tracy's rebellion or resistance simply
reabsorbed into acquiescence? For those of us interested in social change, resistance remains a useful concept, but it needs to be used with care. Sometimes the concept of resistance is used so broadly it is diluted: if resistance is everywhere, then what is not
resistance? Yet if only collective, directed actions, such as an open protest, 'count' as
resistance, then what other potentially subversive activities are missed? In particular,
how might such a narrow definition of resistance neglect the more private and yet still
resistant actions by teenage girls? I argue that how we define and identify resistance
reflects our theoretical location, particularly our understandings of power, subjectivity, agency and 'successful' social change. This position is outlined in the first section
of this chapter. In the second section, specific approaches to resistance are explored in
relation to teenage girls, primarily in school.

The young women's voices included in this chapter were collected through interviews with twelve teenage girls (and their grandmothers) on perceptions and experiences of adolescence, which included some discussion of household and school rules, and their reaction to these rules. Interviewees were located through word of mouth, advertising and announcements in university classes, a high school class and at a hostel for girls, in 2000 and 2001. The girls lived in Toronto, were either white or black, were born in either Canada or the Caribbean and came from a range of socio-economic backgrounds. They ranged in age from thirteen to nineteen. Seven of the young women were interviewed twice. Data were coded along themes of conformity and resistance. As the primary focus of this research was not school rules *per se*, the data is used here to explore theoretical positions rather than to support a conclusive argument.

Conceptualizing Resistance

There are many ways to conceptualize resistance, each of which is linked to distinct theoretical traditions and each of which affects how, when and where spaces of girlhood resistance will be identified. To examine this concept, we need to ask how power, subjectivity and agency are being defined, whether resistance must be conscious and articulated, what or whom is being resisted, and finally, what resistance entails.

What do we mean by power, the self and agency?
How we conceptualize resistance depends on differing understandings of power. Most discussions of power conceive of it in the modernist terms of dominance and submission in which power is possessed by the dominant group and wielded against the subordinate. Often dominant and subordinate are framed in terms of class and/or gender inequality although age-based hierarchies between young people and adults are also applicable. Ontario's zero tolerance policy in schools, requiring standard and inevitable consequences for rule infractions in the name of safety and discipline, might be seen as an example that fits well with such an approach to power. Yet there are others who think about power quite differently. For example, Michel Foucault (1978) frames power not as something to be possessed and enacted upon subjects but as a relation between people. While he identifies a concentration of dominant power relations in institutions and institutional authority, these are the effects of micro power relations in which power is productive and flows through all of us, e.g., through the language that we use, the way we move through time and space, and in our interactions with each other, so dominant and subordinate groups are less clear cut. Students govern themselves and each other, for instance, in their use of language and in classroom interactions. One way young women do this is through the deployment of hierarchies of age, maturity and 'coolness':

> Elizabeth (fifteen, white): I think it's not considered that cool to act older as in being mature in a not fun way, you know being kind of like not support-

ing people who want to just go and do fun things and stuff like that. Like I have a friend who is always jumping around and doing crazy things and some people are kind of like "what's she doing?" and "God, how old is she?" and that's being mature in a dumb way. It's not even being mature at all. You know what I mean, like trying to act above everyone isn't [mature].

Elizabeth's observations draw on fun to produce an alternative, arguably resistant discourse of maturity to counter institutionally supported hierarchies of age that are being used by other girls to govern peers' behaviour. Foucault considers resistance to be integral to such power relations, for "where there is power there is resistance" (1978: 95), but resistance in this example is about local, micro-struggles rather than the large-scale, collective, progressive or revolutionary resistance of a wider social movement.

Resistance implies a degree of agency or intention so we must also consider subjectivity (or the self) and agency, both of which in turn differ between theoretical stances. Modernists tend to see an acting subject present in our very beings—there is a core self inside us which acts. This self may respond angrily to experiences of subjugation which are imposed, for instance (Scott, 1990). Such responses also arise through consciousness-raising, or when we encounter contradictions between ideology and our everyday experiences (Hebdige, 1979). Modernists draw on an understanding of people as rational, internally coherent, acting and pre-discursive (meaning that our selves come before language, structure and culture), though unlike adults, young people are often understood to be in the *process* of attaining or 'discovering' this self. Others have countered that this position assumes the self to be "known and unproblematic across vast cultural and historical differences" (Gal, 1985: 412), thus naturalizing a particular emotional response (e.g., rage) and failing to recognize how a person's multiple investments can undermine their internal coherence.

Postmodernists such as Gal see people as *constituted* or created through language, therefore our selves are produced, and as our discursive contexts change, we also change—an unstable self is not limited to adolescence therefore but ongoing within changing circumstances and the need for shifting identities. Postmodernists would suggest that it is therefore difficult to identify those with power and those without, for we are all embedded in language and our subject positions shift within relations of power. Resistance may be everywhere but it is also hard to pin down. It may arise in the identification of alternative discourses such as Elizabeth's, or from the contradictions in the many discourses that govern and shape us.

Must resistance be conscious and articulated?

Resistance scholars must also ask if those involved in resistance are articulating local or structural oppositions or whether such motives are being imputed by researchers. Youth theorist Paul Willis (1977) suggests that working class English boys' resistance to middle class schooling is evident in their classroom (mis)behaviour, even though the boys do not specifically say they are resisting. Widdicombe and Wooffitt (1995) suggest that such subcultural theorists have, in general, neglected members' accounts of their activities. Studying punk girls, Lauraine Leblanc (2002) argues instead that in order for an action to be identified as resistance, it must be articulated as resistance by those involved. Yet a full disclosure of resistant intent is rare, and is complicated further when people present contradictory positions. Within my interviews, for example, some of the young women were overtly critical of their teachers and cultivated strategies to resist schoolwork yet at the same time had strong investments in their education and in pleasing their teachers. Mediating these positions, Giroux (1983) contends that to be defined as resistant it is necessary that an action involves a hidden or open challenge towards "underlying repressive ideologies" (288). Certainly either an appropriate interpretation must be provided by those involved, or the action must be interpreted through a rigorous examination of the relevant historical and relational conditions, recognizing at the same time that researchers' determinations of what is and is not resistant reflect their own investments, including their political and theoretical locations.

What or whom is being resisted?
This murkiness around resistant intent deepens when we consider targets of resistance: Is there a clear, dominant group being challenged, or are the targets of resistance more dispersed? On the one hand, resistance can have clear and distinct targets. For instance, resisting not only her mother's rules but those of the parents of her friends, Tracy cajoles her friends to stay out beyond their curfews. Then in another realm, she resists the advances of boys by refusing to go out with them at all. While each form of resistance occurs on different terrain, each can potentially be recognized as resistance. On the other hand, what might be resistance to one authoritative group may be acquiescence or conformity to another. When someone resists parental pressures to meet a curfew they may be acquiescing to the pressures of their friendship circle, for example.

One way to negotiate such categorizations is through the use of thick and thin oppositions (hooks and West, 1991) where thick oppositions challenge the more structural, organizational frameworks of society and thin oppositions involve critique but are located in everyday, cultural, micro-practices and not articulated in terms of a fundamental redistribution of power. West suggests that rap, for example, functions "in a thin oppositional mode" (40) because it does not translate into a political movement. Challenges may embody *both* thick and thin oppositions simultaneously, however (e.g., a challenge to the authority of the teacher may at the same time be a challenge to the middle class expectations of the school system), or disrupt one at the expense of the other. Further, in a similar distinction between resistance (thick oppositions) and contestation (thin oppositions), Aggleton (1987) implies a hierarchy of resistances, with contestations seen as less successful. This division neglects to consider the political links between localized and macro power relations, i.e., how Tracy's response to the teacher in the opening quote may also reflect resistance to wider power relations based on age, class, gender and institutional structure. If we assume a diversity of subject positions that we occupy at the same time, the multiple meanings behind any resistant action, and the fragmented and overlapping nature of oppressions or dominations, easy categorizations become complicated.

So then what is resistance?

As we have seen, easy identification of resistance is a difficult task. Is resistance necessarily linked to 'progressive' actions? What of peoples' resistance to progressive ideologies or discourses? Which actions count as resistance—does it depend on a determination of 'success'? How is success evaluated? Such questions are linked to definitions of resistance but also to a researcher's investments in other concepts as well, such as adolescence. Investments in certain discourses of adolescence influence whether their activities are ever identified as resistance, or whether they are explained as rebellion, for instance. In fact, rebellion was raised and naturalized in a number of my interviews.

> Jazz (eighteen, black): …there are a lot of teens that just aren't like that (in trouble a lot) and I don't think they should be looked down upon because all these other teens are being rebellious and lashing out and just hating the world, you know?

> Leah (fifteen, white): People are interested in (popularity, clothes, sex). People want to experience new things, want to experiment, be rebellious maybe.

Rebellion was linked to turbulent adolescent emotions, desires for popularity, and becoming adult. It was also used to explain dyeing your hair, becoming more or less religious, falling behind in school, missing curfew and sneaking off to dances. Rebellion, as both a descriptor of adolescence and an explanation for a range of activities that may take place during adolescence, is thus naturalized as an unorganized, spontaneous, even 'irrational' part of growing up. In contrast, resistance, which is rarely used beyond sociological, cultural studies and activist projects to describe the activities of teenagers (except perhaps in the realm of psychoanalysis), and especially teenage girls, is more often considered to be informed and deliberate, politicized and 'rational'. Consequently, the ease with which any potentially resistant, challenging or subversive activities may be labeled as rebellion undermines young women's agency and political legitimacy.

Indicators of "success" become particularly elusive in instances of accommodation or conformity, which may in fact be acts of resistance. As Öhrn (1993) argues, it is "possible to *use* a subordinate positioning in order to gain influence" (149), a strategy that might be particularly likely among girls and women. For example, Elizabeth describes how it is necessary to manage teachers, even if you think they're wrong.

> 'Cause, because if the teacher gets mad at you, I've never had this happen to me, but it's *so* much harder if the teacher doesn't like you. I know it's so bad,

you shouldn't have to suck up and stuff but for some people it's, the teacher doesn't like them, something happened on the first day and they put up their hand and said "I don't think we should have to do that" and then the teacher will say "Well, that's what we're going to do, so la la la" and then they're on the bad side for the rest of the year and you get kicked out more often for doing the same things people do and don't get kicked out. And it just doesn't look good so I wouldn't ever want to go argue with a teacher, ever.

She proceeds to explain how she will pretend that she likes her teachers. Here Elizabeth is conscious of the power relations in the classroom and chooses a technique that looks like conformity when it may in fact be resistant in its manipulation of the power relationship. Such accommodative practices may be experienced by the young women as resistance (Öhrn), but their effectiveness for creating social change is likely to be disputed and may therefore be rejected as resistance by others.

Operating within a modernist framework, Aggleton and Whitty (1985) are concerned about resistance in terms of effectiveness. As Aggleton elaborates in his later text (1987), in an effective resistance the dominating forces are successfully challenged, while a reproductive resistance inadvertently reproduces the *status quo*. When Tracy talks back to the teacher in the opening quote, for example, this could be seen as an example of a reproductive resistance as it reproduces assumptions of teenage rebellion and need for greater regulation. I expect Aggleton would list conformity as reproductive resistance (if resistance at all). The process by which we determine whether actions are resistant and whether they are successfully so, is affected by previously discussed positions on power, what is being challenged, and what is considered 'effective'—Foucault would counter, for instance, that *all* resistances in turn produce new power relations. Time is also a factor. Schilt (2003) points out instances in which girls acquiesced (to a teacher's sexism and to a boyfriend's sexual advances) only to later address these moments in their home-made zines, which are read and embraced by other girls, sometimes spurring them into "more overt political action" (82). Is this a sufficient challenge to transform acquiescence into resistance?

Despite various attempts to clearly identify kinds of resistance, which actions (and even more so, which desires, thoughts, or words) are considered successfully resistant is much more difficult to identify than some researchers assume and is clearly linked to the paradigm a researcher is working within and their political beliefs about how social change occurs. In my example of Tracy, I have been fairly open with a definition of resistance, giving myself the liberty to identify resistances when they may, in fact, not be intended as such and when, in the grand scheme of things, they may seem to accomplish very little. My own assumptions about power relations between teachers and students, men and women, and between parents and teenagers are evident here, as is my acceptance of a fairly broad definition of resistance and its localized articulation.

Forms Of Resistance

I will now turn to more specific positions on resistance, supported by two tables that draw on and augment Aggleton and Whitty's typology of resistance (1985). Table A summarizes a variety of ways that resistance can be expressed from a modernist position. Table B condenses a number of quite diverse approaches to resistance, each of which can be loosely categorized under the heading of post-modernism.

Resistance I: Speaking Back To Power

Table A: Modernist conceptions of resistance

Forms	Resistance as deviance	Resistance as appropriation	Hidden transcripts	Overt transcripts
Content	'Deviance' as a local, working class response to structural conditions. Unlikely to be articulated or organized.	Taking dominant symbols and using them in new ways to make a statement and to cope with structural conditions. Often ironic and articulated. C/overt strategies.	Hidden, indirect challenges to dominant group or authority. May be collective or individual. Local. Hard to police. May be articulated.	Overt, direct challenges to dominant group or authority. May be collective or individual. Articulated.
Examples	-vandalism -truancy -open and hidden transcripts	-punk girls -goths -Zines	-truancy -unengaged participation -not going to the prom -eye-rolling -Zines	-challenging the teacher or bullies -refusing to stand for the anthem -walk-out to protest school dress code -zines
Evaluation in relation to youth and gender	Some concern that trouble-making is glorified. Work has tended to focus on the activities of boys. May indirectly reproduce or accommodate dominant power relations.	Style central to current, Western adolescence (especially girlhood), yet this may also undermine resistant effects.	Little challenge to *status quo*, may be dismissed as apathy or deviance. May indirectly reproduce or accommodate dominant power relations. Likely form of resistance used by girls.	Often redefined and undermined as rebellion. Differential consequences based on intersecting identifications (e.g., gender or race).

Prominent among modernist conceptualizations of resistance have been traditional, critical cultural studies in which resistance has been identified among working class boys (Willis, 1977; Hebdige, 1979). This tradition can be divided into two categories: resistance as deviance and resistance as appropriation. The first is linked to the works of Phillip Cohen (1972) and Paul Willis (1977), the second to Dick Hebdige (1979). In the first category, boys' "deviant" responses which include truancy, fighting and vandalism, are seen as strategies to deal with the problems they face in dealing with the social structure they live in. Ironically, such responses are only partially successful as their actions in the end reproduce their membership within the working class (Willis, 1977). Willis also provides a good example of the contradictory manifestations and effects of resistance: "while resisting some aspects of dominant ideology in the school, the lads actively reproduced and elaborated other aspects of dominant ideology, such as the devaluation of women and girls" (Gal, 420). In response, Angela McRobbie (1978) in Britain and Jane Gaskell in Canada (1985) have offered research on teenage girls, also in the tradition of British cultural studies. McRobbie found that working class girls question women's roles, but without any associated conceptualization for restructuring these roles. Thus in *their* resistance to middle class schooling they embrace traditional femininity and the ideology of romance and marriage, a response which effectively reproduces their class and gender inequality. Both this and Willis' work draw on Marxist analyses of resistance, with the authors determining what counts as resistance, linking it to the subordinate position of lower class youth and framing it as an oppositional response to a dominant order (embodied in the middle class school).

The second form of youth resistance in cultural studies, according to Leong (1997), is appropriation as resistance, a position more reminiscent of a post-modern approach in which the meanings behind various symbols are contested. Dominant material objects and signs are appropriated by subcultural youth, then reorganized or given new meanings. This position theorizes youth as engaging critically with mass culture and changing it to make it their own, through the use of baby soothers at raves, and teenagers making, buying, selling and trading independent zines, for example (Schilt, 2003). This is, of course, a negotiated resistance in that aspects of dominant culture are both adopted and contested. Leong, however, is skeptical as to the success of such a venture in terms of 'real social change'.

These subcultural theories have been quite prominent in late twentieth century youth studies and reflect a modernist position in a clear division between dominant and subordinate classes. Further, each of these categories of subcultural resistance includes a valuable commitment to agency in the face of political inequalities, and a dedication to social change. In these conceptions youth imbue cultural material with new meaning and shape their cultural environments even in the face of limited resources and ideological domination.

James Scott (1990), also a prominent writer on resistance, draws on Foucault's understanding of power, yet his conceptualization of dominant and subordinate positions and his understanding of subjectivity are quite modernist. Scott's work provides a useful lens for examining the girls' resistance to the age-based power of adults that was evident in my interviews. Rather than being duped to accept domination, Scott believes that resistance is *always* found in relations between dominant and subordinate groups: sometimes it is open or overt and sometimes hidden. Open resistance is direct and visibly challenging to those in positions of dominance. Yet subordinates frequently mask their anger towards dominant groups, only to resist in actions that are evident in 'hidden transcripts,' to escape persecution by those in dominant positions. A prime example of this has already been presented when Elizabeth 'sucks up' to her teachers, even when she dislikes them, in order to get good grades. Another example of hidden resistance would be Jessica (thirteen, white) rolling her eyes behind the teacher's back. Öhrn (1993) found similar patterns in Swedish girls' apparent accommodation at school in which girls drew on gender-related expectations in order to achieve their ends. She found this to be successful for the girls to achieve immediate goals (but not for changing broader power structures) as long as such hidden transcripts did not become outright challenges.

Taylor, Gilligan and Sullivan (1995) similarly distinguish covert and overt resistance though they are concerned that covert resistance is more akin to retreat and therefore more alienating than empowering. Yet as Schilt points out, girls' overt resistance is rare because the consequences for girls who speak out can be too harsh and frustrating. She suggests that girls create an in-between space for themselves, what she calls 'c/overt resistance' "that allows girls to overtly express their anger, confusion, and frustration publicly to like-minded peers but still remain covert and anonymous to authority figures" (81). Schilt provides a compelling argument that girls' zines are an example of such resistance.

In my own interviews, resistance occasionally burst out of the "hidden transcript" into the public realm through clear acts of protest, though not in the collective, organized form some researchers might hope for:

> I: So when those other teachers at the gifted school say "you should know better" and that pisses you off, do you do anything or say anything?
>
> Angela (fourteen, white): …one time I snapped. It was at a different school…the teacher said that to me and I snapped 'cause I've been, I've heard it too many times and I started yelling. I'm like "just because I'm gifted doesn't mean you have to treat me any differently!" and the teacher just like, she just shut up.
>
> Jazz: [my teacher's] like "well if you have a problem you…you tell your mom to come and talk to me" and all my friends go "no no no, you don't

want Jazz's mom to come down here." [I said] "you don't want my mom to come here 'cause oh if my mom comes to this school you will no longer have a job, that's what I told her. You won't have a job, you will be out on the street with your dog." And I got sent to the office.

Scott suggests that overt resistance itself is fairly easy for authorities to identify and address while hidden resistance is more difficult for those in positions of dominance to tackle. Öhrn, however, found that teachers talked about having a more difficult time dealing with girls' overt resistance as they found it difficult to respond to given that it transgressed assumed gender expectations. Girls' overt confrontations ultimately received harsher punishment (than boys') and invariably the girls who were more likely to confront their teachers were working class (1993). Hidden resistance seems to be the preferred tactic for many middle class girls.

Scott's recognition that resistance can be both open and hidden is useful, for it recognizes that what looks like acquiescence may not always be acquiescence. His analysis also gives those involved in such actions the benefit of the doubt: that they understand their subordinate position and the need to resort to strategic tactics. Such strategy can also draw on skills to negotiate the differing positions of various authorities. The following example points to Rita's recognition that rules are enforced differently by teachers and principals, which she uses to her advantage.

Rita (fifteen, black): We do have rules like no bandanas…

I: No bandanas? [Rita's wearing a bandana during the interview]

Rita: Yeah…it's totally annoying because I like to wear my hair…like my hair's short and kind of sticks out and things and sometimes when I wake up in the morning and it's really sticking out I like to just put it in a bandana but I can't do that because of this rule…But sometimes I do it anyways, it's not like the teachers that have this rule but the principal, so if you can go and then as long as the principal doesn't see you, you don't get caught. So I still go sometimes and I wear a bandana and if they said anything I would just take it off.

Similarly, Jess points to the inconsistencies behind the application of rules towards certain students.

Jess: Yeah….She won't let me wear my [sun]glasses in class 'cause I usually wear my glasses inside and she'll make me take them off whereas it's against the rules to wear tank tops and Sarah, I sit at her table, she's probably one of the most popular girls in the entire school and Miss Averon lets her wear a tank top, she doesn't care. She just says "are you cold?" "No." "OK."

These examples underline young people's awareness of inconsistencies among authorities and their willingness to use such inconsistencies in order to challenge authority at both hidden and more overt levels—a negotiation that Scott's analysis recognizes. Yet Scott's analysis assumes that resistance is easy to identify (by the researcher). As I have noted, what I may deem resistance, another observer might characterize instead as teen rebellion, or impudence. Nor does Scott's position complicate oppositions between public/hidden, dominant/subordinate, and public/private: subordinate and dominant may shift and contradict depending on people's locations and intersecting identities. I have focused on hierarchical relations between teachers and students yet, as Jess' observations indicate, other forms of positionality complicate easy categorizations. Shifting locations of popularity, gender, race, age, class and so forth may be salient at different moments in such micro-interactions.

Resistance II: Disruptions

A postmodern position on resistance acknowledges that the self is constructed through discourse (or language). Here, resistance is oppositional but in a more sporadic, diffuse and localized manner than is expressed through organized resistance against a dominating force. While Foucault has been accused of under-theorizing agency and political resistance (Hall, 1996), in his later work he focused on the potential for such diverse, local resistances and alternative discourses. To this end, he was interested in denaturalizing dominant discourses and investigating technologies of the self wherein people can transform their bodies and conduct in order to attain certain ethical ideals, thus also transforming, or producing, their own subjectivities. In this section, however, I focus on several other theorists, namely how Michael Huspek (1993) and Judith Butler (1993) both look to language to locate and understand resistance. In turn, Jose Munoz (1999) uses Butler's discussion of disidentification to locate challenges to dominant power relations. The various positions examined are summarized in Table B.

Michael Huspek's theory of dueling structures (1993) asserts that while we are constructed through language, language also provides potential for resistance. Language constitutes us, though people are differently constituted based on diverse group or class memberships and must therefore negotiate between rival language structures. He frames this as an interdependence of languages and anti-languages. Anti-languages (like Foucault's 'counterdiscourses') are dialects that oppose "standard languages or 'high dialects" (1993: 15). On the one hand, anti-languages can be understood as resistant, with what is dominantly conceived of as negative often understood on the margins as positive: "When, say, 'bad, used by speakers of a subordinate class, takes on the meaning of 'good', the transformation indicates opposition: It is 'our meaning' against 'their meaning'" (Huspek, 1993: 18). On the other hand, languages and anti-languages are rival discourses, so it is in the interdependence and tension *between them* that subjects' agency and resistance arise.

Table B: Diverse post-modern positions on resistance

Forms	Linguistic	Disidentification	Strategic	Redefinition
Content	Gap between speech acts and how they are taken up (Butler 1993). Structures altered through speech and people's conscious negotiation of languages (Huspek 1993).	Taking or misrecognizing a stereotype or dominant image and *redeploying* it differently or disruptively (Munoz 1999).	Consciously "working the system" by strategically deploying pre-established, dominant labels.	Countering dominant definitions through exceptions or alternative discourses, which may slightly reframe and alter discourses.
Examples	Reappropriating hate speech. Negotiation of languages and anti-languages; "bad" vs. "cool" teens.	-Fruitloops -Driving station wagon to the prom (Best 1990)	-deploying discourse of 'experimenting' or 'emotional' teen to accomplish goals	-pointing out exceptions to generalizations about teens -redefinition of adolescence
Evaluation in relation to youth and gender	Flexible speech acts with relative newness to language. Yet resistance without agency? A formulation for inequality, adolescence and language yet dichotomy between language and anti-language.	Infiltrates and distorts dominant discourses, but localized and indirect.	Potential for co-optation and reproduction of categories. Hidden resistance.	Relative newness to language and idea of self-discovery may generate new definitions. Potential for co-optation and reproduction of categories.

Among other rival structures, we might consider adolescent girls as positioned within an interdependence of 'adult' and 'teenage' languages. Such a divide is complicated, of course, as adolescents occupy a marginal social status and yet at the same time adolescence is idealized, temporary and intersected by many other identifications (like gender, culture and class). One possible tension between dominant, adult language and adolescent 'anti-language' is articulated through the language and actions of 'coolness' a category that arose frequently in my interviews, especially as 'badness' was associated with 'coolness'. For Jazz, this offers up a language that may be alternatively read as resistance or rebellion (or both) and that challenges dominant, adult perceptions of ideal behaviour in order to gain peer popularity.

> Jazz: …like I wasn't "yeah I'm a bad teenager" because I actually wanted to be bad but I guess as a teenager being bad is kind of cool so it's just like let me try this and you know, it goes back to the whole popularity thing.

Such popularity is frequently framed by dominant discourses as 'peer pressure'. Jess, in contrast, while interested in being popular, resists 'cool' because of the uncomfortable links she makes between being 'bad' and being 'cool.'

> I: So then what makes somebody unpopular?

> Jess: I think if they don't smoke and that's a bad thing according to *them* [the cool group]. If they're like prudes, and they don't want to perform oral sex on a guy or any kind of that stuff then they're not cool. If they don't want to drink, then they're not cool. If they don't wear the proper clothes then they're not cool. All that kind of stuff.

In Jess' commentary, the language linking 'badness' to 'coolness' is also about concrete class markers (through clothing), age markers (through drinking) and gender inequality (through girls performing oral sex). Thus broader, unequal social structures bolster the anti-languages of adolescent popularity. With anti-languages so embedded in dominant social structures and 'coolness' in part linked to adult social practices, an easy reading of anti-languages as resistance is complicated.

For teenagers themselves, negotiating these rival structures, between the realm of peer relations and that of adult rules, can be difficult and generate various strategies of engagement. In another example, Vienna (sixteen, white) both critiques and consciously moves towards the category of 'cool' that's part of the 'teen world' she claims is quite separate from adults:

> …I feel like I can blend with the rest of them more now. Like I'm really in there…like at my school it's funny and I'm sure this happens everywhere, there's this whole sort of syndrome of "oh I have to be cool" and I guess that's always been around, but it actually is like cool, like mellow, like "oh yeah, what's going on," you know? And "oh yeah, I went to a party on the weekend, na na na na na" you know? And I'd never been like that before because I don't think anyone's actually like that, I think that it's really the facade that people put on because it's cool you know? And so there's, I mean that's really what's going on at my school, everyone acts like that. And sometimes I just want to scream at them "Aaah! Why are you doing that? You're not actually like that." You know it's so superficial. But I don't know, I feel like I can sort of roll with the punches now because I can act like that when I want to. I do feel slightly pressured to act like that because I

> wouldn't have as much acceptance if I didn't but it's kind of fun at the same
> time (laughter), to be just like "yeah I'm cool" (laughter).

Vienna's observations underscore the complicatedness of resistance. Cool may be considered an anti-language, yet one that some teens may attempt to resist (like Jess) or redeploy, like Vienna who is both critical, and accepting, of 'cool'. The gendered nature of cool is again evident here in the emphasis on detachment. Vienna is frustrated by this detachment but also gains pleasure (and caché) in being able to perform it.

In this sense, Vienna's resistance is also about deploying ambiguity so as to walk *between* the spaces of dominant and anti-languages. Similarly, Jazz, while using anti-language and adopting 'cool' throughout her interview, also uses her cool to espouse more dominant expectations, like finishing school:

> I just want to get high school over with so I can say I have my high school
> diploma you know `cause there's so many teenagers I've seen, even teenag-
> ers I know that are my age, even younger than me and they're not even in
> high school—can't even say they have ten credits and I think it's ridiculous
> because I think high school's just a challenge to see if you can get through it
> and I—a lot of people just give up.

For Jazz, this negotiation between dominant and anti-languages is also balancing between other pressures, between values associated with responsible adulthood and those of 'fun' teenagehood, between a white school culture and a resistant black culture, and between racist stereotypes and their disruption. Thus, in those moments when people have to negotiate between rival linguistic structures, we may be able to identify useful spaces of agency, negotiation, and resistance. While Huspek's approach provides a strategy for understanding resistance in terms of rival language structures, he nonetheless emphasizes a dichotomous relationship between languages and anti-languages; the insistence on this dichotomy may prevent him from seeing other potential sources for resistance, such as disidentification, examined below.

Post-modern queer theorist Judith Butler also focuses on language. She suggests that resistance can arise in the gap between what people say and how their "speech acts" are taken up, because there is no guarantee that they will be heard as intended. For example, hate names like 'queer' can be used by those who are the targets of such names in ways that re-appropriate and then apply them in new, more positive ways (Mills, 2000). Butler suggests that our selves are created through language and other relations of power, for these structures bring us into existence (Butler, 1993). But we can also exceed or alter languages and the power relations they reflect: we both 'belong to' and 'wield' power, thus we are able to change it, move beyond it, or use "power against power" (Mills, 2000: 270). The potential for resistance is embedded in our use of language and its vulnerability to being applied differently than intended.

Yet Butler argues that there is also a risk of social 'death' in resistance for if we come into existence through language, then to disrupt or transgress the categories, norms etc. of language (and therefore of power) threatens to dissolve our 'selves'(Mills, 271).

Might teenagers experience a unique relationship to the social because of their relative newness to language and because of social assumptions that adolescence includes experimentation and identity exploration? Adolescents may thus have both a greater investment in dominant language and yet also greater potential for disrupting it, allowing for resistance without as much risk of 'social death' as there is for adults. Teenagers may also be more flexible about inventing new language (and new subjectivities), while adhering to familiar features of language that already frame their sense of being. The invention of language variations, text messaging, and music or fashion alternatives may be an expression of this creative potential.

Butler's work on resistance has been criticized for presenting resistance as accidental, unintentional, and unpredictable rather than something that reflects any kind of agency (Nelson, 1999). Jose Munoz's (1999) notion of disidentification draws on Butler's work in a way that does imply agency. Munoz suggests that people can identify with dominant social forces, counteridentify (challenging the dominant but in a way that then still validates the dominant), or disidentify (working both with and against the dominant, transforming it in the process). When people disidentify, they take dominant signs, roles or discourses and then use them in new ways that disrupt the dominant message, creating something else, something previously unthinkable. Munoz describes disidentification as self-creation, a "survival strategy" for people who are in marginal, or minority, social positions and who consequently fail to identify with dominant positions. They thus need to develop strategies that will "activate their own senses of self" (5), especially through art, in order to cope with their marginality. While 'majoritarian' (dominant) subjects may find it easier to identify with dominant subject positions, people's multiple and conflicting identifications suggest that majoritarians can at times disidentify as well.

Disidentification may be identified in some youth art and performance such as Fruitloops, which is a queer youth cabaret that has been active in Toronto for the last several years, artwork presented by young women at the *Transforming Spaces* conference, and through some zine styles. In my interviews, such transparent examples did not emerge, perhaps suggesting the concept's narrow applicability to specific moments of conscious performance. On the other hand, if we broaden our understanding of performance, it can be understood as constant and on-going in all features of our presentation of self (Butler, 1990). To this end, several areas did emerge in my interviews that could be considered through the lens of disidentification.

Reminiscent of style as resistance (discussed earlier), in my first example, Elizabeth uses clothing to present an image of herself that disrupts expectations:

[In grade eight] I wore really strange things. I went home at lunch and made seashell banners and like draped them around myself and I think it was just important to me to really break out of, not just not wear what I was supposed to but *really* not wear what I was supposed to, it'd be like I know I'm doing this I know, I'm not doing what I'm supposed to be doing...I kind of consider it like a warning, like before I even open my mouth and I'm going to talk to people or whatever, I think it's like a preview...

Elizabeth consciously takes the emphasis on teen fashion and expression, but disrupts expected manifestations of it through exaggeration and anti-branding, challenging assumptions about how she should self-present within both teenage and adult circles. While providing a warning to others, Elizabeth's strategy can also be seen as a mockery of fashion.

In my second example, interviewees eluded some of the more dominant definitions of teenagers as hormonally driven or as social problems (Raby, 2002). They deployed the category of adolescence, specifically female adolescence, differently from what is being presented to them, focusing on themes like having fun, interacting with friends and enjoying a time of less responsibility—emphasizing their own versions of what it means to be a teenage girl. While in these redeployments some dominant discourses of female adolescence are reproduced (e.g., 'girls just want to have fun!'), others (i.e., teens as social problems or at risk) are refused or resisted.

Finally, I was drawn to a pattern of "strategic deployment" in my interviews. Rather than taking a dominant identity or discourse and redeploying it in new and unexpected ways, some of the young women used age-based expectations strategically, to negotiate social situations. This strategy might seem like accommodation and yet is intentionally subversive. Several of the young women I spoke to suggested that they take certain naturalized assumptions (e.g., that adolescence is a time of experimentation) and work with them, using the category 'adolescent' to engage in activities (or to lobby parents for financing of activities) that they suggest would be less available to adults. Descriptions of rebellious adolescence were also used to legitimize confrontation and aspirations to independence, arguing that their activities are simply natural.

Conclusions

This initial exploration of resistance and girlhood raises several key observations. First, regardless of theoretical stance, resistance among girls and young women is likely to be hidden or c/overt—subtle and located in private spaces of interaction. Schilt links this pattern to safety: gendered expectations and gender inequality create situations where girls risk too much in overt challenges. Middle class girls have also learned to present themselves as 'nice', which is incongruous with many conceptualizations of overt political action. If this is indeed the dominant pattern of girls' resistance, researchers are more likely to 'see' girls as agentic and resisting if they are recognizing hidden resistances and, potentially, working within a post-modern framework which seems to offer more latitude for subtleties of resistance in language. Forms of resistance such as disidentification may more easily elude easy cooptation or dismissal by dominant structures than organized walkouts or deviance as resistance, and they may be experienced as successfully resistant by the girls themselves. Yet the potential for such resistance to translate into concrete or dramatic social change is admittedly weak. Resistance through style, strategy and disidentification often seems individualized, private and fleeting.

Second, the dominance of style as the most articulated realm of resistance in my interviews is important to note [see Pomerantz in this volume]. Clothing was a frequent area of expression when interviewees were asked about school rules and violations, for instance. To what extent is this tendency gendered? How much is style a key site of resistance among youth? The importance of style has been frequently noted by those in youth studies and raises a key question: How can resistance through consumption and presentation of self, integral to dominant conceptions of femininity and capitalist subjectivity, be conceived of as resistance at all? Yet it is important to recognize the resistant potential (and intent) in style in order to recognize and value the agency and political engagements of young people, young women in particular, even if it might not look, at first glance, like resistant action and even if it is, ultimately, co-opted.

In terms of theory, some aspects of modernist theories of resistance are attractive: the subject is whole and thus has a clear source of agency. From this theoretical position, girls are situated as subordinate in terms of age and gender (and other potential identifications such as class, race or sexuality). Hierarchies are transparent and avenues for social change, while daunting and elusive, are evident. However, "researchers need to take cognizance of the more nuanced ways in which the ability to shape social action takes place" (Sharpe 2000:4), ways which allow us to identify a much broader range of resistant activity that may better incorporate actions in the lives of teenage girls. Theorists such as Munoz (1999) have attempted to address such nuances although their positions also encounter various criticisms, particularly as these conceptualizations fragment and localize resistance, leaving little potential to understand larger social movements. Ultimately, while modernist and post-modernist positions have quite distinct underlying assumptions, they seem to successfully describe different kinds of resistance, suggesting a need to further develop hybrid conceptualizations. Young women's resistance provides just one site for such explorations but also offers a unique vantage point due to the specific constructions and spaces of adolescence and girlhood that frame young women's experiences and actions.

Chapter Ten

"I'm Going To Crush You Like A Bug": Understanding Girls' Agency And Empowerment

Dawn H. Currie, Deirdre M. Kelly

The extent of feminist literature that associates 'femininity' with altruism and compliance makes it difficult to make sense of girl-inspired violence, exemplified in sensational but rare events such as the murder of Reena Virk.[1] One result is a backlash against projects to empower young women, propelled by claims that girls are already "too empowered" and that boys are now a neglected group.[2] In this chapter we treat such a backlash as reflecting, in part, the failure to fully understand girls' agency.[3] For the past decade, feminist research has portrayed girls as passive, emphasizing a lowering of girls' self-esteem as they experience puberty and problems such as disordered eating, hatred of the female body, and self-destructive behaviours (Pipher 1994). While we do not dismiss the well-documented, albeit small, drop in girls' self-esteem during their "middle years" of school (Kling et al. 1999), this literature can foster the view of girls as, inevitably, "victims" of girlhood.

Our study, *Girl Power*, is an attempt to understand the perils of adolescence through greater attention to how girls develop their own strategies to navigate the transition from girl to young woman (Schilt 2003: 92). We therefore explore girls' agency, expressed through the ways that they negotiate everyday life at school. By connecting agency to girls' subjectivity, we give primacy to girls' (rather than adult researchers') sense of "who they are" and "what they can be." When our research began we were not necessarily interested in peer-based violence. The early stages of fieldwork were designed to sensitize us to the kinds of issues that are relevant to girls at school. We were initially surprised by repeated stories of interpersonal aggression among girls. Referred to as "meanness," the girls maintained that this behaviour is uniquely female. In this chapter, we explore what Merten (1997) calls "the meaning of meanness" for what it tells us about girls' agency 'as girls.'

We begin our exploration with a discussion of academic and popular discourse that claims "relational aggression" as a girl-specific behaviour. We interpret meanness for what it tells us about the gendered nature of power in the highly competitive context of youth cultures. While our interpretation highlights what Connell (1987) calls 'emphasized femininity' as structuring girls' agency, we see it as enabling rather than limiting girls' behaviour. This interpretation has implications for how we think about projects to empower young women.

Our Interview Participants

To inform our interpretation, we draw on an analysis of semi-structured interviews conducted in Vancouver, British Columbia and environs with twenty-nine girls between the ages of eleven and sixteen years. We recruited girls through various referrals. The main criteria included simply a willingness to talk with researchers and parental consent. Efforts were made to ensure a mix of participants along ethnic, racial and class lines. The resulting sample for this chapter consists of eighteen Euro-Canadian girls, five Asian-Canadian girls, and six girls of other racial or ethnic identities. Seven girls came from working-class families, while we classified nineteen girls as coming from middle-class families and three from upper middle-class families. The schools attended by these girls also varied; most were located in middle-class neighbourhoods, but white students did not form the majority at all of these schools.

Meanness As 'Relational Aggression'

As Artz (1998: vi) notes, the vast majority of literature on school violence fails to address girls' agency, perpetuating the belief that violence and delinquency are exclusively male behaviours. This belief is supported by feminist contentions that girls, more than boys, tend to avoid conflict and to resolve moral dilemmas in ways oriented to the preservation of relationships (Brown and Gilligan 1992). If girls' experiences of violence at school are considered, they are likely to be included in terms of sexual harassment. Girls' harassment of each other—if discussed—is characterized as "lateral hostility," "common when members of subordinate groups feel helpless to change the conditions that account for their unjust situation" (Larkin 1997: 71). Chesney-Lind (2002) observes that while researchers took note of girls' aggression decades ago, the scholarly investigation of girls' non-physical aggression and its connections to middle-class, White femininity is much more recent. As Simmons (2002: 69) notes, "The day-to-day aggression that persists among girls, a dark underside of their social universe, remains to be charted and explored. We have no real language for it." Thus, naming "relational aggression" was the first step in recognizing girls' abusive behaviour.

For writers like Simmons, relational aggression refers to "acts that harm others through damage (or the threat of damage) to relationships or feelings of acceptance, friendship, or group inclusion" (21). Relational aggression is closely related to indirect aggression that includes covert behaviour, such as spreading a rumour, that allows the perpetrator to avoid confronting her target, and to social aggression as behaviour that intends to damage self-esteem or social status within a group through practices such as social exclusion. Simmons found relational aggression among girls "epidemic in middle-class environments where the rules of femininity are most rigid" (22). This is because stereotypical femininity emphasizes the importance of relationships in women's lives and negatively sanctions women's competitive behaviour. "Good girls" spend their childhood practicing caretaking and nurturing roles, especially through the friendship networks that allow girls unrestricted access to intimacy. They are socialized away from conflict and expressions of direct aggression. However, girls are at the same time socialized to be empowered, so that:

> ...when anger cannot be voiced, and when the skills to handle conflict are absent, the specific matter [of conflict] cannot be addressed. If neither girl wants to be 'not nice,' the relationship itself may become the problem. And when there are no other tools to use in conflict, relationship itself may become a weapon (31).

Simmons attributes the psychologically harmful consequences of relational aggression to girls' fear of isolation. She argues that because relationships play an important role in girls' social development, fear of abandonment lays the ground for "a different landscape of aggression and bullying [than for that of boys], with its own distinctive features worthy of separate study" (30). Given the dynamics of in/exclusion that motivate girls' behaviour, cliques do play an important role in the "politics of friendships." However, she generally discusses girls' behaviour in terms of their lack of skill for inter-personal relations rather than group dynamics. Thus girls' agency is framed within a negative discourse about what girls' lack, an approach we find problematic.

Like Simmons, Merten (1997) is interested in understanding how girls use covert forms of aggression to manipulate friendship networks. Discussed by the girls in his study as "meanness," he connects this behaviour to competition for popularity. The girls in his study were competing to become or remain popular, a concern that he claims is "nearly ubiquitous among junior high school girls" (176). He addresses the seeming contradiction that although one might expect girls who openly compete for membership in the school's most powerful clique to be considered both mean and unpopular by classmates, the opposite was true. In his school, aggressive girls were popular and, in fact, girls had to be aggressive to become popular. To understand this paradox, Merten considers both the dynamics of popularity and socio-cultural themes. What he finds is a relationship between popularity and meanness:

> Both meanness and popularity had hierarchical aspects and implications. Popularity was an expression and a source of hierarchical position. Furthermore, popularity could be transformed into power, which was also hierarchical. Like popularity, meanness could also be transformed into power.

Hence, power was a common denominator between popularity and meanness (1997: 188).

To Merten, meanness is a "discourse about hierarchical position, popularity, and in-
vulnerability" (188). When something highly valued (such as social power) cannot be
openly expressed, alternative forms of expression are often invoked. Meanness results
from a failure of the culture to allow hierarchy to be explicitly celebrated; it provides a
way for girls to covertly express and experience the feelings of personal power and in-
vulnerability that make popularity so prized. In the end, he links the socio-cultural
construction of meanness to a complex conjunction of fundamental, but often tacit,
issues in mainstream American society (189). Thus, meanness can be seen to result
from the suppression of discourses about tacitly recognized hierarchies.

Merten's work encouraged us because it places girls' behaviours within the everyday dynamics of school hierarchies that regulate adolescent statuses. However
Merten, like Simmons, seems to imply that the gendered nature of this process results
from girls' socialization into an idealized femininity that emphasizes middle-class
"niceness." By implication, girls can be seen as needing to "unlearn" bad behaviours
such as gossip and name-calling, a commonsense suggestion that appeals to concerned adults. As Davies (1989: 6) notes, within socialization theory, the person doing
the socialising—in this case, a teacher or parent—is understood as the active agent. In
contrast, we wanted a way to understand how school-based cultures offer resources
that make the gendered identities of girlhood not simply possible, but also valued by
girls. Valerie Hey (1997) inspired deeper theoretical insight: while focusing specifically
on girls' behaviours, she gives greater emphasis to the heteroreality of school cultures.
As she notes, "the linguistic presence of the patriarchal world in girls' talk alerts us to
the need to theorize girls' relations with each other as *invariably* structured through
assumptions of hetersociality and heterosexuality" (15). While boys may not be physically present as girls negotiate friendship cliques, they sometimes only need to be
present in girls' heads. "In a misogynistic [and heterosexist] world, girls learn to assign
low worth to women and to believe that their greatest importance lies in commanding
the attention of males" (Chesney-Lind 2002: 21).

Following Hey, we explore how relational aggression operates in the service of
constructing (and possibly resisting) the heteroreality of youth cultures. We are interested in how the meanness of girls' everyday behaviour can be understood as a form of
subjectivity and exercise of power. Lacking economic or political power in the school
setting, the one kind of power adolescents do possess is the ability to create status
groups. It is therefore "not accidental that teenagers come to be obsessed with status
systems" (Bettis and Adams, 2003: 129). In this chapter we characterize these status
systems as a discursive economy based on a heterosexist and misogynist currency.

'They Were Just Being Mean': The Discursive Economy Of Meanness

As explained by fifteen year old Emily (Euro-Canadian, middle-class),[4] at school, group affiliation is central to one's social identity because "most people don't define us for who we are, but for who we hang out with." It is not surprising therefore, that processes of in/exclusion dominate peer interaction. Like many other girls, although thirteen year old GG (Euro-Canadian, middle-class) claimed that school can be "fun at times," she also found it "hard because of all the different groups and stuff and trying to fit in." During her interview with GG, Vikki (also thirteen years old, Euro-Canadian middle-class) recounted such an interaction between GG and their friends: "They kind of left her [GG] there without even giving her an explanation. And she was crying. And she came to my house. And I remember telling her 'It's OK" and stuff,' and 'It will be all right' and 'They must have done it for some reason.' They were just being mean."[5] GG was not alone: Being the "odd girl out" was a painful memory for a number of girls. Fourteen year old Erin, for example, recounted a time when, for no apparent reason, her friends abandoned her at lunchtime:

> And they said 'We'll meet you in the courtyard at lunch when lunch starts.' Like, it was a big deal—I had just finished counseling them for like a month about breakups and stuff and they decided they would go to McDonalds instead. And that really bothered me. It was a big problem because Arnie would bother me about it. He'd be 'Like your friends ditched you for McDonalds!' (Euro-Canadian, middle-class)

No matter how inconsequential such conflicts may appear to adults, they influence an adolescent's growing sense of Self. Theoretically speaking, we saw peer groups as collectivities that sustain discourses that orchestrate interpersonal interaction; through them, teenagers make sense of the world and their place in it. We wanted to know how the dynamics of these groups affect girls' subjectivities as their sense of "who I am" and, following from this, "how to be a girl." Although youth cultures have been the subject of extensive research, most of this attention has been directed to boys' groups. Against the legacy of treating girls as incidental to boys' agency, our research focuses on girls' same-sexed cliques, small, tight-knit friendship groups of girls who "hang around together." Not surprisingly, these groups were composed of classmates so that networks were organized by grade levels.

Racialization was also important in group formation, especially when differentiating groups:

> Well, we have geeks which don't associate themselves with people really very much—they just read at lunch and stuff. And then we have—I'm not trying to be racist 'cause I'm not, but there's a lot of Chinese people in our school and there's a group of them who don't really associate like with other people. They just stay as a group. And then there's the popular people* (Vikki).

Like most of the other girls, fifteen year old Amanda, herself Chinese-Canadian, claimed that racialized segregation is a matter of 'language' because at her school the Chinese-Canadian students "don't really talk much, and they have their own little group. They like don't speak English and stuff so then they can't of course communicate with other groups. So then they just stick with their own kind."* Because the emphasis on English fluency 'naturalizes' divisions and segregation, most of the girls discounted racism as important to group dynamics. It interested us that, with very few exceptions, racism did not emerge in girls' descriptions of 'meanness.' Even when fifteen year old Kate—of 'mixed' ethnicity—was singled out because of her 'colour,' she did not see this treatment as mean:[6]

> They're like 'Oh. You're brown but not—but they're not mean about it. They're never really mean people…It's like "Oh you have brown skin. You know, "You're this" or "You're that" just because they're being dumb at the time. Or they're just mad at you. But nothing like "Oh, because you're brown you're bad or you're unacceptable to be with." Nothing like that.

Moreover, in contrast to the racialized segregation that characterized the larger school cultures, most of the friendship cliques interviewed contained a racial and ethnic mix of members. Here we do not claim that racialization is unimportant in friendship dynamics among girls; rather we explore why meanness was reserved for the gendered behaviour that governs same-sexed grouping of girls. Maintaining group boundaries by separating "us" from "them," meanness is about the application of labels that do not simply distinguish between "true friends" and "false" girls, but also between girls who are "cool" and "losers," popular girls who are "pretty" and girls who gain boys' attention because they are "sluts." Meanness embraces a range of practices that include sarcasm, ridicule, name-calling, gossip and, perhaps ironically, "the silent treatment." As a discursive practice, the very act of naming structures the perception that social agents have of their world, thus helping to establish the structure of this world (Bourdieu, 1991). Within this context, several girls claimed that one of the best things about being a girl is that girls can be "bitchy."[7] Fourteen year old Jordan (Euro-Canadian, middle-class), for example, described "cat fights" with girls in younger grades: "It's like, 'Did you hear that she got with somebody?' 'What? Who are you to be saying this?' 'It's not like you were there. How do you know what happened?'" As thirteen year old Shale (Euro-Canadian, middle-class) explained, "It's like an image thing. If you can't be a total good girl, it's cool to be the bitch."

Experiencing this behaviour on the part of "popular" girls in their school, other girls insisted that meanness is gendered. Riva (Iranian-Canadian, upper middle-class) for example, denied that boys acted in similar ways: "maybe they talk behind people's backs but they don't show it as much or they're not—they don't—I don't know. If you say 'Hi' to them they say 'Hi.' But girls can be really cruel." Understanding girls' agency in school cultures therefore required us to come to terms with the dynamics of meanness associated with 'girl culture.' Like Riva, we see meanness as an exercise of power. This exercise can take a number of forms, but typically it involved ridicule and sarcasm about girls' physical appearance:

> Well, Kathy has this really bad problem—she thinks she's fat but she isn't. And her own boyfriend keeps saying that. And they're always bugging her about it. And then Melissa, she thinks she's really ugly, but she isn't—she gets bugged about that a lot. And I don't know. With me they don't really have anything to bug me about, so they make something up. (Twelve year old Liv, Euro-Canadian, working-class)

As Liv suggested, being called "fat" was a common form of name-calling. Girls often teased each other about their weight, especially if they wanted to hurt one another. For example, GG took delight in the idea that some of her classmates would soon enter puberty:

> Like they're both really skinny. And just like I'm waiting for the day when —it sounds mean but—when she starts putting on pounds like she does. Like I'm more chunky than her. I'm like— so she says it as a joke but it still gets to you. Like 'cause a lot of people tease her about being flat [chested] and I'm always there to support her, but she sometimes calls me like a cow and stuff and I'm like "Where did that come from?"…They feel bad about themselves so they have to put down others to make themselves feel better. Also 'cause I think, you know, if they want to make you feel bad that is something you can say—I could totally bring down someone [by talking about her weight].*

The girls' use of this form of ridicule reflects their knowledge that boys prefer girls who are skinny. Fifteen year-old Brooke (Euro-Canadian, upper middle-class), a member of the 'popular' crowd at her school, heard the boys discussing her classmates' weights:

> I hear them a lot, pointing out some of my friends' weights. They'll just be like 'I need a girlfriend.' I'll be like 'Go out with Cindy.' And they're like 'No way!' And I'll go like 'Why?' 'It's just too—she's too big for me.' Kind of like that. You can just tell that someone skinny over someone not as skinny, the skinny one would get the guy.

A perhaps more severe, but also common, form of ridicule is sexual name-calling. The most damaging name was being called a "slut." Sexualized insults often accompanied fights over boys, as evident in this exchange among a group of girls:

> Lydia: We were going out, seeing each other but it was kind of secret. And then this girl found out that I went out with the guy I liked before. And

then she was talking to my brother in the cafeteria. And she goes 'Oh my god your sister is such a slut.' And then my brother told me. And I was like 'I can't believe she said that.' Like, you don't say that to someone older than you, right? because—You don't say that even if—but she thinks she is all hot and stuff and whatever. And we just like—

Jordan: She's ugly.

Lydia: Yeah. She's been gone around. She's—

Forsyth: She is the high school bicycle.

Jordan: She is a walking STD…Ever since then we've been like "Oh my god I smell herpes" when she walks by. And we would like stare her down.* (all fourteen years old and middle-class, one African-Canadian and two Euro-Canadian girls)

A lot is at stake in this kind of name-calling. As Brooke told us, "if word of mouth spreads, people think you're something that you're not." Thirteen year-old Jessica explained that girls "work hard to get certain reputations and they work hard to keep it." In fact, "one girl left our school because she couldn't stand her reputation…She was always getting rude jokes thrown at her over the Internet and all that stuff. And she just couldn't take it anymore and so she left" (Euro-Canadian, upper middle-class). While name-calling could start as conflict between individual girls, meanness is amplified through group participation in gossip. Eleven year-old Missey (Euro-Canadian, middle-class) described gossip as "a bit of a problem": "Like, if I said something to Anna about, say, Sally. It's like if Amy, say, told Carol, then it becomes a problem because people find out and then eventually Sally would find out. And then it becomes a big thing."* As explained by Riva, gossip is linked to the maintenance of a specific friendship network which, in her case, was threatened by her relationship with a guy:

I was pretty good friends with her and then one of the guys from my class were getting really good friends [with me]. It wasn't anything big. And she started—…Well, she was starting to talk behind my back and telling everyone I liked him. Like I would hear from people 'cause people would come and tell me everything and I knew she was doing it. Like one of her friends would come and tell me everything she said. And then I told her and I'm like 'Why would you do that to me? 'We were good friends' and whatever. She said she just felt like it. Like I had forgotten about her by being close to him.

Perhaps ironically, being ignored was not necessarily a positive experience. Meanness could be exercised as "the silent treatment" which, for Riva, meant being snubbed:

One of my friends who's in the popular group—and we were like really good friends—sometimes if she is with somebody else, like she kind of ignores me. And if I ask her something like she gives me a one word answer and she goes away. Stuff like that just kind of makes you upset. They're just so two-faced and they just treat you however they feel like treating you at that time. And that kind of brings you down.

In summary, "meanness" refers to acts of ridicule, name-calling, backstabbing, gossip and social exclusion. Simmons (2002) describes this behaviour as girls' use of friendship as a weapon. While we agree that meanness operates through friendships, we see girls' meanness as an expression of the discursive economy of peer culture. Within that economy, meanness positions the 'other' in a peer hierarchy through a process that robs the 'othered' of control over defining "who she is" and "what she is all about." As a discursive phenomenon, expressions of meanness have the potential to determine a girl's status in the eyes of her peers. Such positioning goes beyond the discursive realm, however, because it regulates membership in peer groupings. It locates individual girls in a gendered economy where currency comes through resources associated with what Connell (1987) calls "emphasized femininity." The resources of this economy include being pretty, being skinny, and behaving in ways that win male attention. Meanness regulates membership in the prized clique of womanhood by controlling (or attempting to control) claim to these resources; as a consequence it polices the boundaries of idealized femininity through surveillance by the male gaze (see Hey 1997). Meanness testifies to the ways in which youth culture, although a sphere of adolescent agency, is mediated by larger societal norms of heterosexism and sexual competition.

How emphasized femininity gives meanness currency becomes obvious in the case of popular girls. As in Merten's (1997) research, popularity was universally associated by the girls in our study with meanness.[8] Despite the fact that girls attended a variety of schools, popular girls were identified as the girls with the power. Thirteen year old Rose (Euro-Canadian, middle-class) was emphatic: "Whenever I think of the word 'popular' I think of people going 'Oh my god, I don't like your clothes. Go away!'"* Fourteen year-old Beverly (Chinese-Canadian, middle-class), for example, complained that popular kids "like to make fun of the unpopular people. Because, like they dress weird or they can't talk like, you know. If you're from Hong Kong, somewhere like that—'You have an accent!'"* Like Merton, we want to know why meanness, a trait despised by so many girls, is associated with popularity as a prized status. In order to solve this riddle we asked what gives meanness currency in the discursive economy of peer culture.

'The Power To Squash People': The Currency Of Meanness

The designation of peers as "popular" is a consistent finding in adolescent research (Simmons 2002). Girls in our study distinguished between two meanings of "popular." They used the word to refer to both kids who were well-liked by their peers as well as members of the "ruling" group. However, as an implicit category in girls' talk, popularity was not always easy to define. For example, Vikki explained "there's the sort of popular people, but they're not—they're not like *not* popular, but they're not *popular*. And then there's the popular people who like go out, and they *do* stuff."* The two meanings of popularity are actually at odds. On the one hand, the girls employ popularity to signal being well liked by peers. On the other, popularity could be used to designate "cool" kids who, in the words of Vikki, 'go out and *do* stuff.' We limit this exploration to the "ruling group" meaning of popular (a meaning contrary to the common sense definition of the term), which we indicate by capitalizing the word from this point onward. Membership in the Popular girls' category is important because, according to GG, if you're not popular, "You're just one of those *other* people." At the same time, being "cool" does not necessarily signal being liked by peers because: "If you're popular there's so much gossiping and like backstabbing, whatever. You know, people don't like people. Then those people who aren't liked don't even know it…They look down on them as if they're not worthy of walking past them, or whatever. That's just like 'Eew'."* (Christine, sixteen year old, Euro-Canadian, working-class, and Kate, fifteen year-old, Euro- and Indo-Canadian, working-class). Although most girls did not like this behaviour, like Riva many simply accepted the contradictory dynamics of Popularity: "I don't even know why they're popular. But that's the way it is."

Although the girls in our study attended a range of schools, their descriptions of Popular girls were consistent: above all, "you have to be cool. And it's hard to say what cool is, but you have to like wear the right clothes and talk the right way" (Liv). Popular girls had to look "perfect," "you know, like all the movie stars and stuff like that. You know, they're all like 'Oh, I'm so fat' and they diet and stuff like that. And then they just get more skinny. And, yeah. I guess that's their whole image" (thirteen year-old Vanessa, Euro-Canadian, working-class). According to fourteen year-old Anna, to be Popular "You have to hang out with the right crowd every day, even though you want to hang out, I don't know, with somebody else." (Filipino-Canadian, working-class). And you have to "keep up" your reputation because "It's like if you do even one little thing wrong, it gets talked about everywhere"* (Vera, fourteen year old Chinese-Canadian, working-class). Virtually every description emphasized that Popular girls are pretty and "not fat." Fifteen year old Mia explained: "They're tall, skinny. Yeah, they tend to wear a lot of like low slung jeans, tank tops that bare their belly a lot…Not all of them are blond but [they] all have long hair" (Euro- and Chinese-Canadian, middle-class). The result is that if a girl sought Popularity, she would have to look and be a certain way. According to Liv it is a combination of dress and the "right" attitude: "It's the clothes that they wear, and their personality. Like if they're not, if they don't go out with anybody or something. Or they don't *want* to go out with guys yet, then they're not considered 'cool.'" A member of the Populars at her school, Brooke argued that "basically, the more guys you know, the more like popular you are." When asked how to maintain Popularity, she replied "Date a certain guy. Not date certain guys. You know. Just hang out with the *right* people, basically."

At virtually all of the schools, girls claimed that having attention from boys is a source of power. At the same time, gaining attention from boys "the wrong way" could earn even Popular girls the label of "slut." The wrong way was often—but not always—through sexualized appearance rather than behaviour. Fourteen year-old Amelia (Euro-Canadian, working-class) described her classmate as a slut because "She goes out with guys, and the way she dresses. She usually wears like these really, really short denim dresses with a denim tank top on and stuff like that, right? She wears lots of makeup and stuff. She tries to make herself pretty." The line between everyday practices of femininity and "being slutty" is very fine. Despite the dire consequences of their labelling, girls' descriptions could be contradictory: "Like, low cut tops and uhm. I don't know…I think that low cut tops are bad, but I don't see anything wrong with showing your stomach. There's nothing revealing about it" (Liv). To us, the distinctions seemed to rest on girls' agency. For example, Amelia explained:

> Amelia: She thinks she's pretty and stuff like that, right? And she'll walk past a couple of grade 10 guys, and then she'll look back and I'll see them glancing at her and stuff like that. Or she'll stand there and she'll start talking to someone else. A whole bunch of guys will be just staring at her, right? It's disgusting.
>
> Shauna: Which part is disgusting?
>
> Amelia: Just *her*. The way she dresses.

The girl in question broke unspoken "rules" about just how much agency girls can express in their pursuit of Popularity. It also shows that girls without the "right looks" can use their sexuality to gain access to the Popular crowd, a tactic described by Brooke. She claimed that: "with girls, you can't—like you can't really get *rejected* from a guy. I mean, like…You know. Like if you're not popular, and if you're not like pretty or whatever, then uhm. Then you can…Like you can get with someone and become 'easy,' kind of." Brooke called this strategy "getting in the back door": "it's a way you get, uhm, kind of *known*. It's a way, a back door into getting into certain groups of people. Because then, if you hang out with like a popular guy, then you'll hang out with all the guys' girlfriends."

Getting "in the back door," however, may not be as easy as it appears. Among other things, Popular girls kept their distance from other girls:

> Like the Popular girls walking down the hall, they don't look at anyone. They don't smile at anyone. They don't say 'Hi' to anyone, for some stupid

reason…It makes other people feel like they're less of a good person, or whatever, which is just totally not true. And like, makes them feel small…I see someone saying 'Hi' to a Popular girl and they just kind of like 'Hi' and roll their eyes at them and walk away. That's mean. (Riva)

In fact, Vikki claimed that some kids are afraid of Popular girls: "She doesn't seem like a bully, but what I've heard, there are some things that she's done that are really nasty. So a lot of people are scared of her. So she kind of finds she's like on top of the Popular people."* Twelve year-old Liv, member of the Popular girls at her school, did not try to hide her unkind treatment of other girls from us. In fact, she bragged, "we're kind of at the top, like the most popular, most known people. But like that doesn't mean that we get along with everybody. Like I know a lot of people that don't like me. And I know a lot of people I don't like…Basically, if someone bugs me I do something about it. And sometimes I hurt them."

While Liv referred to physical aggression, it was more common for group conflicts to be regulated in less direct ways. Popular girls were frequently blamed for rumours:

I find that she can be pretty annoying, or like sneaky, if she wants to start rumours. Stuff like that. Like I've gone through—I was actually pretty far off with Veronica at the beginning of the year, and I had a big problem with her 'cause I heard some things she would say about me. And so I would confront her. And she would lie about it, or whatever.* (Vikki)

Popular girls were blamed, as well, for backstabbing:

Sally: One of them was my buddy last year, but all she talked about was other girls. She was like 'Oh, Caroline this' and 'Caroline that.' And all of this stuff, so—

Marie: And 'Georgina this'—*

This kind of behaviour made girls claim that Popular girls feel that they are better than other kids. Vanessa claimed that Popular girls made their classmates "feel sort of immoral." This is because Popular kids act "superior than you sometimes because they sort of have that power. They feel that they can do whatever they want, and say whatever they want." As a consequence, Popular girls made others like Vanessa feel insecure: "So you kind of feel like you're sort of—like you want to be part of the conversation, but you don't want to let yourself out totally in case you do something stupid, or say something stupid. You know, embarrass yourself."

Given so many negative descriptions of Popular girls, we were curious about how they maintained their high status. Part of the answer lies in the fact that Popular girls were not often challenged.[9] On the contrary, being associated with Popular girls could reap "benefits" among one's peers. Although she "didn't know why," Riva explained that "When like one of my popular friends or whatever is paying me a lot of attention in front of a lot of people, you feel important." Given these types of benefits, many girls aspired to be among the Populars. Onyx (age fourteen, Chinese-Canadian, middle-class) and Grover (age fifteen, Latina-Canadian, middle-class) referred to these girls as "wannabes." However, whether a "wannabe" Popular or not, many girls simply did not want to become enemies of Popular girls. While Riva claimed that she didn't "feel intimidated by them or anything," she also indicated that "I don't really want to make enemies with them. That's like a big thing 'cause if they make up something, it goes all around. Like everyone knows."

The association of meanness with Popularity was so strong that twelve year old Eve (Chinese-Canadian, middle-class) claimed that "you have to put people down to make yourself really popular." Similarly, Vikki maintained that boys are attracted to the kind of girls who were described to researchers as 'mean':[10]

> They can be bitchy. They can be all that. That's why they are those kind of people. And so guys like that 'cause they think that those girls are 'all that stuff' and [that] they are really cool and we like them. And they're all sexy and whatever...Like sometimes you know, you see in the movies when girls are all like bitching at the guys. You'll be like 'blah, blah, blah' and the guy will just go into the kiss sort of thing 'cause he gets turned on by the girl getting like so—all in his space. She's just sort of 'there.'*

For these kinds of reasons it is understandable that some girls admitted "going along" with the behaviour of Popular girls, even though they might otherwise disapprove of meanness.

Toward A Sociology Of Girls' Agency

Adolescent behaviour has interested psychologists for far longer than it has sociologists. Within conventional developmental discourse, "antagonistic interaction" among teenagers is seen as a maturation stage or response to peer pressure. This discourse maintains that antagonism serves a number of social functions: it establishes a social hierarchy, brings nonconformist group members into line and thus reinforces group conformity, and strengthens group identity by clarifying the boundaries between "them" and "us." Sarcasm and ridicule are characterized as adaptive processes that allow adolescents to sort through "what they are" and "what they are not." They ease anxiety by drawing attention to others who are considered inferior and different. One problem is that such a discourse removes adolescence from its social and cultural context, masking the gendered[11] nature of peer interaction. While the notion of girls' relational aggression attempts to correct this omission, it is subject to the limitations of psychological strategies of intervention in general. For example, Simmons (2002) stresses the need for girls to learn better skills for interpersonal interaction. While young people can often benefit from these types of programmes, such an approach views the kinds of behaviours we have discussed in this paper as maladaptive. In contrast, we have shown how "meanness" is an exercise of power in the context of competitive status maintenance. Within this context relational aggression is adaptive; the girls exercising control over inclusion or exclusion in the hierarchy of their peer culture struck us (as they do often do other adults) as "well adapted." If our goal is the empowerment of young women—through the exercise of control over both the discursive and material conditions of their existence—we need to move beyond approaches to resocialize young people. For us, the goal of feminist empowerment is the cultivation of what we call transformative agency, an empowerment that engages girls in projects that work to change the material context of their existence. Such a strategy of intervention that can help redefine the limits of girlhood requires a sociology of girls' agency.

Gendered agency is a complex process that cannot be fully understood without considering the ways in which girls are able to construct alternatives to emphasized femininity. Here we hope to contribute to a sociology of girls' agency by locating relational aggression within the gendered economy of a heteronormative culture based on hierarchy and competition. In a similar move, Merten (1997) notes that by sustaining notions of a meritocracy, school curriculum does not allow this hierarchy to be explicitly recognized because such an acknowledgment would contradict broader educational messages about 'equality.'[12] Women, more than men, are negatively sanctioned for overt competitiveness, leading Merten to conclude that meanness enables girls to experience their popularity while minimizing the risk of losing it, because this covert behaviour allows them to maintain a veneer of "niceness." As Simmons points out, this veneer can prevent adults from recognizing that it may often be the "good girls" —those that appear to be well liked by their peers—who are the agents of adolescent conflicts.

For Merten and Simmons, the discourse of (middle class) femininity shapes and limits girls' agency because it requires girls to act competitively while maintaining an appearance of compliance to cultural norms. Pipher (1994) claims that this kind of duplicity silences girls because they must put their authentic selves aside in order to become what our culture values in women. Girls are told to "be attractive, be a lady, be unselfish and of service, make relationships work and be competent without complaint" (39). Thus our culture trains girls "to be less than who they really are. They are trained to be what the culture wants of its young women, not what they themselves want to become…Everywhere girls are encouraged to sacrifice their true selves" (4). Because Pipher thus equates conventional femininity with loss of Self, her work has inspired a search for the "lost" voice of girls, a search that endorses the notion that, through girls' speaking, adult listeners will hear an authenticity of girlhood, while girls themselves will be empowered to reclaim their "real" Selves. As shown by our research, however, empowering girls to find a "voice" may not be liberatory in the ways Pipher implies; in fact, it can reinforce conventional gender discourses.

Although we also find that girls operate with a sense of "real" Self, we reject the notion of an essential (and idealized) girlhood that exists outside the everyday dynamics of peer cultures, waiting to be "recaptured" through girls' empowerment. While much of the duplicity documented by other research played itself out in our study, one problem is that interpreting this behaviour as a signal of limited agency can reinforce the view of girls as "victims." It also has the potential to foster conventional misogynist thinking about women's behaviour and thus analytically limit our understanding of girls' agency. While we agree that the tenets of middle-class femininity shape the kinds of behaviours we have described, we see them operating as a resource rather than limitation for girls' agency and power. The problem is that, as a resource, the tenets of emphasized femininity authorize girls as objects rather than subjects of desire. What is missing, and what is negatively sanctioned, is girls' desire: while girls are encouraged, as young women, to be sexually desirable, they are negatively sanctioned for expressing sexual agency (see Fine 1997).

Much of this sanctioning occurs through the regulation of girls' dress and bodily comportment. The dilemma to be negotiated by girls is the fact that while "the visibility of the body and flesh is subject to order, surveillance, and regulation, the exposure of the body is fundamental to femininity and social order" (Gleeson and Firth, 2004: 106).This ambiguity gives young women opportunities to actively negotiate exactly how "mature" or how "sexual" they want to appear in particular situations and in relation to other people.[13] At the same time, the double-standard that results in this ambiguity gives rise to the discursive power of girls' meanness: much of the meanness in our study was about girls *doing* power in the discursive economy of peer cultures.[14] Navigating the rules of this economy is precarious: girls must be "pretty" but not "self absorbed"; they must be attractive to boys but not "slutty"; they must be popular among the "right people" but not a "snob"; independent but not a "loner"; and so on. The stakes are high because "Whatever we do it's always wrong" (Hudson, 1984: 31). These girls know that negotiating the double-standard of womanhood is not always under their direct control: the labels that signal femininity can only be applied from the outside because patriarchal culture renders women objects of public scrutiny. Within this context, power is the ability to command in/exclusion by policing the boundaries of idealized femininity. The discursive positioning of other girls within the gendered economy of peer cultures is not a "maladaption" to proper femininity; on the contrary, however abusive this process may become, these practices arise from constructions of an idealized womanhood in the competitive hierarchy of youth cultures.

In closing, what has been identified as girls' relational aggression testifies to the ways in which youth culture, although a semi-autonomous sphere of adolescent agency, is marked by a heterosexist gender hierarchy and the sexual competition of mainstream culture. The seeming duplicity of girls' behaviour mirrors a disjuncture between a discourse of meritocracy as the pedagogical foundation of their education and the everyday reality of how gendered hierarchies operate. In other words, the school itself contributes to what have been identified as the "problematic" behaviours of girls through the everyday exercise of labelling and classifying students. Those in authority scrutinize students not simply for academic "merit," but also according to demeanour and social skills, criteria which are class-based characteristics. The result is a hierarchical ordering of "good" and "problem" students, an ordering that separates those "most likely to succeed" from the rest. Central to this ordering is an ethos of competitive individualism that sustains belief in a meritocracy. On the one hand, this belief maintains that "girls [like boys] can be and do anything." On the other, within youth cultures this message becomes transformed by an implicit understanding of a properly gendered order. While few girls questioned the truism that today "girls can be anything," most were also acutely aware that girls are judged by stereotypical, double standards: girls are judged by their looks, they are seen to be emotionally rather than physically expressive or physically adept, and their reputations can be "ruined" by sexually-demeaning labels. From this perspective, a disjuncture exists between the rhetoric of equality espoused by the school curriculum and the everyday reality of how girls are labelled, classified and—on that basis—achieve 'success.'

To be sure, locating girls' aggression within the everyday context of their schooling complicates how we need to think about projects to empower young women. We suggest that the ways in which girls' agency plays itself out in the context of peer cultures is perhaps more complex than often portrayed. Much of what girls described as "meanness" is often dismissed by adults as, simply, "peer pressure." Perhaps worse, when academics label the "problem" as a developmentally healthy exercise of boundary maintenance, we contribute to its normalization, as evidenced by Brooke's dismissal of sexual name-calling as "high schoolism":

Brooke: Like when a girl gets with a guy she's a slut. When a guy gets with a girl, he's cool.

Shauna: Do you see that as sexism?

Brooke: Humm. I never really thought of it actually as sexism. I thought of it more as just, just as high schoolism.

Brooke's understanding shows the importance of how we name and talk about the non-physical aggression that is common in youth cultures.[15] Although not the focus of our attention, we became aware that boys (at least as described by some girls in our study) also engaged in non-physically aggressive behaviour, such as spreading rumours. It interests us not so much whether boys are competitive in the way attributed to girls, but that their behaviour is not described as "mean" by the girls in our study, or described as "relational aggression" by researchers. What this suggests is that the mandate for "niceness" does not simply encourage covert aggression in girls, but that it also works to gender the meanings we assign to specific behaviours. In this case, it creates an expectation that contributes to the labelling of girls' behaviour but not the identical behaviour of boys. One worry that we have is the possibility that academic emphasis on relational aggression as uniquely female can help to naturalize this behaviour; making it, in the words of Riva: "The way things are."

Notes

1. In 1997, Reena Virk (a fourteen year-old Indo-Canadian girl) was beaten and drowned by a group of youth (seven girls and one boy between the ages of fourteen and sixteen) in a "peaceful" suburb of Victoria, British Columbia. The popular press reported this murder in terms of "girl-on-girl" violence in ways that obscure its connection to the everyday dynamics of sexism and racism. For example, Reena was described as a "troubled" girl, a "misfit" who had stolen another girl's boyfriend and spread rumours. Implicit throughout the coverage is the message that today's girls are "too empowered" and cannot cope with the gains we accredit to feminism. Jiwani (1999; 2000) draws attention to how the racism embodied by this murder was obscured in media accounts, while the racialization of the white girl accused of the murder implicitly worked in favour of her defense.

2. Scholars have critically analyzed this backlash, particularly as it plays out in debates over boys' 'underachievement' in school, in England (Epstein, et al. 1998), the United States (Titus 2004), and Australia (Yates 1997).

3. For a discussion of the moral panic over girls' use of violence, see Chesney-Lind and Irwin (2004).

4. Girls were invited to use "made up" names for their interviews; we employ these pseudonyms in this paper.

5. Some interviews were conducted with girlfriends, allowing spontaneity in the dialogue; these interviews are noted with an asterisk (*). We thank Shauna Pomerantz, who conducted most of the interviews.

6. We can only speculate about why race and racism featured so little in our participants' accounts of other girls' meanness. The girls may have felt it taboo to call someone or something racist, particularly when talking to a white interviewer. From work such as Pyke and Dang (2003)—and from our interviews—we acknowledge that hierarchies operate between and within peer groups.

7. We recognize that 'bitchiness' might also be used to label girls who, in a feminist sense, stand up for their rights or the rights of others. In other words, we do not see this label as simply negative.

8. Unlike Merten (1997), however, we do not assign competition over popularity a causal role in girls' behaviour. While we agree that girls may compete over membership in the Popular

crowd, we see competitive hierarchies themselves—including the ones created when students are assessed by teachers on various aspects of their school performance—as the problem.

9. In the case of fourteen year-old Marianne (Inuit and Euro-Canadian), who was the target of meanness, teachers also did not challenge girls' behaviour.

10. Brooke was among those girls who disagreed. She argued that guys are "not used to someone [if female, that is] standing up to them."

11. We use 'gendered' here as a shorthand reference to inequalities of all kinds, such as those based on 'race,' sexuality, class, physical ability, and age. These multiple axes of subordination and domination intersect in complex ways. Collins' (1990) concept of the 'matrix of domination,' formed by interlocking systems of oppression, captures what we mean.

12. Despite our argument that the school is a context within which inequalities are reconstituted, we acknowledge that schools are among the institutions most committed to gender equality. Nevertheless, a gap exists in the school setting (as elsewhere) between the rhetoric of equality that girls, like boys, can do and be anything and the everyday reality that girls, much more so than boys, are judged based on their looks and vulnerable to attacks on their social worth through sexually demeaning labels. Exposing this gap might allow youth more space to challenge the contradictions and recognize the multiple discourses that shape their gendered identities. More specifically, because 'emphasized femininity' provides currency in the gendered economy where meanness plays out, teachers and other adults need to give young people the language to name this femininity, critique it as well as 'hegemonic masculinity' (Connell 1995), and provide support for other ways of being girls and boys.

13. Gleeson and Firth (2004) interviewed eighteen girls between twelve and sixteen years of age living in Bristol and Cardiff.

14. We acknowledge that the data are far more complex, but given the limits of space here, we have focused on 'meanness' as the most powerful—and surprising—finding.

15. For discussion of what Davies (1993) calls critical literacy, see Kenway et al. (1998).

Chapter Eleven

"Did You See What She Was Wearing?"
The Power And Politics Of Schoolgirl Style

Shauna Pomerantz

"I mean, I guess wearing your clothes is a way of expressing yourself, almost." —Zeni, fifteen, "casual/sporty" style[1]

Far From Clueless: Ad/dressing The "Slut" Look

Blame it on Britney. As teens across the country negotiate the sexually charged territory of high school, more and more of them are doing so in cleavage-baring crop tops and ultra-low-rise pants that show off their pelvic bones. Clothes for girls have never been so skimpy.[2]

—Deborah Fulsang (2002)

In the early twenty-first century, girls' style has become scandalous.[3] The scandal revolves around what is often referred to as the "slut" look, composed of cleavage-baring and midriff-revealing tops, tight low-rise jeans, and hardly-there mini skirts. This style has sparked heated debates across the country, as parents negotiate their daughter's "skin" quotient and students debate their comfort level with the visible thong over fries and gravy at lunch. The controversy has also prompted school administrators to institute a new generation of dress codes for the good of the school's "moral community" (Fine, 1990), banning midriffs, exposed bra straps, cleavage, spaghetti-strapped tank tops, micro mini skirts, and exposed underwear in schools across Canada. These new dress codes tackle concerns raised by parents and teachers, such as, how will boys stay focused with "naked" girls in the classroom? How will girls handle the extra attention that boys offer as a result of the "slut" look? And how will girls be safe from predators and sexual harassment if they dress like they are "asking for it"?[4]

The controversy over girls' style has raged far beyond the walls of the school to become an "incitement to discourse" for the general public.[5] Talk of how girls are dressing "these days" has invaded even the most casual conversations. "Sluts," many people say. Or, "naïve girls" who are "clueless" as to how others are lusting after them, feeling pity for them, or viewing them as voraciously hungry for sexual attention. "Who lets them *out* like that?" people wonder. "Don't girls know the dangers that await them in those outfits?" "Don't girls *know* how they look?" Picking up on this controversy, reporters quickly parlayed girls' style into a "sure thing" in the press. Issues of morality always "play" with the Canadian public—not to mention pictures of scantily clad teenage girls. Where once girls' style was relegated to a back-to-school footnote in the fashion section, it has now become glossy front page news. In big, bold headlines that sometimes stretch across a two-page spread, reporters accuse girls of "dressing like sluts" (Jacobs, 2002: B4) and harbouring a "disturbing hunger" to be "desired, even objectified" (Woodend, 2002; H8).

Others in the press have expressed passive aggressive guilt regarding the "slut" look. In a confessional tone, one male columnist for *The Globe and Mail* writes, "I see really young teenage girls, who I really don't want to think sexual thoughts of, passing by in these things and I really don't know if they want me to stare at their groins or not" (Smith, 2002: R6). Though concerned in tone, the column was accompanied by a sexy picture of a willowy midriff replete with star tattoo, belly piercing, and a great deal of flesh. Another article in *The Globe and Mail* featured a large colour photo of a teenage girl outfitted in red fishnet stockings, cut-off jean shorts, a purple bikini top with silver glitter, and a large heart-shaped tattoo between her breasts. Her face is obscured by a mass of hair that makes her look wild, untamed, and almost animal-like in her wilful attempt to wear what she wants at any cost. The panic-inducing headline next to the photograph reads, "Mom, I'm ready for school!" (Fulsang, 2002: L1).

These images have helped to perpetuate a moral panic surrounding girls' style,[6] one that feeds into a broader discourse that constructs teenage girls as "in-trouble" and "out-of-control."[7] This discourse takes shape around the Ophelia genre, named after Mary Pipher's (1994) wildly successful book, *Reviving Ophelia*. Based on the tragic heroine in *Hamlet*, Pipher views teenage girls as helplessly tossed about by external forces, such as "junk culture," peer pressure, and hormonal changes that turn ordinarily "happy" girls into monsters and victims. Telling stories from her own psychotherapy practice, Pipher weaves together a portrait of girlhood that is "overwhelmed and symptomatic" (13). Pre-adolescent girls, she writes, are full of *joie de vive*, but in adolescence, girls suddenly stray from the path of "ordinary" development to become depressive strangers to both their families and themselves.

While the Ophelia genre charts many significant problems facing girls as they enter adolescence, including date rape, eating disorders, suicide, sexual harassment, and depression, it also fixes girls in a naturalized mould that lacks "any consideration of the effect of social structural forces on individual lives" (Bettie, 2003: 5). As well, only one kind of girlhood is offered up as "typical," creating what Foucault (1978) calls a "regulatory ideal" that normalizes certain ways of being a girl, while demonizing others. Girlhood is thus presented as an immutable category that exists outside of discourse's effect. Made to look inevitable and "natural," girls' development is judged to be either "right" or "wrong" based on a girl's ability to conform to and successfully complete tasks that mark her maturation process as "healthy" (Harris, 1999).

The Ophelia genre grants authority to the moral panic surrounding girls' style. It enables critiques of how girls are dressing "these days" to slip easily and quietly into mainstream consciousness, like an idea that has already been thought. Yet it also works in reverse: the panic over girls' style lends credence to the Ophelia genre, where girls who wear "inappropriate" outfits are acting out their low self-esteem, their desire to be loved, and their voracious hunger for male attention. A modern-day Ophelia in low-rise jeans adds weight to the idea that girls today are "in trouble" and "out of control"—their metaphorical suicides writ large on their descending waistbands. The question Pipher asks has thus become the question on everyone's lips regarding how girls are dressing "these days": "What can we do to help them?"

But moral panic misses the point. Press coverage of girls' style has discursively produced a homogeneous girlhood that comes in one outfit with only one possible meaning. This static reading denies the innumerable ways in which girls use style to negotiate their identities. It also fails to acknowledge that style acts as a "particularly powerful social marker" (Eckert, 1989: 62) within the context of the school, where it forms a "symbolic economy" (Bettie, 2003: 61). In her study of working-class girls, Julie Bettie (2003) describes the significance of this economy as "the ground on which class and racial/ethnic relations were played out" (61), as well as aspects of femininity, sexuality, popularity, and group organization. Style is a shifting and malleable text that enables girls to find each other, to form (dis)identifications, and to distinguish themselves from others. Girls use style to signal "who" they are within groups and as individuals, and how they want to be seen within the social world of the school. But this multifaceted and contextualized understanding of style is lost in the construction of the "slut" look and its accompanying moral panic, where girls' style is emptied of meaning and classified as a "problem."

In opposition to this static reading, I offer an alternative view. Based on a year-long ethnographic study at an urban and multicultural Vancouver high school that I call East Side High (ESH), I explore style in relation to girls' identity construction. I interviewed and observed twenty girls in order to better understand the symbolic economy of style that fluctuated within the school,[8] as well as girls' uses of style in the negotiation of "who" they were and how they wanted to be seen by others. Throughout the school-year, I attended classes with girls, had lunch with them, spent time with them outside of school and at extra-curricular events, and conducted semi- structured interviews. I asked girls how they saw themselves in relation to style, how they wanted others to see them, and what actions they took to ensure that they would be recognized as certain "kinds" of girls and not others. Girls spoke of the impact that style had within the school and its signification in relation to popularity, femininity, gender, class, race, ethnicity, and sexuality. They also spoke of the social categories in which they were both positioned and positioned themselves through style, such as "skank," "prep," "sporty," "punk," "goth," "skater," "hoochie," "wannabe," and a multitude of racial and ethnic designations, such as "Nammer" (Vietnamese), "Flip" (Filipino), "Chink" (Chinese), "CBC" (Canadian-born-Chinese), "ESL" (English-as-second-language), Caucasian, Hispanic, and First Nations.

Far from clueless, girls carefully and creatively used style as a form of embodied subjectivity in order to negotiate their identities. As Chris Weedon (1987) suggests, subjectivity is all "the conscious and unconscious thoughts and emotions of the individual, her sense of herself and her ways of understanding her relations to the world" (32). In order to transcend the mind/body dualism that this definition engenders, Elizabeth Grosz (1994) proposes a model of subjectivity that is embodied. For Grosz, the body is a major aspect of self awareness that must be factored into how we understand ourselves. Agreeing with Grosz, Lois McNay (1999) suggests that the body "is the threshold through which the subject's lived experience of the world is incorporated and realized" (98). The body thus becomes a significant locus of subjectivity.

Yet the body is never naked in society; it is always dressed. As that which makes us socially visible, style forms the "social skin," granting the body visibility and meaning, revealing and releasing the body, cloaking and confining it, shaping it and giving it definitions, borders, and folds (Wilson, 1985). Style fashions the body into a fluid social text that bridges private and public space, or the interiority of the mind and the exteriority of the corporeal self. Style embellishes the body with "a whole array of meanings" (Entwistle, 2001: 33) that it would otherwise not have. As Kaja Silverman (1994) suggests, style is a "necessary condition of subjectivity" (191). As a result, style is an extension of the body and is afforded "all the explanatory power of minds" (Grosz, 1994: vii). For girls—particularly in the school—social visibility is dependent upon style; girls' identities are contingent upon it.

Identity is the contextual and shifting understanding of "who" we are in a particular social, cultural, and historic location. As Stuart Hall (1996) explains, identity is always an "in process" manifestation of "how we have been represented" through discourse, "and how that bears on how we might represent ourselves" (4). Though we are discursively produced through social structural categories, through this production, we also become subjects who are capable of recognizing and reiterating these categories, making them our own and infusing them with creativity, rebellion, and change (Butler, 1990, 1993; Hall 1996). Hall (1996) defines identity as the "point of suture" (5) between discourse and subjectivity, or the structural constraints that shape us and the resulting subjecthood that enables us to shape ourselves. This suturing is made possible through agency. Though, as Bronwyn Davies (1990) suggests, agency is

...never freedom from discursive constitution of self but the capacity to re-
cognise that constitution and to resist, subvert and change the discourses
themselves through which one is being constituted. It is the freedom to re-
cognise multiple readings such that no discursive practice, or positioning
within it by powerful others, can capture and control one's identity. (51)

Girls are thus able to "read the texts of their 'selving'" (Davies, 1997: 274) within the
school and, through that awareness, conceive of themselves differently using style as
a powerful form of embodied subjectivity.

While girls at ESH negotiated their identities in numerous ways, style was one of
the most available, malleable, and talked about forms of embodied subjectivity in the
school. Girls were routinely defined by their style, classified by their style, noticed for
their style, and teased for their style. But they also constantly changed their style,
thought about their style, and used style to position themselves within subject positions or social categories. As social skin, style dictated how girls were seen in the
school, but it also created a way for girls to negotiate that seeing, to reiterate "who"
they were and how they were being viewed by others. As a result, style exemplified the
fluid "double movement" (Gonick, 2003: 10) between discourse and subjectivity,
highlighting the suturing of these two complex social processes in girls' understandings of themselves. In this way, style acted as a membrane of permeability, or a po-
rous covering over the body that enabled girls to transfer something of themselves
into the school's social world (subjectivity), while simultaneously enabling the
school's social world to transfer something of itself into girls (discourse).

By ethnographically attending to girls' uses of style at ESH, I aim to reconcept-
ualize style as a significant form of embodied subjectivity that girls carefully and creatively use to negotiate their identities. But unlike press accounts, determining the
"meaning" of girls' style is not a matter of one simple or linear reading. The symbolic
economy that fluctuated throughout ESH was highly complex and filled with ambiguity. What style meant had everything to do with who was doing the seeing and
who was being seen. But no matter how girls described the meaning of various styles
in the school, one thing was abundantly clear—style mattered (Weber & Mitchell,
2004). As Shen, who modestly described her style as "comfortable," explained: "If you
dress a certain way, people judge you by the way you look, of course, right?
That's—everybody does that. So if you dress like *this*, then you're like *that*." In what
follows, I explore the significance of Shen's equation in three connected social processes at ESH: popularity, experimentation, and individuality. These areas highlight
the ways in which girls used style as a tool for identity negotiation, as well as how
multiple, flexible, and paradoxical girls understood their identities to be.

"A Very Close Line": Negotiating Popularity At East Side High

> "Oh! There's a *very* close line between looking good and looking like a ho."
> —Gianna, eighteen, "in-style" style

ESH is situated in the heart of Wellington, a neighbourhood located in Vancouver's east side. Wellington is known as a funky and community-oriented area full of old and young hippies, gelato parlours, hemp shops, and culturally-themed cafes. But aside from its community orientation, Wellington is also well-known throughout Vancouver for crime, poverty, violence, and drugs. This reputation is rooted in stereotypes about Wellington's immigrant and working-class population. Though Vancouver has a high immigrant population in general, Wellington is viewed as "more" immigrant due to the class divide that exists between east and west. The west side is known for its beautiful homes, "good" schools, beachfront property, and professional residents. The east side is known for cheap housing, "run down" buildings, "bad" schools, drugs, and racially organized gangs. These reputations fix the east side in the public imaginary as "scary" and "dangerous," stigmas that have inundated east side schools.

However it may be constructed within the city, Wellington remains a proud, diverse, and exciting neighbourhood. As a result of its "underdog" status, as well as its cultural vibrancy, the neighbourhood is infused with a sense of community spirit—a feeling that was palpable inside ESH. In the school, over 50 different home languages were spoken and over two-thirds of the student body was first generation Canadian. Within this diverse environment, a range of styles existed that represented the multiplicity of the students. But some styles, of course, were more prevalent than others. At ESH, there were two acknowledged "uniforms" for girls: the "Britney" look and the "JLo" look.[9] The Britney look was so-named for its influence by white pop star Britney Spears. The look—identical to the "slut" look constructed in the press—included tight, low-rise jeans, cleavage- and midriff-baring tops, long hair, and some light makeup.[10] This style was predominantly, though not exclusively worn by white and middle-class or working-class girls.

The "JLo" look was so-named for its influence by Hispanic singer/actor Jennifer Lopez. It was predominantly, though not exclusively, worn by Asian, Italian, and Hispanic working-class girls. The style was defined by a matching pastel tracksuit made of velour. The "suits," as they were called, had low-rise, form-fitting bottoms and tight-fitting jackets.[11] Both the Britney and JLo looks required name brands from expensive stores. Middle-class girls could easily afford such outfits, but they were not off limits to working-class girls, who often held part-time jobs or earned "rewards" from their immigrant parents for keeping up good grades. As a result of their mass marketed appeal, the Britney and JLo looks were the most mainstream of all the styles at ESH and were generally worn by popular girls, defined as those who knew the most people and thus wielded the most power in the school (Bettis & Adams, 2003). Wearing mainstream clothing that marked a girl as popular also meant that she was seen as "preppy" within the school's symbolic economy of style. Preppy, an historically shifting social category, is synonymous with mainstream popularity and refers to "going with the trends" or being "in style."[12] It is also often defined by "emphasised femininity" (Connell, 1987), where girls willingly subordinate themselves to hegemonic masculinity by attracting boys through heteronormative modes of sexuality and beauty.

For those who could afford it (and, of course, wanted it), the preppy subject position offered girls a very specific social standing in the school. It was not just that a girl was viewed as popular (a girl could be popular without being preppy), but rather that she was viewed as a particular "kind" of girl: a girl who looked "good" in the tight and revealing clothing, a girl who looked "sexy," and a girl who wielded power within the heterosexual matrix of the school, where preppy girls set a "normative assumption" (Butler, 1993) for femininity against which all other girls were measured. Preppy girls were seen to emulate the "cultural ideal" that was disseminated through movies, magazines, and music videos. As Shitar, an admittedly unpopular girl with a "punk-ass" style, half-joked, "everyone says, 'Real people don't really look like that!' But you come to our school and you see people really do. Not all of them, but the ones that are important *do*!" Dressing preppy thus automatically linked girls to a particular body type, sexuality, and sexual power. Put another way, preppy girls were most likely to be pretty, thin, "hot," and involved in a heterosexual dating scene.

Standing in ambiguous opposition to the preppy styles at ESH was the abject subject position of "skanky." Skanky was synonymous with "slutty," but did not mean that a girl necessarily "slept around." To be a skank was to show "too much" skin and, more importantly, to show it in the "wrong" way. Yet *who* this rule applied to and *how* often, shifted. Two of the most popular groups in the school were the white and middle-class French Immersion girls and the Asian and working-class "hardcores," so-named for their "tough" attitudes. Though the white popular girls predominantly wore the Britney look and the Asian popular girls predominantly wore the JLo look, each group occasionally wore each others' "uniforms." As a result, the real difference between the groups seemed to hinge on a display of skin, though which group displayed more shifted depending on who I asked. Xiu, a self-described "quiet" Chinese girl with a "really regular" style, explained that the distinction between white and Asian popular girls depended on the midriff, as well as other subtle differences.

> The typical white group I see at school would have their pants all the way
> down to almost where you may see their underwear or lower. They like to
> wear the furry hooded jackets, tight light blue jeans and also, I'm guessing

they are called skater shoes. That is fairly different from the Asian group because the Asian group does not like to show their belly that much. They also wear the hooded jackets with the fur, but their shoes are different. The Asians would go for the Nike Shocks instead of skater shoes.

Yet Dren, a white goth girl who described her style as "alternative," disagreed. As she put it, popular Asian girls wore their pants "so low that you can practically see the hair line." The "skank" label was thus used to form "exclusionary matrices" (Butler, 1993) that created both insiders and outsiders to each racially-defined group.

While popular girls classified each other as "skanky" as a way of forming (dis)identifications, they also used the label to diminish the power of less popular girls in the school. Hispanic girls were routinely held up as the epitome of "hoochie" by white and Asian popular girls. Hoochie was another word for skank, but one that had racial connotations. A "hoochie" style included "glitzy" and "sparkly" clothing that was tight and revealing, lots of makeup with dark lip liner, carefully sculpted eyebrows, dark eye shadow, and heavy mascara. As Dren described it, this look was "total trash" and included "slicked back pony tails" that were "so tight, it looks like they're going to cut off the circulation to their head." And Leah, a popular white girl, acknowledged that while her pants were "tight," they were not "as tight" as the Hispanic girls,

> who have their hair all permed, and they jell it in these curls, and they're known, in my group of friends, as the 'crunchy curl girls'... cause their hair! Like, yeah, you look like you could break it or something. Just crunch! And they wear really like, not-there shirts and really, really tight pants. And those kind of really annoying...platform runners that are kind of in style, but not really. They're white and they've got little platforms. And also they wear those, high heels.

"Skank" was thus a label that emphasised the effects of style as social skin, a label that was carefully used to negotiate the positioning of racial groups in the school, to solidify racial hierarchies, and to emphasise class differences among girls who could not afford to buy the preppy uniforms. Yet, ironically, preppy and skanky looks were almost identical. The distinction between these two subject positions rested on who was doing the seeing and who was being seen—a lesson that Chrissie learned when she saw her status drift from preppy to skanky. Chrissie was thin, pretty, blonde, and in the French Immersion popular group of white girls. She wore the Britney look throughout most of the year, but began to change her style to something "a little more skater" and "tomboy," including baggy cargo pants, skater shoes, hoodies, and baseball caps. When I asked her why her style had suddenly changed, she explained that people thought she was "skanky," even though she thought she was wearing "normal" clothes. When I asked Chrissie what her "normal" style was called, she replied that it was "preppy." But she mentioned that her friends were "getting this impression of me, that I was like, a preppy like, hoochie kind of girl, who went out looking for guys, dressed in tight clothing, or whatever." Here, Chrissie equates preppiness with "hoochie," where previously she considered preppy to be "normal" clothing. Chrissie's preppy clothes included "mini skirts" and "skimpy tops." But lately, when she wore these outfits, she noticed that other girls were "just very blatant—they're like, 'Tramp!'" She suddenly realized that her style was sending messages that she had not intended. "I was like, 'Oh my god. People think I'm someone I'm not at all.' And it really started to bug me."

As a thin and pretty girl, Chrissie drew attention from boys everywhere she went. Many of her friends became jealous of her ability to cause a "stir" and called her "anorexic," "bleached blonde," and "that damn Britney Spears." Some of her friends had even started excluding her from social events. As a result, Chrissie seriously began to consider how she was being seen by others and added new elements of style to her repertoire in order to gain control over her identity at school.

> Yeah. It all kind of adds up, like, I don't want to be some Britney Spears
> skank, blah, blah, blah. I don't want to be known as wanting to go out and
> get attention from guys. I don't like any of that stuff that apparently like, I
> guess like, my overall image presented to people.

But the skater/tomboy wardrobe that Chrissie had begun to cultivate did not erase the Britney look from her repertoire. This reluctance to give up being preppy, however shifting the label may have been, points to the power that the subject position held within the school—a subject position that guaranteed the attention of boys, the envy of girls, and a primary role in the heterosexual dating scene of the school.

But beyond the power she experienced through emphasised femininity, Chrissie also used style to negotiate her identity in relation to what she called "female sexual power." As we sat next to each other in English class one day, I could hear Christina Aguilera's latest hit, *Fighter*, blasting through her disc player. Chrissie admired Aguilera's ability to be sexual, powerful, and to fight against "suppressed female sexuality." She also identified with Aguilera's recent image change from "just another pop star doing whatever" to announcing,

> 'Yeah, I'm not a virgin, blah, blah, blah,' like, everyone can deal with that,
> and sorta just, you know, even if it is slutty, she's not denying it. Know
> what I mean? And like, I always hear guys saying it about, like, um, using
> girls for sex and stuff like that. And what she's doing is just coming right
> back and saying, 'Yeah, *we* can do that too!'

As I listened to Aguilera's commanding voice pound out through Chrissie's headphones, I noted that she was wearing a white mini skirt with a deep slit, a tight pink t-shirt, and strappy sandals with three-inch cork heels. She had recently acquired a nose piercing similar to the one Aguilera had sported on the cover of *Rolling Stone* magazine that month. She enjoyed the power of her sexuality, a power that she equated with expressing herself and challenging the sexual double standard of the boys in the school. But at the same time, her look offered her the power to continue regulating femininity within the school. By multiply locating herself within two styles—the tightness of the preppy look and the bagginess of a more casual, skater look—Chrissie retained the power of her popularity, the power to challenge the sexual double standard, and the power to mitigate her connection to the slippery "skanky" label.

Chrissie's ability to navigate how she was seen at ESH was a common thread in girls' understandings of the school's symbolic economy of style. While it often seemed like a fixed and stable system, girls were aware that they could negotiate "who" they were by using one meaning of style to contradict another, by playing with seemingly entrenched categories, and by using social skin to manoeuvre within their own discursive constructions. Unlike static readings of girls that are offered in the press or through the Ophelia genre, girls at EHS were certainly conscious of the power that style offered them—and they intentionally used it in the negotiation of their identities within the context of the school.

"Different Little Identities": Experimentation And Re-Negotiation

"…if you classify yourself that means you see yourself in *that* way. I see myself as a million things. A million or more. I like to change things."
—Jamie, fifteen, "out-there-but-socially-acceptable" style

Occupying more than one subject position through multiple styles was a strategy that girls often employed to negotiate their identities within the school. Chrissie worked to carefully and creatively position herself within both a preppy and a skater/tomboy style in order to retain the power of popularity, while simultaneously mitigating her "skanky" reputation. Zeni, on the other hand, experimented with an entirely new look in order to re-signify how others saw her. Zeni, a Filipino/Japanese girl with a self-defined "causal/sporty" style, was the grade ten student rep, a sports star, and on the honour roll every year. When she walked down the hall, she said "hi" to almost everyone she passed, but her popularity was bittersweet. Zeni felt trapped in an identity that she did not believe adequately represented "who" she was. Everyone thought she was "Miss Perfect." "And I don't really like it that much," she told me. "It seemed like a joke at first, but then when they keep repeating it over and over again—!"

In order to change how others viewed her, Zeni began diversifying herself across the school, joining different teams, different social groups, and engaging in different activities. She became a "floater" and proudly told me that people were starting to see her in "different ways. Like, people in my guitar class see me as, say, musical. People on my soccer team think of me as, well, soccer. Basketball, just basketball." Surprised by her own ability to cultivate multiple subject positions in the school, she added, "I've got all these different little identities, and I play them when I get there." As a result, Zeni described herself as "different." "That's the proper word," she realized. "I'll talk differently with different groups of people." Conscious of the multiplicity of her identity, she thoughtfully added, "it's just different me-s. Different ways to communicate to them."

But Zeni's diversification into "different little identities" was not complete until she started to experiment with her style. Zeni believed that if she maintained her old "casual/sporty" style, others would continue to see her in the same way and easily "pin" her down. Instead, she made the decision to cultivate a very eclectic and indefinable style. She began shopping at stores that were less popular—buying "unique" articles of clothing and working hard to slip out of her "Gap girl" reputation. As a result, she sometimes wore her pyjamas to school or a "rock star" look, including leather pants, a fitted blouse, a man's tie, and dark sunglasses. Other times, she cultivated a "western" style similar to one Madonna sported in the *Don't Tell Me* video. "I have different looks everyday," she declared. Zeni's different looks added to her "mystery" and kept people from defining her in ways that she did not like. "I don't like people knowing [about me]. I keep people guessing. It's fun. Cause they never know."

While Zeni negotiated how she was seen by others through an eclectic style that was impossible to classify, Leah negotiated her identity by experimenting with a style that she felt could offer her a way out of the preppy subject position she currently occupied. Leah, a white popular girl in the French Immersion group, felt trapped by her well-established Britney look, a look that she referred to as "boring and mainstream." She noted that she never really "liked" her clothes. "I just got them because that's what the stores had and that's what I thought I should have." But Leah longed to experiment with being alternative. At ESH, dressing alternative stood in resistance to the preppy subject position. While preppy styles revolved around mainstream fashions, alternative styles revolved around just the opposite. Alternative girls did not wear labels, did not show much skin, and did not conform to or condone the "uniforms" at ESH.

Leah called her alternative vision the "random" look. The art of randomness, as she explained it, was being able to wear anything you wanted, no matter how "totally weird" it was. For Leah, this philosophy meant having the guts to wear "plaid pants" and a "checked shirt" instead of the "typical" low-rise jeans and tight t-shirts. In an effort to achieve a random style, Leah bought a pair of jeans that were "insanely studded." "I saw them and I was like, 'Wow! These are pretty cool!'"

And it was kind of after that I kind of began to wean out of my normal style. It was just kind of like, yeah, well—buying those jeans, despite the fact that they were tacky and ugly, it was like a revolution. I'm wearing something that not *everyone* in Vancouver's going to have!

She began to troll second hand markets, like *Value Village*, where she picked up "some pretty insane things," including her florescent yellow skirt. When Leah wore this skirt, she received looks from other girls in the hallway, but she did not seem to mind. She knew that it was "weird and tacky. But to me it just says a lot about *me*. It's kind of, it's in your face, but it's kind of subtle at the same time."

While Zeni and Leah carefully and creatively worked to negotiate their identities by experimenting with an obvious shift in style, other girls experimented with style in a more subtle way in order to gain some control over how they were positioned within the school. Both Xiu and Azmera came from strict cultural backgrounds: Xiu came from a traditional Chinese family and Azmera's single mother was a devout Muslim from Kenya. Both girls used style to shift the view others had of them within these cultural positionings. Xiu's own style was in keeping with her "quiet" Chinese, CBC status. As a Canadian-born-Chinese girl, Xiu was careful to wear clothing that did not make her look like a "Honger," or someone who was born in Hong Kong. The distinction between Canadian-born and ESL was an important one to her and required attention to subtle modifications, such as wearing the "right" cut of jeans. In order to achieve a CBC look, Xiu wore comfortable slacks, moderately loose-fitting jeans that were dark blue with a slight flare, "regular" runners, and loose-fitting sweaters and t-shirts that did not reveal any skin. But this positioning did not stop Xiu from thoughtfully—though cautiously—enacting subtle modifications to how she was seen by others at ESH. In order to occasionally break free of her "quiet" and "studious" reputation, Xiu wore the colour black—a colour that suggested "a secret, mysterious look, and that's the kind of look I'd like to keep." She saw black as a way to add maturity and sophistication to her traditional, Chinese identity. Her experimentation with black caused her friends to get "totally get confused" about "who" she "really" was. After a moment's reflection, Xiu admitted to "enjoying" this confusion as it added some "mystery" around her identity at school.

Like Xiu, Azmera also felt that she blended "in with the crowd," because, as she put it, "I look like an average person." Azmera and her mother had lived in Canada for nine years and struggled with Azmera's desire to break free from Muslim traditions. In order to do the things that "other girls do," Azmera felt she had to lie to her mother about where she was and who she was with. But even though they disagreed on how a "good" girl should act, they did not disagree on how one should dress. Azmera wore a style that made her mother happy: no-name brand jeans, sweaters, and comfortable clothing that did not cost a lot of money. In accordance with her mother's point of view, Azmera did not condone the Britney look that her friends sported: "The way some girls can dress and their parents can let them out of the house looking like that! And I don't agree with that either."

Though she did not want to look like her friends, Azmera enjoyed subtly enhancing her identity as the "nice" Muslim girl who "couldn't hurt a fly." She experimented with different looks that she felt were chic and modern. For Azmera, those looks meant putting together "outfits" that were not "regular," such as her favourite boots, "the jean ones with the diamond sparkles on them," her light blue pants that she folded up in the 1950s retro look that was *en vogue* at the time, a shirt with sparkles on it, "and my hat. I love hats too." These subtle enhancements were enough to offer her the "boost" she needed in the school, where she sometimes felt invisible next to the ultra-thin Asian girls whom she admired for looking so "fashionable." As she explained, "if you're a girl, and you want like, a good reputation with the girls, you kind of just have to like, you have to dress good. You have to keep up a high standard." According to Azmera, that standard meant "dressing like an Asian girl." Though she did not "agree with" the Britney look, she did not have a problem with the JLo suits that most preppy Asian girls wore. But when I asked Azmera if she would ever shop at Aritzia, the store that carried the "right" kind of suits, she replied, "Aritzia? Um, it's too expensive and I'm like, a bargain shopper! Like I could probably find the same pair of pants that they have at Aritzia at another store. Just cheaper."

While girls experimented with different styles in order to shift how they were perceived by others in the school, they were also limited by the "forced choices" (Davies, 1990: 46) they had to make within cultural and financial constraints. A forced choice suggests that while girls had agency to carefully and creatively negotiate their identities, they were also positioned with economic, cultural, and religious realities that meant a girl could not simply buy whatever she wanted or wear whatever she felt like wearing. These decisions were mitigated by structural constraints that white, middle-class girls did not necessarily have to contend with. Girls from immigrant families often had to negotiate their family's traditions, while second and third generation Canadian girls did not. And, of course, each family had its own unique set of expectations that offered yet another level of complexity as girls negotiated the social space between home and the school.

But even within cultural, generational, and economic constraints, girls readily used style to negotiate identity by experimenting with a look or an item of clothing that was incongruous to what others had become accustomed to seeing. Subtle modifications worked just as well as overt ones, depending on the symbolic economy of style that fluctuated within each social group. While Leah felt it necessary to shift between preppy and alternative looks, Xiu felt that wearing black was risky enough. Experimentation thus enabled girls at ESH to both literally and metaphorically try something on, perhaps retreating the next day, perhaps moving deeper into a new subject position, or perhaps incorporating an altogether new way of being into a firmly-established identity.

"Not Just another Number": Dressing As An Individual

> "I'm pretty unique. I think everybody thinks they're unique, right?"
> —Shen, sixteen, "casual" style

While girls used style in order to negotiate popularity and to experiment with multiple ways of being in the school, they also used style to create a lasting impression on others—something at which Dren was an admitted expert. Teachers and students all knew Dren, if not by name, then by style. She was "that *goth* girl" to just about everyone and wore a very distinctive uniform in all-black, including gossamer tops, flowing skirts, tall lace-up boots, chain belts, studded dog collars, skull rings, dark eye make-up, a lip and eyebrow piercing, and dyed black hair. Dren's style was her "baby." "I've kind of cultivated it," she said of her look. "It's something that not a lot of people have and it makes me different and I'm proud of it 'cause it's my own." Dren explained why she went to the lengths that she did in order to stand out at ESH.

> I'm like, my own person and I don't look like everyone else. I don't act like everyone else and I don't follow the same herd as everyone else. Something that like, makes me different in a way that maybe I'll be remembered. I mean, maybe in a couple of years, when I leave ESH, they'll be all, 'Remember that goth girl? That Dren girl? Remember that goth chick who used to walk around with her chains?' you know?"

Like Dren, Abby also carefully thought about how she could engrain herself in people's minds. Her "bad-ass/school-girl/business-woman" style was meant to ensure that people would "look through the yearbook like seventeen years later, and go, 'Oh, that was Abby! She was weird!'" Abby wore pinstripe pants, denim skirts, high-heeled Mary-Jane shoes, tall striped knee socks in bright colours, pinstripe blouses, and the occasional suit jacket. She modelled herself after the stylized characters in Tim Burton's animated film, *The Nightmare Before Christmas*. This look came to her when she saw a pair of wildly-coloured striped stocks in a store window one day, an article of apparel that she called her "salvation." The style suddenly clicked in her mind: "It was like, '*Yes!*' I could be style-y! I could be in Halloween-town. *Yes!*" Abby realized that being "obscure" was a sure-fire way to create a lasting impression at ESH, even if she was admittedly unpopular in the present. She reasoned that no one would remember the "preppy girls who all look the same and they're all conformed to what the style of the time was." Like Dren, what made Abby proud of her style was that people always commented on how creative it was. "You know, people say, like, 'Oh wow! That's like, a really original outfit' or whatever. I always get really gloating and like, '*Yes!* They said I was original!'"

For other girls at ESH, creating an impression meant wearing a style that generated respect and intimidation. Gwen was one such girl who quietly commanded respect from girls at ESH by purposefully cultivating a "gang" identity. Because Gwen was First Nations, white and Asian girls perceived the black bandana she occasionally wore around her head as a symbol of gang membership. Gwen's style was a "punk-slash-prep" hybrid that she carefully organized depending on the day of the week. When she had classes in the First Nations program,[13] she wore clothing that she defined as "more punk," including dark colours, baggy tear-away pants with one leg rolled up over her knee, studded wrist cuffs, and dog collars. But when she attended mainstream classes, she wore brighter colours, flared jeans, and tucked-in tops in order to "fit in." As a supplement to this hybrid style, Gwen also sometimes wore a black bandana tied around her forehead or her wrist.

Knowing that the girls in her mainstream classes would be intrigued by the gang symbol, Gwen enjoyed the attention that it brought her. White and Asian girls ran up to her to ask about her gang affiliation. "They're like, 'Are you in a gang?' Just be like, 'How tough are you? You ever kicked anybody's ass?'" Though Gwen told me that the bandana did not have any real meaning in her life, she was well aware of its signification within the symbolic economy of style at ESH, where gang bandanas were known to be red, black, and blue. "I only wear the black one," she noted. "I think red's the most dangerous one." This justification suggests that Gwen did not need to be thought of as too tough—just tough *enough* to imbue her with a sense of power and authority. Interestingly, Gwen never confirmed her involvement in a gang when she was asked. She simply adorned herself with an element of style that made it possible for others to slot her into their preconceived notion of First Nations girls, using her discursive production within the school to her advantage.

Gwen's identity as a "gang girl" was ambivalently located in her desire to fit in with the preppy girls in her mainstream classes. She both wanted their approval *and* wanted them to feel intimidated by her tacit association to violence. But for Ratch, there was nothing tacit about her desire to appear intimidating at ESH. "I know that when I walk down the street," she proudly told me, "people look away. They try not to make eye contact with me. They kind of get this like, nervous look, like I'm like, carrying a knife and I'm going to chop off their head or something!" Ratch's punk style consisted of a mini-skirt held together by safety pins (known as a bondage skirt), ripped fishnets, black converse sneakers, and a punk band t-shirt (usually the Sex Pistols or the Slits). Her style, combined with her tall, broad physique and wild mane of hair, created an aura of confidence that very few girls at ESH had the ability to pull off.

Dressing punk was a declaration of power that Ratch wore like a badge of honour. "I used to be scared of doing lots of things," she said of her pre-punk days. "Like, I would never think of going into a mosh pit because I might get kicked in the head or something.[14] But now I like, go in there and like, I've had my face bashed into other people and stuff, and it doesn't phase me." I asked Ratch if she enjoyed sporting an intimidating style. "I love it," she declared. "I don't dress like this because of self-defence and whatever, but it does take a lot of pressure off me, cause I'm not going to get mugged like, most likely. A lot of my friends who dress like everyone else, or whatever, get mugged like, get hassled all the time." Ratch's intimidating style made it possible for her to talk back to just about anyone in the school. "Yeah, I'm pretty comfortable with myself," she asserted. Explaining her confidence in relation to style, she added:

> If you're confident with who you are, you can pull off anything. Like, people are like, 'Wow, a lot of people who do that, a lot of people can't pull it off!' But it's just being comfortable. It's being confident in what you wear. Cause if you dress like [me], you have to have a lot of confidence, or people are going to be like, 'What the *fuck* are you doing?'"

While negotiating popularity necessitated forming identifications with others through similar, recognizable styles, standing out meant cultivating a style that was unique at ESH, one that was not easily executed or emulated. Highly familiar with the symbolic economy of style that fluctuated within the school, Dren, Abby, Gwen, and Ratch were able to negotiate their identities by consciously and obviously moving into uncharted territory within particular social settings. While Gwen's choice of a bandana colour or Abby's striped socks may have held no recognizable meaning outside of the school, inside, these choices became contextualized as part of a complex and shifting system of signification—a context that infused seemingly random and irrelevant elements of style with meaning, power, and politics.

"I Have My Style": Revisiting A Moral Panic

> "I don't have anything else. Like, I don't have like a big talent or anything. I don't have a sport I love, or, I'm not really good at school. I don't have millions of friends. I have my style. I can make clothes. I play with things. It's my hobby." —Shitar, "punk ass" style

It seems impossible to imagine that anyone who has ever spent even a little bit of time in high school could suggest that girls' style is devoid of meaning—no matter how slippery or ambivalent such meanings may be. The moral panic surrounding girls' style in the press thus smacks much more of backlash than it does of genuine concern. Are boys' cultural practices so consistently derided? The ease with which girls' style has been dismissed suggests that the real panic is over girls' new found power within the social sphere. Where once girls went unrepresented in both the academic and popular presses, now girls are the focal point of anthologies such as this one, conferences, and publications that celebrate the innumerable subject positions that girls can currently access (Pomerantz, Currie & Kelly 2004). But for every "girl power" rally call that is issued, girls are simultaneously reminded that they are performing girlhood "incorrectly" and that they have a "moral" obligation not to lead boys astray by being too powerful, too sexy, or too resistant to emphasised femininity. These reminders surface in the form of girl-specific syndromes, neuroses, and moral panics that let boys off the hook, yet continue to heap responsibility onto girls for maintaining order and civility.

This backlash against girls' newly minted social power continues to work the age-old trope that girls are cultural and consumer dupes. The moral panic surrounding girls' style plays into this indictment by suggesting that girls are far too "clueless" to know what they are buying and will, therefore, buy anything. And if girls will by anything, how can their choices have any real meaning? While there can be no denying the overwhelming impact of consumer culture in girls' lives, the dupe argument overlooks consumer culture as a hegemonic sphere where marketers must attract and sustain the attention of the targeted audience. While girls may want to buy the latest and hottest outfits sported by their favourite pop stars on MuchMusic and MTV, they are not blindly allegiant or easily tricked. Their consent must be won by marketers, whose ideas are often shot down in shopping malls and school hallways. This power forces marketers to be aware of girls, who will ultimately decide whether or not a style succeeds or fails. The power to consume or not to consume is one that girls exercise vigilantly and with purpose. As they carefully and creatively negotiate their identities in the school, girls ask themselves how they want to fit into its symbolic economy—an economy that, like consumer culture, is a hegemonic sphere where battles of transformation are fought and won daily.

Conclusion

The goal of this chapter has been to highlight the complexity of schoolgirl style and its multifaceted and shifting connotations. In so doing, I have aimed to situate girls' style within the very place where it takes on meaning as a powerful and political system of slippery significations—namely the school. Inside the school, overt and covert negotiations take place that are contingent upon the meanings that are created within its social world, meanings that differ from city to city, neighbourhood to neighbourhood, and school to school. This contextualized understanding of style enables a deeper understanding of girls' identities as complex and constantly on the move. It also showcases girls' awareness of how they are perceived by others and their creative efforts to shape and shift these perceptions. Girls at ESH kept their subject positions in play and readily negotiated new, hybrid, and experimental subject positions as a way to gain some control over how others perceived them, and how they perceived themselves.

As social skin, style thus functions as a significant form of embodied subjectivity for girls. It points to the intricate social processes in which girls are engaged on a daily basis, including consumer culture, the school and its social world, identity negotiation, and the discursive construction of girlhood. By denying the importance of their cultural practices, girls' attempts to make meaning out of their complicated lives goes unnoticed and undocumented. A Canadian girlhood studies that seeks to take girls' attempts at meaning-making seriously must work to highlight these connections by focusing on the cultural practices that girls themselves deem to have meaning in their lives. Toward that end, I leave the last words to Abby, who resented the way in which girls were represented in the press, particularly their construction as "clueless."

> I hate the fact that people judge without having talked to all teenage girls…cause I'm definitely not like that and my friends are mostly all definitely not like that. And so, it's just really bad, you know? Like, I'm sure if [adults] went out and talked to some people, they'd go: I guess [girls] are a lot smarter than we thought they were.

Notes

1. All the girls' names are pseudonyms.

2. Fulsang is referring to the influence of Britney Spears, whose 1999 smash, *Baby One More Time* (Jive Records), propelled her into the limelight. The video featured Spears in a schoolgirl uniform, but with a twist; she knotted her white blouse just under her breasts to reveal her midriff. Though Spears did not "invent" the visible midriff, she did much to popularize it as a mainstream style, as did her forerunners, Madonna and the Spice Girls.

3. Girls' and women's style has always pushed the envelope of social acceptability (flapper skirts and hot pants come to mind). Historically, it was "indecent" for a woman to show her ankles, calves, upper arms, knees, and thighs. And during the sexual revolution of the 1960s and 1970s, girls and women wore micro mini skirts and tube tops that easily rivalled the "skimpiness" of today's outfits.

4. Here, it should be noted that girls are always vulnerable to sexual assault and sexual harassment, no matter what they wear. Occurrences of these problems have not gone up as a result of current fashion trends and forcing girls back into "modest" clothing will certainly not make sexual assault and sexual harassment go away or make girls any less vulnerable as targets of violence.

5. "Incitement to discourse" is an expression used by Michel Foucault.

Chapter Twelve

From The Curse To The Rag:
Online gURLs Rewrite The Menstruation Narrative

Michele Polak

The Curse. My Friend. Aunt Flow. Bloody Mary. On the Rag. My period. That time of the month. My little red-headed cousin from the country. Surfing the crimson wave. Riding the cotton pony.

I begin this chapter by noting some of the many euphemisms North American culture has used for menstruation. I named only ten, but could have easily filled an entire paragraph with the colourful phrases that name this biologically female function. It is surprising how the preteen girl is expected to navigate around menstruation discussions, especially when mainstream North American culture so readily assumes known context. Catherine Driscoll (2002) notes that the coming of menstruation "is mostly figured as a physical change not necessarily heralded, signalled, or followed by any change in identity." However, the ideology of menstruation in Western culture indicates that such a change for adolescent girls "is often represented as social or psychological rather than physiological" (91) and the language codification by the culture of such an event is certainly one indication. The narrative of menstruation has been shrouded in secrecy, fear, discretion and embarrassment and has trickled down through generations of women. The perpetuation of such a narrative is pervasive in the feminine hygiene industry's widespread advertising.

For contemporary adolescent girls who are enmeshed in the mixed media images of popular culture, such a narrative becomes part of the framework that constructs girlhood. In my research on girls' online home pages, I began seeing a rewriting of the menstruation narrative, one that constructs a different conversation from the one of my own adolescence. While the ads of contemporary girls' magazines promote a discourse of euphemisms masking the issues of menstruation, girls online have taken to rewriting the familiar menstruation narrative; the one that teaches secrecy and discretion in relation to menstruating bodies. Girls online are creating a *new* narrative that is unflinchingly descriptive and seethingly honest—using a platform that allows for girls' voices in a communal space—often creating celebratory moments. While the feminine hygiene industry places the product uncritically for consumption, girls are using online spaces to ask—and answer—issues about menstruation that are not being circulated elsewhere. In reality, "girls want to know what it *feels* like to be menstruating" (Golub, 1992: 49, emphasis mine) and they are using online spaces to work through such issues.

In analyzing the current discussions of menstruation that girls are having online, I needed to go to the sources that are helping to (re)create this new and evolved narrative. I wanted to note the process that adolescent girls follow—from awareness through advertising to purchasing products—to try to understand exactly what type of discourse was forming and what new narrative was emerging from the remnants of the old. Since much of this is being created in a new textual space, it is the specifics of language that I am most interested in.

I began my research by collecting feminine sanitary product inserts and packaging and by reading ads in teen magazines. I sent out a request for samples to female colleagues and family members, and within days my mailboxes were spilling over with Tampax and Playtex bags, inserts, box tops and torn pages from *Teen*, *Seventeen* and *YM*. I had Carefree pantiliner packages stuck to student folders and Always Thin Ultra Flexi-Wings filed with my electric bill. Interestingly, almost every woman who sent me her feminine sanitary product packaging wanted to talk about their periods: particularly their first periods. I began to realize that given a platform, women are willing to talk about menstruation; we *need* to talk about menstruation. Yet, most of us are women who have been menstruating for more than ten years. If women have a need for such discussion, what about the preteen girl at the onset of puberty? What are they learning about menstruation and how are they learning? Like adult women, "girls really want to hear that they are not alone, that they are not the only ones who feel a sense of foreboding that their social ambitions, indeed their entire identity, can be derailed by their bodily anarchy" (Baumgardner and Richards, 2000: 192). Except now, girls have a space to voice such needs. By using online space, girls are not only writing a new menstruation narrative but they are ripping the familiar menstruation narrative of secrecy and discretion apart.

That I began this chapter with euphemisms is telling. We seldom hear the word "menstruation." I know I have never directly said, "I'm menstruating," nor have I heard other women say it, much less girls (who often can't pronounce it). Discussions about menstruation fall into the category of cultural taboo, ranked just under incest for social acceptance. Women don't discuss their periods in mixed company. Karen Houppert (1999) notes that there is no embarrassment when buying a box of Kleenex, but that shame surrounds buying feminine sanitary napkins. She analyzes this concept with an analogy: "Blood is kinda like snot. How come it's not treated that way?" (4)

Presently, as in the past, "nearly every religious and cultural tradition stigmatizes menstruating women" (Merskin, 1999: 944). We seldom celebrate its arrival or mark it with anything more than an "X" on our calendars. The negation surrounding menstruation is deeply rooted in religious, scientific and medical histories and altering that ideology would involve changing dominant thought patterns. By the end of the nineteenth century, the medical field began to analyze and categorize menstruation and decided it had less to do with sexuality and more to do with hygienic standards as new germ theories coded menstrual fluid as a health risk. Commercially-made feminine sanitary napkins replaced homemade rag napkins, giving rise to the feminine hygiene industry (Brumberg, 1997: 38). Tampax delivered the first tampon in July of 1936, and today the feminine hygiene industry is an eight billion dollar (US) industry worldwide (Houppert, 1999: 13).

It is no coincidence that the industry is so profitable. From day one, industry brands have used advertising and in-school programs to educate girls on the upcoming changes to their bodies. Most likely, "the industry's point of view is the only one young girls hear in the schools" (81). That "puberty film" preteen girls see in most North American schools is still being shown, only now there are newer versions created by corporate sponsors. The emphasis placed on menstruation education has come from the product makers, and the education carries with it marketing language. Information about that first period is seldom found at home; parents are often uncomfortable discussing menstruation with their daughters and if they do, it is "to emphasize selecting a sanitary product" but not about the responsibilities of menstruation itself (Brumberg, 1997: 54). Girls are left feeling unprepared and search for "information about menstruation from other sources" (Kissling, 1996: 294). The feminine hygiene industry works hard at getting that information to them. The result is the perpetuation of a commodified and coded language of menstrual myths, which Houppert suggests is "promoting a whole culture of concealment" (1999: 14). Instead of speaking openly to girls about what menstruation is and preparing them for the changes in their bodies and their emotions, we seem to be tied to the notion of keeping menstruation a secret. Girls learn early that menstruation beliefs "are negative, reflecting cultural stereotypes rather than personal experiences" (Golub, 1992: 19) and this ideology has effectively thrived for generations. The question remains: where do girls discuss menstruation and learn about the topic? What is available for them?

How am I supposed to get my groove on when I'm majorly stressed that
my defunct pad's gonna skip a beat? —Always, magazine advertisement

When I began comparing advertisements pulled directly from teen magazines, I learned that there are very clear, recurring themes that structure these ads. As Driscoll argues, "the feminine adolescent body is constructed in girls' magazines as a range of desires trespassed upon by a variety of physiological imperfections" and this becomes clear in the rhetorical structure in which these ads are created (2002: 94). None of the ads I reviewed dared stray too far from the ideology that menstruation is something that should be kept hidden for fear of repercussions. Discretion is to be used at all times when menstruating, a conventional femininity with attention paid to hetero-normative behaviour is the only way to define *girl*. Without the aid of proper feminine sanitary protection, a girl can forget any sort of socializing or actually *living* while menstruating. The narrative is clear here: managing menstruation is crucial to sorting through adolescent identity and the printed advert uses marketing rhetoric to bring that point home. As my interest focuses on how the current generation of girls may be navigating through the menstruation narrative, I limited my analysis to contemporary advertising and randomly selected ads from popular teen magazines from 2001 to 2004. Many of the same ads were repeated in different magazines. It is important to note that the majority of ads were strategically located within the magazine—on right-side pages—clearly indicating the importance of the product in relation to the reader. Flip open any teen magazine and you will find yourself directly looking at the feminine hygiene industry's "best of the best."

Word use is perhaps the most obvious connection between these ads: *trust*, *security*, and *comfort* are all readily-identifiable terms used across product lines and brands. The use of specific language reinforces the idea that without these products, girls will not feel *fresh*, thus disabling their ability to socialize and integrate with their peers. Fear and discretion are confirmed as the proper code of conduct for the menstruating girl. Houppert found that "the menstrual product industry…plays on insecurities—Am I leaking? Will this pad show?—and develops ad campaigns to maximize these fears" (36) and I did indeed find this notion of concealment (based on fear) in many of the advertisements I read. In promoting their Compak brand, a tampon with a collapsible applicator, Tampax boasts that the product is "small enough to keep out of sight" and "protection and discretion in the palm of your hand" (Tampax, sleeve). Another ad for the same product says, simply: "Discreet. Small. Extends and protects. Only you'll know it's a tampon" (Tampax, Dimes). The message is clear: without this brand's tampon, a menstruating body is sure to be discovered.

In many of these ads, the narrative depicts menstruation as something that needs to be "conquered" and with the right product any teen girl can become empowered to manage messy leaks, drips or spots, thus perpetuating the importance of secrecy where menstruation is concerned. Tampon ads specifically promote this concept of management, "reinforcing menstrual taboos while reassuring girls that they can control the menstruation process" (Driscoll, 2002: 96). Management has to do much with that sense of concealment, not allowing anyone (outside of the girl herself) to realize that a menstruating body even exists. For this purpose, feminine hygiene ads are careful about what is shown of the product in their design. Few ads will actually show a tampon or sanitary pad, and if they do it is through an illustration as opposed to a photograph. Only o.b. tampons have been consistent in using images of the actual product in their ads. Since their marketing ploy is that the tampon is used without an applicator, it is to their advantage to show the complete product. Other brand's non-applicator tampons are shown in their wrapper to accentuate their small size. And it is all about size. The smaller the tampon, the easer to hide. "Hiding" is germane here; most of the ads reinforce the product's ability not to be recognized. Discretion is emphasized over comfort of use. The goal is to show that though a girl is menstruating, her "condition" can go undetected with the proper product.

Detection and concealment are crucial to the menstruation narrative. Many ads place girls in social situations (usually in relation to boys) and illustrate that if the product is used properly and discreetly, security is guaranteed (and no boy will ever find out she's menstruating). It is boys who need to be kept oblivious. Perpetuating norms of conventional femininity, many of these ads promote a fixed hetero–normative identity: a girl is "normal" when she follows proper social codes. Identity is at stake here—an ignorance of the menstruating body is a sign of non-recognition of the body. As adolescents are already struggling with their newly-forming identity, to deny girls recognition of the self is to deny identity. As Merskin (1999) notes, "allegorical images (such as hearts and flowers) are associated with feminine hygiene products in order to signify freshness and delicacy" (947), thus inscribing the norms of stereotypical femininity onto the menstruation narrative. These ads have become "a kind of social guide" (955) for teen male/female relationships. In one Tampax ad, a cartoon drawing of three boys (one carrying flowers) is titled, "Just like the Tampax Multipack, it's good to have variety" with the adjacent text listing the benefits of the product's multi-pack packaging, stressing that "'those days' are even easier to handle. And that's good, because you've got your hands full with all those men" (Tampax, boys). In an Always ad, another cartoon depicts a girl standing in front of a large store display of feminine sanitary pads labelled with names like "Monster Maxis," "Titanic," and "Power Pads." A boy is seen in the distance walking up the isle. Balloon text above the girl's head reads: "I've only got about a nanosecond before Mr. Major Drugstore doll strolls by…and here I stand like a googly-eyed pad-freak. How'm I going to pick the right pad before I self-combust from utter and total embarrassment?" (Always, Samantha). Houppert comments that "the copy tells us, if boys are privy to their periods, the girls can kiss romance good-bye" (74). The perpetuation of such ideology enforces an ideal image that girls must maintain when menstruating.

Image plays a key role in how many of these ads are structured and the relation between image and identity is clear: if a girl is anything less than how the culture has historically defined "feminine," she places herself in a position of possible rejection by a boy. According to Merskin (1999), "bodies of girls and women are given meanings that suggest that there are times when they are unattractive" (954) and this is a consistent theme in many of the ads I viewed. In one Always sanitary pad advertisement, the text reads, "Spring dance. And you have your period. The good news is, your hormones make you feel more attracted to the caring, sensitive types. So, there's no better time to check him out!" (Always, Dance). The relationship between body image and identity to a girl's physiology during menstruation further reinforces the connection to the feminine. In another Always ad, "8 Signs your pad is all about protection" the text boasts: "You can catch a guy checking your rear end and the words 'Oh my God!' don't cross your mind!" (Always, 8 signs), combining the scripts of image *and* fear of detection. Maintaining a clean (and fresh) image is part of the narrative mythology that has been passed on through generations. Brumberg (1997) reasons that "modern mothers typically stress the importance of outside appearances for their daughters: keeping clean, avoiding soiled clothes, and purchasing the right equipment" (30) and since "menstruation instruction…often relies entirely on a curriculum created and peddled by sanitary protection companies," it is most likely how mothers came to this conclusion in the first place (Houppert, 1999: 81).

According to many of these ads, the "right equipment" is required to lead a more active lifestyle. Many maintain that girls are passive while menstruating and that only through proper product use will freedom follow, allowing the uncertain girl to participate in social and athletic events (Merskin, 1999: 954). All of the Playtex ads I viewed had some sort of activity theme pivotal to both the design and the written text. In one, a group of teens are playing on the beach. The header text reads: "Me? Miss out on the fun? That's not an option with Playtex Tampons" (Playtex, Beach). In another: "Awesome day! Can't believe I nearly bailed 'cause I was scared to use a tampon" (Playtex, Raft). In one Always ad, the layout is text-based; with half the page in repetition of the word "Sit" and the other half, "Dance." Only the line, "Stand-Up Protection" (Always, Sit) divides the design. There is a constant motif which contributes to the menstruation narrative here: without the proper product, menstruation will keep a girl passive and thus, unsocial. Without social interaction, there is no possibility that girl will meet boy.

> There are scientific studies that have concluded that tampons contribute to
> the cause of TSS. The reported risks are higher to women under 30 years of
> age and teenage girls. —Playtex tampons, package insert

By publishing such ads in teen magazines, the feminine hygiene industry can guarantee instant recognition of their product, thus leading to successful sales. It is at this point that a language shift occurs within the narrative. Ads in teen magazines are designed to draw in the female audience early, to create a potential consumer from youth to menopause. However, as Driscoll (2002) notes, "The girl of girls' magazines is in the field of puberty and yet not in control of it—she is in need of instruction, guidance, and helpful illustrative models" (95); once the product has been purchased, girls are faced with having to use it without clear guidelines for instruction. Since "tampons are now the primary product being advertised to girls" (Merskin, 1999: 953), it is likely that a box of tampons will be purchased by a girl sometime within her first five years of menstruating. In contrast to the advertising with which they have become familiar, however, the product's inserts and packaging maintain a very serious tone and inform the user of how to use the product with no specific attention paid to audience.

First-time users of sanitary pads, for example, are instructed by the packaging with either drawings or one-line sentences that state simply, "Peel middle adhesive strip and center pad on panties" (Stayfree, package wrapper). They do not state where specifically the pad should be placed, nor do they specify how the pad should be positioned. Any woman who has used sanitary pads knows how precarious that placement needs to be to avoid slipping and bunching. An inexperienced girl must navigate through much of this on her own. Imagine her confusion when confronted with "flexi -wings" or the thong pantiliner. Sanitary pad product lines often focus more attention on the package text and the product characteristics than they do usage. Girls are able to judge all of the benefits of a sanitary pad from the packaging—"Four Wall Protection" (Stayfree, package wrapper) or "Double Barriers" (Carefree, package box)—but knowing that a product is longer or wider is not helpful when placement is not specifically defined.

More daunting than sanitary pads, of course, is tampon usage. Insertion instructions vary per product, and some within the product line. Tampax, for example, includes a detailed drawing of their tampons on every insert yet the labelling changes. However, how the tampon is held is differently described: from a "contoured easy-to-hold grip" (Tampax Pearl), to "grooved ridges" (Tampax Satin), to "finger grip rings" (Tampax Regular) to a "grooved finger grip" (Tampax, package insert). The language becomes very clinical: insertion of the tampon should begin at the "vaginal opening" inserting "at a slight upward angle, approximately...forty-five degrees" (Tampax, package insert). A Playtex insert notes, "You should gently slide the applicator inside your vagina until your fingers touch your body" (Playtex, package insert). It is likely that a nervous twelve or thirteen year old girl is going to struggle with much of this terminology, especially if she is unfamiliar with the dynamics of her own anatomy. While every insert sheet I reviewed does include some attention to the first-time tampon user with a "Frequently Asked Questions" segment, this information is limited; drawings are of the side view of tampon insertion, not of female genitalia. Of all the product line insertion sheets I reviewed, only Tampax addresses the issue of actually labelling genitalia. This is not on every insert, however; of seven different inserts from products produced by Tampax in my collection, only one (Tampax Satin) addresses the first-time user in this way.

What may be perhaps most confusing to the new tampon user, however, is not the lack of detail on how to insert a tampon but the warnings of Toxic Shock Syndrome (TSS), a disease associated with tampon usage. By American and Canadian law, every tampon box insertion sheet must include a written caution. Every insert sheet I reviewed included very specific warnings about TSS. One insert included the text: "WARNING: Important information about Toxic Shock Syndrome (TSS)," outlined in a box in the middle of the page with a large font (Playtex, package insert). Several different Tampax insert sheets list instructions for tampon insertion on one whole side of the sheet with information about TSS on the reverse. While tampon ads boast of the comfort and discretion of tampon usage, there are no legal requirements that force the industry to include this information anywhere but on the inside of the product packaging. For many first-time tampon users, it is only after they purchase the product that they learn of this risk. If girls are only warned of the dangers of tampon usage by insertion sheets, they risk missing the the message if they have turned away from the instructions for lack of understanding the language.

There is a fragile connection here between the language that perpetuates the familiar menstruation narrative through advertising and the information that is provided for product usage. Sorting through the differences is difficult without the proper information to work through the associations. What I have found available for girls in terms of current menstruation education consists either of a one-day health class at school, various *Our Bodies, Ourselves*-type texts, and/or product advertising. Since most contemporary girls' mothers have been fed the menstruation narrative from these very same sources, discussions beyond the familiar narrative are not always forthcoming. While some mothers (or sisters or aunts) may share tips, most "menstruation education today tends to be rather intellectual, emphasizing anatomy and physiology, reproductive capacity, and menstrual hygiene" (Golub, 1992: 48). The menstruation narrative that is available for girls is one that limits uninhibited discussions and is defined by set rhetorical structures. As Elizabeth Kissling (1996) found in her research on girls and menstruation, girls in her study "perceived a lack of information resources, and often felt too shy or self-conscious to use available resources they did recognize" (298), suggesting that girls not only need more information on menstruation, but that they *want* more information. These discussions are indeed occurring. As I argue in the section that follows, a new space is opening, one that is shared among a community and in the company of other girls.

Thanks for making me not seem so weird. —Hello84Kitty, *bolt.com*

Today, much collaborative girl activity takes place online. This space is accessed by computer savvy *gURLs* who can build web pages in minutes and keep methodical daily weblogs about anything from dating to school activities. Space for women on the Internet has been largely established within the last decade, and gURLs do use the computer, logging on to contact friends they've met in message board forums and in chat rooms. Sherry Turkle (1999) found in her research of online communities that "the computer is not simply valued as the carrier of an idea, but as a means to increase a community's self-knowledge" (346) and gURLs are using the Internet to create such spaces for knowledge sharing. gURLs claim this space early; some begin creating websites as young as age eight and they hone their skills well into adulthood. There is a meshing of public and private space online for gURLs, a place to be honest yet anonymous without fear of the repercussions that may occur in a physical space. The body is removed so identity becomes malleable and gURLs can interact in any venue they choose. Driscoll (2002) notes that online, "significations of gender are mutable and disposable" allowing a girl to acknowledge her gender position without being constrained by the pre-written gender discourse from culture (277). In her research of gURLs homepages as a site for sexual expression, Stern (2002) argues that "the amalgam of private authorship and anonymous global readership offered by the WWW [World Wide Web] enables girls to speak both confidently and publicly about a conventionally taboo topic" (266). If such authorship is creating a space for frank discussions about sexual identity and awareness, such a space can be created for conversations about the menstruation narrative; especially considering that "for many girls, friends are among the most valued information sources, filling in the gaps of conventional menstrual education" (Kissling, 1996: 304). For gURLs, online space has become such a source.

The topic of menstruation comes up often in gURL-dominated chat rooms and in asynchronous message boards. It is common to see menstruation-related "posts" on a message board—an online text message sent to a "thread" which lists posts in linear fashion under one topic heading—on both websites created for teens and also gURL-specific websites. In sites such as *LiveWire Teen*, ("Peer answers. Peer support. Period.") forums for teen discussion include "Teen Health & Wellness" with threads focusing specifically on menstruation questions alongside other health-related topics. *bolt.com*, another teen website, lists forums for menstruation discussion under "Dealing & Health" with a sub-forum entitled, "PMS/Period." On gURL-focused websites such as *gURL.com*, menstruation discussions may occur both in message board forums and in other spaces within the site such as "Help Me Heather," an advice forum directed by one of the adult website owners. Menstruation discussions are occurring and in quantity; on a random day as I began my research, I noted eleven feminine sanitary product-related posts on a *bolt.com* forum and twenty-six menstruation-related posts on *gURL.com*. With all of this conversation occurring in only a twenty-four hour period, it seems only likely that a rewriting of the menstruation narrative will follow.

Rewriting the familiar menstruation narrative—the one fuelled by the feminine hygiene industry and perpetuated by mothers, grandmothers and consumer culture —is what has been happening in online communities. Here, gURLs are not only freed from the trappings of discretion but they are also learning new ideas about how the narrative may be rewritten. These are communities that consist of gURLs of all ages and backgrounds, so younger gURLs are benefiting from the experience of their own peers. Recognition of identity is occurring here; questions that are asked with timid hesitation by younger gURLs are answered with supportive comments and encouragement from older gURLs, responses enforcing the idea that menstruation is one thing they have in common and no question is too silly or too embarrassing to ask:

> OK i have a question. I started my period just recently. It came the first two months but it never came in march. I am still a virgin so i dont know whats wrong. If anyone might know please write a response! (MonkeChic88).

> Don't worry, nothing is wrong with you. Within the first few years of your period you might skip a month or two from time to time, it's completely normal (StarDust2211).

Issues concerning menstruation that are assumed learned via euphemisms or shared medical knowledge are often made more clear online:

> doctors ask is your period regulated, wtvr on a regular cycle...i mean i know whne o expect mine but its 3 weeks apart then 6 weeks apart—is that nriomal?? or means i am not regulated yet? I've had for 2.5 yrs...(rodaho).

> regulated means that it comes on a regular cycle. if it was irregular, it would come at a different time every month and would be unexpected (SpaceyBaby).

Note the online discourse here: this is computer language that these users are well versed in; acronyms and misspellings are part of the language style, as are screen names for anonymity. Not only are gURLs getting answers to their questions, they are getting it in their own language.

Online, the menstruation narrative is up for discussion with discussions concerning issues that are never addressed in feminine hygiene advertisements. In addition, questions are met with support, an acknowledgment that such issues are not new to the experienced gURL. It is in these communities that the preteen gURL will learn about menstrual blood, and that it is sometimes a dark color, but never the blue fluid that is depicted in ads:

> Hey people I want to know how to get blood out of sheets and if anyone knows can blood be brown? (Sammybells).

Any information, in addition to what the industry provides, that can be passed along is going to be well received. While tampon insert sheets may respond to difficult insertion questions with "remove the tampon and try again with a new one," the experienced girl can suggest another alternative:

I can't get um in!! Any suggestions? (nextluckygirl)

Find the smallest ones possible and try using vaseline to help push them up there. I think the plastic applicators are the best (meggie_54).

The "delicate" nature of the familiar menstruation narrative is not represented online; there are no euphemisms used:

well if we used home made pads, where would you put them when you are at the movies or someting? (incubus07190)

lol, that sounds really weird, i just use toilet paper. lol (irishluck7)

that's so funny! i thought i was the only one that did the toilet paper thing! now i don't feel so stupid! (imwithstupid87)

Such realities for contemporary girls may not be the same realities that mothers and grandmothers recognize. For gURLs, online space helps establish a shared base of knowledge:

What do I need to carry…in my bag for school, like details(not brands) on everything that should be in my trapper keeper/small purse all day at school (atjuedes)

just keep an extra pad on hand and a pair of panties in your locker. that should do you (blaubenthal).

You can't carry a backpack in school?? Why? (Airi_n_Hpotter)

at my school we couldnt! i think its because you can keep like a gun or something (Cafe_Mocha).

As gURLs start to recognize the problems within the familiar menstruation narrative, they become aware of the limits of the narrative as well. It is in these realizations that such a narrative is rewritten. Often, gURLs recognize that the knowledge passed onto them by their mothers is not the information they actually need:

i was talking to her the other day nad she found a lil box of tampons and she freaked!! shes like omg your not using them, if u do your not a virgin no more, no ones going to marry you this and that, and im like, ma your full of crap and i left, god, its just a da.mn tampon (mbabee).

Your mom is dumb (murderbabybirds).

Turning to other gURLs for advice, however, does not necessarily remove an older female presence from the online gURLs' real life experiences. Often, gURLs encourage including mothers, sisters and grandmothers in the menstruating experience:

please help me I am scared of tampons they make me nervouse and the problem is I don't know y? please help wat if I have to go swimming one day wat do I do! (Vro/freakd)

Hey...okay look here's the deal if you have an older sister or maybe like just
your mother, tell them ur situation. Then maybe they can stand outside the
bathroom door and sort of direct you. If it's that bad, and you cant get help,
know that plenty of woman use tampons without being scared and just let
yourself know its not a big deal (*Mel*).

Online, gURLs are sure to educate each other to make up for the shortcomings of the
familiar narrative:

okay I've only had my period once, and i used pads cause i was too scared to
try tampons...i know they're safe and easy and everything but i dont get
how they work...where do you put them in? (i dont know any of the fancy
names for down there btw) is there a hole or something? the one you uri-
nate from? and how often do you need to change it? (ticklemeelmo240)

okay right well there should be a diagram or something to tell you were to
put it in the box....you insert it into your vagina...not the whole you uri-
nate from tho! the one below it! you change it evry 4–8 hours or when it's
leaking or when you feel it's ready to be changed! but don't go over 8 hours
cuz that's a risk of tss! (sarah354)

In addition, with the vast variety of ages and experiences that constitutes the online
gURL community, posters are almost always guaranteed an answer to their questions
with confirmations or corrections added as threads grow:

I'm scared to use tampons 'cause of toxic shock (Reginald).

Oh yeah, but that's only if you put them in wrong (ThePurpleRoom).

Actually it happens when girls/women wear high absorbency tampons. So
try getting the minimum absorbancy that you can for your flow cycle
(Theophania).

With a new narrative, gURLs face managing menstruation in a different way than
how the advertising teaches them to manage it; the prevailing concern is not about
hiding the menstruating body as much as it is about finding the right product and
how to use it properly. By sharing facts and/or experiences with a product, gURLs are
able to make decisions for themselves concerning how they stand in relation to the
marketing of one product over another:

without regard to the brand of tampon...which type do you think is better?
the ones with plastic applicators or the ones with carboard applicators?
(Blondie110)

the plastic applicators are better. just easier to put in. (RaiderChick001)

plastic all the way. cardboard sucks! (sassyren-a)

The feminine hygiene industry has recognized the impact of online space for girls. Tampax has created *beinggirl.com* and Kimberly-Clark's Kotex brand's *girlspace.com* offers websites full of quizzes, polls and forums for menstruation discussion. gURLs continue to be targets of marketing, evidenced by how the product is consistently worked into the webpage design layout. On message board forums for teens or those specifically created for gURLs, product loyalty emerges only as a recommendation and not a hard sell. On *gURL.com*, for example, easing fear is the priority, not product brand names:

> Putting a tampon in seems like a daunting task, doesn't it? I know for me it was…Anyway relax. I know, I know that's easy to say and hard to do. This is what I did and it worked. Buy a brand for teens—like slim fit, gentle glide, peral glidem etc. shop around, ask your frineds or your mom. Plastic applicators are easier to insert (kathy109).

And on *bolt.com*:

> I recommend using tampax. I do not recommend O.B until you get used to putting in a tampon with an applicator (Krisy1301).

> Uhm, you could use playtex silkglide or tampax pearl. I think those are the easiest ones to put in. You just pull on the string to get it out. It's not a big deal really….truth is, if you use silkglide, you'll probably fall in love with them (OrEohunny2005).

> i just tried kotex security…they're pretty good…same with tampax and playtex…but i really couldn't feel the kotex ones, and they don't leak (devillish_angel).

It is common for threads to offer such a variety of suggestions with the kind of high volume visits these topics receive.

What is perhaps the most common issue that arises in online gURL communities are discussions about embarrassment. While the familiar menstruation narrative teaches girls discretion about their menstruating bodies, the rewritten narrative that gURLs are creating teaches that all girls have similar experiences and that sharing them is the best way to understand and embrace the learning that comes with menstruation. In this way, a sense of identity begins to grow, the same identity that is denied girls by the familiar/old or conventional menstruation narrative. Sharing, as gURLs argue, is part of the process:

> Could you guys post your embarrassing stories about your periods…I dont know…Hearing about other people kinda makes me feel better for all the stupid crap Ive done (MissSexy76110).

Issues that were once a hindrance to the generation before are shrugged off by gURLs in the realization of how common incidents relating to menstruation are:

pads are loud. You might as well say hey im on my period *crinkle Crackle* i have the shhhh wrappers…they are alright but i dunno… (BluesMagenta).

Ha, I remember I used to be so freaked about people hearing the RRRRRRIP of the pad and packaging. My friends and I would turn on the water loud and start washing our hands if one of us was changing a pad and there were others in the bathroom. You get over it. Now it's like, who gives a shit? (lex-a).

Unlike feminine hygiene product advertisements, no language taboos are in use here, nor are euphemisms; if the new product user is ashamed or embarrassed about menstruation, gURLs move right past the embarrassment and give the poster the information she needs with no hesitation:

What are OB tampons like…arnt they just like playtex…confused (ki-ki11).

they don't have applicators… BLECH! (Mejane-a)

never tried them but yeah, how do you get them in if they dont have applicator?? (sassyren-b)

You just put them in (ditto2001).

wouldnt your finger get all…ya know? (krispykremewiss)

bloody? yes (Mejane-b).

Given that girls do read teen magazines (in abundance) and the contemporary girl is part of a media-soaked generation, it is inevitable that "spillage" from consumer culture will continue to make its mark on the menstruation narrative. As gURLs are rewriting, the constant references to what is being fed to them as feminine hygiene "education" is always up for discussion. Since so much of the narrative that has been passed down continues to inscribe conventional feminine ideals, this seems to be the base topic from which gURLs begin a restructuring of the narrative. Boys and relating to boys remains an issue in the menstruation narrative, no matter who is doing the writing. With gURLs however, the rhetoric of staying clean and fresh—and particularly around boys—is no longer valid. One dominant theme among gURLs is to post about a boyfriend or male friends who are "OK" learning about menstruation:

Have any of you guys talked to your boyfriends about your periods ? (or your ex boyfriends) I told my boyfriend he's cool with it but he really hates pads and he really hates when I'm like "oh man I have cramps" he's like "oooooooh ooook then I think I'm gonna go" I told him everything about it he knows when it is how long it last and stuff. Have any of you girls told your guys ? how did they react ? (lovergirl_03_30)

As some gURL communities do form on teen websites that are not exclusive to girls, menstruation is up for discussion for every member of the community, including boys:

> My gf talks to me about her period. Its no big deal. Guys understand thats what girls are all about (lostguy).

Shattering the old narrative are the many, many requests concerning *how* to tell boys about menstruation:

> um, If anyone can help me too, I have a new bf—and if somthing comes up about period—can I just say "its that time of the month" and nothing else to because they dont want to hear about it, is taht ok? (sparkarumpa)

gURLs are no longer hiding (or hiding behind) their menstruating bodies:

> hey!…okay my bf can always tell for some reason?!…he doesnt really mind that i talk abou it…like the other day i was goin to the bathroom an he saw me…i was havin super bad cramps an he came out an gave me a giant hug an kiss an asked if i was okay…hes so sweet!!*…but guys really dont mind when we talk about it- almost all of them have sisters =) (stacey2008).

Nor are they allowing for the perpetuation of silence or non-recognition of identity where the menstruating body is concerned:

> Well…yeah i told my boyfriend…im actually quite open about my period…ill tell anyone…lol…if someone asked me whats wrong? ill say…im on my period…ya happy? i dont really care. (thugladee).

> The GUYS are uncomfortable with it…a tampon fell out of my backpack, and of course I wasn't embarassed (who cares?), but the guy was like… uhh, you dropped something. I was like, what is it? It was under the desk and I couldn't see it. And he said "It's umm…it's right there…under the desk." God, they can't even say tampon? He was bright red and doing a nervous laugh. I found it funny (lex-b).

Of course, the implications of online discussions about menstruation are plentiful. First and foremost, girls with no computer access are excluded completely. Internet usage remains a privilege and unless a girl has access to a computer at home, school or public library, she is left out. However, computer access does not guarantee that every girl online becomes a gURL; without strong computer skills, a user may lack the knowledge to travel through chat rooms and message boards. Consideration also needs to be made of the sources of advice. Since online communities are often open forums, anyone can offer guidance and opinion. As much as anonymity is an attraction for a gURL to create identity, it is as much a safety hazard when such an identity is masked. Given that cyberethics concerning identity is still a new debate, such teen communities can become a predatory space and sometimes dangerous for girls.

Gender interaction in such communities, however, seems to be productive where the menstruation narrative is concerned. Boys are getting answers to questions they never knew how to ask, or *who* to ask as the familiar menstruation narrative ignores them completely. It should be noted, however, that while boys may be reading threads about the topic, few actually participate in discussion unless they have an actual question or an applicable comment. As far as receiving backlash or negative responses from boys concerning menstruation, like any online gURL community, this is space very much protected by a generation of girls that have found a platform for voice and they will not be silenced. gURLs know when a post is not "real" either by tone, context or style of language and they will react by "trolling" the offender out, making note of the presence and then ignoring a post (or posts) completely. Since netspace is so much about interaction and community, being ignored eventually sends the offender elsewhere.

What is lacking in these menstruation discussions is often professional medical advice. Many of these girls post issues that may require medical attention, such as signs of infection or prolonged periods. The benefits of the diversity of online communities, however, are the array of suggestions that are offered for discomfort and overall health. In addition to conventional medical advice, holistic treatments for curing cramps are posted, thus never limiting a gURL in her options. That gURLs are moving away from (or in some cases, not recognizing) conventional medicine may be yet another rewrite of the menstruation narrative, a return to a place in which women are more in tune with the patterns of their menstrual cycles and are inclined to consider whole body healthcare. While advice is what is most sought-after in menstruation discussions, it should be noted that with such an age range among gURLs, the experience of older gURLs often prompts recommendations of speaking with a female family member, usually a mother. In fact, seeking outside help beyond the online community is the most common advice provided in these menstruation discussions.

If navigating through the menstruation narrative is difficult enough for adult women, it is much more so for the preteen girl. That so many women anxiously wanted to speak with me about their menstrual cycles at the beginning of my research is a testimony to how badly a shift in this cultural ideology toward menstruation needs to happen. As Driscoll (2002) notes, "menstruation in discourses on girlhood, feminine adolescence, or female puberty articulates revelation, explication, reassurance, and disgust" (92) and these dichotomies are what is being offered to the adolescent girl for education in menstrual health. It is in online spaces that the familiar menstruation narrative is up for being rewritten by a new generation of gURLs who are beginning to challenge the mythologies that have existed for over a century. We can only hope that this space opens up for girls who are excluded and for the adult women who are looking for a space of their own. Perhaps as this narrative is being rewritten, we will look to menstruation euphemisms as a part of our past.

Web and Product Notations

Always, 8 signs. Advertisement. *Seventeen*. June 2002.

Always, dance. Advertisement. *Twist*. March 2003.

Always, package wrapper. Procter & Gamble. Bag of 32 Thin Ultra Flexi-Wings Pads. Accessed March 2003.

Always, Samantha. Advertisement. *Teen People*. Feb 2001.

Always, sit. Advertisement. *YM*. Nov 2004: 27.

http://www.bolt.com

http://www.discussion.kimberly-clark.com

http://funkyteen.com

http://www.golivewire.com

http://www.gurl.com

http://messageboards.gurl.com

http://www.golivewire.com

Carefree, package box. Personal Products Company. Box of 18 Panty Shields. Accessed October 2004.

Playtex, beach. Advertisement. *YM*. Nov 2004: 20.

Playtex, Frisbee. Advertisement. *Girl's Life*. Feb/March 2002: 25.

Playtex, raft. Advertisement. *Girl's Life*. Feb/March 2003.

Playtex, package insert. Playtex Products, Inc. Accessed March 2003.

Stayfree, package wrapper. Personal Products Company. Bag of 18 Ultra Thin Maxi Pads. Accessed March 2003.

Tampax, Boys. Advertisement. *Sugar*. April 2002.

Tapmax, Dimes. Advertisement. *YM*. Sept 2003: 159.

Tampax, package insert. Tampax Corp. Printed, 2000. Accessed, March 2003.

Tampax Pearl, Regular, Satin. Package inserts. Procter & Gamble. Printed, 2002. Accessed, March 2003.

Tampax, sleeve. Advertisement. *Teen People*. March 2001: 151.

Chapter Thirteen

Pretty In Panties:
Moving Beyond The Innocent Child Paradigm In Reading Preteen Modeling Websites

Sophie Wertheimer

"Vicky" faces the camera. She kneels down, legs slightly parted, head tilted to the side.[1] Wearing a red polka dot bikini and clutching a teddy bear in her left hand, her painted lips part to reveal the faint shadow of a smile. Her heavily lined blue eyes staring directly into the lens, and in turn, at her viewer, she seems oblivious to the modeling set—a floor and wall painted of white—that surrounds her. Instead, she appears absorbed in the moment, posing for the camera with a demeanour and look of appealing nonchalance, one not so distant from that of the fashion models who inhabit the pages of *Vogue*. She is preserved on virtual celluloid, and for a monthly membership fee of $19.95 (in American funds), you can see hundreds of additional pictures of her, wearing colourful outfits, practicing yoga, lying down on her stomach or her back, but always posing, always looking straight into the camera.

"Vicky" is ten years old and she is but one of the countless North American girls (predominantly white and between the ages of seven and twelve) who have found their way onto the internet as part of the phenomenon of preteen modeling websites. Making their first appearance in the late 1990s, media coverage on the topic credits Webe Web, a Florida based corporation also specializing in adult pornographic sites, with their initial creation. As a spokesperson for the company reports,

> [T]he child modeling sites were inspired by a birthday party thrown for a friend's nine-year-old daughter. Pictures of the Spice Girls-themed party were posted on the Internet, and within a week they were getting 20, 000 page views a day...The company started charging for the site, which morphed into Jessithekid.com (Scheeres, 2001).

"Jessi the Kid" garnered a high degree of popularity and success, making it obvious that there was a substantial market for these images, and new websites soon began making their appearance. Less than a decade later, the internet now houses hundreds if not thousands of them.[2] While many of these websites continue to be owned and operated by private entrepreneurs, a number of them are also run by the girls and their family members or guardians themselves.[3]

Furthermore, "Jessi the Kid" seems to have created the template for all subsequent preteen websites, such that very little diversity is to be found amidst the pages. All have a similar "feel," brightly coloured and reminiscent of the pin-up girl. All have similar content as well. Though certain images feature the models with friends or in larger groups, each girl usually poses alone on her own individual website. While preview pages are accessible free of cost, offering a dozen or so pictures of the model in various outfits and poses, the remainder of the site is accessible to paying members only. In exchange for fees, members are granted access to new images (updated monthly or more often) and archived photos, hundreds of images of the model posing in various outfits—from bikinis, leotards, to shorts and halter-tops. Members are also granted access to videos, chat rooms, and wish lists from which they can select gifts to send to the girls.

Heralded by their makers as "portfolios" for the girls to advertise their modeling services, these websites have garnered some controversy since their appearance in cyberspace. Though the models are always "fully" clothed (or at least have their genitals and breasts covered), news media have been quick to criticize, and have accused preteen modeling websites of promoting child pornography and pedophilia.[4] Not without reason. As a *Daily News* article remarks, they "are set up just like porn sites, with all but a few pictures hidden in a members-only area accessed by credit card for twenty to thirty dollars a month. Billing, viewers are assured, will be discreet" ("Parents Exposing Kids on Soft-Porn Web Sites," 2002). Beyond their design, these websites feature images of little girls made up and looking lasciviously to the camera, making it difficult to read "Lil' Miss Amber," "SammiJo" and "Jessi the Kid," without seeing sexual connotations.

I first heard about preteen modeling websites in the summer of 2003, while watching an episode of *Oprah* (Oprah, 2003). My curiosity immediately aroused, I quickly jumped online to try and locate these websites for myself. They were surprisingly easy to find: a simple google of the term "preteen model" linked to hundreds of individual home pages. As I clicked away, taking free tours and seeing the images of these petite preteen bunnies I found myself feeling simultaneously repulsed and fascinated by them. Reading in these sites what to me were clear sexual overtones, I could not help but feel appalled, angered even, by the sheer existence of them; not to mention how easy they were to find. Paradoxically, as I clicked away, I also felt drawn to them, wanting to see more, wanting to know more.

Intrigued by the sites and my strong visceral reaction to them, I began reading about the preteen modeling phenomenon in newspapers and on the internet, while also discussing matters with friends and colleagues. It became increasingly apparent that I was not alone in experiencing such a strong response to them. More often than not they seemed to trigger reactions very similar to my own: an avalanche of emotions in both degree and range. I began to wonder why we (as individuals and members of a wider North American culture) were reacting so very strongly to these images. What exactly was it that managed to stir up so many contradictory feelings and emotions, and to such a strong level? Was it the medium? Or the message?

My fascination launched me into a research inquiry that would lead me to explore academic literature surrounding childhood, girlhood, sexuality and culture within the North American context. The more I read, the more I realized that the pre-teen modeling website phenomenon was not an isolated occurrence, but rather came to be positioned in a much broader social, cultural and discursive framework; one shaped by very specific understandings of childhood.

This chapter begins by tracing the North American construction of the child, one I argue is fraught with contradictions whereby the child is perceived as embodying asexual innocence while simultaneously finding herself eroticized in countless cultural texts. Situating the preteen modeling websites in relation to the myth of the innocent child, I investigate why they manage to elicit such strong reactions. Reading these websites within the paradigm of childhood innocence, I argue that the girls who model for them are rendered passive objects as opposed to active meaning-makers and agents in their own right. In the second section I attempt to move beyond the child as innocence paradigm, offering ways to read these websites and girls' participation in them as providing the models with forms of empowerment and pleasure, albeit problematically.[5]

Mapping The Murky Terrain Of North American Childhood

It is difficult to remain unaffected by the image of a prepubescent girl in a bikini; lips painted into a pulpous red pout, and legs stretched open towards the camera lens. It is almost impossible to remain unaffected because it seems to work in direct opposition to our understanding of the girl-child. Indeed, as Lea Redfern (1997) notes, in the North American context, "children are constructed as, above all else, innocent. Innocence is understood as a freedom from, or an absence of, guilt and sin; it conveys ignorance, artlessness and naivety" (52).

In fact, the equation of the child with innocence seems to have become so prevalent and ingrained in our culture that many authors have even ascribed to it the status of myth. This is one of the key tenets in Henry Giroux's work on children and culture, in that he posits that the myth of the innocent child is "constructed around the notion that both childhood and innocence reflect aspects of a natural state, one that is beyond the dictates of history, society and politics" (Giroux, 2000: 265). Such a perspective has come to dominate most discursive accounts and constructions of childhood in Western culture.[6]

However, children have not always been so innocent. The origins of this conflation can be traced back (with debate) to the nineteenth century, when changing social
conditions allowed children to be moved from the factories and streets into schools
and other social institutions (Jenkins, 2004: 23). Progressively segregated from the
world of adults, children increasingly came to be regarded as separate and distinct entities. Childhood, as Giroux notes, was rendered a world "untainted, magical, and ut-
terly protected from the harshness of adult life" (1999: 265).

One of the realms where the 'child as innocence' paradigm has manifested itself
particularly strong is in relation to sexuality. Although earlier twentieth century
thinkers such as Sigmund Freud and Benjamin Spock advocated for understanding
children as possessing their own inherent sexuality, one not so distant from that of
adults, it seems that society has been reluctant to include this attribute in its understanding of the child (Jenkins, 1999: 209-230).

According to Laurence O'Toole, this may in part be due to the "uncivilized character" of children's sexuality, "which appears to be without barriers, failing to observe
the distinctions between the masculine and the feminine, the oral and the anal" (1998:
235). Presenting an affront to the heteronormative model of sexuality so valued in
North American society, O'Toole argues that it is necessary for the child's polymor-
phous sexuality to be denied or repressed, because it also challenges the assumed "nor-
mality" of heterosexuality.

Furthermore, in a society where sexuality is viewed as what Walkerdine calls an
"adult notion," (1996: 325) and largely premised on underlying Christian, and in
turn, Victorian equations of sexuality with guilt and sin, "a child's knowledge of the
sexual [becomes] antithetical to their innocence" (Redfern, 1997: 52).[7] Any demon-
stration of sexuality on the part of the child, any remote association between the two,
becomes highly taboo. For the myth of childhood innocence to be preserved, the child
must be rendered—and kept—asexual at all costs.

Though the myth of the innocent asexual child persists as the dominant paradigm in understanding and representing childhood within the North American context, this is not tantamount to saying that other representations or constructions of
childhood have remained non-existent. For instance, recent years have also witnessed
an increase in discourses and representations related to deviance in children, for example with concerns surrounding violent crimes perpetrated by young children
(Woodson, 1999). Labelled by Woodson as *the monstrous child*, alternative discourses
of childhood come to simultaneously strengthen and threaten the myth of the innocent child, exemplifying what children ought not to be and not to do. Furthermore, often depicted as belonging to a category of otherness, whether in relation to race, class,
psychological or physical health, these alternative discourses also come to reify an assumption intrinsic to the myth of the innocent child, namely that she is most often
white, middle class, physically attractive and female. As Giroux (1998) notes,

> In short, the discourse of innocence suggests a concern for all children but
> often ignores or disparages the conditions under which many children are
> forced to live, especially children marginalized by class or race who, in ef-
> fect, are generally excluded from the privileging and protective invocation
> of childhood (32).

As our own childhoods (or at least my own!) have taught us, there is excitement to be
found in what is taboo or prohibited. Paradoxically, while much has been invested towards building and preserving the notion of the innocent, asexual child, Western culture has also rendered the child an object of desire.[8] As Walkerdine (1996) contends,
the erotically appealing prepubescent girl is a leitmotif within Western culture and
one that is not particularly new. For instance, Nabokov first published his influential
novel *Lolita*, about a middle-aged man and his attraction to a girl on the brink of puberty, in 1955. Before this time, the 1930s were marked by the immense popularity of
Shirley Temple. One of the critics of this young starlet, Graham Greene, once described
her as "a fancy little piece, wearing trousers with the mature suggestiveness of a
Dietrich: her neat and well-developed rump twisted in a tap-dance: her eyes had a
sidelong searching coquetry" (153).

The eroticization of the girl-child has not subsided. Quite the contrary: the image
of the innocent but alluring (white, middle-class, female) child only seems to have mul-
tiplied. Examine, for instance, Coppertone suntan lotion, where a cute little blond-
haired girl laughs as her underwear is pulled down by a dog. Or turn on the television or
flip through a magazine. "Popular images of little girls as alluring and seductive, at once
innocent and highly erotic, are contained in the most respectable and mundane of locations: broadsheet newspapers, women's magazines, television adverts" (Walkerdine,
1996: 326). Indeed, as Anne Higonnet (1998) notes,

> The sexualization of childhood is not a fringe phenomenon inflicted by per-
> verts in a protesting society, but a fundamental change furthered by legiti-
> mate industries and millions of satisfied consumers. By the 1990s, the
> image of the child has become perhaps the most powerfully contradictory
> image in Western consumer culture, promising the future but also turned
> nostalgically to the past, trading on innocence but implying sexuality, si-
> multaneously denying and arousing desire (153).

The appeal of the eroticized child has not only permeated visual culture, but has also
made its way into countless other cultural texts, endlessly reproduced and rewritten.
In his (1998) book *Erotic Innocence*, James Kincaid traces the many sites—from advertisements, to jokes about notorious child-lover Michael Jackson—where discourses
and images of sexualized children are circulated. He suggests that

> ...our culture has enthusiastically sexualized the child while denying just as
> enthusiastically that it was doing any such thing. We have become so en-

gaged with tales of childhood eroticism (molestation, abduction, and pornography) that we have come to take for granted the irrepressible allure of children (13).

Kincaid also pinpoints a pattern that seems to have occurred in tandem with the increased eroticization of children: the rise in concerns surrounding the issue of child abuse. Though "discovered" and institutionalized in the 1960s, the fear of child abuse, and more specifically child sexual abuse, has become so pervasive that many authors have positioned it within the framework of the moral panic (Wilkins, 1997). "Characterized by a wave of public concern, anxiety, and fervour about something, usually perceived as a threat to society," Wilkins advances that moral panics often manifest a "level of interest totally out of proportion to the real importance of the subject" (Wilkins, 1997).

Of course, within North American society children certainly have been and continue to be victims of abuse. But the fear and obsession with this issue has become so omnipresent that it has even changed the way children are raised and educated. For example, many American schools have instituted "no-touch" policies, which include "forbidding male teachers from changing diapers or being alone with children and prohibiting caregivers, both male and female, from holding children in their laps while reading, or even hugging a child who has fallen off a tricycle" (Levine, 2002:182).

However, as Scheper-Hughes and Stein (1999) note, "the 'choice' of child abuse as a master social problem of our times also includes a strong 'choice' for only certain forms of child abuse—battering and sexual abuse—and a *selective inattention* to other forms—specifically, poverty-related neglect" (190). Pervasive as they may be, discourses surrounding child abuse, rather than providing a comprehensive image of the various forms of abuse that affect children, tend to focus on cases of sexual abuse, and more particularly sexual abuse by strangers. This process of selective inattention allows for the production of the ultimate Big Bad Wolf, the fundamental threat to the child: the pedophile. He is the grown man who loiters in public parks and schools, waiting to lure children away with candy, to use and discard them as he pleases. He has been vilified and dehumanized, as is well reflected in the following statement made by a lawyer specializing in defending children: "The predatory pedophile is as dangerous as cancer. He works quietly, and his presence becomes known only by the horrendous damage he leaves" (qtd. in Levine, 2002: 23).

Though child abuse in the form of pedophilic "stranger-danger" has and continues to affect children, the focus on this particular manifestation of abuse obscures the reality that most cases of abuse against children occur within the home. This finds itself well illustrated in Canadian statistics about child sexual abuse. A 2003 report indicates that "only 10% of the victims under the age of 6 and about 10% of victims aged 6 to 13 were sexually assaulted by a stranger while this was the case for almost one-fifth of victims aged 14 to 17" (Statistics Canada, 2003). In this sense, the moral panic diverts our attention "from the intense emotional fabric of the isolated nuclear family in which the overwhelming majority of abusive situations originate" (Silin, 1997: 222-3).

Beyond this, many authors suggest that the preoccupation, if not obsession, with this particular type of abuse also serves

> to displace other collective unconscious anxieties and contradictions in American society…[and] masks the (American society's) complicity (and collective responsibility) in the implementation of local, national and international policies that are placing our nation's, and indeed the world's children at great risk (Levine, 180).

The pedophile can therefore be understood as a scapegoat upon which society projects its fears in relation to childhood, perceived as increasingly under threat in a world of incessant newness and uncertainty, where risk seems to have become the modus operandi.[9] And within this framework, where the innocent child has also become the child-at-risk, the new medium of the internet, (attractive but greatly unknown) has come to be understood and discussed.

Indeed, this new and mostly unknown medium has come to be positioned as presenting yet another threat to the sanctity of childhood. While discussions surrounding children and the internet have certainly praised the value and opportunities offered by this medium in enhancing children's access to information and knowledge, they have also tended to center around its negative implications, real or imagined, in the lives of children.[10] As Holloway and Valentine (2003) note,

> some commentators argue that the relatively unregulated nature of cyberspace means that sexually explicit discussions, soft and hard core pornography, racial and ethnic hatred, Neo-Nazi groups and paedophiles [sic] can all be found in the space dubbed by some on the moral right an 'electronic Sodom' (74).

Because there seems to be an almost automatic assumption that where there is a threat to children, there is also a child abuser lurking not far behind, discourses of pedophilia and the internet have taken on monumental proportions—to the extent that Oprah Winfrey has called the web "open season for pedophiles" (Oprah, 2003). Through its largely unregulated nature, the internet has come to be understood as an ideal site for the circulation of child pornography, the luring of children into the production of pornography and other types of sexual abuse. While there have been reported cases of pedophilic web-rings, and although the internet certainly harbours child pornography and virtual communities of individuals that consume it, actual occurrences seem to have been blown out of proportion. As Lumby (1997) contends, it is possible to apply the framework of moral panic to concerns surrounding sexual predators and access to pornographic material on the web. Rather than reflecting the actual extent of the threat that the internet presents, these discourses mobilize around middle-class concerns surrounding parenting and the family, pointing to "broad cultural anxieties about the way the labile world of the internet and the possibilities of virtual life are changing traditional social hierarchies, including the boundaries between adults, adolescents and children" (45).

From this brief and by no means comprehensive account of the prevalent paradigms and discourses that inform our understandings and perceptions of "the child," it becomes rather obvious that childhood as a discursive construct is an extremely murky terrain, one fraught with myths, expectations, projections and contradictions. Seen in this light, the complex and contradictory responses to images of prepubescent girls in bikinis perhaps are not so surprising after all.

Indeed, the images on these websites present a direct affront to the myth of the innocent child, in that they explicitly project a highly eroticized image of her. In challenging the innocence of the child, these images become read as reflecting the child-at-risk, and inevitably conjure up the spectre of abuse and, by extension, that of the pedophile. This certainly seems to be the principal leitmotif in media coverage of this phenomenon, as the images are constantly referred to as forms of child pornography (without the nudity), and assumed to "have a primary audience of pedophiles" (*Daily News*, 2002).

Furthermore, while the images on these websites may represent another level on the erotic-child continuum—constructed, circulated and consumed in many other of our cultural texts—they seem to strike us as much more "real" than the Coppertone baby or the picture of the pretty little girl eating ice cream in a car commercial. As Higonnet (1998) notes, "knowing a child is professional helps," creating an "awareness that a role is being played, a role that does not affect the 'real' child" (147). The images on these websites are not of 'professional' models, produced and circulated in a context of assumed regulation and protection to render unrelated products and services more enticing. Rather, with their "amateur" aesthetic, these are images of the "little girl next door," that could "just as well have been from a backyard birthday party" (Brunker). They are not printed in a magazine or billboard, but are circulated on the internet; a world largely defined by its unregulated nature.

Finally, the intent behind these images is not to sell a product or service, but rather to sell the images themselves. "These Web sites don't sell products, they don't sell services—all they serve are young children on a platter for America's most depraved" (Brunker). However, as Higonnet remarks, "a child marketed as a public spectacle is intended to provoke some kind of desire, perhaps ultimately for a product or service, a cosmetic or an athletic ideal, but inevitably for himself or herself along the way" (1998: 147). This begs the question as to why these websites elicit such strong reactions while the Coppertone baby has yet to be dislodged from bottles, advertisements and billboards throughout North America (and perhaps even the world).[11]

Higonnet describes Western culture's bad habit of equating image with reality; one that even informs the legislation surrounding child pornography (1998: 162-3). The act of looking at the image of the child in an erotic manner therefore automatically indicates or results in an actual act of abuse. Similarly, extrapolating from anti-pornogra- phy feminists' claim that "pornography is the theory, rape is the practice," Jenkins (2001) offers the corollary: "child pornography is the theory, molestation is the practice" (4).

Of course, the association between erotic images of children and actual acts of pedophilia is not unfounded. As the Brunker points out, "David Westerfield, charged in San Diego with murdering [seven]-year-old neighbor Danielle Van Dam, had 64,000 pictures of children on his computer." This is not an isolated case, in that many child sexual abusers have been found to "collect" pornographic or erotic images of children. However, as Rettinger (2000) illustrates, for the most part, it appears that just as few molesters actually consume erotic images of children, consuming such images rarely results in the sexual molestation of children. "A simple, direct causal link between pornography and sexual offending is not supported by the literature" (18), a point echoed in Higonnet's claim that "there is simply no consistent or reliable evidence that looking at an image all by itself can make a person commit an action, even the action represented in the image" (177).

Despite the data, this profoundly rooted articulation affects the way in which we view preteen modeling websites. The models may be clothed, but we read the images as erotic and thus assume that this desire will be acted upon and that the models will become victims of sexual abuse. "These sites are like an amusement park for pedophiles…and sooner or later, they will want to go for a ride" (Thompson). However, considering their magnate popularity, some of these sites garnering "thousands of hits per day," (Daily News) "Lil Amber's' fan club at one time [having] more than 9,000 members," (Brunker) it seems improbable that all these "fans" are molesting children in reality. Sometimes, a fantasy is arousing precisely because it is just that; because it is unreal while simultaneously transgressing very real taboos. Neil Levy (2002) even argues that "a case can be made for the opposite view: that allowing virtual porn will reduce the amount of harm to actual children, by providing an acceptable outlet for dangerous desires" (320).

Dangerous desires that are apparently shared by many. The immense popularity of these websites resonates with Higonnet's claim that "the sexualization of childhood is not a fringe phenomenon inflicted by perverts in a protesting society" (153). Indeed, not only do these websites offer images that we as a society have grown accustomed to seeing, but ones that we have come to find extremely appealing. According to Silin, "the pedophile, who we demonize even as we construct, marginalize as we normalize, distance as we bring closer, has become a primary vehicle for expressing/repressing our own erotic interests in children" (1997224-25). Beyond troubling us because they present a direct affront to the innocent child paradigm, one that "can only end in abuse," these websites touch a nerve because they offer us images we like to see, and hate ourselves for liking. Whether or not we are erotically titillated by the images, we read sexuality and eroticism into them. Because ascribing any form of sexuality to children is so taboo, we cannot help but experience extremely strong emotions and reactions as a result.

I must emphasize that in no way do I wish to negate the reality of child abuse —sexual, physical, verbal and even institutional—in vilifying these sites or the predatory pedophiles we assume to be lurking behind them. However, we avoid questioning the wider structures that have rendered the child erotically appealing in the first place. Perhaps it would prove more productive to turn a critical eye on the social parameters that create such a big market for these websites and renders participation in them attractive to both the girls and their parents. In the process, we might also gain a more comprehensive and realistic understanding of the social, cultural, institutional and familial issues that continue to make children victims of physical, psychological and sexual violence; moving away from a pattern whereby the "surveillance of images substitutes for the care of real children" (Higonnet: 189).

Granted, these websites force us "to the realization that the cultural geography of childhood can no longer be envisioned as a happily-ever-after, never-never land of innocence and light" (Woodson: 42). Rather than clinging desperately to our antiquated and problematic discourses, paradigms and reactions, perhaps in this moment of realization we can find ways to move in different directions.

Moving Beyond The Child As Innocence: Play, Empowerment and Pleasure As Possible Paradigms

In the conclusion to his book *Erotic Innocence*, Kincaid (1998) reminds us that

> We have been so busy reinventing the child as being at risk sexually that we
> have allowed the happy child to wander out of our range. We have made
> the child we are protecting from sexual horrors into a being defined exclu-
> sively by sexual images and terms: the child is defined as sexual lure, the
> one in danger, the one capable of attracting nothing but sexual thoughts.
> The laughing child has been replaced in our cultural iconography by the
> anxious, fretting child—really, a grotesquely sexy little adult (283).

Within this framework, where the child is "marked as innately pure and passive, children are ascribed the right to protection but are, at the same time, denied a sense of agency and autonomy" (Giroux, 2002: 2). Lacking the power to make their own voices heard, they remain condemned to being viewed as passive victims in need of constant protection from adults.

Though I may be critical of these childhood paradigms and how they construe and constrict children, I understand that the very same accusations could be directed against my own work. In the process of situating preteen modeling websites and reactions to them within the paradigm of childhood innocence, I too have continued to construct her as an object of inquiry as opposed to an active subject in her own right. In the remainder of this chapter, I wish to move beyond the paradigm that views these girls as passive objects in need of protection to one where preteen models become active subjects invested with agency and intention. Operating under the assumption that children are meaning-makers in their own right who actively seek power for themselves, I offer speculations as to how participation in these websites may be viewed as both empowering and pleasurable to their models, albeit not unproblematically given the context in which they occur.

While my discussion of childhood is premised on the assumption that notions and experiences of childhood are culturally constructed and historically specific, one aspect of childhood does prove to be universal: most children eventually grow up and become adults. In order to become "adjusted" citizens, children must learn and practice the rules and norms accepted and promoted by their society. "Children ultimately must be integrated into the more broadly conceived sense of order and generality that comprises adult society" (Jenks qtd. in Woodson: 33). Within families, schools, social environments, and their exposure to the media, children are progressively socialized, taught what it means to be a boy or a girl, and how one is expected to act accordingly. "Childhood is [therefore] a time when children are to be developed, stretched and educated into their future adult roles, clearly through the institution of schooling but also through the family and wider social and civic life" (Holloway and Valentine, 2002: 2).

Beyond the family, school and media, another one of the sites where this process of socialization occurs is in the act of playing. For example, Gary Cross (1997) traces the history of Western toys and how they are positioned within a wider social and ideological framework. Turning his attention to dolls, Cross posits that these have adorned the environments of young girls for centuries, allowing them to learn "their expected gender roles by making their dolls into protagonists of the domestic dramas of modern caregiving, conviviality, and consumption. They rehearsed the worlds of the caring mother, dear friends, and modern shoppers" (67). Although Cross mostly alludes to the porcelain lady doll, with delicate hair and lace dress, I believe this proposition also holds true of their modern counterparts (like the plastically voluptuous *Barbie* or the scantily clad *Bratz*). Indeed, doll play remains a key tool in helping girls learn the gendered roles and expectations of their cultures and societies.

Furthermore, as Chris Richards (1995) notes, play not only allows the child to learn and negotiate the conventions and assumptions that circulate in her environment, it also provides a flexible space to begin experimenting with present and future identities. In his case study, he observes his daughter's dancing to Disney's *The Little Mermaid*. Richards (1995) suggests that "young children constantly engage with and, in the mode of play, enact identifications associated with the sexuality of adolescence and early childhood" (142). He posits that dancing to "adult" popular music, with all its sexual under- and overtones, allows young girls to play at "being someone older, more sexual, more accomplished, more knowing, and briefly, trying out the rules of the game in which they appear to act" (147).

This point is echoed by Gerard Jones (2002), who emphasizes the importance of fantasy play in children's development. Responding to concerns regarding the often violent nature of children's games, he posits that these forms of play are in fact important and necessary. Play provides children with a sense of power and control, also enabling them "to pretend to be just what they know they'll never be. Exploring, in a safe and controlled context, what is impossible or too dangerous or forbidden to them is a crucial tool in accepting the limits of reality" (11).

Considering that North American culture is "so overloaded with sometimes contradictory messages about how one is to be, what one should believe, what is right and wrong, how one should look" (Ganetz, 1995: 78)—and this especially in relation to girls—play thus offers a key site to begin negotiating certain of the fears and tensions intrinsic to one's cultural and social environment. "It is one of the fundamental ways in which all of us deal with uncertainty" (Bloustien, 2003: 2-3). This belief seems to have been the driving force behind the *Barbie* doll, as recounted by her creator Ruth Handler who noted that:

> …watching her daughter play convinced her that girls were inevitably curious and worried about female adulthood and its obvious signifiers and that they craved ways to help them play through their feelings. "I realized that experimenting with the future from a safe distance through pretend play was very important part of growing up," she said." I believed it was important to a little girl's self-esteem to play with a doll that has breasts. (qtd. in Jones, 2002: 94)

Handler's quote also directs our attention to the importance of play in relation to the body. While play is often a highly embodied and physical activity, it can allow the child to develop her corporeality and sense of identity. Echoing Richards' observations and emphasizing the need to "respect the power that girls feel when they thrust and jump and sing," Jones posits that emulating Britney Spears can serve as a potent locale to explore and "be" in one's own body (Jones, 2002: 93). Through dance or other forms of embodied play like dress-up, children learn the limits and possibilities of their own physicality, also coming to use their body as a tool for the creation of the present and future self. The body becomes a site for expression, autonomy and intention, as well as "a source for their own personal pleasure in their strength and suppleness" (Richards, 1995: 78).

Allowing children to learn and negotiate social rules and expectations while also offering a site for the embodied development of identity, play can therefore be defined as a highly strategic activity. Gerry Bloustien (2003) draws from her ethnographic research with young Australian girls to illustrate this point. Having provided them with cameras to record their lives and thoughts, she defines her informants' process of video-diary making as a form of "strategized play," one that is

> closely tied to identity, notions of the self and ways of dealing with uncertainty. It is a concept of embodied play that equates with pleasure but not triviality. This type of play has taken a very particular form since the advent of the camera, the phonograph and now the complexities of even more elaborate technologies of mechanical reproduction (Bloustien, 1999: 19).

Clothing could also be appended to this list of technologies. Indeed, as Hillevi Ganetz (1995) remarks, fashion has come to play an increasingly central role in the lives and play of girls. She notes that "clothes provide women with possibilities to transform themselves, to be mobile, to experiment with themselves and the female role which the androcentric model has ascribed to them" (73).

Strategized play thus offers a space where the body becomes a central locale for expression and experimentation with different selves and subjectivities, through the help of technologies such as clothing, toys and cameras. A number of parallels can be drawn between these definitions of play and the preteen models' activities. While adults read eroticism into these websites and assume sexually abusive situations, a child has not yet assimilated all these social scripts and may view things from a different perspective. It is possible to speculate that in dressing up and posing, the models engage in a form of strategized play, "trying out various forms of identity and the relations to the body that they might entail" (Richards, 1995: 147). Just as they do when they dance to Britney Spears or *The Little Mermaid*, these girls are finding a space to begin enacting and negotiating certain tensions and contradictions inherent to their society's construction of girlhood, adulthood and sexuality, and how they wish to take them up in their own lives.

In the process, they also learn "that to be female is hard work and that it requires constant self-surveillance of the body to meet a ubiquitous female ideal" (Bloustien, 2003: 78). Indeed, within North America, girls are brought up in a society where looks matter. Ours is a culture that has made beauty, especially women's beauty, a cult, complete with accompanying myths, rituals, and iconography. The beautiful woman is prized and revered, adorning every magazine cover, every fairytale fantasy. She is also objectified, commodified, and sexualized in the process. As Jones (2002) points out, though adults may "tell them that looks, popularity, trendiness, pleasing boys don't matter—but the real life of children's society shows them that they do matter" (95). As Angela McRobbie (1984) notes,

> It is indeed a great irony of the female labour market that those fields which are held out as promising of the greatest rewards socially and financially [modeling, acting and dance], have consistently depended on the exploitation of the most traditional sexual qualities. In each of them the body is sharply in focus and with it appropriate gestures and appropriate presentation. What is more, it is in these fields that girls are, quite unrealistically, given the most encouragement to succeed (148).

While this particular text precedes my own by two decades, McRobbie's claim continues to resonate quite strongly. Just as many girls dream of becoming models, pop stars or Hollywood actresses, physical appearance continues to play an important role in one's professional success and advancement. Of course, the emphasis on beauty and self-sexualization can certainly be read as a sign of oppression, creating a pattern whereby "girls look at the world through concepts of male sexuality so that even when they are not looking at male sexuality as such, they are looking at the world within its frame of reference" (Van Roosmalen, 2000: 223).

However, there is always more than one side to any story. There is both pleasure and power to be found in rendering oneself desirable, and little girls are certainly not oblivious to this dynamic. For instance, in her ethnographic examination of tween girls' readings of Britney Spears, Melanie Lowe (2003) notes that "while the girls feel offended and angry when women's bodies are objectified in media, many of them are surprisingly empowered by the idea that women themselves might choose to use their own bodies for personal or—in the case of Britney Spears—professional gain" (123).

Similarly, Walkerdine (1996) contends that the script of the eroticized girl is one of the only alternatives girls can find to the hegemonic innocent child paradigm. She states that,

> The popular cultural place which admits the possibility that little girls can be sexual little women provides a place where adult projections meet the possibility for little girls of being Other than the rational child or the nurturant quasi-mother, where they can be bad. It can then be a space of immense power for little girls and certainly a space in which they can be exploited, but it is not abuse (331).

Girls participating in preteen modeling websites also appear to take pleasure in the process of dressing up, looking "pretty" and being photographed. In fact, as one preteen model photographer contends, "it's not like we're having to kidnap these girls and drag them in front of the camera...they send emails and put up notices on the Web, begging to be photographed" (Thompson). While they may not understand the ramifications of their participation in the same way adults do, the models know that their images are being circulated, "they know that there are people out there looking at the pictures" ("Thorny Legal Issues Raised by Effort to Ban Child Modeling Sites"). Within a context where "the aestheticization of the body is, in our culture, the very core of being a woman," (Ganetz: 92) the girls come to understand that there is a certain degree of power and pleasure to be drawn from rendering the public self desirable. Though these might not be the forms of empowerment that we most want to bestow on young girls, they remain one of the few options where girls can gain a sense of power and control.

Indeed, as Woodson (1999) reminds us, "children have no voice in government or laws affecting their well-being. They have no vote in school curricula or testing, or in the reconfiguration of welfare. Fundamentally, children exercise no control over their bodies or their environments" (41). As Jones (2002) echoes, "of all the challenges children face, one of the biggest is their own powerlessness" (65). Yet children actively seek power and agency, finding it where they can. Of course, this occurs in everyday activities, in the music and television programs they consume, in their choices of friends and games, in their interaction with figures of authority. But the areas where girls can make their voices heard remain quite limited, and the websites provide one outlet.

Whether or not their participation in these websites yields fame, it can certainly prove to be very lucrative. The owners of Webe Web boast that "their web sites each make at least $1,000 a month for the girls" (Sherman). Money that—according to most parents—goes toward "fattening their college funds" although significant portions of the earnings probably benefit parents and web companies as well (*Daily News*). Still, it remains that preteen modeling offers the prospect of significant financial gain. Of course, this proves to be problematic in that these earnings are made within a paradigm of commodification, whereby both the child and the image of the child are increasingly located in a capitalist framework of consumption. Just as children of this age range excite "marketing executives, who lust after the increasingly generous allowances of the twenty-seven million tweens in America" (Cross, 2004: 11), so too have recent years witnessed young girls' sexuality becoming "commodified —in advertisements, magazines, music, television and movies, in the economic lures of the sex trade, and in the simple day-to-day affirmation of the value males place on females as sexual beings" (Van Roosmalen, 2000: 203). Still, it remains that these girls are earning considerable amounts of money (more than other options such as babysitting or selling lemonade ever could); something that can certainly provide a sense of power and agency within a capitalist milieu.

Finally, this framework allows us to move beyond seeing the girls as either passively consumed (by their audience) or as active consumers (of the clothes they wear and the gifts they are sent), to viewing them as actual *producers* of culture in their own right. As Kearney (1998: 119) notes, "the lengthy association of femininity and females with the practices of consumption and consumerism, an association which has served to further reinforce the notion of production as a masculine and male activity also informs the girls' representations as cultural producers" (291). Drawing from her ethnographic examination of girls' zine production, Anita Harris (2004) quotes one of her respondents who states: "to be able to produce something was very exciting…I felt electrified." She comments further that "participating in their own cultures is an active engagement rather than simply making another consumer choice. These young women break down barriers between consumption and production" (Harris: 173-4).

Granted, participation in these websites can be read as feeding into the hegemonic cultural paradigms of patriarchy and capitalism that create a market for and valorize images of sexualized girls. But as George Lipsitz notes, "[t]oday's youth culture proceeds from a different premise. Instead of standing outside society, it tries to work through it, exploiting and exacerbating its contradictions to create unpredictable possibilities for the future" (Lipsitz qtd. in Kearney: 198). While contributing to a dominant paradigm whereby girls' sexuality becomes objectified and commodified, it remains that in participating in these websites, girls move from being mere consumers to actual producers of culture. This process not only subverts traditional associations, but it can prove to be a source of both power and pleasure for preteen models.

Returning To The Initial Gut Reaction

Having traveled through this deconstruction and intellectualization of preteen modeling websites and the different ways in which they can be read, I feel it is important to return to my initial gut reaction, and trace what has become of it in the process of thinking about, researching, and writing about it here. What do I think about these websites now? What feelings do they incite?

I would like to say that I have made my peace with preteen modeling websites; that they no longer stir in me contradictory emotions of anger, revulsion and attraction. Alas, this is not the case. Though I can now view them from a more critical and informed perspective, I remain highly conflicted and troubled by the images of these petite preteen bunnies.

At the heart of this persistent dis-ease lies many unanswered questions. While this chapter hopefully provides an examination of the preteen modeling phenomenon and the different readings one could have of them, it also makes its extreme complexity glaringly apparent. Preteen modeling websites are situated at a fraught intersection where girlhood, sexuality, innocence, power, adulthood, society, culture, and so much more coalesce. It is a site ripe with potential for endless inquiry. For instance, interviews and ethnographic work with the girls, parents, and all others involved in preteen modeling might yield some insight into what renders participation in these websites appealing. Similarly, additional research into how these websites are distributed and consumed also strikes me as another important area of inquiry.

While my discussion has attempted to re-place a modicum of agency into the models' hands, I remain uneasy with these websites and girls' participation in them. They remain located within a patriarchal framework, one whereby images of girls and women are commodified and sexualized. Additionally, these texts further reify the standards of ideal beauty dominant to North American society. Though there certainly is room within this framework for young girls to find and employ empowerment and agency, it remains—perhaps irrevocably—problematic, limited, and certainly not ideal.

Indeed, in the process of researching these websites, I have often wondered how I would react should my own hypothetical daughter want to participate in them. Would I allow her to become a preteen model? Pending a discussion of these issues throughout her modeling career, and an insistence that I remain actively involved in the production of her website at all stages of the process, I might eventually acquiesce. However, I would admittedly much prefer to see my daughter becoming involved in activities like zine production, or theatre acting. Of course, a critical eye could be turned on these activities as well. Yet from my perspective as an feminist-inflected adult, I deem them preferable in terms of the forms of empowerment they may provide, in that they are not so obviously linked to a patriarchal and capitalist models of commodification and sexualization.

I have argued that these websites should not be automatically read as signalling or creating sexually abusive situations, but they nonetheless conjure up the spectre of abuse. While no public accounts of abuse have been reported in relation to preteen modeling websites, I still see the reflection of this "reality" in their image. They render obvious the difficult position that children have come to be located in North American society, as individuals devoid of their own sexuality, yet simultaneously infused with adult fantasies of power and domination. These websites continue to trouble me, because they cannot help but remind me of the realities of child abuse: a reality that countless girls continue to experience on a daily basis.

While it is important to acknowledge the many forms of violence that children are exposed to, it is also paramount that we move beyond the paradigm of childhood innocence that continues to construe children as passive and vulnerable victims who can do very little for themselves. In fact, it is important to do so for the very welfare of children, in that we may actually be causing them more harm than good. As Silin (1997) notes,

> In our overzealous attempts to protect children, we deny their sexuality and their agency...Kitzinger notes that we would be more effective advocates for children if we empowered them to come to their own defense, to realize their own strategies and skills of protection—if we saw them as strong rather than as weak, sexual rather than without desire (225).

Similarly, Ost (2002) argues that in insisting on children's innocence, not only do we further reinforce their association as "objects of innocence, the one aspect of childhood that may be of the greatest attraction to the child sexual abuser," but we also create a climate where shame is cast onto the child's body (457-8). As Higonnet notes, "When every photograph of a child's body becomes criminally suspect, how are we going to avoid children feeling guilt about any image of their bodies?" (1998:180).

The time has come for the formulation of new childhood myths. Whether labelled Kincaid's *laughing child* or Higonnet's *knowing children*, these myths acknowledge children as having "bodies and passions of their own" (Higonnet, 1998: 207). These are paradigms that move beyond the constraining lens of idealized innocence and asexuality, giving flesh to the child. Flesh that can be certainly be damaged—sexually, physically, psychically—not only by pedophiles, but by the institutions, ideologies and social and cultural constructs that continue to define, constrain and determine what children are and what they can do. But also flesh that experiences joy, pleasure, power, pain, desire, and this in manners and to degrees not so distant from those of adults. Moving beyond our initial gut reactions of outrage and anger, we need to orient ourselves towards a more accountable and comprehensive understanding of the child, as well as society's and our own roles in shaping and constraining her. We need to create new myths wherein hopefully adults, but especially children, can find more room to operate, understand, change and affect themselves and the world around them.

I would like to thank Monika Kin Gagnon who supervised a directed study on youth culture in the context of which I wrote the initial draft of this paper. I also want to acknowledge the generous support of Candis Steenbergen and Yasmin Jiwani, who have provided me with ample and highly useful suggestions and feedback in the process of writing a chapter on the contentious issue of girls and sexuality.

Notes

1. I use the name "Vicky" as a pseudonym, but not in reference to any preteen model in particular.
2. Though it is impossible to provide an exact quantity of preteen modeling websites, at the time of writing this chapter I had seen more than two hundred different sites. Furthermore these sites link to others and seemingly incessant linkages would suggest that that many more hundreds also exist.

3. As I write this, I have yet to encounter an academic article that examines preteen modeling websites.

4. This finds itself well reflected in the titles given to articles and special reports about these websites: "Selling Innocence," (Deborah Sherman. NBC 6 News); "Parents Exposing Kids on Soft-Porn Web Sites," (*Daily News*); "Underage and Selling their Sexuality on the Web" (Doug Thompson, *Capitol Hill Blue*).

5. I feel it important to make a few clarifications about the terms I will be using throughout: Though "childhood" is a vast term, I use the term in reference to later childhood, from the age of seven approximately to the onslaught of puberty. I also use this term in reference to girls more particularly, in that very often discourses about the child (as innocence, eroticized, and threatened) are premised on an underlying assumption of child as feminized. The term "girl-hood" (and "girl") appears in the second section when I use literature more specifically from the area of girl studies, and because I am talking about but rather the experiences of the preteen models themselves. Though my study is focused on the experiences of girl children more particularly, I make this distinction in order to emulate the terms employed in the literature from which I draw, while assuming there to be much overlap between the two. Like "childhood" and "girlhood," definitions of the term "preteen" vary depending on the source. I use preteen only in reference to the websites, referring to young girls between the ages of seven and twelve. The term preteen is most probably used by the websites in an erotically charged manner (like "barely legal" and similar internet-porn lingo), and so I prefer to keep my own use of the term to a minimum, preferring childhood or girlhood instead.

6. For additional discussions of the mythology of the child as innocence, see the work of Higonnet (1998) and Kincaid (1998).

7. The influences of Christian and Victorian ideologies and mores on the development of current Western paradigms of childhood are traced in the work of Jenkins (2001) and Holloway and Valentine (2000).

8. For a discussion of the eroticization of the child, and particularly the girl-child, see Higonnet (1998), Walkerdine (1996) and Kincaid (1998, 1999).

9. For a discussion of the 'at-risk' child, see Best, 1990. The first chapter of Harris' (2004b) *Future Girl* addresses the 'girl-at-risk.'

10. For a discussion of the debates surrounding children and the internet and their polarization into "nightmares and utopias," see Buckingham, 2000.

11. Many inquiries concerning child molesters have found that instead of using explicit child pornography, they often "report using "non-pornographic pornography" as a source of fantasy. These materials included advertisements, mail order catalogues, children's movies...and television programs" (Howitt qtd. by Jill Rettinger, 2000).

Chapter Fourteen

I Am (A) Canadien(Ne): Canadian Girls And Television Culture

Michele Byers

The first part of this title reflects the difficulty of injecting gender identity into discussions of Anglo-Canadian youth culture. The bracketed use of French is an attempt to locate the gendered subject who often disappears in discussions of nation and national concerns.[1] My aim in what follows is to reinsert girls into the national imaginary, as well as to insert Canadian programming into discussions of television representations of youth culture. The focus of this chapter is an examination of the way girls are represented in three fictional Canadian television series: *Degrassi Classic* (made up of *Degrassi Junior* High and *Degrassi High*) *Degrassi: The Next Generation* and *Renegadepress.com*. These texts provide alternatives to the more hegemonic and highly gendered brands of national identity offered by Canadian television productions and provide moments of disruption to the equally highly gendered logic of many popular American teen series.

Much work on television to date has focused on texts that are produced in the United States. These televisual images circulate most widely, and have the highest global currency, but they are produced within a particular national context. Mainstream American representations of girls convey a limited range of American girlhoods, and do not offer space for the articulation of what Grant and Wood (2004) describe as "a distinctly Canadian voice" (16), even though they circulate widely in Canada. This national context is central to the type of content American television series contain, the characters they feature, the issues they tackle, and how these issues are dealt with. This became apparent, for example, when *Degrassi, The Next Generation* included a story arc about a character deciding to have an abortion in their 2003 season. The N, the American cable network which houses *The Next Generation*, decided not to air the episodes, which caused little stir when aired on CTV, the series home network in Canada. American TV producers, who discussed the issue of abortion in Kate Aurthur's (2004) article for the *New York Times*, demonstrate that the type of story arc produced on *The Next Generation* would not likely have been made in the U.S. This was also true almost two decades ago when a *Degrassi Classic* episode about abortion aired on the CBC, but was edited before being broadcast on PBS in the United States.

The importance of studying popular representations of girls is apparent in the growing number of scholarly and popular works that take this as their central focus. Until now, very little of this work has examined Canadian girls and texts.[2] In this chapter, I focus on how these particular Canadian dramas tell stories about girls that are distinctly Canadian. It is not that these stories exhaust all the tales about Canadian girls there are to tell, that they equally privilege the voices of all Canadian girls, that they tell stories that are without ambiguity and contradiction, or that will not resonate with Canadian or non-Canadian girls. But they do tell stories about girls in a voice whose distinction includes its national location, and the way that this location is intimately connected to the socio-cultural, political, economic, historical, and technological contexts that influence the stories television can tell, how it tells them, and the people it chooses to bring them to life.

International scholars like Angela McRobbie (1994), Sherrie Inness (1999), and Catherine Driscoll (2002) for example, have addressed the problematic relationship between girl cultures and feminism, as well as the ambivalence of understanding girls as passive in the face of pressures of media consumption. This chapter looks at the way feminist language, and different or shifting conceptions of feminism, make their way into Canadian television culture, and tries to an open space from which to engage in a critical discussion about Canadian television more generally. I suggest that the representations offered by these dramas represent moments of disruption in a televisual landscape in which girlhood is often hegemonically circumscribed within particular narrative limits.[3]

It is important to stress that a disruption is an alternative, not a complete rupture. The presence of these series does not spell a miraculous televisual liberation for girls from more hegemonic girlhood narratives offered by such series as *Beverly Hills, 90210, The O.C.,* or *One Tree Hill.* Nor do these Canadian series offer unilaterally liberatory representations of girlhood (just as the American shows noted above do not offer unilaterally hegemonic ones). Like most television narratives, they offer us different notes of ambivalence, contradiction, and complexity. As Ella Shohat and Robert Stam (1994) insist, there are no "perfectly correct texts" or "perfect characters"; instead we have to search out those moments of what I am here calling disruption (11). Thus my purpose is not to identify 'good' texts about girls and to position them against texts about girls that are 'bad,' as this suggests that a template exists for a 'better' image of girls than the ones that currently exist and that the insertion of this better image into the television landscape will result in a better world for girls (Walters, 1995). Rather, what I hope to suggest is that the texts on which I focus offer different narratives that need to be studied for the different stories and images of girlhood they include (and exclude), but also to mark their moments of contradiction and ambiguity. Just as Herman Gray (1995) asks how "blackness" circulates within

American television, I ask how 'girlness' labours to construct particular meanings within Canadian television texts that are produced at particular moments in our cultural history.

Two And A Half Decades Of *Degrassi*

Degrassi is a Toronto-based television franchise that, in one form or another, has been airing on Canadian television for twenty-five years. The *Degrassi* series (of which there are five) have an impressive pedigree, having been nominated for (and won) a variety of national and international awards including international Emmys and Prix de la Jeunesse. The series have all been funded through a variety of public and private trusts, as is typical of Canadian television, including Telefilm Canada, The Bell Fund, Canadian Television Fund, and The Canadian Film and Video Production Tax Credit. The *Degrassi Classic* series (hereafter cited as *DC* and referring to *Degrassi Junior High* and *Degrassi High*) aired on the CBC, a public broadcaster, from 1987 to 1991, and received part of its funding from the American PBS. The series has been seen in over 150 countries.

From its inception, the series' creators attempted to build a television series about 'real' kids played by real kids. The importance of this cannot be underestimated when it is common practice in the United States to have teenaged characters played by young adult actors, often in their twenties. For example, the cast of *Beverly Hills, 90210*, which aired at the same time as *DC*, ranged in age from seventeen to twenty-nine (average age of twenty-one) in 1990, when the series first aired and the characters were sophomores in high school (grade ten). The cast of *The O.C.*, another popular, more recent, prime-time soap, features actors who ranged in age from seventeen to twenty-five (average age of twenty-two) during the 2003 first season, well before the characters' senior year in high school. By contrast, the actors in *DC*'s large ensemble were between fourteen and seventeen (most were fifteen) when the series aired in 1987 and the characters were supposed to be in grades seven and eight. Casting real young people in TV series about youth is important. Teens look like teens, not like adults. Casting adults to play teen girls sends confusing messages to teen viewers about girls' bodies and ways of behaving.

DC successfully integrated explicitly political issues and language, often linked to second wave feminism, into its dialogue and story arcs. Several *DC* characters described themselves as feminists and fought for a variety of girls' and women's rights. While language and story arcs are important markers of political commitment and ideological positioning, the way that characters are represented is equally important. The girls on *DC* were consistently presented as strong and competent, and included more visible social differences among them than was (and continues to be) found on many youth TV series. Included were Black and bi-racial girls, girls from Italian, Greek and Jewish cultural backgrounds, working-class girls, fat girls, punk rock girls, and girls using wheelchairs.

It is important to note that *DC* was produced during a period when there were few other series of its kind in circulation. In the years immediately following, American series like *Beverly Hills, 90210* and *Saved by the Bell* hit the television screens. Although all of these shows focus on teens and, to a certain extent, the social issues that impact their everyday lives, the political and social justice emphases that permeated *DC* were less in evidence, as was the social difference of the actor/characters on the American shows that *DC* helped to inspire. But the *DC* series had far less visibility than either of these shows and in critical discussions of teen series, especially of the early years of this most recent phase of the genre's development, *DC* is often entirely overlooked. And while certain narrative conventions established on *DC*, particularly the focus on the peer group and the "dramas" of adolescence, have been fully incorporated into the genre, the American series have provided the wider parameters of "teen TV" that continue to be followed: the casting of adult actors as teens, the homogenization of the cast in terms of beauty as well as race, ethnicity, and class, and the displacement of storylines involving politically-sensitive social issues from central to peripheral characters (Simonetti, 1994). The more marginal position of *DC* when compared to these other series is likely due, at least in part, to the fact that it aired on PBS (and the CBC) rather than on one of the major networks (*90210* aired on FOX, *Saved by the Bell* on NBC) and the association of PBS with education rather than entertainment. This was further entrenched by the fact that many students were introduced to *DC* through their junior high school curriculum.

But fans tend to foreground the differences between *DC* and the American series described above as central to their perception of the series continued importance within the teen television genre, also noting the Canadian series' greater realism in the casting of average looking teens, location shooting, and willingness to tackle social issues that are taboo on American television, especially abortion (Smith 2005, also see the *Degrassi* page at www.jumptheshark.com). And yet, while *DC* was direct in its foregrounding of political issues, its stories were not without their own ambivalences, contradictions, and stereotypes. For example, head writer Yan Moore has noted that a central story arc from *Degrassi Junior High* was to involve a character who would become pregnant. Initially, three characters were considered: Stephanie (Nicole Stoffman) and Caitlin (Stacie Mistysyn), who were core characters, and Spike (Amanda Stepto), a then marginal member of the ensemble. According to Moore, Stephanie "was too obvious, she dresses [like] provocatively and we didn't want to say something about 'those girls.' Caitlin, we thought, Caitlin couldn't get pregnant" (personal interview, 2003). Two things stand out in this discussion. One, the reason why Caitlin "couldn't" get pregnant was because she was not one of "those girls." She belonged to the category of nice, smart, well-behaved, middle-class girls. Second, Spike is also one of "those girls," she is from a working-class single parent family, her mother was a teen parent, and Spike is a punk rocker, a subculture originally associated with working class youth rebellion.

The significance and ambivalence of choosing a character through whom to enact a specific and politically-sensitive narrative arc on a television series is highlighted in this example, which is only one of many I could have drawn upon. Choosing to tell this story via a secondary character who disappeared after her pregnancy or the birth of her child would have created a very different type of narrative than the one presented on *DC*. Spike (and her daughter Emma) is, in fact, part of a meta-narrative that spans four of the five *Degrassi* series. Yan Moore's comments suggest that the series writers and producers were keenly attuned to the ways their narrative choices would be interpreted by viewers. While they avoided stereotyping "those girls" who dress and act provocatively, in constructing Spike, whose character only really develops through the pregnancy story arc, other stereotypes about class, education and subcultural identity are drawn upon.[4] The story that would have been told if Caitlin *had* become pregnant and chosen to keep her baby, as certainly does happen in some middle-class families, would have been another powerful choice, although perhaps one that would have been less comfortable for the writers and producers and perhaps for some viewers as well.

Degrassi: The Next Generation (hereafter cited as *TNG*) began airing on CTV in 2001, without any American funding partners. *TNG* followed the casting style established by *DC*; its actors were between twelve and sixteen (mostly fourteen and fifteen) during the first season (2001), which followed the same grade organization as *DC*. It currently airs in several countries, and has a large and ardent following among teenagers in the United States. As Ben Neihart (2005) points out in *The New York Times*: "when the first episode of Season four…had its premiere on the N…it came in as the highest-rated program of the night among teenagers in all of broadcast and cable television, beating out even super mainstream youth shows like *Joan of Arcadia* and *8 Simple Rules*." (42). Changes in the location of the series in terms of which network chooses to broadcast it and when, are significant. In Canada the series moved from a public to a major private broadcaster. In the U.S., *TNG* is found on a specialty cable station with a reach of about forty-million families. Despite the smaller audience than it might have found on network television, as Neihart's quote suggests this has not stopped *TNG* from being highly competitive with similar programs being aired on the networks. *TNG* is clearly well positioned to offer competing discourses about adolescence within the mainstream, more so than its progenitor or most other Canadian media texts.

By 2001, ideas about girlhood and empowerment had been fully incorporated into the everyday lexicons of media producers and consumers, and images of empowered girls and women on television—for instance the heroes of *My So-Called Life*, *Buffy the Vampire Slayer*, and *Sex and the City*—were regularly produced, lauded, and critiqued.[5] At the same time, while the media incorporated many ideas borrowed from feminism, the word itself appeared to sit less comfortably in the mouths of young girls and it was heard less often in the television texts produced for them than was true of series like *DC* that aired a decade and a half earlier. In *DC* you can see the seeds of the third wave feminism, but the voice of the story is still very much of the second wave. This is not surprising, given that most of the *DC* writers and producers grew up in the second wave generation. The links and continuities, as well as the tensions, between feminisms and generations are evident in the transition from *DC* to *TNG*, in the desire of the new cohort of *Degrassi* writers to avoid "copying what came before, [but] finding one's own way" (Baumgardner and Richards, 2000: 130). Their vision offers many empowering, feminist narratives both dramatic and mundane. However, they tend not to use feminist or political language as regularly and explicitly as did *DC*; perhaps this reflects (the perception) that young girls less readily accept this type of language today. And yet, many *TNG* story arcs tell tales that are feminist and, while they are not without their own contradictions, these are stories that are not often told on mainstream teen television.

Now at the end of its fourth season, *TNG*, working with a slightly smaller cast/ensemble than *DC*, represents young women and men equally as central characters. The characters are somewhat more generically middle-class than was the case on *DC*, they are better looking in a mainstream way, and they have better wardrobes; that is, they are more in keeping with the style trends of the day. Racial difference is slightly (visually) more foregrounded on *TNG*, although these identities are rarely seen as problematic or associated with marginalization. Two of the main eight female characters are Black (one of the two is Muslim (Somali) and another is Filipino; a secondary character is an Asian girl adopted into a white family. There is also a character who identifies as Ukrainian, one whose step-father is Jewish and whose biological father is gay, and another who is physically distinguished by being a few dress sizes larger than most girls we see on TV today. The two remaining main female characters have been raised by single-mothers, one of whom is an alcoholic. Thus, while at first glance *TNG* seems to be moving in a direction of greater homogeneity, it consistently represents the type of differences among girls that might be found in an urban Toronto high school, although not every type of difference is accounted for (an impossible task) and the ones highlighted tend to be those that will be familiar to viewers.

It is worth noting that *TNG*'s more generic middle-classness may be seen as "trumping" any issues associated with racial difference (Gray, 1995). For example, interracial relationships, dealt with quite critically on *DC*, are largely ignored when characters of different races date on *TNG*. And while issues of racism were part of large story arcs on *DC*, on *TNG* they are more likely to be treated as "very special" events in a style familiar from teen series in the U.S. (Wilcox 2001). However, when compared to many other series currently being produced for youth audiences, the differences found on *TNG* are broad and subtle. Popular youth series produced in the U.S., from *The O.C.*, to *Joan of Arcadia*, to *One Tree Hill*, create landscapes populated by young people cleansed of virtually all visible difference.[6] The point is not to laud *DC* or *TNG* as "better" than the American series, but to point out the deep ambivalence in this type of representation on all these series. As I discuss elsewhere with Rebecca Haines (forth-coming, 2005), although *DC* created a very compelling story arc about the difficulties encountered by Michelle (Maureen Mckay) and BLT (Dayo Ade) as an interracial cou-ple, the series did follow conventional narrative forms by choosing to tell the story of a white girl and black boy, and making Michelle's (white) family the focus of the arc's tensions, while BLT's family was virtually invisible. Further, the couple's eventual breakup after which they each dated characters of their own "race" was left uninterrogated. On *DC* by contrast, Ashley and Jimmy and Emma and Chris' (again white girls and black boys) interracial relationships are never discussed in terms of race, which remains primarily unmarked (as is Jimmy's later relationship with Hazel, who is black and Muslim).

TNG's story arcs, however, are very girl-friendly, and tell stories that are often omitted from other youth programming, which contributes to its distinctly Canadian voice. One of the most compelling *DC* story arcs involved the pregnancy of four-teen-year-old Spike. *TNG* starts with the entry of Spike's daughter, Emma (Miriam McDonald), into junior high. Thus, right from the start, two female characters are the series' lynchpin. The series' pilot episode, "Mother and Child Reunion," dealt with the issue of cyberstalking, and put Emma at its centre. Emma was also at the centre of a story about menstruation (she gets her first period at school and, after having to change out of her bloodied skirt, unashamedly tells the whole class when they tease her for wearing old gym shorts), politics (she lobbies both against the objectification of cheerleaders and the use of genetically-modified foods in the school cafeteria), and "sex bracelets" (an older boy encourages her to engage in oral sex, she then contracts gon-orrhoea). Each of these story arcs takes on an important social issue for girls and com-municates it in a compelling way. For instance, the political episodes force Emma to make complex choices that include getting suspended, demonstrating that girls can and should be politically active. The sex bracelet episode uses the word "blow job" in a frank way and shows that oral sex has real consequences, even for a 'good girl' like Emma.

Emma is not the only female character to have such complex, girl-centered stories built around her. Ashley's (Melissa McIntyre) experimentation with drugs ends up with the loss of her friends, she goes through a style change which forces her to think about what is worth giving up for a boy, and she has to deal with finding out that her boyfriend is bi-polar. Manny (Cassie Steele) decides she is tired of being a good girl and wants to be "hot," after which she loses her virginity, becomes pregnant, has an abortion, and must face public ridicule at school. Terri (Christina Schmidt) is embarrassed about being a plus-sized model; later she becomes involved in an abusive romantic relationship that ends with her in a coma. Hazel (Andrea Lewis) struggles to be proud of her Muslim heritage. Paige (Lauren Collins) is date raped and eventually takes her rapist to court. And Ellie (Stacey Farber) deals with her problems by cutting herself, eventually leaving her alcoholic mother and moving in with her boyfriend. Each of these stories puts the experience of a young female character at its centre, bringing the audience into her world.

It is not just the stories themselves that are compelling; the way that these stories are told is equally important. The date rape story arc involving Paige is an excellent example of the importance of narrative. Early in the second season, the writers created a two-part episode dealing with the rape itself and its aftermath. At the end of the season, Paige was forced to confront her rapist, which led her to decide to press charges against him. A season went by, and then in the two-part opener for the fourth season, the court date finally came up. After being pressured by her rapist, Paige worried that perhaps she should abandon the court case; finally, she decided to pursue the charges, although she ultimately lost the court battle. This story is compelling for a number of reasons aside from its dramatic content. It unfolds over a realistic timeline. Paige is not saved by a valiant boyfriend; she does not heal or develop amnesia after a day or two. She learns that "no means no," that she was not responsible for the rape, and that the rapist should be punished. Paige gains strength from confronting her accuser, but the series does not sugar-coat the situation for its viewers. The rapist is not convicted; he goes off to University with no record, potentially to rape other young women. This does not give us the type of resolution we are use to seeing on television, where 'bad' guys are punished and the innocent are vindicated, but it still shows Paige being empowered and encourages girls to take action immediately if they are raped. The date-rape story arc is one that has been featured on other teen TV series, although in mainstream (American) series the rape survivor is often a secondary character. If a central character is the intended target of rape, her rapist is usually thwarted, or if the rape occurred, it happened in the past. Usually, the rapist gets what he deserves. TNG avoids the pitfall of many narratives about rape, by making the rapist someone who is known to Paige, rather than a stranger.[7] And by making this a story that arced over the course of three seasons, the series also highlights the long-term consequences of rape on young women's lives.

None of this is to say that even in its representations of girls *TNG* avoids ambivalence and contradiction. For instance, why did they choose to make Hazel a core character on the series rather than Fairuza (Jacqueline Rose) who was a starring guest player in the episode ("Don't Believe the Hype") in which Hazel "comes out" as a Muslim after the school's International Day. Fairuza is Iraqi and wears a hijab to school, and during the school event her display is defaced by the word "terrorist." Hazel pretends she is Jamaican because she fears being marginalized in the way Fairuza was. While the episode invites discussion of topical issues around prejudice towards the Muslim community, and presents this community as visibly diverse since Hazel is Somali and Fairuza, Iraqi, it also evidences its own deep conflicts about the representation of these issues and their integration into television narratives. Thus, Fairuza, the guest star, bears the burden of representing Otherness. The cultural currency that is to be gained for representing Otherness at all is available for the series, but the core character, despite the fact that she has now "come out," never mentions anything about being Muslim again (Ono 2000). Fairuza makes Muslim Otherness visible in a highly provocative way that could not have been hidden in other episodes as was possible with Hazel. Thus we know from the second season on that Hazel is Muslim, but because this aspect of her identity is marginalized, the audience does not have to "deal" with this fact; Fairuza disappears into the background.

New Kid On The Block: *Renegadepress.com*

Renegadepress.com (hereafter cited as *Renegade*) aired its first thirteen episodes in 2003, and nine more in the winter of 2005. It is filmed, and takes place, in Regina, Saskatchewan. Although less information is available about the cast of *Renegade* than any of the *Degrassi* series, its actors seemed to range from fifteen to seventeen during its first season, when their characters were in high school. Like the *Degrassi* series, *Renegade* is funded through a variety of public and private trusts, including The Bell Fund, Canadian Television Fund, SaskTel New Media Fund through SaskFilm, Canadian Heritage, and The CTV Saskatchewan Program Development Fund. Unlike them, *Renegade* only airs in Canada, and is not run on a major network. *Renagade* currently airs on smaller, more specialized stations like APTN (Aboriginal Peoples Television Network) and TV Ontario. Thus although *Renegade* produces some fascinating story arcs, the possibility that these will be truly disruptive or even that they will figure substantially in discussions of teen television is limited by their lack of circulation outside of specialized viewing audiences in Canada. This is in contrast not only to American teen programming, but to the *Degrassi* series as well.

Renegade clearly follows from the *Degrassi* tradition, telling stories about teens from their perspectives, using age-appropriate actors, taking a no-holds-barred approach in its choice of subject matter, and avoiding closure. Produced during the same period as *TNG*, *Renegade* also takes a strong position on many social and political issues, but is also less inclined to use explicitly political language than was *DC*. There are seven core characters on *Renegade*, three of whom are young women: Zoey (Ksenia Solo), an upper-middle-class white girl; Carmen (Barbara Mamabolo), a Black girl who is a model; and Crystal (Rachel Colwell), who is Aboriginal.[8] There is also a secondary character, Hema (Agam Darshi) who is Indo-Canadian and eventually reveals she is a lesbian, and another, Melaine (Tatiana Maslany), who reveals she is Muslim (Serbian) in season two. In season two, a fourth girl, Patti (Ingrid Nilson), who is white, was also added to the cast. The inclusion of an Aboriginal character is especially significant, since Aboriginal youth are among the most under-represented in North American television (see Miller, forthcoming). Crystal is also presented without the burden of stereotypes about Aboriginal peoples in Canada. Although the series does not ignore the realities of poverty, violence, and discrimination of Aboriginal peoples and communities, Crystal is presented as an average, middle-class girl, who happens to be Aboriginal.[9] Gray (1995), in his work on representations of "blackness" in 1980s American television, notes that middle-classness is often used to make viewers comfortable with social difference and one of its effects is that it displaces broader questions of "economic and social disparities and constraints" (81). Drawing on Stuart Hall's notion of a "politics of reversal," Gray suggests that *The Cosby Show* achieved such widespread popularity because middle-classness made its characters universally appealing to white audiences, a strategic choice. Gray reminds us that finding authentic images of difference is important, but that interrogating the often deeply conflicted and multiple potential meanings through which these representations labour is even more so.

Renegade clearly broadens the televised landscape of representations of Canadian girls, particularly with its inclusion of Crystal. Many of the series' episodes feature lead story arcs that focus on girl-centred issues. The primary way that the series connects to these issues is through its premise that the characters are all involved with an online video newspaper they run called *Renegadepress.com*; many of the stories involve issues the characters encounter in their everyday lives and investigate for the newspaper. Although this can be problematic, in that the issues are highlighted by staging special events that often—but not always—require "guest stars" to initiate, they also intersect with the personal lives of the core characters.

What is particularly impressive about *Renegade*'s story arcs is that they have managed to follow *Degrassi*'s lead, but have also dealt with unique issues: girls bullying, the pro-ana movement, fights against the installation of video-surveillance cameras in high schools, breast-enhancement surgery, Aboriginal heritage, lesbianism and bi-sexuality, unions, white power, as well as a variety of issues raised specifically by the increasing availability of internet technologies, such as suicide on the net and young girls using webcams as a form of sex free prostitution. The manner in which girl-centred narratives are organized is very important on *Renegade*. The series has been successful, in my view, in telling unusual stories that are important to girls in a compelling way that is graphic but not exploitative. For instance, in "Skin Deep" Carmen is shocked to learn that a friend (Amanda, played by *TNG*'s Lauren Collins) is going to receive breast implants as a gift for her sixteenth birthday because she wants to be a model. Carmen, a model herself, is forced to address the value placed on conventional feminine attractiveness, the increasing use of cosmetic surgery to enhance girls' "beauty," and the privilege that she herself has exacted because she is beautiful in a conventional way. Carmen begins with the following attitude: "her body, her choice," but with Zoey's (one of the newspaper's star reporters) encouragement and her own discovery that Amanda is getting implants because she is depressed and thinks they will be good for her "mental health," Carmen begins to see things in a different light. The camera zooms in on photos of "breast implants gone bad" that Zoey has downloaded from the Internet; they are presented to the viewer in Technicolor detail. Carmen brings Amanda the pictures in an attempt to get her to change her mind, but she responds by asking Carmen if her (Amanda's) body is fine, would she be willing to trade in her own? The episode ends with Amanda lying on a gurney, giving the anaesthesiologist the okay to put her to sleep. Here, as we have often seen on *Degrassi*, closure is refused as the narrative presents us with an ambivalent position: breast implants are presented to the viewer as a problematic choice, and yet Amanda decides to go through with the operation.

In "A Very Thin Edge," Zoey worries that her friend Melaine may be anorexic. Mel tells Zoey that she is not anorexic; like other "pro-anas," she tells Zoey: "I don't want to recover...Anas are proud of their lifestyle choice. They are completely in control of their bodies." Zoey begins doing research about pro-ana, but the more she reads, the more she begins to identify with the group's idea of power, self-control, and choice. Carmen, who has had an eating disorder, tells Zoey: "Anorexia is not a lifestyle. It is not a choice. It's a horrible disease and it kills people," as she shows Zoey pictures of anorexics on-line. Again, the camera zooms in on the photos, this time of an emaciated woman. Zoey immediately links the popularity of anas to the way thin women's bodies are valued in Western society. What Zoey reads on the pro-ana site is deeply disturbing, as is the way she gets caught so easily in the pro-ana universe. In a quest to help her friend, Zoey tracks down "Silvermaiden" (Vanessa/Elyse Levesque), the host of the pro-ana website, and finds a very sick girl under constant care. When Carmen and Zoey go and see Vanessa, hoping for an interview, the girl can hardly sit up. Carmen asks: "How can you be in control when you can't even leave the house?"

The last scenes show Vanessa hooked up to an IV. We also see Mel, trying to run on her 200-calorie a day diet.

Both the breast implant and pro-ana narratives employ a highly ambivalent discourse of choice, specifically framed as "my body, my choice," that is used in ways that might be said to actually foreclose on girls' choices. The "choice" discourse is strongly connected to a woman's right to control her body reproductively and to be free of sexual and physical violence so pervasive within patriarchy, which makes its use here problematic. Girls should have the right to choose their own paths and to control their own bodies, but those choices cannot be understood outside of the social, cultural, political, and historical worlds girls live in. In these worlds girls often feel that they are invisible and worthless if they do not conform to impossible standards of beauty. They have little space to exercise their own free will, and cosmetic surgery and pro-ana are examples of things that girls may turn to, to reassert control. Thus the choice discourse is deployed here as an act of resistance against adult authority. Although *Renegade* gives space for the articulation of this discourse, it also offers a counter-discourse that points to the limits these resistance tactics offer, and the way that they potentially reinforce rather than subvert the curtailment of girls' power.

Renegade tells many stories in which girls' experiences are highlighted and in which girls' identities are not relegated to stereotypes. That does not mean, however, that these stories are not without the contradictions and ambivalences raised in relation to the other series. The choice to make Hema a lesbian (in "A Very Thin Edge"), for example, is unusual, first, because while gay male characters have become more visible on teen series, lesbian youth are still largely invisible. Second, Hema is a conventionally attractive, very feminine young Indian woman, who defies many stereotypical media depictions of lesbians. However, Hema is a secondary character, whose Otherness (like that of Fairuza) never has to be incorporated into the everyday experiences of the series' core characters or its story arcs. Her marginal identity is thus contained in this single episode. Further, the doubling of Hema's Otherness across the axes of both race and sexual orientation, on top of the marginalization of the character within the overall diegesis, is an important and also not unusual televisual strategy. As I have written elsewhere (1998) about the youth series *My So-Called Life*, these axes of difference complicate one another, but the ways in which this works is rarely explored on television. Lesbians of colour are largely invisible on the TV screen and off it; providing moments of visibility for these identities is important. But the series reveals its ambivalence in its choice to tell this story and yet to make its central character marginal to any wider meta-narratives. *Renegade*'s narrative goes beyond that of many other teen series by interrogating the particular pressure Hema feels from her family who want her to find an Indo-Canadian boyfriend, and then allows her to articulate her own particular struggles to define herself and to come out in a way that will allow her to claim both her racial/ethnic and queer identities.[10] At the same time, while this type of "special event" is useful in bringing particular issues (ones often erased from televisual representation) into the public sphere, the special guest star status of its key character largely subdues the possibilities of its overall impact (McCarthy, 2003).

A similar critique can be made of a first season story arc involving Crystal. In a strikingly similar set up to the episode involving Hazel and Fairuza discussed above, the *Renegade* episode focuses on a class assignment that involves discussing the students' "heritage." Unlike *TNG* episode, where the existence of this type of event is left uninterrogated, Crystal and her friends approach their assignment cynically, seeing it as a "one-off" celebration by their school of the more problematic social differences that permeate their everyday experiences. At the centre of this narrative arc is Crystal's desire to hide her heritage because she does not want to be "the Native kid." Instead, she decides to tell her classmates that she is Italian. Like the *TNG* story arc, Crystal chooses an ethnic identity that she sees as being more desirable than her own and she trades on the superficiality of her school's event (and aspects of Canadian multicultural policy) by assuming that her classmates will accept her identity based on her ability to present them with ethnic food. Also like *TNG* story arc, the issue of racism is presented as an internalized one; Crystal, like Hazel, is the one with the problem. Where Hazel is contrasted with Fairuza, whose body, more marginal within the series' diegesis, becomes the receptacle of racist sentiment that can be dispatched at the end of the episode, on *Renegade* Crystal is contrasted with the Aboriginal gang members at her school. Both girls recognize that their differences from these more visible Others is arbitrary and seek to hide their identities in order to protect themselves from the potential racism of their classmates and communities. Although Crystal, again like Hazel, appears to come to terms with her identity at the end of the episode, it remains very peripheral to her character. The episodes that deal with Aboriginal identity and community focus primarily on the experiences of her brother, Jack.

In these episodes the viewer is confronted with complex issues, which are examined from several sides, and whose primary players are girls. Zoey, the intellectual over-achiever, and Carmen, the beauty queen, are often called upon to offer different points of view, although not always the ones we expect. Hema and Crystal offer narratives that enlarge the arena of social difference on Canadian television. The topics covered in these episodes have not received much coverage on teen TV, they are compellingly dramatic, and lack the type of closure we come to expect from mainstream television. Like *TNG*, which refuses its viewers the satisfaction of seeing Paige's rapist jailed, *Renegade* denies us Amanda's last minute change-of-heart about her implants, and suggests that Zoey could not convince Mel or Vanessa to give up pro-ana. None of these characters is reducible to a simple stereotype, but that does not mean that the ways in which they are presented is unproblematic. The series is not without its own contradictions and moments of deep ambivalence, which surface especially clearly in the deployment of the choice discourse, and in the "special" status of certain characters and character traits.

Conclusion

At the start of this chapter, I suggested that American television often circulates as the generic that stands in for the stories of all people, in a way that other television narratives cannot. It is important to applaud Canadian television texts that, although by no means perfectly meeting the needs of all, create spaces for girls in the Canadian landscape, and tell their stories in particular, but distinctly Canadian, voices. To be clear, it has not been my intention to suggest that these more counter-hegemonic, girl-friendly narratives completely rupture the more hegemonic and likely more familiar iconography of mainstream Canadian television, or that they do the same thing within the broader matrices of teen television culture. Neither is it my intention to suggest that these images are somehow "perfect" and offer representations that are unproblematic, unambivalent, and without contradiction. Rather, what I wish to emphasize is that despite these contradictions, these series do offer important disruptions and alternatives to the more conventional narratives and representations of girls' lives offered on mainstream teen television.

For their many similarities, *Renegade* and *TNG* are quite different in the way that they are situated within television, at both the national and international levels. *Renegade*, at present, is available only to a small national market, whereas *TNG*, now attracts millions of viewers every week in Canada and abroad, and can hardly be called a marginal show. Especially after the coverage it has received in major publications like *The New York Times*, *TNG* is on the cultural radar (and may not even be identified as Canadian, especially by new viewers). Clearly, there is money to be made in providing the type of alternative models of identity and narratives about youth culture that *TNG* produces. In this sense, *TNG* has a greater opportunity to effect change in the lives of a greater number of viewers than *Renegade* as well as within the medium and genre. And it does this, at least in part, because Canadian cultural products do not have to adhere to the same rules that govern the production of mainstream American television series. On the other hand, while covering such "taboo" topics as abortion mark *TNG* as different and contribute to both its success and cache, the American network still has (and uses) the right to edit what it does not like out of the episodes that air south of the border.

Both *TNG* and *Renegade* are important Canadian youth series because they make girls and girl-centred narratives central to way they tell stories and to the stories they tell. They imagine girlhood in particular Canadian contexts; these images are similar to, but also different from, the more visible, widely circulated fare produced primarily in Hollywood. Among the unique qualities of these series are the fact that they consistently have girls playing girls, they touch on (and, indeed, often delve deeply into) taboo topics, they present their narratives in complex ways, using multiple voices, the characters often have to face real consequences for their actions, and they do not offer us stories that end simply, with a sense of closure that makes us feel better. But these same relations of power and context also influence the type of narratives that *TNG* and *Renegade* produce in more problematic ways. For instance, I have tried to show how both of the series often opt for narratives about identity and difference (for instance race and/or ethnicity) that use quite conventional strategies such as employing special guest stars or subsuming everyday aspects of difference except in episodes that address issues of identity as their primary story arcs. This often means sidelining characters whose inclusion in the centre of the narrative would necessitate a much more complex exploration of the everyday experience of living in bodies that embody race, gender, or sexual orientation in different ways. The contradictory nature of these discourses and their deep ambivalence surfaces in the choice of narratives and characters to highlight, but also in the way that issues of, for instance, choice and resistance, are scripted into these narratives as well.

As the political pendulum swings further right in the United States, Canadian television narratives such as these offer the possibility of injecting discourses about important social and political issues that effect girls and women back into the television landscape, where they all too often fade into the background or disappear entirely.[11]

Notes

1. This is not a new insight. In the 1970s, Angela McRobbie noted that the work her (mostly male) colleagues were doing in the early days of the Birmingham School was primarily a way of imagining male homosocial landscapes where active female bodies were virtually non-existent. This work, which included writings by Stuart Hall, Paul Willis, Dick Hebdige, and Paul Gilroy, "led to an emphasis on four areas of key importance...race; state and nation; sexuality and representation; education and ethnography" (181). Especially in early works as exemplified by Hall and Tony Jefferson's *Resistance Through Rituals*, (1976), subcultural youth identities are often unproblematically consolidated as male.

2. For an example of this type of work whose focus is Canadian drama, see my chapter "Have Times Changed?: Girl Power and Feminism on *Degrassi*" in my anthology *Growing Up Degrassi: Television, Identity and Youth Cultures* (2005).

3. I do not address the question of what individual viewers do with or how they understand and negotiate the meaning of a particular television text. However, theories of reception (Fiske, 1987) have long acknowledged that audiences often interpret television texts in ways that radically diverge from the expectations of their producers.

4. Stephanie is also from an educated, middle-class family. Her acting out is presented as something she does directly in opposition to her parents' rules; she brings her provocative clothes

and make up to school and dresses in the bathroom, changing again before she goes home. She also tires of this "look" after a relatively brief period of time. This is in contrast to Spike who seems much more invested in her subcultural identity and who maintains it through the end of the *DC* series, although by the time she reappears on *TNG* she is much more conventional looking. Spike, like her mother, also becomes a hairdresser and is a single mother, but she is firmly represented as middle-class as is her daughter Emma. This is in keeping with the increased homogenization of *TNG*'s cast towards a middle or upper-middle-class identity.

5. See, for example, Sherrie Inness' (1999) discussion of *Xena: Warrior Princess* and the many articles on *Buffy* found in volumes edited by Kaveney (2002), Wilcox and Lavery (2002), South (2003), and other volumes on powerful women on television by Early and Kennedy (2003), and Heinecken (2003).

6. Relatively invisible differences may be included. For instance class differences may be included, but usually have little impact on a character's actual lifestyle; non-sexually active gay characters (primarily gay male characters) or secular non-Christian characters may also be featured.

7. Of course, the fact that Paige's rapist is a popular, good-looking, wealthy "jock" does fall back on a stereotype about the type of men who rape, one that is familiar from other teen series like *Beverly Hills, 90210*.

8. Carmen's racial/ethnic background is ambiguous. Her name, Carmen Roverez, suggests she may be Latina or bi-racial. The male characters, it should be noted, include a poor white boy (Ben Lalonde/Nolan Funk), an Indo-Canadian boy (Ishan Dave/Sandi Bhutella), and an Aboriginal boy (Jack Sinclair/Bronson Pelletier), and a forth character whose background has not yet been highlighted but whose family name (Cherniak) suggest he might be Jewish or Eastern European (Oscar/Shawn Ecker). In the 2005 season, Lalonde's character disappeared.

9. Another series lead, Jack (Bronson Pelletier), is Crystal's brother. The story proffered by the series is as follows: both children were born on a reserve. Their parents had substance abuse problems. The father eventually became sober, left to attend school, and took Crystal with him. Jack stayed with his mother, who also became sober, but was sent to live with his father after some gang-related trouble. Their father runs the Native Centre in Regina.

10. A recent Canadian series, *Godiva's*, featured a similar story arc involving an upper-middle-class Indo-Canadian young man (Ramir/Stephen Lobo) whose family was endeavouring to set him up with "appropriate" Indo-Canadian women. In one episode the woman to whom he is introduced is, he feels, perhaps perfect for him: beautiful, successful (she is a doctor), intelligent, charming, and sexy…as well as meeting the expectations of his parents. However, she reveals soon after that although she is willing to marry him, she is a lesbian. Here, she is willing to marry in order to provide her family with the appearance of conventional, heterosexual domesticity. Despite what he now knows, Ramir also decides to announce their engagement to make his parents happy. The conflation of this narrative about closeting with race/ethnicity maintains, at least on one level, the myth that ethnic Canadian communities are more traditional, controlling and homophobic than conventional (white, Anglo-Christian) "Canadian" families (Bannerji 2000).

11. More about these series can be found on their interactive websites: www.degrassi.tv and www.renegadepress.com.

Coda

The problem with editing a book called *Girlhood: Redefining the Limits* is that there seem to be no clear limits on how to end it, even allowing for the fact that we have mostly stayed within the borders of Canada and Canadian girlhoods.

Perhaps we could start with our own self-interrogation: does this book indeed redefine the limits of Girlhood Studies? We think it does in several ways. First of all, it opens up new spaces for thinking about the contexts in which girls grow up. The contributors to this volume have been writing about girlhoods that span a range of differences and that involve active struggles of resistance and redefinition.

What other questions can we ask of Canada in terms of girlhood? There are many girlhoods remaining that need spaces for voice; that need articulation both from the immediate standpoint and in combination with the historic, contemporary and theoretical confluences of that body of cumulative work dealing with girlhoods. The collected works in this anthology reflect the interlocking and intersecting influences of societal, institutional forces in conjunction with the individual agency that girls are able to reflect and refract in their lived realities. It is this nexus of social forces and individual agency that continues to demand further interrogation especially in revealing how the limits of girlhood themselves are defined and redefined in response to prevailing social forces.

What we would hope is that such a perspective might inspire others to take on similar (national) orientation: what does a South African girlhood in the twenty-first century look like? What does it mean to be girl in Russia a decade after the fall of communism? To be a Muslim girl post-9/11? Clearly these are not questions that can be answered in one book, let alone one chapter, but they are questions that emerge and ultimately lead us to exploring other fascinating trajectories around globalization, transnational and diasporic communities, globalization, hybridized identities and the blurring of gender boundaries. Yet, we are cognizant of the fact that this anthology merely scratches the surface. Much more needs to be done and we hope that what is offered here are glimpses into areas that could be explored further.

When we redefine the limits, we see that there are no limits both horizontally and vertically. To borrow Clifford Geertz's (1973) notion of going thick and deep, there are certain cross cutting themes in the lives of girls and young women that 'shout out' to be explored in limitless ways—across geographic borders, across historical eras and so on. Indeed, as we found in organizing the chapters of this book, when certain thematic areas emerged, there could be a whole book just on that one subject—sex trafficking, gender violence, hope, play, sexual debut, sexuality, menstruation and so on. This is not to say that girlhood scholars are not taking on single issues in global ways, as evident in the numerous works cited in this volume, but only that there is clearly much more work that can be done to reveal and reflect on the full complexity of girlhoods.

We think that this anthology goes some way to redefining the limits of what it means for women scholars of any age to engage in research that is so clearly rooted in the past (our own) and the future (the lives of baby girls and pre-schoolers, pre-adolescent girls, adolescent girls and young women). While this is only an emerging area of scholarship—some of the works that are presented here offer illuminating insights into the ways in which we recapture the past. Perhaps the offerings here highlight the myriad possibilities and problematic encounters that define the process of girlhood. Ultimately though, we are cognizant that what we have chosen to compile here reflects to some degree our own preoccupations with the problems and possibilities that marked our own girlhoods. And in that sense, we hope to have redefined the limits of girlhood by drawing upon those experiences and learnings that shaped and continue to form our gendered lives and our encounters with other girls across race, sex, time and place.

Yasmin Jiwani, Candis Steenbergen and Claudia Mitchell, Montréal, Québec

References

Aapola, Sinikka, Marnina Gonick, and Anita Harris. *Young Femininity: Girlhood, Power and Social Change*. Houndsmill, Basingstoke and NY: Palgrave Macmillan, 2005.

Aboriginal Healing Foundation (AHF). "Where are the Children?" 2005. http://www.wherearethe children.ca/en/home/html.

————. *Aboriginal Healing Foundation Program Handbook*. Ottawa: AHF, 1999.

Aggleton, Peter. *Rebels Without a Cause?* London: The Falmer Press, 1987.

Aggleton, Peter and Geoff Whitty. "Rebels Without a Cause? Socialization and Subcultural Style Among the Children of the New Middle Classes." *Sociology of Education*. 58 (Jan 1985): 60-72.

Alder, Christine and Anne Worrall, eds. *Girls' Violence: Myths and Realities*. Albany: State University of NY Press, 2004.

Alexander, M. Jacqui, and Mohanty, Chandra Talpade. Introduction to *Feminist Geneologies, Colonial Legacies, Democratic Futures*. NY: Routledge, 1997: xii-xiii.

Allen, Paula Gunn. *The Sacred Hoop: Recovering the Feminine in American Indian Traditions*. Boston: Beacon Hill, 1986.

Allen, Robert C. "Reader-Oriented Criticism and Television." In *Channels of Discourse*. Chapel Hill and London: University of North Caroline Press, 1987: 74-112.

Almeida, Rhea, Rosemary Woods, Theresa Messineo, Roberto Font and Chris Heer. "Violence in the Lives of the Racially and Sexually Different: A Public and Private Dilemma." *Journal of Feminist Family Therapy*. 5.3/4 (1994): 99-126.

Amnesty International. *Stolen Sisters: Discrimination and Violence against Indigenous Women in Canada*. London: Amnesty International Secretariat, 2004.

Amselle, Jean-Loup. *Branchements: Anthropologie De L'universalité Des Cultures*. Paris: Flammarion, 2001.

Anderson, Benedict. *Imagined Communities*. NY: Verso, (1983) 1991.

Anderson, John. "Aboriginal Children in Poverty in Urban Communities: Social Exclusion and the Growing Racialization of Poverty in Canada." Presentation to the Subcommittee on Children and Youth at Risk. March 19, 2003. http://www.ccsd.ca/pr/2003/aboriginal.htm.

Anderson, Kim. A *Recognition of Being: Reconstructing Native Womanhood*. Toronto: Second Story Press, 2000.

————. "A Canadian Child Welfare Agency for Urban Natives: The Clients Speak." *Child Welfare*, 77.4 (1998): 441-460.

Anisef, Paul, and Kenise Murphy Kilbride. "The Needs of Newcomer Youth and Emerging 'Best Practices' to Meet Those Needs—Final Report." Joint Centre for Excellence on Research on Immigration and Settlement, *CERIS Report*, 2000.

Appadurai, Arjun. "The Production of Locality." *Modernity at Large: Cultural Dimensions of Globalization*. Minneapolis and London: University of Minnesota Press, 1996: 178-199.

Arat-Koc, Sedef. "Hot Potato: Imperial Wars or Benevolent Interventions? Reflections on 'Global Feminism' Post September 11th." *Atlantis*. 26.2 (2002): 433-44.

Armstrong, Jane. "No-Name Ship Found Crammed With Asians" *The Globe and Mail*. 21 July 1999.

Artz, Sibylle. *Sex, Power, and the Violent School Girl*. Toronto: Trifolium Books, 1998.

Aujla, Angela. "Others in Their Own Land: Second Generation South Asian Canadian Women, Racism, and the Persistence of Colonial Discourse." *Canadian Woman Studies*. 20.2 (2000): 41-47.

Aurthur, Kate. "Television's Most Persistent Taboo." NY *Times*. 18 July 2004.

Avard, Denise, and Louise Hanvey. *The Health of Canada's Children: A CICH Profile*. Ottawa: Canadian Institute of Child Health, 1989.

Attarian, Hourig and Yogurtian, Hermig. (Producers). *Survivor Stories, Surviving Narratives: Pergrouhi's Story* [Video documentary]. Montreal: Par Productions, 2002.

Azam, Sharlene. *Rebel, Rogue, Mischievous Babe*. Toronto: HarperCollins, 2001.

Bannerji, Himani. *The Dark Side of the Nation: Essays on Multiculturalism, Nationalism and Gender*. Toronto: Canadian Scholars' Press Inc, 2000.

Barry, Richard. "Sheltered "Children": The Self-Creation of a Safe Space for Gay, Lesbian, and Bisexual Students" in Lois Weis and Michelle Fine, eds. *Construction Sites*. NY: Teacher's College Press, 2000: 84-99.

Batth, Indy. "Centering the Voices from the Margins: Indo-Canadian Girls' Sports and Physical Activity Experiences in Private and Public Schools." Master of Arts Thesis, University of British Columbia, 1998.

Baumgardner, Jennifer and Amy Richards. *Manifesta: Young Women, Feminism, and the Future*. NY: Farrar, Straus and Giroux, 2000.

Belenky, Mary Field. *Women's Ways of Knowing: The Development of Self, Voice, and Mind*. NY: Basic Books, 1997.

Berman, Helene, and Yasmin Jiwani. "In the Best Interest of the Girl Child: Phase II Report." The Alliance of Five Research Centres on Violence, 2002.

Bertram, Corrine, Julia Hall, Michelle Fine and Lois Weis. "Where the Girls (And Women) Are." *American Journal of Community Psychology*. 28.5 (2000): 731-755.

Bessant, Judith. "From Sociology of Deviance to Sociology of Risk: Youth Homelessness and the Problem of Empiricism." *Journal of Criminal Justice*. 29 (2001): 31-43.

Best, Amy. *Prom Night: Youth, Schools and Popular Culture*. NY, Routledge, 2000.

Best, Joel. *Threatened Children: Rhetoric and Concern About Child-Victims*. Chicago: University of Chicago Press, 1990.

Bettie, Julie. *Women Without Class: Girls, Race, and Identity*. Los Angeles: University of California Press, 2003.

Bettis, Pamela and Natalie Adams, eds. *Geographies of Girlhood: Identity In-Between*. Mahwah: Lawrence Erlbaum and Associates, 2005.

————. "The Power of the Preps and a Cheerleading Equity Policy." *Sociology of Education*. 7 (2003): 128-142

Blackburn, Mollie "Understanding Agency Beyond School-Sanctioned Activities" *Theory Into Practice*. 43.2. (2004): 102-110.

Bloustien, Gerry. *Girl Making: A Cross-Cultural Ethnography on the Process of Growing Up Female*. NY: Berghahn Books, 2003.

————. "It's different to a mirror 'cos it talks to you': Teenage Girls, Video Cameras and Identity." In Sue Howard, ed. *Wired-Up*. London: UCL Press, 1999: 115-133.

Blumenfeld, Warren. "Gay/Straight" Alliances: Transforming Pain to Pride" in Gerald Unks, ed. *The Gay Teen*. NY: Routledge. 1995:113-121.

Boal, Augusto. *Theatre of the Oppressed*. London: Pluto Press, (1971) 2000.

Boodram, Chris. *Building the Links: The Intersection of Race and Sexual Orientation*. Ottawa: Egale, 2003.

Bouchard, Pierrette, and Natasha Bouchard. ""Miroir, Miroir..." La Précocité Provoquée De L'adolescence Et Ses Effets Sur La Vulnérabilité Des Filles." *GREMF*. 87 (2003).

Bouchard, Pierrette, Jean-Claude St-Amant, and Jacques Tondreau. "Filles Et Garçons Dans Le Système D'éducation: Les Nouveaux Mythes Et La Réalité." *GREMF*. 12 (1995).

Boucher, Kathleen. ""Faites La Prévention, Mais Pas L'amour!": Des Regards Féministes Sur La Recherche Et L'intervention En Éducation Sexuelle." *Recherches Féministes*. 16.1 (2003): 121-58.

Bourdieu, Pierre. *Language and Symbolic Power*. John B. Thompson, ed, Gino Raymond and Matthew Adamson (trans). Cambridge: Harvard University Press, 1991.

————. *Ce que parler veut dire: l'économie des échanges linguistiques*. Paris: Fayard, 1982.

Brah, Avtar. *Cartographies of Diaspora: Contesting Identities*. NY: Routledge, 1996.

Britzman, Deborah. "What is this Thing called Love?: New Discourses for Understanding Gay and Lesbian Youth" in Suzanne deCastell and Mary Bryson, eds. *Radical In<ter>ventions: Identity, Politics and Difference/s in Educational Praxis*. Albany: SUNY Press, 1997.

Brown, L. "New Peekaboo Outfits Flunk Schools' Dress Code: Tank Tops, Other Revealing Attire on the Hit List." *Toronto Star*. 29 May 1998: A1.

Brown, Lyn Mikel, and Carol Gilligan. *Meeting at the Crossroads: Women's Psychology and Girls' Development*. Cambridge, MA: Harvard University Press, 1992.

Brumberg, Joan Jacobs. *The Body Project: An Intimate History of American Girls*. NY: Random House, 1997.

Brunker, Mike. "Young 'Model' Sites Feel the Heat: Porn, Sexual Exploitation Charges Leveled Against 3 Operators." *MSNBC News*. http://www.msnbc.msn.com/id/3078759/.

Buckingham, David. *After the Death of Childhood: Growing Up in the Age of Electronic Media*. London: Polity Press, 2000.

————, and Julian Sefton-Green. *Cultural Studies Goes to School*. London: Taylor and Francis, 1995.

Burman, Michelle J., Susan A. Batchelor and Jane A. Brown. "Researching Girls and Violence: Facing Dilemmas of Fieldwork." *British Journal of Criminology*. 41 (2001): 443-459.

Butler, Judith. *Bodies that Matter: On the Discursive Limits of "Sex"* NY: Routledge, 1993.

————. *Gender Trouble: Feminism and the Subversion of Identity*. NY: Routledge, 1990.

Byers, Michele, ed. *Growing Up Degrassi: Television, Identity and Youth Cultures*. Toronto: Sumach Press, 2005.

(campbell), njeri-damali. "Emotions, Organizing, Truth Telling and Change." *Love (in)tention: Creating Action.* Laurentians, 2004.

Cardinal, Linda. "Ruptures et Fragmentations de l'Identité Francophone en Milieu Minoritaire; Un Bilan Critique." *Sociologie et Sociétés.* 26.1 (1994): 71-86.

Caron, Caroline. "La Presse Féminine Pour Adolescentes: Une Analyse De Contenu." M.A. Université Laval, 2003a.

————. "Que Lisent Les Jeunes Filles? Une Analyse Thématique De La "Presse Ados" Au Québec." *Pratiques psychologiques* 3 (2003b): 49-61.

Carr, Wilford, and Stephen Kemmis. *Becoming Critical: Education, Knowledge and Action Research.* London: The Falmer Press, 1986.

Chansonneuve, Deborah. *Reclaiming Connections: Understanding Residential School Trauma among Aboriginal People.* Ottawa: Aboriginal Healing Foundation, 2005.

Charbonneau, Johanne. "La Maternité Adolescente: L'expression Dramatique D'un Besoin D'affection Et De Reconnaissance." *Possibles* 22.1 (1998): 43-55.

Chesney-Lind, Meda. *The Female Offender.* Thousand Oaks: Sage, 1997.

————, and John Hagedorn, eds. *Female Gangs in America.* Chicago: Lake View Press, 1999.

————. "The Meaning of Mean." *Women's Review of Books.* (November 2002): 20-22.

————, and Katherine Irwin. "From Badness to Meanness: Popular Constructions of Contemporary Girlhood." in Anita Harris, ed. *All About the Girl.* NY: Routledge (2004): 45-58.

Christian-Smith, Linda K., ed. *Texts of Desire: Essays on Fiction, Femininity and Schooling.* London: Falmer, 1993.

Cohen, Phil. "Subcultural Conflict and Working Class Community." *Working Papers in Cultural Studies.* 2 (Spring 1972): 5-51.

Cohen, Stanley. *Folk Devils and Moral Panics: The Creation of the Mods and Rockers.* London: MacGibbon and Kee, 1972.

Collins, Patricia Hill. *Black Feminist Thought: Knowledge, Consciousness, and the Politics of Empowerment.* NY: Routledge, 1991.

Connell, R. W. "Encounters with Structure." *International Journal of Qualitative Studies in Education.* 17.1 (2004): 11-28.

————. *Masculinities.* Berkeley: University of California Press, 1995.

————. *Gender and Power.* Stanford: Stanford University Press, 1987.

Conseil du Statut de la Femme. *Des Nouvelles D'elles: Les Jeunes Femmes Du Québec.* Gouvernement du Québec, 2002.

Côté, Jocelyne. "Brève Généalogie De Discours Sur Les Mères Adolescentes: Le Cas De L'administration Québécoise De La Santé Publique." *Anthropologie et Sociétés.* 21.2/3 (1997): 287-301.

Cottle, Simon., ed. *Ethnic Minorities and the Media.* Buckingham: Open University Press, 2000.

Cross, Gary. *The Cute and the Cool.* NY: Oxford University Press, 2004.

————. *Kid's Stuff.* Boston: Harvard University Press, 1997.

Cummings, Joan-Grant. "Collaboration and the People's Movements: An Oxymoron or a Revolutionary Imperative." Presentation to the McGill-McConnell Management Programme, Montreal, 2001: 6.

Currie, Dawn H. *Girl Talk: Adolescent Magazines and Their Readers*. Toronto: University of Toronto Press, 1999.

Dallaire, Hélène, and Geneviève Rail. "Parole Aux Jeunes Francophones: La Problématique De L'équité En Éducation Physique." *Canadian Woman Studies*. 15.4 (1995): 47-52.

Dame, Linda. "Live Through This: The Experiences of Queer Youth in Care in Manitoba." *The Canadian Online Journal of Queer Studies in Education*. 1.1 (2004). http://jqstudies.oise.utoronto.ca /journal/viewarticle.php?id=2andlayout=html

Davies, Bronwyn. "The Concept of Agency: A Feminist Poststructuralist Analysis." *Social Analysis: Journal of Culture and Social Practice*. 29 (1990): 42-53.

————. "The subject of Post-Structuralism: A Reply to Alison Jones. *Gender and Education*, 9.3 (1997): 271-284.

————. *Shards of Glass: Children Reading and Writing beyond Gendered Identities*. Cresskill, NJ: Hampton Press, 1993.

————. *Frogs and Snails and Feminist Tales: Preschool Children and Gender*. St. Leonards, Australia: Allen and Unwin, 1989.

Davies, Lorraine, Julie Ann McMullin, and William R. Avison. *Social Policy, Gender Inequality and Poverty*. Ottawa: Status of Women, 2000.

Davis, James Earl. "Forbidden Fruit: Black Males' Constructions of Transgressive Sexualities in Middle School." In William J. Letts and James T. Sears, eds. *Queering Elementary Education*. NY: Rowman and Littlefield, 1999.

DeBlase, Gina L. "Missing Stories, Missing Lives: Urban Girls (Re)Constructing Race and Gender in the Literacy Classroom." *Urban Education*. 38.3 (2003): 279-329.

de Jesús, Melinda L. "Fictions of Assimilation: Nancy Drew, Cultural Imperialism, and the Filipina American Experience." In Sherrie Inness, ed. *Delinquents and Debutantes*. NY: NY University Press, 1998: 227-46.

Denov, M. and K. Campbell. "Casualties of Aboriginal Displacement in Canada: Children at Risk Among the Innu of Labrador." *Refuge*. 20.2 (2002): 21-33.

Downe, Pamela. J. "'The people we think we are': The Social Identities of Girls Involved in Prostitution." In Kelly Gorkoff and Jane Runner, eds. *Being Heard: The Experiences of Young Women in Prostitution*. Halifax: Fernwood, 2003: 46-68.

Driscoll, Catherine. *Girls: Feminine Adolescence in Popular Culture and Cultural Theory*. NY: Columbia University Press, 2002.

————. "Girl Culture, Revenge and Global Capitalism: Cybergirls, Riot Grrls, Spice Girls." *Australian Feminist Studies*. 14.29 (1999): 173-193.

Durand, Jean-Pierre, and Robert Weil, eds. *Sociologie Contemporaine*. Paris: Editions Vigot, 1994.

Durham, Meenakshi Gigi. "Displaced Persons: Symbols of South Asian Femininity and the Returned Gaze in U.S. Media Culture." *Communication Theory*. 11.2 (May 2001): 201-17.

————. "Girls, Media, and the Negotiation of Sexuality: A Study of Race, Class, and Gender in Adolescent Peer Groups." *Journal and Mass Communication Quarterly*. 76.2 (Summer 1999a): 193-216.

————. "Articulating Adolescent Girls' Resistance to Patriarchal Discourse in Popular Media." *Women's Studies in Communication*. 22.2 (Fall 1999b): 210-29.

Early, Francs and Kathleen Kennedy, eds. *Athena's Daughters: Television's New Women Warriors*. Syracuse: Syracuse University Press, 2003.

Eckert, Penelope. *Jocks and Burnouts: Social Categories and Identity in High School*. NY: Teachers College Columbia University, 1989.

Edelman, Murray. "The Construction and Uses of Social Problems." *Constructing the Political Spectacle*. Chicago: University of Chicago Press, 1988: 12–36.

Eisen, Vitka and Mary Kenyatta. "Cornel West on Heterosexism and Transformation: An Interview." *Harvard Educational Review*. 66.2 (1996): 356–367.

Entwistle, Joanne. "The Dressed Body." In Joanne Entwistle and Elizabeth Wilson, eds. *Body Dressing*. Oxford; NY: Berg, 2001: 33–58.

Epstein, Debbie, J. Elwood, Valerie Hey and J. Maw, eds. *Failing Boys? Issues in Gender and Achievement*. Buckingham: Open University Press, 1998.

Fanon, Frantz. *Black Skin, White Masks*. Translated by Charles Lam. NY: Grove Press, 1967.

Fatila, Rita. "Rita Fatila's Secret Survival Weapons" *Fireweed*, 59/60. (1997): 35.

Fédération des Femmes du Québec. *S'unir Pour Être Rebelles*. Montréal, 2003.

Fine, Michelle. "The Public" in Public Schools: The Social Construction/Constriction of Moral Communities." *Journal of Social Issues*. 46.1 (1990): 107–117.

————. "Sexuality, Schooling, and Adolescent Females: the Missing Discourse of Desire." In Mary Gergen and Sara Davis, eds. *Toward a New Psychology of Gender*. NY: Routledge, 1997: 375–402.

Finkelhor, David and K. Kendall-Tackett. "A Developmental Perspective on the Childhood Impact of Crime, Abuse, and Violent Victimization." In Dante Cicchetti and Sheree L. Toth, eds. *Developmental Perspectives on Trauma: Theory, Research, and Intervention*. Rochester: University of Rochester Press, 1997: 1–32.

Fisher, John. *Reaching Out: A Report on Lesbian, Gay and Bi-sexual Youth Issues in Canada*. Ottawa: United Church of Canada, 1999.

Fisk, Robert. *Pity the Nation: Lebanon at War*. London: Oxford University Press, 1992.

Fiske, John. *Television Culture*. NY and London: Routledge, 1987.

Foucault, Michel. *The History of Sexuality. Volume I: An Introduction*. NY, Vintage Books, 1978.

————. *Discipline and Punish*. Translated 1977. NY: Pantheon, 1975.

————. *Power/Knowledge: Selected Interviews and Other Writings. 1979-1979*. Edited by C. Gordon. NY: Pantheon, 1980.

————. "The Order of Discourse, Inaugural Lecture at the Collège De France." In Robert Young, ed. *Untying the Text*. Boston: Routledge and Kegan Paul, 1981: 48–78.

Fournier, Michèle, Marie-Marthe Cousineau, and Sylvie Hamel. "La Victimisation: Un Aspect Marquant De L'expérience Des Jeunes Filles Dans Les Gangs." *Criminologie*. 37.1 (2004): 149–65.

Fournier, Suzanne and Ernie Crey. *Stolen from our Embrace: The Abduction of First Nations Children and the Restoration of Aboriginal Communities*. Vancouver: Douglas and McIntyre, 1997.

Fraser, Nancy. "The Uses and Abuses of French Discourse Theories for Feminist Politics." In Nancy Fraser and Sandra Lee Bartky, eds. *Revaluing French Feminism*. Bloomington and Indianapolis: Indiana University Press, 1992: 177–194.

Freire, Paulo. *Pedagogy of the Oppressed*. Translated by M.B. Ramos. NY: Continuum, (1970) 1988.

Fulsang, D. "Mom, I'm Ready for School!" *The Globe and Mail*. 28 September 2002: L6.

Furger, Roberta. *Does Jane Compute?* NY: Warner Books, 1998.

Gaardner, Emily, and Joanne Belknap. "Little Women: Girls in Adult Prison." *Women and Criminal Justice.* 15.2 (2004): 51-80.

————. Tenuous Borders: Girls Transferred to Adult Court." *Criminology.* 40.3 (2002): 481-517.

Gal, Susan. "Language and the 'Arts of Resistance'." *Cultural Anthropology,* 10.3 (1985): 407-424.

Galeano, Eduardo. *The Book of Embraces.* (Cedric Belfrage, trans.). NY and London: Norton, 1992.

————. *Days and Nights of Love and War.* NY: Monthly Review Press, 2000.

Ganetz, Hillevi. "The Shop, the Home and Femininity as Masquerade." In Johan Fornas and Goran Bolin, eds. *Youth Culture in Late Modernity.* London: Sage Publication, 1995: 72-99.

Garrison, Ednie Kaeh. "U.S. Feminism—Grrrrl Style! Youth (Sub)Cultures and the Technologies of the Third Wave." *Feminist Studies* 26.1 (Spring 2000):141-170.

Gaskell, Jane. "Course Enrollment in the High School: The Perspective of Working-class Females." *Sociology of Education.* 58 (January 1985):48-50.

Gay, Lesbian and Straight Education Network. *School Related Experiences of LGBT Youth of Color: Findings from the 2003 National School Climate Survey.* 2003. www.glsen.org

Geertz, Clifford, ed. *The Interpretation of Cultures.* NY: Basic Books, 1973.

Gilbert, Brian (Director). *Not Without My Daughter,* USA: 1991.

Gilligan, Carol. *Mapping the Moral Domain.* Cambridge: Harvard University Press, 1988.

Giroux, Henry. *Stealing Innocence: Youth, Corporate Power, and the Politics of Culture.* NY: St.Martin's Press, 2000.

————. "Stealing Innocence: The Politics of Child Beauty Pageants." In Henry Jenkins, ed. *The Children's Culture Reader.* NY: NY University Press, 1999: 265-282.

————. "Nymphet Fantasies: Child Beauty Pageants and the Politics of Innocence." *Social Text* 16.4 (Winter 1998): 31-53

————. "Theories of Reproduction and Resistance in the New Sociology of Education: A Critical Analysis" *Harvard Educational Review.* 53.3 (1983): 257-293.

Gleeson, Kate and Hannah Frith. "Pretty in Pink: Young Women Presenting Mature Sexual Identities." in Anita Harris, ed. *All About the Girl.* London: NY (2004): 103-114.

Golub, Sharon. *Periods: From Menarche to Menopause.* London: Sage, 1992.

Gonick, Marnina. *Between Femininities: Ambivalence, Identity, and the Education of Girls.* Albany, NY: State University of NY Press, 2003.

————. "The 'Mean Girl' Crisis: Problematizing Representations of Girls' Friendships." *Feminism and Psychology.* 14.3 (2004): 395-400.

Gore, Dayo, Tamara Jones Folayan, Joo-Hyun Kang. "Organizing at the Intersections: A Roundtable Discussion of Police Brutality Through the Lens of Race, Class and Sexual Identities." In Andrea McArdle and Tanya Erzen, eds. *Zero Tolerance.* NY: NY City Press, 2002: 251-269.

Gouin, Rachel. Action Strategy Meeting 2004: Mini Report. Montreal: POWER Camp National / Filles d'Action, 2005.

Grant, Agnes. *Finding my Talk: How Fourteen Native Women Reclaimed their Lives after Residential School.* Calgary: Fifth House, 2004.

Grant, Peter S. and Chris Wood. *Blockbusters and Trade Wars: Popular Culture in A Globalized World*. Vancouver/Toronto: Douglas and McIntyre, 2004.

Gray, Charlotte. *Flint and Feather: The Life and Times of E. Pauline Johnson, Tekahionwake*. Toronto: Harper Canada, 2002.

Gray, Heather, Samantha Phillips and Ellen Forney. *Real Girl/Real World: Tools for Finding Your True Self*. Seattle: Seal Press, 1998.

Gray, Herman. *Watching Race: Television and the Struggle for "Blackness."* Minneapolis: University of Minnesota Press, 1995.

Grewal, Inderpal and Caren Kaplan, eds. *Scattered Hegemonies: Postmodernity and Transnational Feminist Practices*. Minneapolis and London: University of Minnesota Press, 1994.

Griffin, Christine. "Good Girls, Bad Girls: Anglocentrism and Diversity in the Constitution of Contemporary Girlhood." In Anita Harris, ed. *All About the Girl*. NY and London: Routledge, 2004: 29-43.

Gross, Larry, Steven K. Aurand and Rita Adessa. *Violence and Discrimination against Lesbian and Gay People in Philadelphia and the Commonwealth of Pennsylvania*. Philadelphia: Philadelphia Lesbian and Gay Task Force, 1988.

Grosz, Elizabeth. *Volatile Bodies: Toward a Corporeal Feminism*. Bloomington: Indiana University Press, 1994.

Guidon, Geneviève. "Quelques Opinions Personnelles Sur Le Féminisme." *Possibles*. 22.1 (1998): 56-62.

Hage, Ghassan. *White Nation: Fantasies of White Supremacy in a Multicultural Society*. NY and Australia: Routledge and Pluto Press, 2000.

Hall, Stuart. "Introduction: Who Needs Identity?" In Stuart Hall and Paul Dugay, eds. *Questions of Cultural Identity*. London: Sage, 1996: 1-18.

————. *Policing the Crisis: Mugging, the State, and Law and Order*. NY: Holmes and Meier, 1978.

————, and Tony Jefferson. *Resistance Through Rituals*. London: Hutchinson, 1976.

Hamilton, Graeme. "Suspect Confessed to 'Racist, Nazi Beliefs'." *National Post*. Montreal. May 29, 2001.

Handa, Amita. "Caught between Omissions: Exploring 'Cultural Conflict' among Second Generation South Asian Women in Canada." Ph.D. Thesis, University of Toronto, 1997.

————. *Of Silk Saris and Mini-Skirts: South Asian Girls Walk the Tightrope of Culture*. Toronto: Women's Press, 2003.

Haraway, Donna J. *Simians, Cyborgs, and Women: The Reinvention of Nature*. NY and London: Routledge, 1991.

Harris, Anita, ed. *All About the Girl: Culture, Power, and Identity*. NY: Routledge, 2004a.

————. *Future Girl: Young Women and the Twenty-First Century*. NY: Routledge, 2004b.

————. "Revisiting Bedroom Culture: New Spaces for Young Women's Politics." *Hectate*. 27.1 (2001): 128-139.

————. "Everything a Teenage Girl Should Know: Adolescence and the Production of Femininity." *Women's Studies Journal*. 15.2 (1999): 111-124.

Hatfield, Michael. *Concentrations of Poverty and Distressed Neighbourhoods in Canada*. Ottawa: Human Resources and Development Council, 1997.

Hebdige, Dick. *Subculture: the Meaning of Style*. London, Routledge, 1979.

Heinecken, Dawn. *The Warrior Women of Television*. NY: Peter Lang, 2003.

Herbert, Carrie. *Talking of Silence: Sexual Harassment of Schoolgirls*. London: Falmer Press, 1989.

Hernández, Daisy, and Bushra Rehman, eds. *Colonize This! Young Women of Color on Today's Feminism*. NY: Seal Press, 2002.

Hey, Valerie. *The Company She Keeps: An Ethnography of Girls' Friendship*. Buckingham: Open University Press, 1997.

Higonnet, Anne. *Pictures of Innocence: The History and Crisis of Ideal Childhood*. London: Thames and Hudson, 1998.

Hirsch, Marianne. *Family Frames*. Cambridge, MA: Harvard University Press, 1997.

Holloway, Sarah and Gil Valentine. *Cyberkids*. London and New York: Routledge Falmer, 2003.
————. "Children's Geographies and The New Social Studies." *Children's Geographies*. Routledge: NY and London, 2000: 1-28.
————. *Cyberkids*. London, NY: Routledge-Falmer, 2003.

Hollows, Joanne. *Feminism, Femininity and Popular Culture*. Manchester and NY: Manchester University Press, 2000.

hooks, bell. *Killing Rage: Ending Racism*. NY: Henry Holt and Company, 1995.
————. *Outlaw Culture: Resisting Representations*. NY and London: Routledge, 1994.
————. *Teaching to Transgress*. London: Routledge, 1994.
————, and Cornel West. *Breaking Bread: Insurgent Black Intellectual Life*. Boston: South End Press, 1991.

Houppert, Karen. *The Curse: Confronting the Last Unmentionable Taboo: Menstruation*. NY: Farrar, Straus and Giroux, 1999.

Howell, Jayne. "Turning out Good Ethnography, or Talking out of Turn? Gender, Violence and Confidentiality in Southeastern Mexico." *Journal of Contemporary Ethnography*. 33.3 (2004): 323-352.

Hudson, Barbara. "Femininity and Adolescence." in Angela McRobbie and Mica Nava, eds. *Gender and Generation*. Basingstoke: Macmillan, 1984: 18-34.

Human Rights Watch. *Hatred in the Hallways: Violence and Discrimination Against Lesbian, Gay, Bisexual, and Transgender Students in U.S. Schools*. NY, 2001.

Huspek, Michael. "Dueling Structures: The Theory of Resistance in Discourse." *Communication Theory*. 3.1 (1993): 1-25.

Hylton, John H. *Aboriginal Sexual Offending in Canada*. Ottawa: Aboriginal Healing Foundation, 2001.

Imam, Umme Farvah. "South-Asian Young Women's Experiences of Violence and Abuse." In Hazel Kemshall and Jacki Pritchard, eds. *Good Practice in Working with Violence*. London: Jessica Kingsley Publishers, 1999: 128-48.

Indian and Northern Affairs Canada. *Aboriginal Women: A Profile from the 1996 Census*. Ottawa: Ministry of Indian and Northern Affairs, 2001.

Inness, Sherrie A. *Tough Girls: Women Warriors and Wonder Women in Popular Culture*. Philadelphia: University of Pennsylvania Press, 1999.
————, ed. *Delinquents and Debutantes: Twentieth-Century American Girls' Cultures*. NY: NY University Press, 1998a.

————, ed. *Millennium Girls: Today's Girls around the World*. Lanham, Boulder, NY, Oxford: Rowman and Littlefield Publishers Inc., 1998b.

————, ed. *Running for Their Lives: Girls, Cultural Identity, and Stories of Survival*. NY: Rowman and Littlefield Publishers, 2000.

Isin, Engin F. "Introduction: Democracy, Citizenship and the City." In *Democracy, Citizenship and the Global City*. London: Routledge, 2000: 1-22.

Jack, Agness. *Behind Closed Doors: Stories from the Kamloops Indian Residential School*. Penticton, BC: Theytus Books, 2001.

Jacobs, M. "Girl Power means Dressing Like a Slut." *The Edmonton Sun*. 12 October 2002: B4.

James, Carl E. "'Up to No Good': Black on the Streets and Encountering Police." In Vic Satzewich, ed. *Racism and Social Inequality in Canada*. Toronto: Thompson Educational Publishing Inc., 1998: 157-76.

Jenkins, Henry. *Beyond Tolerance: Child Pornography on the Internet*. NY: NY University Press, 2001.

————. "The Sensuous Child: Benjamin Spock and the Sexual Revolution." In Henry Jenkins, ed. *The Children's Culture Reader*. NY: NY University Press, 1999: 209-230.

Jenson, Jane. "Mapping Social Cohesion: The State of Canadian Research." Canadian Policy Research Networks. SRA-321/CPRN Study No. F/03, 1998. http://www.cprn.org.

Jenson, Jane. "Globalization, Social Cohesion and Citizenship: The Challenges." Canadian Policy Research Networks, 2002. http://www.cprn.com/family/works_e.htm.

Jiwani, Yasmin. "War Talk": Representations of the Gendered Muslim Body Post 9-11 in *The Montreal Gazette*." In Jo Anne Lee and John Lutz, eds. *Situating "Race" and Racisms in Space, Time, and Theory*. Montreal: McGill-Queens University Press, 2005: 178-203.

————, "Liminality and Location: Observations and Reflections on the Opening Plenary at the Transforming Spaces Conference." In Candis Steenbergen, ed. *Transforming Spaces: Girlhood Agency and Power*. Montreal: POWER Camp National/Filles D'Action, 2004: 18-21.

————, Nancy Janovicek, and Angela Cameron. "Erased Realities: The Violence of Racism in the Lives of Immigrant and Refugee Girls of Colour." Vancouver, CA: FREDA, 2001.

————. "The Denial of Race in the Murder of Reena Virk." The FREDA Centre for Research on Violence against Women and Children, April 2000.

————. "Erasing race: the story of Reena Virk." *Canadian Woman Studies*. 19.3 (1999): 178-184.

Johnson, Norine G., Michael C. Roberts and Judith Worell, eds. *Beyond Appearance: A New Look at Adolescent Girls*. Washington, DC: American Psychology Association, 1999.

Jones, Gerard. *Killing Monsters: Why Children Need Fantasy, Super-Heroes, and Make Believe Violence*. NY: Basic Books, 2002.

Juteau, Danielle. "Ambiguités de la Citoyenneté au Québec." Conférence Desjardins, prononcée dans le cadre du programme des Études sur le Québec de l'Université McGill. Montreal: 2000a: 1-26. http://www.ulg.ac.be/cedem/downloads/DJ2WP.PDF.

————. "What True Pluralism Requires." *Options Politiques*. (January-February, 2000b). 70-72.

Kaputikian, Silva. *Girs mna hishatakogh* [Let My Writing be a Testimony]. Antelias, Lebanon: Publishing House of the Catholicosate of the Holy See of Cilicia, 1996.

Karaian, Lara., Lisa Rundle, and Alison Mitchell, eds. *Turbo Chicks: Talking Young Feminisms*. Toronto: Sumach Press, 2001.

Kearney, Mary Celeste. "Producing Girls: Rethinking the Study of Female Youth Culture." In Sherrie Inness, ed. *Delinquents and Debutantes*. NY: NY University Press, 1998: 285-309.

Keating, Analouise. "Forging El Mundo Zurdo: Changing Ourselves, Changing the World." In Gloria E. Anzaldúa and Analouise Keating. *This Bridge We Call Home*. NY: Routledge, 2002: 519-30.

Kehily, Mary Jane. *Sexuality, Gender and Schooling*. London: Routledge Falmer, 2002.

Kelly, Deirdre M., Shauna Pomerantz and Dawn Currie. "Skater Girlhood and Emphasized Femininity: 'You Can't Land an Ollie Properly in Heels.'." *Gender and Education*. in press.

Kent, G. "Ban on Blue Hair Drives Family to Court." *Calgary Herald*. 7 August 1999: A5.

Kenway, Jane, Sue Willis, Jill Blackmore and Leonie Rennie. *Answering Back: Girls, Boys, Feminism in Schools*. NY: Routledge, 1998.

Kenway, Jane, and Sue Willis, eds. *Hearts and Minds: Self-Esteem and the Schooling of Girls*. London, NY, Philadelphia: The Falmer Press, 1990.

Khan, Shahnaz. "The Veil as a Site of Struggle: The Hejab in Quebec." *Canadian Woman Studies*. 15.2/3 (1995): 146-52.

Kingsley, Cherry and Melanie Mark. *Sacred Lives: Canadian Aboriginal Children and Youth Speak Out about Sexual Exploitation*. Ottawa: Human Resources Development Canada, 2000.

Kincaid, James. "Producing Erotic Children." In Henry Jenkins, ed. *The Children's Culture Reader*. NY: NY University Press, 1999: 241-253.

————. *Erotic Innocence: The Culture of Child Molesting*. London: Duke University Press, 1998.

Kirmayer, Lawrence J. "Landscapes of Memory: Trauma, Narrative, and Dissociation." In Paul Antze and Michael Lambeck, eds. *Tense Past: Cultural Essays in Trauma and Memory*. NY: Routledge, 1996: 173-198.

Kishchuk, Natalie. Girls Club at Verdun Elementary: Evaluation Report, 2004-2005. Montreal: POWER Camp National/Filles D'Action, 2005.

Kissling, Elizabeth Arveda. "'That's Just a Basic Teen-Age Rule': Girls' Linguistic Strategies for Managing the Menstrual Communication Taboo." *Journal of Applied Communication Research*. 24.4 (1996): 292-309.

Kling, Kristen, Janet Shibley Hyde, Carolin J. Showers and Brenda N. Buswell. "Gender Differences in Self-Esteem: A Meta-Analysis." *Psychological Bulletin*. 125.4 (1999): 470-00.

Kroll, Ian, and Lorne Warneke. *The Dynamics of Sexual Orientation and Adolescent Suicide: A Comprehensive Review and Developmental Perspective*. Calgary: University of Calgary, 1995.

Kuhn, Annette. *Family Secrets*. London: Verso, 1995.

Kumashiro, Kevin. "Reading Queer Asian American Masculinities and Sexualities in Elementary School." In William J. Letts and James T. Sears, eds. *Queering Elementary Education*. NY: Rowman and Littlefield, 1999: 61-70.

————. "Queer Students of Color and Antiracist, Antiheterosexist Education: Paradoxes of Identity and Activism." In Kevin Kumashiro, ed. *Troubling Intersections of Race and Sexuality*. NY: Rowman and Littlefield, 2001: 1-25.

Kunz, Jean Lock, and Louise Hanvey. "Immigrant Youth in Canada." Canadian Council on Social Development, 2000.

Ladha, Azmina N., ed. *Re-Righting Reality: Young Women on their Search for Self.* Vancouver: The FREDA Centre for Research on Violence against Women and Children, 2003.

Lamb, Sharon. *The Secret Lives of Girls: What Good Girls Really Do—Sex, Play, Aggression, and their Guilt.* NY: Free Press, 2002.

Lambert, Pierre-Yves. "Racisme, Ethnocentrisme et Discrimination au Canada." *Nouvelle Tribune.* Bruxelle, June 1997. n.p. http://users.skynet.be/suffrage-universel/camiqc.htm.

Lamda Legal Defense and Education Fund. *A Guide to Effective Statewide Laws/Policies: Preventing Discrimination against LBGT Students in K–12 Schools.* 2001. www.glsen.org.

Lane, Phil, Judie Bopp, and Michael Bopp. *Aboriginal Domestic Violence in Canada.* Ottawa: Aboriginal Healing Foundation, 2003.

Leblanc, Lauraine. *Pretty in Punk: Girls' Gender Resistance in a Boys' Subculture.* New Brunswick: Rutgers University Press, 2002.

Lees, Sue. *Sugar and Spice: Sexuality and Adolescent Girls.* London: Penguin Books, 1993.

Leschied, Alan, and Anne Cummings. *Female Adolescent Aggression.* Solicitor General: Canada, 2002.

Leong, Laurence Wai-Teng. "Cultural Resistance: The Cultural Terrorism of British Male Working-Class Youth." *Social Theory.* 12 (1992): 29-58.

Lesko, Nancy. "The Curriculum of the Body: Lessons from a Catholic High School." In Leslie G. Roman and Linda K. Christian-Smith with Elizabeth Ellsworth, eds. *Becoming Feminine.* London: Falmer Press, 1998: 123-142.

———. "Denaturalizing Adolescence: The Politics of Contemporary Representations." *Youth and Society.* 28.2 (1996): 139-161.

Levine, Judith. *Harmful to Minors: The Perils of Protecting Children from Sex.* Minneapolis: University of Minnesota Press, 2002.

Levy, Neil. "Virtual Child Pornography: The Eroticization of Inequality." *Ethics and Information Technology* 4 (2002): 319-323.

Livingstone, Sonia M. *Young People and New Media.* London: Sage, 2002.

Lomawaima, K. Tsianina. *They Called it Prairie Light: The Story of Chilocco Indian School.* Lincoln: University of Nebraska Press, 1994.

Loutzenheiser, Lisa and Lori MacIntosh "Citizenships, Sexualities and Education." *Theory into Practice.* 43.2. (2004): 151-158.

Lowe, Melanie. "Colliding Feminism: Britney Spears, "Tweens," and the Politics of Reception." *Popular Music and Society* 26.2 (2003): 123-140.

Lumby, Catharine. "Panic Attacks: Old Fears in A New Media Era." *Media International Australia.* 85 (November 1997): 40-46.

Maguire, Patricia. "Uneven Ground: Feminisms and Action Research." In Peter Reason and Hilary Bradbury, eds. *Handbook of Action Research.* Thousand Oaks: Sage, 2001: 59-69.

Mac an Ghaill, M. "(In)visibility: Sexuality, Race and Masculinity in the School Context." In Debbie Epstein, ed. *Challenging Lesbian and Gay Inequalities in Education.* Buckingham: Open University Press, 1994: 152-176.

Maguire, Patricia. *Doing Participatory Research: A Feminist Approach.* Amherst: Center for International Education, 1997.

Mahtani, Minelle. "Interrogating the Hyphen-Nation: Canadian Multicultural Policy and 'Mixed Race' Identites." *Social Identities.* 8.1 (2002): 67-90.

Makler, Andra. "Imagining History: A Good Story and a Well-Formed Argument." In Nel Noddings and Carol Witherell, eds. *Stories Lives Tell*. NY: Teachers College Press, 1991: 29-47.

Mallon, Gerald P., Nina Aledort, and Michael Ferrera. "There's No Place Like Home: Achieving Safety, Permanency and Well-being for Lesbian and Gay Adolescents in Out-of-Home Care Settings." *Child Welfare*, 81.2 (2002): 407-440.

Mangle, Sarah. "Making Space for Girls." In Lori McNulty, ed. *The Youth Friendly City: The World Urban Forum, Vancouver Working Group Discussion Paper*. The Environmental Youth Alliance, March 2004.

Martinez, Dorie Gilbert. "Mujer, Latina, Lesbiana: Notes on the Multidimensionality of Economic and Sociopolitical Injustice," *Journal of Gay and Lesbian Social Services*. 8.3 (1998): 99-112.

Martinot, Steve. *The Rule of Racialization: Class, Identity, Governance*. Ed. Stanley Aronowitz. Philadelphia: Temple University Press, 2003.

Mata, Fernando and John Valentine."Selected Ethnic Profiles of Canada's Young Age Cohorts." Strategic Research and Analysis Multiculturalism Program, Citizen's Participation and Multiculturalism) Ottawa: Dept. of Canadian Heritage, 1999.

Mazzerella, Sharon R. *Girl Wide Web: Girls, the Internet and the Negotiation of Identity*. NY: Peter Lang, 2005.

————, and Norma Odom Pecora. *Growing up Girls: Popular Culture and the Construction of Identity. NY*, Peter Lang, 1999.

McCarthy, Anna. "'Must See' Queer TV: History and Serial in *Ellen*." In Mark Jancovich and James Lyons, eds. *Quality Popular Television*. London: BFI Publishing, 2003: 88-102.

McEvoy, Maureen and Judith Daniluk. "Wounds to the Soul: The Experiences of Aboriginal Women Survivors of Sexual Abuse." *Canadian Psychology*, 36(3) (1994): 221-234.

McNay, Lois. "Gender, Habitus and the Field: Pierre Bourdieu and the Limits of Reflexivity." *Theory, Culture and Society*. 16.1 (1999): 95-117.

McRobbie, Angela. *Feminism and Youth Culture: From 'Jackie' to 'Just Seventeen.'*. NY: Routledge, (1991) 2000.

————. "Dance and Social Fantasy." In Angela McRobbie and Mica Nova, eds. *Gender and Generation*. London: MacMillan Publishers, 1984: 130-161.

————. *Postmodernism and Popular Culture*. NY: Routledge, 1994.

————. *'More!* New Sexualities in Girls' and Women's Magazines', in I Curran, D. Morley and V. Walkerdine (eds) *Cultural Studies and Communications*. London: Arnold, 1996.

Mendez, Juan. "Serving Gays and Lesbians of Color Who are Survivors of Domestic Violence" *Journal of Gay and Lesbian Social Services*, 4.1 (1996): 53-59.

Merskin, Debra. "Adolescence, Advertising, and the Ideology of Menstruation." *Sex Roles*. 40.11/12 (1999): 941-957.

Merten, Don E. "The Meaning of Meanness: Popularity, Competition, and Conflict among Junior High School Girls." *Sociology of Education*. 70 (1997): 175-191.

Miles, Robert and Malcolm Brown. *Racism*. Second Edition. NY: Routledge, (1989) 2003.

Miller, Jim. *Shingwauk's Vision: A History of Native Residential Schools*. Toronto: University of Toronto Press, 1996.

Miller, Mary Jane. *Outside Looking In*. McGill-Queen's University Press, in press.

————. *Turn Up the Contrast: CBC Television Drama Since 1952*. Vancouver: University of British Columbia Press, 1987.

Million, Dian. "Telling Secrets: Sex, Power and Narratives in Indian Residential School Histories." *Canadian Woman Studies*. 20.2 (2000): 92-104.

Milloy, John S. *A National Crime: The Canadian Government and the Residential School System, 1879-1986*. Winnipeg: University of Manitoba Press, 1999.

Mills, Catherine. "Efficacy and Vulnerability: Judith Butler on Reiteration and Resistance." *Australian Feminist Studies*. 15.32 (2000): 265-279.

Minh-ha, Trinh T. *Woman, Native, Other: Writing Postcoloniality and Feminism*. Bloomington: Indiana University Press, 1989.

Mitchell, Claudia, and Jacqueline Reid-Walsh. *Seven Going on Seventeen: Tween Culture within Girlhood Studies*. NY: Peter Lang Associates, 2005.

————. *Researching Children's Popular Culture: The Cultural Spaces of Childhood*. London and NY: Taylor and Francis, Routledge, 2002.

Mohanty, Chandra Talpade. *Feminism Without Borders: Decolonizing Theory, Practicing Solidarity*. Durham, NC: Duke University Press, 2003.

————. "'Under Western Eyes' Revisited: Feminist Solidarity through Anticapitalist Struggles." *Signs*. 28.2 (2002): 499-535.

Moran, Bridget. *Stoney Creek Woman: The Story of Mary John*. Vancouver: Arsenal Pulp Press, 1997.

Munoz, Jose Esteban. *Disidentifications: Queers of Colour and the Performance of Politics*. Minnesota: University of Minnesota Press, 1999.

Narayan, Uma. *Dislocating Cultures/Identities, Traditions and Third World Feminism*. London and NY: Routledge, 1997.

Nasrin, Taslima. *Meyebela: My Bengali Girlhood*. Translated by Gopa Majumda. Steerforth Press, 1998.

NEA. "Making the Grade For all Students" *NEA Today*, 17.4 (1999).

Neihart, Ben. "…OMG!< >I Love Ellie and Ashley.< >…Craig Is Totally HOTTTT.< >DGrassi Is tha Best Teen TV N da WRLD!<" *The NY Times Magazine*. 20 March 2005: 40-45.

Nelson, Lise. "Bodies (and Spaces) do Matter: The Limits of Performativity." *Gender, Place and Culture* 6.4 (1999): 331-353.

Newman, Zoë, and Kelly O'Brien. Special Issue: "Revolution Girl Style" *Fireweed*. 59/60 (Fall/Winter 1997).

Nicholson, Linda J., ed. *Feminism/Postmodernism*. NY: Routledge, 1989.

O'Brien, Carol-Anne. "The Social Organization of the Treatment of Lesbian, Gay and Bisexual Youth in Group Homes and Youth Shelters." *Canadian Review of Social Policy*. 34 (1994): 37-57.

Odem, Mary E. *Delinquent Daughters: Protecting and Policing Adolescent Female Sexuality in the United States, 1885-1920*. Chapel Hill, NC: University of North Carolina Press, 1995.

O'Nell, T. (1989). "Psychiatric Investigations among American Indians and Alaska Natives: A Critical Review." *Culture, Medicine and Psychiatry*. 13 (1989): 58-87.

Ong, Aihwa. (1999). "Flexible Citizenship: The Cultural Logics of Transnationality." In Aihwa Ong, ed. *Flexible Citizenship*. London: Duke University Press, 1999: 1-26.

Ono, Kent. "To Be A Vampire on *Buffy the Vampire Slayer*: Race and ("Other") Socially Marginalizing Positions on Horror TV." In Elyce Rae Helford, ed. *Fantasy Girls*. Lanham: Rowman and Littlefield, 2000: 163-186.

Oprah. "Controversy Over Young Girls Modeling Online." Host: Oprah Winfrey. NBC/Global, 28 April, 2003. http://www.oprah.com/tows/pastshows/200304/tows_past_20030428.jhtml.

Orenstein, Peggy. *Schoolgirls: Young Women, Self-Esteem, and the Confidence Gap*. Toronto: Anchor Books Doubleday, 1994.

Orion Center. *Survey of Street Youth*. Seattle, WA, 1986.

Osborne, Brian S. "Landscapes, Memory, Monuments and Commemoration: Putting Identity in its Place." *Canadian Ethnic Studies*, 33.3 (2001) 39-77.

Ost, Suzanne. "Children at Risk: Legal and Societal Perceptions of the Potential Threat that the Possession of Child Pornography Poses to Society." *Journal of Law and Society*. 29.3 (September 2002): 436-60.

O'Toole, Laurence. *Pornocopia*. London: Serpent's Tail, 1998.

Palmer, Sally and Walter Cooke. "Understanding and Countering Racism with First Nations Children in Out-of-Home Care." *Child Welfare*, 75.6 (1996): 709-725.

Park, Peter. "What is Participatory Research? A Theoretical and Methodological Perspective." In Peter Park, M. Brydon-Miller, Budd Hall and Ted Jackson, eds. *Voices of Change*. Westport: Bergin and Garvey, 1993: 1-20.

Phillips, Lynn M. *Flirting with Danger: Young Women's Reflections on Sexuality and Domination*. NY: NY University Press, 2000.

Pipher, Mary. *Reviving Ophelia: Saving the Selves of Adolescent Girls*. NY: Balantine, 1995.

Pollack, Shoshana. "Reconceptualizing Women's Agency and Empowerment: Challenges to Self-Esteem Discourse and Women's Lawbreaking." *Women and Criminal Justice*. 12.1 (2000): 75-87.

Pomerantz, Shauna, Dawn Currie and Deirdre M. Kelly. "Sk8er Girls: Skateboarders, Girlhood, and Feminism in Motion." *Women's Studies International Forum*. 27.5/6 (2004): 547-557.

Potter, Roberto Hugh and Lyndy A. Potter. "The Internet, Cyberporn, and Sexual Exploitation of Children: Media Moral Panics and Urban Myths for Middle-Class Parents?" *Sexuality and Culture*. 5.3 (June 2001): 31-48.

Potvin, Maryse. "Second-Generation Haitian Youth in Quebec. Between the 'Real' Community and the 'Represented' Community." *Canadian Ethnic Studies*. 31.1 (1999): 43-73.

Pratt, Geraldine. "Between Homes: Displacement and Belonging for Second Generation Filipino-Canadian Youths." *Research on Immigration and Integration in the Metropolis: Working Paper Series*, no. 02-13 (2002).

Pyke, Karen D., and Tran Dang. "'F.O.B.' and 'Whitewashed': Identity and Internalized Racism among Second Generation Asian Americans." *Qualitative Sociology*. 26.2 (2003): 147-72.

Quéniart, Anne, and Julie Jacques. "L'engagement Politique Des Jeunes Femmes Au Québec: De La Responsabilité Au Pouvoir D'agir Pour Un Changement De Société." *Lien Social et Politiques—RIAC*. 46 (2001): 45-53.

Raby, Rebecca C. "A Tangle of Discourses: Girls Negotiating Adolescence." *Journal of Youth Studies* 5.4 (2002): 425-48.

Rand, Erica. *Barbie's Queer Accessories*. Durham: Duke University Press, 1995.

Rattansi, Ali. "Western" Racisms, Ethnicities and Identities in a "Postmodern" Frame." (n.p.) In Ali Rattansi, and Sallie Westwood, eds. *Racism, Modernity and Identity*. Cambridge: Polity Press, 1994: 136-155.

Razack, Sherene H. *Looking White People in the Eye: Gender, Race, and Culture in Courtrooms and Classrooms*. Toronto, Ontario: University of Toronto Press, 1998.

————. "From the 'Clean Snows of Petawawa': The Violence of Canadian Peacekeepers in Somalia." *Cultural Anthropology* 15.1 (2000): 127-63.

————, ed. *Race, Space and the Law: Unmapping a White Settler Society*. Toronto: Between the Lines, 2002.

————. *Dark Threats and White Knights: The Somalia Affair, Peacekeeping and the New Imperialism*. Toronto: University of Toronto Press, 2004.

Redfern, Lea. "The Paedophile as Folk Devil." *Media International Australia* 85, (November 1997): 47-55.

Rettinger. Jill. *The Relationship Between Child Pornography and The Commission of Sexual Offences Against Children: A Review of the Literature*. The Research and Statistics Division of the Department of Justice of Canada. March, 2000.

Richards, Chris. "Room to Dance: Girls' Play and 'The Little Mermaid'." In Cary Bazalgette and David Buckingham, eds. *In Front of the Children*. London: British Film Institute Publishing, 1995: 141-150.

Royal Commission on Aboriginal Peoples (RCAP). *Report of the Royal Commission on Aboriginal Peoples*. Ottawa: The Ministry of Indian and Northern Affairs, 1996.

Rumbaut, Ruben G. "Assimilation and Its Discontents: Between Rhetoric and Reality." *International Migration Review*. 31.4 (1997): 923-60.

————. "The Crucible Within: Ethnic Identity, Self Esteem, and Segmented Assimilation among Children of Immigrants." *International Migration Review* 28.4 (1994): 748-94.

Russell, Stephen. and Nhan Truong.. "Adolescent Sexual Orientation, Race and Ethnicity, and School Environments: A National Study of Sexual Minority Youth of Color." In Kevin Kumashiro, ed. *Troubling Intersections of Race and Sexuality*. NY: Rowman and Littlefield, 2001: 113-130.

Sanders-Phillips, Kathy, Peter A. Mosian, Stacy Wadlington, Stacey Morgan, and Kerry English. "Ethnic Differences in Psychological Functioning among Black and Latino Sexually Abused Girls," *Child Abuse and Neglect*. 19.6 (1995):691-706.

Sandoval, Chela. *Methodology of the Oppressed*. Minnesota: University of Minnesota Press, 2000.

Saskatchewan Women's Secretariat. *Profile of Aboriginal Women in Saskatchewan*. Regina: Saskatchewan Women's Secretariat, 1999.

Savin-Williams, Ritch C. "Verbal and Physical Abuse as Stressors in the Lives of Lesbian, Gay Male and Bi-Sexual Youth." *Journal of Consulting and Clinical Psychology*. 62 (1994): 261-269.

Scanlon, Joseph. "The Sikhs of Vancouver: A Case-Study of the Role of the Media on Ethnic Relations." Paris: Unesco Press, 1977.

Scheeres, Julia. "Girl Model Sites Crossing the Line?" *Wired*. July 23, 2001. http://www.wired. com/news/ebiz/0,1271,45346,00.html.

Scheper-Hughes, Nancy and Howard F. Stein, "Child Abuse and the Unconscious in American Popular Culture." In Henry Jenkins, ed. *The Children's Culture Reader*. NY: NY University Press, 1999.

Schilt, Kristen. 'I'll Resist with Every Inch of my Breath: Girls and Zine Making as a Form of Resistance' *Youth and Society*. 35.1 (2003): 71-97.

Schooler, Deborah, L. Monique Ward, Ann Merriwether, and Allison Caruthers. "Who's That Girl: Television's Role in the Body Image Development of Young White and Black Women." *Psychology of Women Quarterly*. 28 (2004): 38-47.

Schultz, Katherine. "Identity Narratives: Stories from the Lives of Urban Adolescent Females." *The Urban Review*. 31.1 (1999): 79-103.

Scott, James C. *Domination and the Arts of Resistance*. New Haven: Yale University Press, 1990.

Sears, James. "Black Gay or Gay-Black: Choosing Identities and Identifying Choices." In Gerald Unks, ed. *The Gay Teen*. NY: Routledge, 1995: 135-157.

Sedgwick, Eve. *Epistemology of the Closet*. Berkeley: University of California Press, 1990.

Seiter, Ellen. *The Internet Playground*. NY: Peter Lang, 2005.

Serequeberhan, T. "Reflections on In My Father's House." *Research in African Literatures*, 27(1) (1996): 110-118.

Sharpe, Joanne, Paul Routledge, Chris Philo and Ronan Paddison. "Entanglements of Power: Geographies of Domination/resistance." In Joanne P. Sharp, Paul Routledge, Chris Philo and Ronan Paddison, eds. *Entanglements of Power*. London: Routledge, 2000.

Shohat, Ella. "Area Studies, Gender Studies, and the Cartographies of Knowledge." *Social Text*. 72.20 (2002): 67-78.

————, and Robert Stam. *Unthinking Eurocentrism*. NY and London: Routledge, 1994.

Silin, Jonathan. "The Pervert in the Classroom." In Joseph Tobin, ed. *Making A Place for Pleasure in Early Childhood Education*. New Haven: Yale University Press, 1997: 214-234.

Silverman, Kaja. "Fragments of a Fashionable Discourse." In Shari Benstock and Suzanne Ferriss, eds. *On Fashion*. New Brunswick, N.J.: Rutgers University Press, 1994: 183-196.

Simmons, Rachel. *Odd Girl Out: The Hidden Aggression in Girls*. NY: Harvest Books, 2003.

Simonetti, Marie-Claire. "Teenage Truths and Tribulations Across Cultures: *Degrassi Junior High* and *Beverly Hills 90210*." *Journal of Popular Film and Television*. (Spring 1994).

Smith, R. "Cleavage, fine. Bellies, well, okay. But groins?" *The Globe and Mail*. 21 September 2002: R6.

Snider, Kathryn. "Race and Sexual Orientation: The (Im)possibility of these Intersections in Educational Policy." *Harvard Educational Review*. 66.2 (1996): 292-302.

Sohoni, Neera. *The Burden of Girlhood: A Global Perspective*. Oakland: Third Party, 1995.

Sofronoff, Kate, Len Dalgliesh, Robert Kosky. *Out of Options: A Cognitive Model of Adolescent Suicide and Risk-Taking*. Cambridge and NY: Cambridge University Press, 2005.

Solis, Jocelyn. "Re-thinking Illegality as a Violence Against, not by Mexican Immigrants, Children, and Youth." *Journal of Social Issues*. 59.1 (2003): 15-31.

South, James B., ed. *Buffy the Vampire Slayer and Philosophy*. Peru, Illinois: Open Court Publishing CompaNew York, 2003.

Spain, Chy Ryan. "An Interview with Dena Underwood" in Kevin Kumashiro, ed. *Troubling Intersections of Race and Sexuality*. NY: Rowman and Littlefield, 2001: 55-60.

Spivak, Gayatri Chakravorty. *In Other Worlds*. NY and London: Routledge, 1988.

Stasiulis, Daiva. The Active Child Citizen: Lessons from Canadian Policy and the Children's Movement. *Citizenship Studies*. 6.4 (2002): 507-537.

―――. "Relational Positionalities of Nationalisms, Racisms, and Feminisms." In Caren Kaplan, Norma Alarcon, and Minoo Moallem, eds. *Between Woman and Nation*. Durham: Duke University Press, 1999: 182-218.

Statistics Canada. *Aboriginal Peoples of Canada*. 2003. Http://www12.statcan.ca/english/census01/products/analytic/companion/abor/canada.cfm#2

―――. *Children and Youth as Victims of Violent Crime*. A report produced by Statistics Canada. http://www.statscan.ca/Daily/Englis/030725/d030725a.htm.

―――. *Women in Canada, 2000: A Gender-based Statistical Report*. Ottawa: Statistics Canada, 2001.

Steenbergen, Candis., *et al*, eds. Special Issue: "Young Women: Feminists, Activists, Grrrls." *Canadian Woman Studies*. 20/21.4/1 (Winter/ Spring 2001).

―――, ed. *Transforming Spaces: Girlhood, Agency and Power*. Montreal: POWER Camp National/Filles d'Action, 2004.

Sterling, Shirley. *My Name is SEEPEETZA*. Vancouver: Douglas and McIntyre, 1992.

Stern, Susannah. "Sexual Selves on the World Wide Web: Adolescent Girls' Home Pages as Sites for Sexual Self-Expression." *Sexual Teens, Sexual Media*. Mahwah: 2002: 265-285.

Surrey, Janet L. "Relationship and Empowerment." *Women's Growth in Connection*. NY: The Guilford Press, 1991.

Talburt, Susan. "Constructions of LGBT Youth: Opening Up Subject Positions." *Theory into Practice*. 43.2 (2004): 116-121.

Tanenbaum, Leora. *Slut! Growing Up Female with a Bad Reputation*. NY: Seven Stories, 1999.

Tatum, Beverly. *Why are all the Black Kids Sitting Together in the Cafeteria? And Other Conversations about Race*. (Fifth edition). NY: Basic Books, 2002.

Taussig, Michael. *Defacement: Pubic Secrecy and the Labor of the Negative*. Stanford: Stanford University Press, 1999.

Taylor, Jill McLean, Carol Gilligan and Amy Sullivan. *Between Voice and Silence: Women and Girls, Race and Relationship*. Cambridge: Harvard University Press, 1995.

Thobani, Sunera. "Nationalizing Citizens: Bordering Immigrant Women in the Late Twentieth Century." *Canadian Journal of Women and the Law*. 12.2 (2000): 279-312.

"Thorny Legal Issues Raised by Effort to Ban Child Modelling Sites." *Computer Crime Research Center Website*. http://www.crime-research.org/news/2002/09/Mess1802.htm.

Tincknell, Estella, Deborah Chambers, Joost Van Loon, and Nichola Hudson. "Begging For It: "New Femininities," Social Agency, and Moral Discourse in Contemporary Teenage and Men's Magazines." *Feminist Media Studies* 3.1 (2003): 47-63.

Titus, Jordan J. "Boy Trouble: Rhetorical Framing of Boys' Underachievement." *Discourse*. 25.2 (2004): 145-69.

Todd, Sharon. "Veiling the 'Other', Unveiling our 'Selves': Reading Media Images of the Hijab Psychoanalytically to Move Beyond Tolerance." *Canadian Journal of Education*. 23.4 (1998): 438-51.

Tolman, Deborah L. "Daring to Desire: Culture in the Bodies of Adolescent Girls" In Janice Irvine, ed. *Sexual Cultures and the Construction of Adolescent Identities*. Philadelphia: Temple University Press, 1994: 250-84.

Toronto District School Board. *Equity Foundation Statement and Commitments to Equity Policy Implementation*. Toronto: Toronto District School Board, 2000.

Torres, Sara., ed. *That Body Image Thing: Young Women Speak Out!* Ottawa: CRIAW, 1999.

Turkle, Sherry. "Commodity and Community in Personal Computing." *High Technology and Low-Income Communities*. In Donald Schon, Bish Sanyal and William Mitchell, eds. Cambridge: MIT Press, 1999: 337-347.

Twine, France Winddance. "Brown Skinned White Girls: Class, Culture and the Construction of White Identity in Suburban Communities." *Gender, Place and Culture* 3.2 (1996): 205-24.

Urquiza, Anthony J., and Beth L. Goodlin-Jones. "Child Sexual Abuse and Adult Revictimization with Women of Colour." *Violence and Victims* 9.3 (1994): 223-31.

United Nations Development Program (UNDP). *Putting Promises into Action: Campaign for Children*. NY: United Nations, 2000.

Ussher, Jane and Julie Mooney-Somers. "Negotiating Desire and Sexual Subjectivity: Narratives of Young Lesbian Avengers" *Sexualities*. 3.2 (2000) 183-200.

van Dijk, Teun A. "Elite Discourse and Racism." *Race and Ethnic Relations*. California: Sage, 1993.

Van Parijs, Philippe. *Sauver La Solidarité*. Paris: Les éditions du cerf, 1995.

Van Roosmalen, Erica. "Forces of Patriarchy: Adolescent Experiences of Sexuality and Conceptions of Relationships." *Youth and Society* 32.2 (December 2000): 200-227.

Varney, Joan Ariki. "Undressing the Normal: Community Efforts for Queer Asian and Asian American Youth" in Kevin Kumashiro, ed. *Troubling Intersections of Race and Sexuality*. NY: Rowman and Littlefield, 2001: 87-104

Violet, Indigo. "Linkages: A Personal-Political Journey with Feminist-of-Colour Politics." In Gloria E. Anzaldúa and Analouise Keating, eds. *This Bridge We Call Home*. NY: Routledge, 2002: 486-94.

Von Schulthess, Beatrice. "Violence in the Streets: Anti- lesbian assault and harrassment in San Francisco." In Gregory M. Herek and Kevin T. Berrill, eds. *Hate Crimes*. London: Hutchinson, 1992: 65-75.

Waldram, James B. *Revenge of the Windigo: The Construction of the Mind and Mental Health of North American Aboriginal Peoples*. Toronto: University of Toronto Press, 2004.

Walkerdine, Valerie. *Daddy's Girl: Young Girls and Popular Culture*. Cambridge, Mass.: Harvard University Press, 1997.

————. "Popular Culture and the Eroticization of Little Girls." In Henry Jenkins, ed. *The Children's Culture Reader*. NY: NY University Press, 1998, 254-64.

————. *Schoolgirl Fictions*. NY: Verso, 1990.

Walters, Suzanna Danuta. *Material Girls: Making Sense of Feminist Cultural Theory*. Berkeley and Los Angeles: University of California Press, 1995.

Ward, Janie Victoria, and Beth Cooper Benjamin. "Women, Girls, and the Unfinished Work of Connection: A Critical Review of American Girls' Studies." In Anita Harris, ed. *All About the Girl*. NY: Routledge, 2004: 15-27.

Weber, Sandra, and Claudia Mitchell. *Not Just Any Dress: Narratives of Memory, Identity and the Body*. NY: Peter Lang, 2004.

Weedon, Chris. *Feminist Practice and Poststructuralist Theory*. Oxford, NY: B. Blackwell, 1987.

West, Cornel. *Race Matters*. Boston: Beacon Press, 2001.

Wideen, Marvin, and Kathleen A. Barnard. "Impacts of Immigration on Education in British Columbia: An Analysis of Efforts to Implement Policies of Multiculturalism in Schools." Vancouver: Vancouver Centre of Excellence, January 1999.

Wilchins, Ricki.A. *Read My Lips: Sexual Subversion and the End of Gender*. Ithaca, NY: Firebrand Books, 1997.

Wilcox, Rhonda. "There Will Never Be a 'Very Special' *Buffy*: Buffy and the Monsters of Teen Life." *Slayage*. 1.2 (2001). www.slayage.tv.

————. and David Lavery, eds. *Fighting the Forces: What's at Stake in Buffy the Vampire Slayer*. Oxford: Rowman and Littlefield Publishers Ltd., 2002.

Wilkins, Julia. "Protecting Our Children from Internet Smut: Moral Duty or Moral Panic?" *The Humanist* 57.5 (September-October 1997): 4–8.

Willis, Paul. *Learning to Labour: How Working Class Kids Get Working Class Jobs*. NY: Columbia University Press, 1977.

Willis, Jane. *Geneish: An Indian Girlhood*. Toronto: New Press, 1973.

Wilson, Elizabeth. *Adorned in Dreams: Fashion and Modernity*. London: Virago, 1985.

Wine, Jeri Dawn and Janice L. Ristock, eds. *Women and Social Change: Feminist Activism in Canada*. Toronto: James Lorimer and Co., 1991.

Wiseman, Rosalind. *Queen Bees and Wannabees: Helping Your Daughter Survive Cliques, Gossip, Boyfriends, and Other Realities of Adolescence*. NY: Crown Publications, 2002.

Wolf, Diane L. "Family Secrets: Transnational Struggles among Children of Filipino Immigrants" *Sociological Perspectives*, 40.3 (1997), 457–482.

Woodend, D. "Girl Power." *The Vancouver Sun*. 23 November 2002: H8, H9.

Woodson, Stephani Etheridge. "Mapping the Cultural Geography of Childhood or, Performing the Monstrous Child," *Journal of American Culture* 22.4 (Winter 1999): 35.

Wyss, Shannon. "This was my hell": The Violence Experienced by Gender Non-Conforming Youth in US High Schools" *International Journal of Qualitative Studies in Education*. 17.5 (2004): 731-735.

Yates, Lynn. "Gender Equity and the Boys Debate: What Sort of Challenge Is It?" *British Journal of Sociology of Education*. 18.3 (1997): 337-47.

Yuval-Davis, Nira. "Citizenship, Territoriality and the Gendered Construction of Difference." In Engin Isin, ed. *Democracy, Citizenship and the Global City*. London and NY: Routledge, 2000: 172-188.

About The Contributors

Hourig Attarian is a researcher and educator. She is a Ph.D. Candidate in the Faculty of Education, McGill University, in Montréal, Québec.

Helene Berman is an Associate Professor in the School of Nursing at the University of Western Ontario and a Research Associate with the Centre for Research on Violence Against Women and Children. She is co-editor of *In the Best Interests of the Girl Child* (with Yasmin Jiwani, 2002).

Michele Byers is an Assistant Professor at Saint Mary's University. She is the editor of *Growing Up Degrassi: Television, Identity and Youth Cultures* (Sumach Press, 2005).

Dawn H. Currie is Professor of Sociology and past Chair of the Women's Studies Programme at the University of British Columbia. She is the author of *Girl Talk: Adolescent Magazines and Their Readers* (University of Toronto, 1999).

Pamela J. Downe is an Associate Professor of Women's and Gender Studies at the University of Saskatchewan. Her publications include *leishmaniasis, Modelos de enfermedades,* (Universidad Autonoma de Yucatan), and *Gendered Intersections,* an edited volume (with Lesley Biggs, Fernwood Publications, 2005).

Tatiana Fraser holds a BA in Women's Studies from the University of Ottawa and a Masters of Management for National Voluntary Sector Leaders from McGill University. She co-founded POWER Camp in 1995, and is currently the Executive Director of POWER Camp National.

Marnina Gonick is Assistant Professor of Language and Literacy Education and Women's Studies at the Pennsylvania State University. She is author of *Between Femininities: Ambivalence, Identity and the Education of Girls,* (SUNY Press) and co-author of *Young Femininity: Girlhood, Power and Social Change* (Palgrave Press).

Rachel Gouin is a doctoral candidate at McGill University where she is researching young women's learning as they engage in social action. Dedicated to her role as mother, student and activist, she is happy to be bilingual, and negotiates the boundaries of the two *official* languages that occupy her brain.

Yasmin Hussain is currently the Research Coordinator for the "Intersecting Sites of Violence in the Lives of Girls" project at the Centre for Research on Violence Against

Women and Children in London, Ontario. She enjoys working with children in the af-ter-school homework/learning support programmes in the community. The children have reacquainted her with the joy of colouring with crayons!

Yasmin Jiwani is Associate Professor in the Department of Communication Studies at Concordia University. Her publications include *Rural Women and Violence in BC* for the Department of Justice Canada, and *Violence Prevention and the Girl Child* for the Status of Women Canada (Phase I and II). She is also the author of *Discourses of Denial: Mediations of Race, Gender and Violence* which will be published by UBC Press in 2006.

Deirdre M. Kelly is Professor in the Department of Educational Studies at the University of British Columbia. She is the author of *Pregnant with Meaning: Teen Mothers and the Politics of Inclusive Schooling* (Peter Lang, 2000) and *Last Chance High: How Girls and Boys Drop in and out of Alternative Schools* (Yale University Press, 1993).

Azmina Ladha is about to finish her final year of school at Osgoode Hall. She has worked at the FREDA Centre for Research on Violence against Women & Children in Vancouver, and in 2004, she developed Go Girls, an activity-based leadership program for marginalized young women.

Jo-Anne Lee teaches in the Women's Studies Department at the University of Victoria. She co-edited *Situating Race and Racisms in Space, Time and Theory* (McGill-Queen's, 2005). She is the President of the Canadian Research Institute for the Advancement of Women and the founder of Anti-dote, a network for multi-racial girls and young women in Victoria.

Rian Lougheed-Smith is currently entering her second year at Mount Allison Univer-sity. Rian is also an artist, a writer and a past volunteer/participant in research and is currently working at the Muriel McQueen Research Centre on Violence.

Barb MacQuarrie is the Community Director at The Centre for Research on Violence Against Women and Children. Currently she is a National Coordinator for the research initiative, "Intersecting Sites of Violence in the Lives of Girls."

Sarah Mangle worked with POWER Camp National as Network Director as the Girls' Club Coordinator. A recent graduate of Concordia University with a BFA in Studio Art, Sarah is an artist, musician, and writer.

Claudia Mitchell is a James McGill Professor in the Department of Integrated Studies in Education at McGill University. She is the co-author of *Researching Children's Popular Culture: Cultural Spaces of Childhood* (Routledge, 2002) and the co-editor of *Seven Going on Seventeen: Tween Studies in the Culture of Girlhood* (Peter Lang, 2005); *Not Just Any Dress: Dress, Body and Identity* (Peter Lang, 2004); and *Just who do we think we are: Methodologies for Self-Study* (Routledge-Falmer, 2005).

Michele Polak is currently a doctoral student at Miami University of Ohio. She attributes most of her work to her nieces: Amanda, who first showed her aunt that there is a whole girl world online that she never knew existed, and Nicole who will talk about her period to anyone, anytime, anywhere.

Romy Poletti is completing her final year in the Media, Information and Technoculture program at the University of Western Ontario. Her interest in girls' and women's issues led her to work on the Identifying Intersecting Sites of Violence in the Lives of Girls study.

Shauna Pomerantz is completing her Ph.D. in the Department of Educational Studies at the University of British Columbia. Her dissertation, entitled, *Dressing the Part: Girls, Style, and School Identities*, is a year-long ethnographic study of how girls negotiated their identities at an urban and multicultural high school in Vancouver.

Rebecca Raby is an Assistant Professor in the Department of Child and Youth Studies at Brock University. Her girlhood included building forts in the woods and sneaking to the store for candy. As well as sporty things like squash, her spare time includes writing short stories about childhood.

Candis Steenbergen is completing her Ph.D. in the Humanities: Interdisciplinary Studies in Society and Culture at Concordia University in Montréal, where she is working on her dissertation investigating the interplay between generational rhetoric, nostalgia, and feminisms in Canada. She is the editor of *Transforming Spaces: Girlhood, Agency and Power*. (POWER Camp National/Filles d'Action, 2004).

Fathiya Wais traveled from the horn of Africa to this native land in February 1991. Known for her sharp humour and spirited personality, Fathiya has completed a diploma in social sciences (University of Ottawa) and is currently pursuing graduate studies in Anthropology.

Ashley Ward has just finished her second year in the Print Journalism Program at Centennial College. She is also a successful reporter who has been published in the *East Toronto Observer* and *The Courier*. She has been involved with the Centre for Research on Violence Against Women and Children for the past three years.

Sophie Wertheimer is currently pursuing her Ph.D. in Communication Studies at the University of Calgary. *Pretty in Panties* is strongly informed by her experiences as a woman who was a little girl not so long ago; who remembers vividly the complexities, pains and pleasures of growing up girl in Canada.

Hermig Yogurtian lives in Montréal. Now the mother of two adolescent girls, she is (still) trying to come to grips with her own girlhood, and a few others that came and went before hers, and made it what it was.

Also Available from BLACK ROSE BOOKS

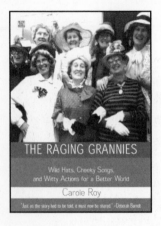

RAGING GRANNIES: Wild Hats, Cheeky Songs, and Witty Actions for a Better World
Carole Roy

an Amelia Bloomer Project finalist, sponsored by the Feminist Task Force of the America Library Association

Bursting with adventures, protest songs, photographs, Granny profiles, and Granny wisdom, this is the tale of the Raging Grannies: their beginning and growth, the invention of their identity, the educational and bold potential of their activism, and their impact on issues, stereotypes, media, and people.

Unique in form and content...fills a gap in feminist literature. Roy's examination of strategies of satire and humour is ground-breaking. —Deborah Barndt, co-editor of *Just Doing It: Popular Collective Action in the Americas*

CAROLE ROY is a long-time activist. She holds an MA in Women's Studies, from York University, and a Ph.D. in Adult Education, from University of Toronto.

355 pages ♀ paper 1-55164-240-9 $24.99 ♀ cloth 1-55164-241-7 $53.99

WOMEN AND RELIGION
Fatmagül Berktay

While taking women's subjectivities and their reasons for their taking to religion into account, this book focuses mainly on the *functions* of religion, the way it relates to women; its contribution to gender differences; and the status of women within it, particularly the relationship between gender on the one hand, and power and social control on the other, and within this context, the meanings attributed to the female body. The author examines why, in all three monotheisms the gender of God is male and what the impact of this is on our thoughts vis a vis gender definitions, the nature of authority and power structures.

Undertaken as well, is an exposition of contemporary Fundamentalism in both its Protestant and Islamic variants (in America and Iran).

FATMAGÜL BERKTAY is an associate professor with the Department of Philosophy, and teaches feminist theory at the Women's Research Center, both of the University of Istanbul, Turkey. She is a contributor to *Being a Women, Living and Writing*.

240 pages ♀ paper 1-55164-102-X $24.99 ♀ cloth 1-55164-103-8 $53.99

OBSESSION, WITH INTENT: Violence Against Women
Lee Lakeman

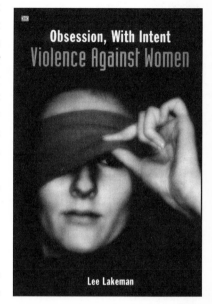

Obsession, With Intent is an investigative report into one hundred cases of violence against women; in *all* cases the women tried to get help from the system. It is a harrowing account of individual women's stories, their understanding of the danger they faced, their attempts to get help, the incompetence and/or indifference they met, and, in those cases where someone was willing to prosecute, their vulnerability under/within the law. It reviews 911 procedure, from how the emergency operator evaluates the call, to the police (how, or if, they collect evidence), to prosecuting attorney, to court, to sentencing.

Among the many narratives are "domestic dispute" cases, sexual assault cases, and cases of murder. The landmark decision, in the case of Jane Doe who fought for and won the right to sue the Toronto police force for the way in which they routinely dealt with rape victims is examined, as are a number of sexual assault cases—some high profile, some occurring more than forty years ago. Accounts of the serial killers Bernardo and Pickton are chilling, as are the other numerous accounts of impending murder. (As early as 1997 Picton had been charged with confining, and repeatedly stabbing, Wendy Lynn Eisteler, but charges were dropped and Picton released; the prosecutor judged that there was no likelihood of a conviction—the victim was "a drug-addicted prostitute." Thirty more women would die.)

Recognizing that violence against women is one of the strongest indicators of prevailing societal attitudes towards women, *Obsession, With Intent* screams out for social change regarding violence against women at the individual, the institutional, and the political level.

LEE LAKEMAN works at the Vancouver Rape Relief and Women's Shelter. She has organized Take Back the Night marches, neighborhood confrontations of abusive men, and anti-violence lobbies petitioning government representatives. She is a contributor to *Not For Sale: Preventing the Promotion of Prostitution*.

256 pages, bibliography, index
Paperback ISBN: 1-55164-262-X $24.99
Hardcover ISBN: 1-55164-263-8 $53.99

Also Available from BLACK ROSE BOOKS

"LOVE OF SHOPPING" IS NOT A GENE: Problems With Darwinian Psychology
Anne Innis Dagg

Focusing on the problems present in much Darwinian psychological research—flawed data, faulty analysis, and political motives—Innis Dagg, an eminent and outspoken critic of this ideology, first presents an overview of the theory and its popularity both among professionals and lay people, then she examines concepts of social behavior —based on 'genes vs culture'—including: aggression in the form of rape, infanticide, homicide, gang violence and war, and general criminality; homosexuality in both the human and the animal world; and race, IQ, and environment. In the end, a new perspective, which acknowledges the complexity of life by placing at its center the living organism, in its environment, rather than the gene, emerges.

ANNE INNIS DAGG has an MA in Genetics and a Ph.D. in Animal Behavior. She is the author of numerous books, including *The Feminine Gaze: A Compendium of Non-Fiction Women Authors and Their Books.*

 256 pages ♀ paper 1-55164-256-5 $24.99 ♀ cloth 1-55164-257-3 $53.99

See also:
> ECOLOGY OF EVERYDAY LIFE: Rethinking the Desire for Nature, *Chaia Heller*
> EMMA GOLDMAN: Sexuality and the Impurity of the State, *Bonnie Haaland*
> FEMINISM: From Pressure to Politics, *Angela Miles, Geraldine Finn, editors*

---

send for a free catalogue of all our titles

C.P. 1258, Succ. Place du Parc
Montréal, Québec
H2X 4A7 Canada

or visit our website at http://www.blackrosebooks.net

to order books

In Canada: (phone) 1-800-565-9523 (fax) 1-800-221-9985
email: utpbooks@utpress.utoronto.ca

In United States: (phone) 1-800-283-3572 (fax) 1-651-917-6406

In UK & Europe: (phone) London 44 (0)20 8986-4854 (fax) 44 (0)20 8533-5821
email: order@centralbooks.com

Printed by the workers of

for Black Rose Books
